Irish nationalism and European integration

MANCHESTER
1824

Manchester University Press

Irish nationalism and European integration

The official redefinition of the island of Ireland

KATY HAYWARD

Manchester University Press

Manchester and New York

distributed in the United States exclusively
by Palgrave Macmillan

Copyright © Katy Hayward 2009

The right of Katy Hayward to be identified as the author of this work has been asserted by her in accordance with the Copyright, Designs and Patents Act 1988.

Published by Manchester University Press
Oxford Road, Manchester M13 9NR, UK
and Room 400, 175 Fifth Avenue, New York, NY 10010, USA
www.manchesteruniversitypress.co.uk

Distributed in the United States exclusively by
Palgrave Macmillan, 175 Fifth Avenue, New York,
NY 10010, USA

Distributed in Canada exclusively by
UBC Press, University of British Columbia, 2029 West Mall,
Vancouver, BC, Canada V6T 1Z2

British Library Cataloguing-in-Publication Data
A catalogue record for this book is available from the British Library

Library of Congress Cataloging-in-Publication Data applied for

ISBN   978 0 7190 7278 9   *hardback*

ISBN   978 0 7190 7279 6   *paperback*

First published 2009

18 17 16 15 14 13 12 11 10 09   10 9 8 7 6 5 4 3 2 1

The publisher has no responsibility for the persistence or accuracy of URLs for external or any third-party internet websites referred to in this book, and does not guarantee that any content on such websites is, or will remain, accurate or appropriate.

Typeset in Sabon
by Servis Filmsetting Ltd, Stockport, Cheshire
Printed in Great Britain
by the MPG Books Group

Dedicated with love to my parents, Jan and Jonathan,
and my sisters, Nats and Abi,
for Littlecombe

Contents

Figures and tables

Figures

Tables

Preface

How has it been possible for successive Irish governments to not only accept but actively promote two of the largest challenges to traditional conceptions of Irish nation-statehood, i.e. the handing over of state sovereignty to the European Union and the retraction of the constitutional claim over Northern Ireland? This book argues that, rather than indicating a pragmatic retraction of nationalism, such decisions (and their justification on the public stage) reveal the unique power and continuing relevance of nationalism to Irish and, indeed, European politics today.

As the most detailed study to date of Irish official discourse in the late twentieth century, this book reveals how Irish governmental elites changed their definition of Irish nation-statehood in response to EU membership. This redefinition of Ireland's identity, borders and governance was made all the more necessary by the Troubles and the related challenges to the credibility of Irish official nationalism. However, this process has not taken the form of 'Europeanisation' or of a simple replacing of 'old' concepts with 'new' ones. Rather, whilst conceptions of identity, borders and governance inspired by the European Union (EU) have been employed to help find more widely acceptable conceptions of Irish nation-statehood in relation to Northern Ireland, the Irish governmental elite has affirmed traditional conceptions of identity, borders and governance when conceptualising the position and prospects of Ireland in the EU. Thus, Irish official discourse appears to have been used not only to accommodate both traditional and new conceptions of nation-statehood, but also to make them appear mutually complementary.

Acknowledgements

This book is based on original research funded by a doctoral research scholarship from University College Dublin and completed through post-doctoral research fellowships from the Irish Research Council for the Humanities and Social Sciences and the Institute of Irish Studies' International Research Initiative at Queen's University Belfast. I am immensely grateful for this funding support, which made the whole venture possible.

This book could not have been written without the support of Alan Sharp when fostering the original ideas at Magee. I wish to pay particular tribute to Brigid Laffan, Elizabeth Meehan and John Coakley, who have provided invaluable guidance, advice and insight throughout. Warm thanks, too, to Tom Garvin and Tobias Theiler, whose intellectual contributions were enlightening albeit, on occasion, wonderfully diverting. I am indebted to the Institute for British-Irish Studies (University College Dublin) for access to its collected papers, the Geary Institute for its provision of resources, and the Dublin European Institute for its unique super-collegiate legacy.

I have cherished the counsel and encouragement of Sylvia Adair, Francis Byrne, Brendan W. Devitt, John F. T. Gibbons, Gervase Holdaway, Kevin Howard, Muiris MacCárthaigh, Claire Mitchell, Don and Sheila Shaw, Wanda Wigfall-Williams and Gillian Wylie. Young Elsa and Rosa have marvellously demonstrated both the truth and the lie of the Irish proverb 'two shortens the road'. The journey's end was only made conceivable and attainable by my beloved friend and husband, Colin Shaw.

Particular thanks to the staff at Manchester University Press and the National Library of Ireland for their kind assistance.

And a final note of appreciation to KSO and KCSM for all that jazz.

Biographical notes

Ahern, Bertie (Patrick Bartholomew) (b.1951): Fianna Fáil TD for
Dublin Central (then Dublin Finglas) since 1977, he was Minister for
Labour in 1987 and 1989 and played a leading role in negotiations with
the Progressive Democrats on coalition partnership in 1987 and 1991.
Ahern was an early supporter of Haughey within the party and supported him against the challenge from Reynolds and others in late
1991. After sacking Reynolds as Minister for Finance in 1991,
Haughey handed the position to Ahern. He was one of just two cabinet
ministers to remain in their posts once Reynolds assumed the premiership in January 1992 and, when Reynolds resigned in 1994 following
the collapse of the Fianna Fáil/Labour coalition, Ahern succeeded
Reynolds unopposed. Somewhat surprisingly for a man known to have
such good negotiating skills, Labour could not be persuaded back into
coalition with Fianna Fáil and Ahern sat in opposition for three years.
Ahern won the general election in June 1997 and formed a government
in coalition with the Progressive Democrats; the same coalition won
again in 2002 and in the 2007 election Fianna Fáil retained power with
the aid of a dramatically reduced Progressive Democrat party, the
Green Party and Independent TDs. Bertie Ahern resigned as Taoiseach
on 6 May 2008.

Andrews, David (b.1936): son of Todd Andrews, Andrews became
Fianna Fáil TD for Dún Laoghaire in 1965. Lynch appointed him
Minister of State in the Department of Foreign Affairs in 1977. His min-
isterial career was stymied by the fact that he backed George Colley
against Haughey in the 1979 party leadership election, and he did not
return to the frontbenches until 1992, when he was briefly Minister for
Foreign Affairs for Albert Reynolds before Fianna Fáil went into coali-
tion with Labour. Andrews was first Minister for Defence in Bertie
Ahern's government but was soon returned to Foreign Affairs to succeed
Ray Burke. Andrews was a lead negotiator for the Irish government in

the Good Friday Agreement. He retired as Minister for Foreign Affairs in 2000.

Bruton, John (b.1947): one of the youngest ever TDs, Bruton was elected for Fine Gael for the Meath constituency in 1969 and was appointed Minister for Finance by Garret FitzGerald in 1981. The Dáil defeat of Bruton's controversial budget of February 1982 led to the early collapse of the coalition government. On the coalition's re-instatement in November 1982, Bruton was moved to the Ministry for Industry and Trade, to return to the post of Minister for Finance following a cabinet reshuffle in 1986. Again, Bruton's budgetary proposals led to controversy and the coalition split once more in 1987. On Garret FitzGerald's resignation, Bruton became deputy party leader (to Alan Dukes) and, in 1990, stood unopposed as Fine Gael leader. The party's poor fortunes at the national polls continued in the 1992 election and it was only because of the Fianna Fáil/Labour coalition's premature collapse in late 1994 that Bruton became Taoiseach, with the support of Labour and Democratic Left. Bruton's partnership with Labour's Dick Spring as Tánaiste and Proinsias De Rossa (Democratic Left) was a surprising success and Fine Gael made gains in the 1997 election, but not enough to counter the losses to its coalition partners. Bruton resigned from the party leadership in 2001 and subsequently became, along with De Rossa, an Irish Parliament representative to the European Convention on the Constitution, as well as National Parliament Representative on the steering committee of the Convention. In 2004, following resignation from the Dáil, he was appointed EU ambassador to the United States.

Burke, Ray (b.1943): elected Fianna Fáil TD for Dublin North in 1973, Burke was Minister of State in Lynch's second government and held various ministerial positions (Environment; Energy; Industry; Justice; Communications) in the Haughey administrations. He was not appointed to the cabinet by Reynolds, but was made Minister for Foreign Affairs by Bertie Ahern in June 1997. He resigned as minister and TD in October 1997 over allegations he received corrupt payments, subsequently a matter for tribunal inquiry.

Butt, Isaac (1813–79): a Protestant from Donegal, Butt's political career saw him move from Conservative Unionism (and Orangeism) towards liberalism in thought and affiliation. He became an advocate of a federal solution to the British–Irish relationship and founder of the Irish Home Rule League in 1873, from which he resigned shortly before his death.

Carson, Edward (1854–1935): Dublin-born Protestant with a prominent political career in Ireland, north and south, and Britain. Unionist MP for the University of Dublin (1892) and for Belfast Duncairn (1918–21). Leader of the Irish Unionist Party (1910–21), he led the campaign against Home Rule, including the Ulster Covenant of 1912. Solicitor-General for Ireland (1892); appointed Attorney-General (1915–16); joined the cabinet (1917–18) but resigned on discovery that Prime Minister Lloyd George was drafting an all-Ireland Home Rule Bill (Foster, 1989: 465).

Collins, Gerry (b.1938): Fianna Fáil TD for Limerick, Collins held positions of Minister for Posts and Telegraphs, Minister for Justice and Minister for Foreign Affairs (1982, 1989–92) in the Lynch and Haughey administrations. In his latter ministerial role, Collins served as President of the Council of the European Economic Community (EEC) in 1990. He supported Haughey right up to his resignation and was excluded from Reynolds' cabinet (retiring as a TD in 1997). Collins was an MEP from 1994 to 2004.

Collins, Michael (1890–1922): a member of the Irish Republican Brotherhood and participant in the Easter Rising, Collins joined the executive of Sinn Féin in 1917 under de Valera's presidency. He was elected MP in 1918 for Cork South and sat in Sinn Féin's Dáil Éireann. In 1919 he was nominated Minister for Finance by de Valera, elected president of the IRB, and became a director of intelligence for the IRA, thus taking a leading role for republicans during the Irish War of Independence. Following the truce, he deputised Griffith in negotiations with the British government, leading to the Anglo-Irish Treaty of 1921. Collins' attempts to find a compromise between the pro- and anti- Treaty divisions in Sinn Féin failed and he led the Provisional Government and its army against the anti-Treaty IRA during the Civil War, during which he was killed in an ambush.

Cosgrave, Liam (b.1920): son of W. T. Cosgrave, he became a Fine Gael TD for Co. Dublin aged 23 and was made Minister for External Affairs in the coalition government of 1954, in which role he chaired meetings of the Council of Ministers for the Council of Europe. He succeeded Dillon as party leader in 1965 and became Taoiseach of the Fine Gael/Labour coalition government in 1973. He resigned as party leader following defeat in the 1977 general election and retired from politics in 1981.

Cosgrave, W. T. (1880–1965): imprisoned for his active role in the Easter Rising, Cosgrave won a parliamentary seat (Kilkenny by-election) for Sinn Féin whilst in prison in 1917 and won the Carlow-Kilkenny seat in the general election of the following year. On the pro-Treaty side in 1921, he succeeded Collins as Chairman of the Provisional Government in 1922, becoming the first President of the Executive Council of the Irish Free State in December 1922. In April 1923, following the split within Sinn Féin, Cosgrave led the resulting pro-Treaty party of Cumann na nGaedheal, which was to be the governing party of the Irish Free State until 1932. The following year, in opposition, Cosgrave oversaw the creation of Fine Gael (from Cumann na nGaedheal, the National Centre Party and the National Guard) and led it until his retirement in 1944.

Costello, John A. (1891–1976): Attorney-General 1926–32, in which role he represented Ireland at meetings of the League of Nations; 1933 elected Cumann na nGaedheal (Fine Gael) TD for Co. Dublin. In 1944 he became Fine Gael spokesperson on External Affairs. After the 1948 election, he became Taoiseach of a coalition led by Fine Gael (whose leader Richard Mulcahy was not acceptable as Taoiseach for some coalition partners). In his times as Taoiseach (1949–51, 1954–57), Ireland left the British Commonwealth (when the External Relations Act was repealed and the Republic of Ireland Act passed) and later joined the United Nations.

Cowen, Brian (b.1960): Cowen was elected Fianna Fáil TD for Laois-Offaly in 1984. He supported Albert Reynolds' bid for the party leadership in the early 1990s and held ministerial positions (Labour; Energy; Transport; Health) in Reynolds' government. On return to government (under Ahern) in 1997, Cowen was made Minister for Health and Children and succeeded David Andrews to the position of Minister for Foreign Affairs at a time (2000) of continued negotiations over 'sticking issues' in post-GFA Northern Ireland. He was made Minister for Finance in 2004 and, following the poor showing of the Progressive Democrats in the 2007 general election, Tánaiste. Cowen succeeded Bertie Ahern as leader of Fianna Fáil and Taoiseach in May 2008, forming the 28th Government of Ireland just six weeks before the referendum on the Lisbon Treaty.

Craig, James (also Viscount Craigavon) (1871–1940): Belfast-born, MP from 1906 to 1921, when he succeeded Carson as leader of the Unionist Party and became Northern Ireland's first Prime Minister until his death in 1940. Although he was a parliamentary secretary 1919–21, Craig was never as comfortable in wider British politics as Carson. He was actively involved in organising Ulster Volunteers against Home Rule.

De Valera, Éamon (1882–1975): born in New York and raised in Limerick, a member of the Gaelic League, Irish Volunteers and the Irish Republican Brotherhood, he held a position of responsibility during the

Rising for which he was imprisoned until 1917. On his release, he took a parliamentary seat for Sinn Féin in an east Clare by-election and the following year led the party to victory in the general election. Although officially president of the first Dáil Éireann, de Valera was absent (due to imprisonment or fundraising in the US) for much of its nativity and he resigned from that position following the Dáil's narrow ratification of the Anglo-Irish Treaty. He was nominal leader of the anti-Treaty forces during the Civil War, after which he was interned until 1924. He resigned from Sinn Féin whilst still its leader (because it rejected his proposal to accept the Free State Constitution) and founded Fianna Fáil in 1926. The following year he swore the Oath of Allegiance in order to become a TD. In 1932, Fianna Fáil gained a parliamentary majority, making de Valera Taoiseach. His dismantling of the 1921 Treaty from the position of government culminated in the 1937 Bunreacht na hÉireann. The following year he was elected President of the Assembly of the League of Nations but his international standing was soon damaged by his policy of neutrality during the Second World War. De Valera held the position of Taoiseach (with two three-year gaps of inter-party governments) until 1959, when he was replaced by Seán Lemass and moved to Áras an Uachtaráin as President of Ireland until 1973.

Devlin, Joseph (1871–1934): Belfast-born Devlin was active in the anti-Parnellite Irish National Federation and then the United Irish League before being elected MP for the Irish Parliamentary Party in Kilkenny North in 1902 and for Belfast West in 1906. He followed the party line (including Redmond's position on the War) until 1918, when he opposed the compromise with southern Unionists following the Irish Convention. From 1918 until his death, he led the Nationalist Party in Northern Ireland, first in Westminster (in a policy of abstention) and then from 1929 in Stormont. Devlin played a crucial role in the revival of the Ancient Order of Hibernians in Ireland.

Dillon, James (1902–86): son of John Dillon, the last leader of the Irish Parliamentary Party, James Dillon became TD for the National Centre Party (later merged into Fine Gael) for Donegal West in 1932 and, from 1937, for Co. Monaghan. He was Minister for Agriculture in Costello's coalition governments (1948–51, 1954–57) and became leader of Fine Gael in 1959 until his resignation following narrow defeat by Lemass' Fianna Fáil in the 1965 general election.

Dillon, John (1851–1927): Dublin-born, MP for County Tipperary 1880–83 and for Mayo East 1885–1918. Joined the anti-Parnellite Irish National Federation after the split in the Irish Parliamentary Party, and later replaced Justin McCarthy as its leader. Supported Redmond on the Irish Party's reunion and supported the third Home Rule Bill in 1912. He became leader of the Irish Party in March 1918 and withdrew it from the Commons one month later in protest at the extension of conscription to Ireland. In an event that mirrored the fortunes of the Irish Parliamentary Party as a whole, Dillon lost his seat to de Valera in the 1918 election.

FitzGerald, Garret (b.1926): the son of Desmond FitzGerald (1888–1947; London-born Irish Volunteer, Sinn Féin then Cumann na nGaedheal TD, first Minister for External Affairs of the Irish Free State), FitzGerald had a relatively high profile as a writer and lecturer on economics before being elected to Seanad Éireann in 1965. He was elected Fine Gael TD for Dublin South East in 1969 and was soon active as a liberal member of the parliamentary party. He was appointed Minister for Foreign Affairs in Cosgrave's coalition government of 1973, a role in which he made a particular impression in the EEC, including holding Ireland's first Presidency. FitzGerald assumed leadership of Fine Gael in 1977, overseeing an exceptional growth in the party. Fine Gael formed a coalition government with Labour following the 1981 election but FitzGerald was forced to ask President Hillery to dissolve the Dáil in late January 1982 following the defeat of Bruton's hairshirt budget. Fine Gael lost just two seats in the subsequent February election and was in a relatively strong position to resume power in the election of November that same year alongside Labour. FitzGerald's reformist agenda – in a range of matters from British-Irish relations to contraception – met substantial opposition; his economic policies towards 'fiscal rectitude' were the most unpopular of all. Fine Gael lost nearly a third of its seats in the 1987 election and FitzGerald resigned as party leader, remaining as a TD for a further five years.

Gavan Duffy, George (1882–1951): English-born Gavan Duffy came to Dublin in 1917 when he was called to the Irish bar and defended several Irish republicans, including Roger Casement. He was subsequently elected as Sinn Féin MP (South Dublin) in 1918, and was sent by de Valera, with Seán T. O'Kelly, as envoy of the Irish Republic to the Paris Peace conference. He was a reluctant signatory to the Anglo-Irish Treaty and Minister for Foreign Affairs for the fourth Ministry of the Second Dáil Éireann in 1922, but resigned from office the same year. He continued to have a notable legal career, unofficially advising de Valera on the 1937 Constitution and serving as President of the High Court.

Griffith, Arthur (1872–1922): member of the Gaelic League and Irish Republican Brotherhood, he founded Sinn Féin in 1905 and became its president in 1908 until replaced by de Valera in 1917. He was elected an MP for Sinn Féin in 1918 although his relationship with the party leadership was tense. He took a strong pro-Treaty stance after his involvement in negotiations and was voted President of Dáil Éireann for a short period immediately after its ratification.

Gwynn, Stephen (1864–1950): prolific author, member of the Gaelic League, and MP (Galway City, 1906–18) for the Irish Parliamentary Party, for which he led much of the pro-Home Rule Act publicity in face of the Sinn Féin challenge. Perhaps his greatest act in this regard was following Redmond's call (and his own as member of the Irish Recruiting Council) and enlisting with the British Army during the First World War, where he had a distinguished military career. He returned to take Redmond's place in the Irish Convention negotiations. After failing to win a seat in the 1918 elections, Gwynn turned to political commentary, becoming Ireland Correspondent for such papers as the *Observer*.

Harney, Mary (b.1953): appointed by Lynch to Seanad Éireann in 1977, Harney was elected to Dáil Éireann in 1981 for Fianna Fáil (Dublin South/Mid West). She broke ranks with the party leadership by voting in favour of the Anglo-Irish Agreement and was later one of the founding members of the breakaway Progressive Democrats. She succeeded Des O'Malley as party leader in 1993 and entered coalition government with Bertie Ahern four years later, becoming Tánaiste (until 2007). She has held ministerial responsibility for Enterprise and Health.

Haughey, Charles (1925–2006): born in Mayo to parents from Co. Derry, Haughey became a TD for Dublin North Central on his fourth attempt in 1957 and was quickly appointed to the junior ministry by Lemass, becoming Minister for Justice in 1961 (during which time he dealt a strong hand against the IRA and its border campaigns, introducing special military courts and overseeing internment for IRA prisoners) and Minister for Agriculture in 1964. In 1966 he declared himself a candidate for the leadership of Fianna Fáil on Lemass' retirement but later stepped aside on the Taoiseach's advice in order to support the compromise candidate of Jack Lynch. He was rewarded with the position of Minister of Finance. Haughey was sacked from this position by Lynch in May 1970 over the 'Arms Crisis' and remained on the backbenches until 1975, when Lynch appointed him spokesman for Health and Social Welfare. Haughey held ministerial responsibility for this post when Fianna Fáil was re-elected to power in 1977. He beat Tánaiste George Colley in the leadership election following Lynch's resignation in 1979, thus becoming Taoiseach. Haughey failed to gain a majority in the June

1981 election but regained power following the premature collapse of the FitzGerald administration in February 1982 through the support of four left-wing (Independent and Workers' Party) TDs. However, these TDs withdrew their support for Fianna Fáil over its planned spending cuts and Haughey lost power again in November 1982. He returned as Taoiseach of a minority government in 1987 (having depended on the casting vote of the Ceann Comhairle [Speaker]), following parliamentary defeat in a Dáil vote, he called an election in 1989, this time depending on Desmond O'Malley's Progressive Democrats (a breakaway party from Fianna Fáil) as coalition partners. Haughey resigned as party leader and Taoiseach in January 1992 following growing disquiet within the Fianna Fáil and was succeeded by Albert Reynolds, whom he had sacked from the post of Minister for Finance a few months earlier for his declaration of opposition to Haughey. He retired from politics the same year although the rest of his life was dogged by scandal relating to unethical payments he received whilst in power.

Healy, Timothy (1855–1931): Healy's political career is characterised by variety. Healy's political career saw him elected as an Irish Parliamentary Party MP for, variously, Wexford, Monaghan, South Londonderry, north Longford and (for the Irish National Federation in 1892) north Louth. Following the split in the IPP, Healy was expelled from both the pro-Parnellite Irish National League and the anti-Parnellite Irish National Federation. In 1911 he took the parliamentary seat in his native Cork for the anti-IPP All-for-Ireland League. He resigned his seat in favour of the Sinn Féin candidate in 1918 and was recommended by Cosgrave for the position of Governor General of Ireland, which he held from its creation in 1922 until his resignation in 1927.

Hobson, Bulmer (1882–1969): a Quaker from Co. Tyrone, Hobson was a founding member of the Irish Volunteers and sat on the Supreme Council of the Irish Republican Brotherhood. He sided with MacNeill against the Easter Rising, and later became a civil servant in the Free State.

Hyde, Douglas (1860–1949): a Protestant from Co. Roscommon, Hyde is best known for founding the Gaelic League and for being the first to hold the position of President of Ireland following the dissolution of the office of Governor General through the 1937 Constitution.

Lemass, Seán (1899–1971): he joined the Irish Volunteers in his youth, and subsequently participated in the Easter Rising, the War of Independence (for which he was interned 1920–21) and, for the anti-Treaty republicans, the Civil War. He was elected as TD for Sinn Féin for

Dublin City in 1924 and soon after joined de Valera in leaving Sinn Féin to found Fianna Fáil. He served as Minister for Industry and Commerce (Minister for Supplies during the Emergency) under de Valera in all his governments until 1959, when he succeeded de Valera as leader of Fianna Fáil and Taoiseach until 1966.

Lynch, Jack (1917–99): Cork-born Lynch had an illustrious reputation as a Gaelic Athletic Association footballer and hurler, only retiring inter-county competition some years after being elected as Fianna Fáil TD for Cork in 1948. He soon became an assistant and speech writer for de Valera and was appointed a parliamentary secretary in 1951. From 1957, he held ministerial posts for Education, the Gaeltacht, Industry and Commerce and, in 1965, Finance. When Lemass retired in 1966, there were a substantial number of prospective leaders within a restless Fianna Fáil, and Lynch was persuaded to stand as a compromise candidate against George Colley. His first period in office was a time of upheaval in Irish politics, with the rising Troubles in Northern Ireland and Ireland's entry into the EEC. He lost the election of February 1973 to the Fine Gael/Labour coalition but returned a significant majority for Fianna Fáil in 1977. Nonetheless, power struggles within the party led to his early resignation in December 1979, just before completing his term as President-in-office of the Council of the EEC.

MacBride, Seán (1904–88): former Chief of Staff of the anti-Treaty IRA and founder of the republican socialist party Clann na Poblachta, for which he was elected TD for Dublin County (South-West) in 1944. He became Minister for External Affairs in Costello's first inter-party government and played a key role in Ireland's withdrawal from the Commonwealth. MacBride left the Dáil in 1957, after which time he played a significant role in international affairs, including in the Council of Europe, the Organisation for Security and Co-operation in Europe, the United Nations and Amnesty International (which he founded). He was awarded the Nobel Peace Prize in 1974.

McCarthy, Justin (1830–1912): a Liberal and Home Rule MP for Longford (1879–86, 1892–1900) and Londonderry (1886–92), he chaired the anti-Parnellite Irish National Federation at its inception.

O'Donnell, Liz (b. 1956): former deputy leader of the Progressive Democrats, O'Donnell was TD for Dublin South in 1992 until 2007 and helped negotiated the PDs into coalition government with Ahern's Fianna Fáil. She was made Minister of State in the Department of Foreign Affairs and was involved in the negotiations around the Good Friday Agreement.

O'Higgins, Kevin (1892–1927): Sinn Féin MP for Laois (then Queen's County) from 1918 and one of the original members of Cumann na nGaedheal, O'Higgins' rose rapidly within the political rankings, holding the position of assistant Minister for Local Government in the first and second Dáil Éireann and (as a strongly pro-Treaty member) Minister for Economic Affairs in the Provisional Government, Minister for Justice (1922–27), first vice-president of the Executive Council from December 1922 and briefly Minister for External Affairs. As Minister for Justice, he was responsible for the establishment of the Civic Guard (becoming An Garda Síochána) and the execution of many republican prisoners during the Irish Civil War. For this latter role, he was assassinated by the anti-Treaty IRA in July 1927.

O'Neill, Terence (1914–90): born and educated in England to an aristocratic family from Ulster, O'Neill was elected to Stormont for the Unionist Party in 1946. In 1963 he became party leader and succeeded Lord Brookeborough as Prime Minister for Northern Ireland. His reformist policies and conciliatory gestures (such as the meetings with Lemass and Lynch) were unpopular with many members of his own party. The increasing unrest around the civil rights movement, growing paramilitary activity and internal dissidence within the UUP made O'Neill's position untenable and he resigned as party leader and Prime Minister in April 1969.

Parnell, Charles Stewart (1846–91): Wicklow-born Protestant, elected MP for the Home Rule League in 1875 and soon became associated with radicalism and parliamentary obstructionism. He became party leader in 1880 and founded the Irish Parliamentary Party two years later. Parnell's able tactics as a parliamentarian were central to Gladstone's decision to introduce the first Home Rule Bill (Foster, 1989: 359).

Pearse, Patrick (1879–1916): a young member of the Gaelic League and one of the first members of the Irish Volunteers. His membership of the Irish Republican Brotherhood led to him taking a leading role in the Easter Rising.

Plunkett, Horace Curzon (1854–1932): a Protestant from Co. Meath, Plunkett moved from being a unionist of Anglo-Irish heritage to a staunch Irish nationalist. He was a Conservative MP for South Dublin from 1892 to 1900 but became convinced of the need for Home Rule after the failure of the Irish Council Bill in 1908. He chaired the Irish Convention (1917–18), seeking to find agreement on implementing the third Home Rule Act. In seeking compromise between nationalists, unionists and Britain, and as an alternative to partition, he founded the

Irish Dominion League, proposing a united Ireland within the British Commonwealth. He was a senator in the post-Treaty Seanad Éireann, but turned in later life to his other interest of agricultural co-operation.

Redmond, John (1856–1918): Nationalist MP from 1881 until his death in 1918. After the Irish Parliamentary Party's split and Parnell's death, Redmond led the Parnellite minority Irish National League from 1891, during which time he worked constructively with Irish Unionists in Westminster, such as Plunkett, and later became leader of the reunited Irish Parliamentary Party in 1900. Redmond played a crucial role in the introduction of the third Home Rule Bill of 1912 and his trust that it would be implemented after the First World War (which caused its suspension in 1914) caused him to encourage Irish volunteers to join the British Army.

Reynolds, Albert (b.1932): after a successful and varied business career, Reynolds was elected TD for Longford-Westmeath in Fianna Fáil's landslide election victory of 1977. Reynolds supported Haughey in the wrestle to replace Lynch as Fianna Fáil leader in 1979, and was rewarded with ministerial positions of Posts and Telegraphs, Transport (1980–82), Industry and Energy (1982) and Industry and Commerce (1987–88). In 1988, he replaced Ray MacSharry (who became European Commissioner) as Minister for Finance and played a key role in negotiating agreement with the Progressive Democrats to support Fianna Fáil in government after the 1989 election. Following growing disquiet within the party about Haughey's leadership, Reynolds announced he would stand for election should Haughey resign and subsequently backed a motion of no confidence in the Taoiseach. He was sacked for this action but shortly afterwards won the leadership election and premiership following Haughey's resignation in January 1992. Reynolds held onto the position of Taoiseach after the general election a year later through coalition agreement with Labour. The government survived a series of storms (some of which related to Reynolds' decisions in business) but by late 1994 Dick Spring led the Labour Party out of government (following disagreement over the Taoiseach's nominated appointee for President of the High Court) leaving Reynolds little choice but to resign.

Saunderson, Edward (1837–1906): Fermanagh-born Liberal MP for Cavan from 1865, only to switch to the Conservative Party four years later on a difference of principle with Gladstone over Disestablishment. He lost his seat in 1874 but became Conservative MP for North Armagh in 1885 until his death. Leader of Parliamentary Unionists (1888) and

Irish Unionist Alliance (1891), as well as a prominent Orangeman, Saunderson played crucial role in organising Ulster resistance to Home Rule.

Spring, Dick (b. 1950): Labour Party TD for Kerry North 1981–2002, leader of Labour Party 1982–97, Spring participated in four coalition governments right from his first day as a TD. First, briefly, as a junior minister (1982) and then as Tánaiste and Minister under FitzGerald 1982–87. He returned to government in 1993, this time as Tánaiste and Minister for Foreign Affairs in Reynold's coalition government – positions he retained following the collapse of the coalition and the election of Bruton's 'rainbow coalition'.

Intergovernmental agreements on Northern Ireland, 1973–2002

Sunningdale Communiqué (Sunningdale Agreement) (December 1973): the outcome of talks between the two governments (of Liam Cosgrave and Ted Heath) and representatives of the SDLP, UUP and Alliance Party (as members of the new power-sharing Executive of Northern Ireland under Brian Faulkner). Sunningdale was specifically about the introduction of an 'Irish dimension' to government in Northern Ireland. Its proposals for a Council of Ireland and all-island Consultative Assembly were extremely controversial and became the focus of a sustained united campaign by unionists, leading to the anti-Sunningdale coalition (United Ulster Unionist Council) winning all but one seat for Northern Ireland in the February 1974 general election and to the Ulster Workers Council strike in May 1974. This pressure, plus disagreement within the UUP, led to the collapse of the Northern Ireland Executive and the restoration of direct rule in May 1974. For detailed analysis of the Irish government's role and motivation in the talks, see Farrington (2007).

Anglo-Irish Agreement (Hillsborough Agreement) (November 1985): Garret FitzGerald and Margaret Thatcher signed the AIA, one of the most controversial intergovernmental agreements on the status of Northern Ireland. It provided an institutional outlet for the Irish government to take an advisory role in Northern Ireland, through the Anglo-Irish Intergovernmental Conference and a Permanent Secretariat of the DFA based at Maryfield. It also stated that there would be no change in the constitutional status of Northern Ireland without 'majority consent' within Northern Ireland – a provision that has been included in every major intergovernmental agreement since.

Downing Street Declaration (Joint Declaration on Peace) (December 1993): building on the talks and declarations between John Hume (SDLP) and Gerry Adams (SF), this joint statement by Albert Reynolds and John Major affirmed Northern Ireland's right to self-determination and pledged the commitment of the two governments to finding a constitutional settlement, including an all-island arrangement by 'mutual consent'. The declaration included the statement that the two governments, 'consider that the development of Europe will, of itself, require new approaches to serve interests common to both parts of the island of Ireland, and to Ireland and the United Kingdom as partners in the European Union'.

Framework Documents ('A New Framework for Agreement') (February 1995): subtitled, 'A shared understanding between the British and Irish Governments to assist discussion and negotiation involving the Northern Ireland parties', the Framework Documents were announced by John Bruton and John Major, making note of the ceasefires of the IRA and Loyalist Military Command. They confirmed the centrality of the principles of self-determination and consent, the use of exclusively democratic and peaceful means, and protection of the rights and identities of 'both traditions in Ireland' in any settlement.

Good Friday Agreement (Belfast Agreement) (April 1998): following on from protracted multi-party negotiations, the GFA was between the two governments (as contained in the incorporated British-Irish Agreement) and all main parties excepting the DUP. It contained proposals to institutionalise the relationships of the three 'Strands' – within Northern Ireland, north-south, and between Ireland and the UK – in a power-sharing arrangement.

Abbreviations

AIA	Anglo-Irish Agreement
DFA	Department of Foreign Affairs
DL	Democratic Left
DUP	Democratic Unionist Party
EC	European Community
ECHR	European Court of Human Rights
ECSC	European Coal and Steel Community
EEC	European Economic Community
EMS	European Monetary System
EP	European Parliament
ERDF	European Regional Development Fund
ERM	Exchange Rate Mechanism
EU	European Union
FF	Fianna Fáil
FG	Fine Gael
GFA	Good Friday (Belfast) Agreement
GIS	Government Information Service
HOC	House of Commons
IBIS	Institute for British-Irish Studies
ICTU	Irish Congress of Trade Unions
IDL	Irish Dominion League
IPP	Irish Parliamentary Party
IRA	Irish Republican Army
IRB	Irish Republican Brotherhood
ITGWU	Irish Transport and General Workers' Union
L	Labour Party (Ireland)
MLA	Member of the Legislative Assembly
NATO	North Atlantic Treaty Organization
NI	Northern Ireland
PD	Progressive Democrats
RTÉ	Radio Telefís Éireann

SDLP	Social Democratic and Labour Party
SEA	Single European Act
SF	Sinn Féin
TD	Teachta Dála (Member of Dáil Éireann)
TEU	Treaty on European Union (Maastricht Treaty)
UCD	University College Dublin
UN	United Nations
US/USA	United States of America
UUP	Ulster Unionist Party
UWC	Ulster Workers' Council

1

Introduction

The 'Birth of a New Ireland' was announced just in time for the new millennium, on 2 December 1999, by the *Irish Times*. The spur for this declaration was the signing of commencement orders in Dublin, giving effect to the 1998 multi-party and 1999 British–Irish Agreements and devolving power to the new north–south and British–Irish bodies. That same day in Belfast, the Northern Ireland Executive met for the first time, whilst President Mary McAleese lunched with the Queen in London and made promises to return the favour soon. But it was the formal amendment by Taoiseach Bertie Ahern of Articles 2 and 3 of Bunreacht na hÉireann (the Constitution of Ireland), which had claimed sovereignty over Northern Ireland, that garnered the most enthusiastic rhetoric in Ireland that day. Echoing public optimism and desire for a settlement, the *Irish Times* leader hailed the occasion as 'a more momentous day' than any other in Ireland's political history. In contrast to the 'incomplete constructions' of Northern Ireland and the Irish Free State/Republic and the congruent 'simplistic and majoritarian politics of the past', the new institutions were said to at last acknowledge 'the diversity of culture, of race, of religion, of identity, which span this island'. Twenty-first century Ireland looked set to be an increasingly complex nation-state, and one that would require a highly nuanced national ideology to be maintained.

A new Ireland for a new Europe?

In fact, the blueprint for this seismic shift in Ireland's political landscape had been sketched in the language of mainstream Irish nationalism for quite some time. As this book will show, political leaders in Ireland had become adept at employing descriptors of nation-statehood that enabled it to become modernised, globalised, renewed. Of specific significance in this process of redefinition has been Ireland's membership of the European Union. This, it shall be argued, provided both the practical means and the conceptual tools for the nation-state to remain not just relevant but crucial in a changing political, social and economic environment. This, as Milward (1992) observed, is a process that is vital to the momentum and integrity of European integration itself and features in all member-states. However, the case of Ireland is particularly illuminating because the peculiarities of national history have endowed its official nationalism with a powerful, actual significance. That is to say, Irish official discourse on the meaning of Irish nation-statehood has always, regardless of the intentions or circumstances of the actor concerned, had implications for the contested status of Northern Ireland and the conflict associated with it. By inspiring a new type of language for Irish political leaders to talk about and engage with Northern Ireland, the European Union has indirectly proffered a means for the revivification of Irish official nationalism as a pillar of the peace process. Evidence of this is present even in the aforementioned *Irish Times* leader, whose use of terms such as 'diversity', 'partnership' and 'understanding' has become well established in Irish official discourse on Northern Ireland, which has in turn been integral to speeches by political actors on the subject of European integration.

There is a second core dimension to this relationship between nationalism and European integration in Irish official discourse; this is also premised on the assertion that the redefinition of the nation-state through membership of the European Union (EU) is directed towards its maintenance rather than its disappearance. Although the EU has enabled the innovation necessary for the continued legitimacy of official nationalism in a changing context, discourse about the EU itself has been characterised by traditionalism. The EU has been presented by successive generations of Irish politicians as being for the benefit of the Irish nation-state. When making a case for further European integration, as at times of referendums on European treaties, governing politicians tend to rely on core tenets of Irish nationalism rather than fresh concepts inspired by the EU.

It is argued herein that the challenges posed to Irish official nationalism by the need for accommodation in/with Northern Ireland and in/with the European Union have been to a notable degree met together in Irish official discourse on the two. A connection is thus made, as Bertie Ahern (29 March 2001b) put it, between the processes of 'transformation in Ireland and in Europe'. The central aim of this book is to explore the nature of this connection and, indeed, this transformation through an analysis of the discourse of Irish political leaders as they have sought to build a 'new Ireland' alongside a 'new Europe'. Before explaining the devices used in this book to investigate this transformation, the next section of this chapter summarises its core theoretical propositions.

The dynamics of nationalism

Official discourse and nationalism

One of the core functions of official nationalism is to present an image of the nation-state to its insiders and outsiders. It is in this particular process of representation that official discourse comes into play. Official discourse has been defined as texts (written or spoken) produced by the political elite to 'place, fix and orient subjects to desired positions' (Burton and Carlen, 1979: 46). This relates to the governmental elite's role of defining the orientation, norms and goals of a political system (Weber, 1968). By analysing texts presented by members of the government, it is possible to critique the government's public position on the subject. Indeed, rather than being overcome by (or even ignoring) its inherent paradoxes, analysis of official discourse directly engages with official nationalism as it is publicly presented. In this sense, official discourse acts a window on the governmental elite's accommodation of the range of elements that compete for influence in the political realm (including the dynamics of European integration or the peace process in Northern Ireland). Indeed, by examining the textual articulation of official nationalism, discourse analysis cuts across the divisions imposed by the constructivist/essentialist debate through assessing nationalism on its own terms or, at least, in the same conceptual realm. Thus, it is possible to accurately profile 'Ireland' as it is portrayed in official nationalism.

Nevertheless, it is conceded even at this early point that official discourse is just one of innumerable factors that may contribute towards an individual's perception and opinion of national and international affairs. Moreover, official discourse is brought into the realm of public discourse via the media, and the means by which official discourse is mediated inevitably influences the recipient's perception of the message of the governmental elite. For this reason, the propositions made here are admittedly grand and yet come with strict caveats. This work is intended to illuminate and elaborate a particular dimension of the relationship between official nationalism and European integration. It does not claim to identify a deterministic or causal connection between political actors, the language they use (i.e. official discourse), the topics they talk about (i.e. European integration and nation-statehood) and the actions of the audience (i.e. voting public). Rather, it seeks to offer an insight into one important aspect (i.e. Ireland's official conceptualisation) of the vibrant complexities of the EU–nation-state nexus.

Nationalism and change

The role that official nationalism plays in conceptualising the relationship between European integration and nation-statehood is related to the process of 'imagining' the nation-state itself. Anderson's (1991) description of the nation as an 'imagined political community', though well-worn, is helpful here as it neatly describes the communion between members of a nation as being one which 'lives' in their minds (p. 6). This collective imagination is continually fed by images and concepts about nationhood; the nation's political elite are a crucial source of such discourse. Indeed, it may be said that the primary concern of official nationalism, as the elite-led legitimising ideology of the nation-state, is to shape and maintain this 'imagining'. Changes in the perceived meaning, significance and context of the nation-state as an imagined political community are of particular interest here, as we move to consider the redefinition of the state in the late twentieth century.

Members of the nation-state will still relate to it in essentially the same way and perceive it as a stable, enduring entity (this, after all, is a core tenet of nationalism), but this is only possible because official nationalism continually adapts to an evolving context.[1] The integrity of Irish nationalism, for example, has been enhanced rather than damaged by a declining emphasis on rural, Gaelic and Catholic identities in response to the realities of modern Ireland. Membership of the European Union has involved its own particular challenges to the traditional conception of the nation-state elaborated in official nationalism. Due to the responsive nature of official nationalism, every member-state has been required to be 'reimagined' in the light of European integration. The success of this process has varied according to the particular nature, focus, role, challenges, dynamics etc. of official nationalism in each member-state. The fact that the relationship between Irish nationalism and European integration has historically been a seemingly comfortable one – and the problems that the governmental elite of some EU member-states, notably Denmark and the United Kingdom, have had in this regard – point to the continued centrality of the *national* conception of politics. The governmental elite may be able to construct a new conception of nation-statehood but, drawing on one insight of ethnosymbolic theories of nationalism (see Armstrong, 1982; Smith, 1986), this can only be done using the tools and resources available to them in their particular context.

It is in this way that official nationalism enables a sense of continuity to exist alongside processes of change – all new conceptions have to be seen to be the natural development of existing conceptions, not their

Table 1.1 Traditional and new conceptions of identity, borders and governance

Official discourse	Identity	Borders	Governance
Traditional framework of the nation-state	Nation	Territory	State
New framework of the European Union	Community	Space	Polity

replacement. This relates to the need to establish a centre ground between the theories of European integration and nationalism which conceive the relationship between the EU and the nation-state being one of inherent competition. The next chapter contains a critique of such theories of the 'replacement' or the 'reaffirmation' of the nation-state by the EU and suggests a more holistic model of 'symbiosis' between the two in the realm of official nationalism. This symbiosis is explained in this book through the use of a triform model, which shows the three thematic areas addressed and affected by nationalist discourse.

Triform model: identity, borders and governance

In this book, the triform model is used to aid analysis of the way in which the political systems of the nation-state or the EU are depicted in official discourse. It is primarily intended to provide a simple diagrammatic overview of the key points being raised in the text. The theoretical foundations of this model are explored in detail in chapter 2; its inclusion at this stage facilitates comprehension of the core elements and areas of change that we are particularly concerned with here. It relates to three specific characteristics of a national political system: *identity, borders* and *governance*. The strength and dynamism of a political system lies in the ways in which the elements of identity, borders and governance become interconnected. The meaning and form of these elements are interpreted in the 'traditional' model of nation-statehood as being expressed through *nation, territory* and *state*. Official nationalism brings these three elements together in the concept and practice of nation-statehood. On the other hand, official discourse has presented European integration as developing in the same three core areas of identity, borders and governance, but in this context, the new context produces the concepts of *community, common space* and *polity* (see table 1.1). The way in which these 'traditional' and 'new' concepts are elaborated and connected in official national discourse constitutes the core focus of this book.

The nation-state under pressure

The significance of the Irish case

The role of official discourse in balancing the imagination of the nation-state and its reimagination in the light of European integration is examined here in the case of Ireland during its first thirty years of European Union (EU) membership (1973–2002). Ireland is a valuable case study for examining the relationship between European integration and nation-statehood in official nationalist discourse. First, Ireland has been frequently lauded as a 'model' and 'successful' member-state of the European Union, not only and not least by Irish politicians.[2] Yet, as outlined at the start of this chapter, Ireland, north and south, has also been seen as exemplifying the continued potency of nationalism. Given this often tense and sensitive context, Ireland has apparently demonstrated a remarkable reworking of official nationalism as a facilitator of agreement and accommodation. Thirdly, official Irish nationalism appears to have facilitated a positive approach to EU membership alongside upholding positive conceptions of nation-statehood. Relatively low levels of knowledge on the European Union in Ireland have been generally accompanied by positive perceptions of EU membership.[3] This suggests that popular opinions of the EU in Ireland have been determined less by concrete information on the EU itself than by *impressions* of the impact of EU membership on Ireland. Such impressions of EU membership are, to a significant degree, shaped by official discourse. Official discourse encompassed the pressures on conceptions of nation-statehood, interpreted them and used them positively. The ability of the governmental elite in Ireland to present European integration as, more than compatible, *complementary* to Irish nation-statehood is particularly significant given the circumstances of the elaboration of official Irish nationalism since the late 1960s. The next section of this chapter gives a brief overview of the type of challenges faced by the Irish governmental elite when seeking to define the Irish nation-state in a context of upheaval.

Internal and external pressures on Irish official nationalism

The internal pressures on Irish nationalism are those that may be seen as arising essentially but not exclusively from developments in Northern Ireland from 1968 onwards. These began with the civil rights movement and escalated to an increasing polarisation of society into 'nationalist' and 'unionist' 'communities' of distinct political, national and religious loyalties and identities, with violent consequences. One reason such events in Northern Ireland led to pressure on official Irish nationalism was that its traditional discourse of nation-statehood was seen as being of direct pertinence to the situation in the province. These principles (enshrined, but open to interpretation, in the 1937 Constitution of Ireland, specifically Articles 2 and 3) were an exclusive conception of Irish national identity, a belief in the territorial integrity of the island of Ireland and the ideal of independent sovereign statehood over the nation and its territory. Pressure was placed on Irish official nationalism as these principles were interpreted by some as giving the Irish government a constitutional as well as moral responsibility to intervene in the developments in Northern Ireland.[4] Such pressures, therefore, may be seen as demanding an adherence to the traditional narrative of Irish nationalism, i.e. a sovereign state for thirty-two-county historic Irish nation.

Events in Northern Ireland at this time precipitated the return of virulent nationalism into the spotlight on the European stage as well as in Ireland itself. For the conflict in Northern Ireland appeared to epitomise much of what the ideal of European integration had been defined against, namely violent division on the grounds of nationalism. The entry of Ireland and the United Kingdom into the EEC in 1973 enhanced the 'European' significance of events in Northern Ireland. Ireland's accession to the EEC was largely a response to developments that integrally affected Ireland's position yet were perceived to be beyond the control of its government. Continuing emigration from Ireland, the need to expand markets for exports, declining incomes for agricultural producers and the reverberations of the Cold War were among the external factors that placed pressure for change on the traditional interpretation of Irish nation-statehood. Such pressures were behind an awareness of the need for a more inclusive and outward-looking national identity, a vision of territorial borders as bridges (as opposed to barriers) for integration and a conception of statehood in line with a context of what would come to be termed interdependence. The development of the EEC epitomised such external pressures for change in the conceptualisation of nation-statehood.

Thus, events in Northern Ireland placed pressure on the Irish government elite to maintain and act upon a traditional discourse of nation-statehood; at the same time, it needed to develop a new discourse of nation-statehood in response to developments in the EEC and the international community. Official Irish discourse has enabled Irish nation-statehood to appear unremittingly fundamental in a perpetually altering context. Whilst events in Northern Ireland placed pressure for the active realisation of the traditional tenets of Irish nationalism in the early 1970s, by the late 1990s official Irish nationalism was using *new* interpretations of Irish nation-statehood to address the issue of Northern Ireland. This new discourse has been influenced by the development of European integration; hence, the connection between the ideals of the EU and those of a 'new Ireland', as seen above in the use of terms such as 'diversity' in official Irish discourse regarding both Northern Ireland and the EU. In parallel, the pressures of European integration, which have represented *new* conceptions of politics (and, by implication, nation-statehood) since the early 1970s, have been addressed through an emphasis on *traditional* elements of Irish nation-statehood in official discourse that deals with EU. In brief, Irish official discourse has been able to reconcile nation-statehood with European integration by finding symbiosis between the two in the realms of identity, borders and governance.

The study in comparative setting

Is Ireland unique?

Is Ireland exceptional in being able to meld official nationalism and European integration so successfully? The degree to which such a symbiotic relationship between national and supra-national ideologies is unusual is in large part due to the circumstances of Ireland's accession to the EEC. That is to say, Ireland's relative youth as an independent nation-state and its post-colonial status and close dependence on Britain meant that the balance of what Ireland stood to lose by not joining or by joining the EEC weighed much more heavily on the side of the former. The questions of loss of sovereignty and the imposition of constraints arising from economic co-operation etc. simply did not apply to Ireland in the same way as to the other eight members. The situation of Ireland and, of course, the EU has changed dramatically since 1973. The 2004 round of major European enlargement means Ireland is far from the only post-colonial member-state, it is far from the smallest and far from the youngest either. The speeches given by Taoiseach Bertie Ahern in January 2001 to chambers of commerce in Malta and Cyprus refer to Ireland's own experience of colonialism and division whilst carefully lauding the EU's role in moving beyond this historical legacy. This type of balancing act encapsulates the decision by the Department of Foreign Affairs and the Department of the Taoiseach to depict Ireland as a 'model' for the new (particularly small-sized) member-states. Such a tactic has been part of a conscientious effort to carve an Irish niche in the spreading European landscape. Although the mantle of a post-colonial developing nation neither fits nor suits twenty-first-century Ireland (especially since it has become a net contributor to the EU coffers), it could still not line up with other long-term member-states as a powerhouse of European integration. The idea of being a 'model' member-state enables the Irish state to show how far it has come whilst leading others along the same path. This tactic depends on the conceit of a comfortable fit between Irish official nationalism and the project of European integration. This has endured, according to the results of Eurobarometer surveys as well as official discourse, even in the wake of referendum rejections and a surge in economic standing.[5] Indeed, it has even outlasted the Euro-enthusiasm of many of the new member-states (Sitter and Henderson, 2006). The answer to why the marriage of Irish nationalism and European integration has remained a comparatively happy and stable one long after the honeymoon period lies at least in part in the particularities of Irish official nationalism.

One of the most definitive elements of Irish nationalism has been the irredentist claim held over the territory of another member-state. Although EU member-states have long histories of border conflicts and contested territorial rights, the fact that Ireland's claim over Northern Ireland was enshrined in the Constitution until its amendment in 1998 made it a particularly unusual case. The violent conflict in Northern Ireland – by far the most destructive within the EEC/EU – made Irish official irredentism all the more incongruous. Nonetheless, the limited attempt made by the EU to encourage agreement between Ireland and the United Kingdom has been premised on the Irish claim having a certain legitimacy (for example, the 1984 Haagerup Report for the European Parliament on the situation in Northern Ireland).[6] The main impact of the EU with regard to peace on the island of Ireland has been in the form of direct funding of community-level ventures in Northern Ireland and the border region. Its influence at the elite level has been much less direct; indeed, it has been mediated through the discursive and innovative input of certain (mainly nationalist, north and south) key players (Hayward, 2007). Much of the inspirational discourse that has played a part in changing political relations on the island of Ireland has made use of the European Union as 'the best example of conflict resolution in the world'.[7]

The grand narrative of the project of European integration itself centres upon the choice of European nation-states to turn relationships with their neighbours from conflict towards productive negotiation. With the example of post-war Franco-German relations at the heart of this discourse, and perhaps lessons from the Irish case in mind, the European Union has more recently sought to address border conflicts between prospective member-states (as in the failed attempt at agreement in pre-accession Cyprus) and between member-states and their neighbours (as in the case of Greece and Turkey), and even with associated states (as in Israel and Palestine). Comparative studies of such cases have shown that the influence of the EU in relation to conflict or contention between states is still inescapably conditioned by the national context (for example, Diez *et al.*, 2008). Nonetheless, meta-level analyses suggest that the EU can indirectly affect the conceptual delineation and significance of national borders, and this has consequences for the formation of community identities in Europe (Delanty, 2006). It may also directly affect the most contentious of border issues between states, i.e. irredentism; Kornprobst's (2007) analysis of the cases of Ireland and the Federal Republic of Germany shows that claims over the territory of another state may be retracted as a consequence of change in the 'ideational environment'. What he terms the 'dejustification' of irredentist claims is made possible through a combination of the normative/ ideational and the pragmatic dimensions of inter-state co-operation that the European Union entails. This study brings these two dimensions together in showing how national politicians have mediated the EU's influence for ideological change in relation to Irish identity, borders and governance.

Other analyses of national discourse in Europe

Aside from the national peculiarities of the Irish case and the subsequent changes to EU policy towards similar cases, the methodology of analysing official discourse in order to investigate the EU–nation-state relationship could be applied to great effect elsewhere. As yet a relatively novel methodological approach to understanding European integration, discourse analysis has tended to be applied in European studies to investigate *either* European policies *or* national identities. A leading example of the latter is Marcussen *et al.*'s (1999) study of 'the evolution of French, British and German nation state identities'. Marcussen *et al.* examine discourses of party elites in the three member-states 'in order to understand their identity constructions with regard to the nation state and to Europe'. Their research has three core hypotheses, which are upheld in their conclusions. First, resonance: 'new visions of political order need to *resonate* with pre-existing collective identities embedded in political institutions and cultures in order to constitute a legitimate political discourse'. Second, interests: 'political elites select ideas in an instrumental fashion' according to their perceived interests, particularly during 'critical junctures' (i.e. when there is a perceived crisis situation). Third, socialisation: once views have become consensual amongst the political majority, they are internalised and institutionalised by elites and become resistant to change (Marcussen *et al.*, 1999: 615–16). These hypotheses are informed by social identity theory and self-categorisation theory, based in social psychology as well as social constructivism, and the study is predominantly focused on elaborating these theories rather than analysing the elite discourse. Nevertheless, one key point of the study is also pivotal to this research, namely that there are different 'Europes' just as there are different nation-states due to the way in which national governmental elite discourse functions in relation to both.

Thomas Diez's (1999) study goes further in considering the formation of a 'European identity' as part of the discursive construction of an 'internal' EU political space. Rosamond (1999) too employs discourse analysis to investigate European integration, but this time in the construction of an 'external' context for the EU. Rosamond highlights the operation of specific discourses, such as globalisation, in constructing an external context in order to justify the pursuit of certain policies at an EU level. In this way, Rosamond seeks to show the significance of discourse in policy-making in the European Union. This theme was expanded upon and developed in Radaelli and Schmidt's (2005) collection of ground-breaking work on the role of discourse in policy change in Europe. They place discourse as a crucial link between agency and structure in the process of European integration. According to Radaelli and Schmidt (after Schmidt, 2000) there are two types of discourse involved in European policy-making. First, the political elite use co-ordinative discourse in order to reach agreement on policy matters. Then communicative discourse is used to present the policy programme to the public; this is the type of discourse we are most interested in here. As Radaelli, Schmidt *et al.* (2005) repeatedly acknowledge, the role of discourse does not override other factors, such as institutional constraints and national interests, but examining it does help to gain a deeper comprehension of ideational and interactive processes involved in political change. Whilst Radaelli and Schmidt's (2005) collection is structured around EU policy areas (such as banking regulation, security and defence, and telecommunications), they do recognise the need for nation-based studies to show the impact of these discourses in practice. This study intends to address this need.

Other analyses of political/conceptual change in Ireland

It is worth turning at this point to briefly consider notable studies that have similarly taken a constructivist approach to the history and politics of the Irish case study in particular. O'Mahony and Delanty (1998), Hanafin (2001), MacLaughlin (2001) and English (2006) are all concerned with the role of nationalism in the development of the Irish nation-state in concept and practice. English's work traces the historical roots of Irish nationalism through to the present day and concludes that it will remain a powerful force in Irish politics for the foreseeble future. The others share an emphasis on the symbolic, cultural, identity and ideological aspects of nationalism – also a feature of Graham's (2001) 'deconstruction' of 'Ireland'. As a literary critic, Graham (2001) explores conflicting interpretations of 'Ireland' in postcolonialism, historical revisionism, feminism and postnationalism. Indeed, Graham's *Deconstructing Ireland* is not unlike Kearney's *Postnationalist Ireland* (1997), not least in that Kearney also attempts to 'deconstruct' the Irish nation in philosophical and cultural terms. However, the ultimate claims made by Kearney (1997: 1) are more politically oriented, namely to 'reinterrogate [the] critical implications' of nationalism. Kearney places his postnationalist Ireland firmly in a European context, as does McCall (1999) in his dissection of the possibilities the EU offers for reconstructing communal identities in Northern Ireland. The significance of the EU for reimagining the relationship *between* Ireland and Northern Ireland is emphasised by Goodman (2000). Goodman's study is grounded in a socio-economic analysis of the implications of European integration on north-south relationships in Ireland. He concludes that the Good Friday Agreement (GFA) (1998) represents the necessary state-level recognition of the convergence between north and south that has been occurring since the 1950s.

As to the cross-border dissemination of influence and ideas among politicians towards peaceful co-operation, we acknowledge that this study investigates just one (albeit relatively uncharted) dimension, i.e. southern official discourse. Therefore, this book could at best claim to complement Catherine O'Donnell's (2007) detailed and insightful analysis of the relationship between Fianna Fáil and Sinn Féin since the Troubles. O'Donnell convincingly demonstrates the significance of Fianna Fáil's adherence to core republican principles despite the rhetorical change that facilitated its driving role in the peace process. This tactic enabled it to encourage Sinn Féin's engagement in the process and, moreover, to have some influence in the critical alteration of that party's discourse. This modified language allowed Sinn Féin to be brought into the centre of political negotiation and, ultimately, power in Northern Ireland (Shirlow and McGovern, 1998). On the constitutional nationalist side, the work of Peter McLoughlin (2006) and Michael Cunningham (2008) has begun to show the importance of the 'political journey' of John Hume and the power of the language he has used to plot a new course for political dialogue about the Northern Ireland problem. John Hume and the Social Democratic and Labour Party's (SDLP) concepts of both north-south relations and European Union certainly had an impact on the discourse of the main political parties in the south and (perhaps in part through this southern channel) on their political opponents in the north too. Gilligan (2007) shows the importance of Hume's 'identity talk' in the 1980s and its influence on Fine Gael and initiatives such as the New Ireland Forum and the Anglo-Irish Agreement. Subsequent public reception of new identity narratives within Northern Ireland is, according to Walker (2007), essential for its post-conflict society. Although it is beyond the scope of this book to trace the patterns of cross-insemination in Irish nationalism's ideological change, the very fact that it has been an all-island affair has been crucial to finding agreement. Instead, this book brings the themes of these studies together within the European context, arguing that there would have been no agreement at all were it not for the ability of the Irish political elite to construct a discursive symbiosis between nation-statehood and European integration.

Chapter summary

The key proposition of this book is that Irish official discourse has been able to pose European integration and nation-statehood as mutually complementary. It thus seeks to highlight the richness of the interweaving elements of official nationalism and European integration in official discourse as an arena for exploring the nation-state–European Union relationship. This is achieved by dividing the book into three parts. The first part of this book consists of a chapter (2) on official nationalism and its relationship to European integration and a chapter (3) on official discourse and the use of discourse analysis as a methodological tool in studying official nationalism.

Chapter 2 applies the triform model outlined above to official nationalism and European integration, considering in detail the way in which each element of identity, borders and governance is presented in the 'traditional' conception of the nation-state and the 'new' conception of the European Union. As well as outlining the basic 'framework' (i.e. supporting structure) of the nation-state and the European Union in the three core areas of identity, borders and governance, this chapter prepares the way for the consideration of the 'narrative' (i.e. supporting story-line) and the 'model' (i.e. inspiring ideal) of the nation-state and the EU as presented in Irish official discourse. The final section of chapter 2 outlines three alternative theories of the way in which European integration relates to the nation-state and its conceptualisation before highlighting the reasons as to why the theory of 'symbiosis' is most appropriate for this research. Pivotal to the concept of 'symbiosis' is the acknowledgement of the central position of national governmental elites in maintaining, developing and legitimising the nation-state and the European Union.

The connection between concept and practice in this process is encapsulated in 'discourse'. Chapter 3 elaborates the theoretical origins and tenets of discourse theory and analysis before considering in detail the function and the value official discourse in the processes of official nationalism and European integration. As a methodological approach, discourse analysis reflects a particular conception of the role and meaning of discourse in relation to political practice and change. Following an overview of other studies in the areas of nationalism and European integration which have used discourse theory and analysis, the final section of chapter 3 outlines in detail the way in which it is applied in this research.

The significance of context in shaping official nationalism and its approach to European integration makes it necessary to locate an examination of contemporary official nationalism within in its historical and political framework. The second part of this book fulfils this requirement, with its overview of the development of official nationalism in Ireland. Chapter 4 analyses the period from the first Home Rule Bill to the Irish War of Independence (1886–1921) during which competition between the three broad versions of nationalism in Ireland – unionist, constitutional and republican – intensified around their conceptualisations of the framework, narrative and ideal models of the Irish nation. Developments in international affairs, particularly in Europe, had the effect of altering the focus and appeal of each of these versions of nationalism in Ireland. As a result, the need to find a middle ground between constitutional and republican nationalisms shaped the development of official nationalism in the independent Irish Free State after 1922.

The struggle of the new governmental elite to construct a nation-state in the context of disagreement within Ireland and tensions beyond Ireland is examined in chapter 5. This includes the changes made to official national discourse as successive governments sought to reconcile the ideals of nation-statehood with the 'incomplete' reality of the nation, territory and state over which they had jurisdiction. The way in which Irish official nationalism develops in relation to its internal and external contexts constitutes the focus of this chapter. The development of official nationalism first centred upon the process of nation-building, i.e. legitimising the state through its association with the Irish nation, and then on the process of state-building, i.e. consolidating the structures of the state. The growing conception of the twenty-six-county state as a nation-state had significant implications for its relationship with Northern Ireland and with other states, particularly Britain. This conception is integrally related to the definition of the Irish nation, territory and state which, the chapter shows, changes substantially over this fifty-year period. This leads into an overview of the core pressures placed on the definition of Irish nation-statehood by events in Northern Ireland and Europe. The position of Irish official nationalism in relation to both the Troubles in Northern Ireland and the process of European integration in 1972 is outlined in preparation for the in-depth analysis of the way in which Irish official discourse addresses these two areas that occurs in the final part of the book.

Through detailed analysis of official national discourse in the period 1973 to 2002, the third part of the book considers the ways in which the accommodation of new dynamics of European integration occurred alongside the assertion of traditional tenets of Irish nation-statehood. This analysis is divided into three chapters (6–8), focusing on the way in which official discourse has addressed each of the three themes of identity, borders and governance in the context of EU membership and conflict in Northern Ireland. Each chapter examines the 'reimagination' of these elements in relation to the three core aspects of official discourse: framework, narrative and ideal model. The core argument is that the conception of Irish identity (nation), borders (territory) and governance (state) associated with a traditional nationalist approach to Northern Ireland has actually been applied by Irish official discourse to justify Ireland's position in the new context of European integration. In parallel to this, the conception of identity (community), borders (space) and governance (polity) that has been associated with the process and project of European integration has been used in Irish official discourse to explore new paths for progress in Northern Ireland.

The implications of the centrality of official discourse in ensuring a comfortable 'fit' between Irish official nationalism and European integration have been apparent in referendums on European treaties, all of which between 1972 and 1998 were passed successfully, in accordance with the wishes of the governmental elite. The circumstances of the defeat of the first Nice Treaty referendum are considered in detail in the conclusion of this book. The outcome of this referendum (and the 2008 Lisbon referendum, see Afterword) has implications not only for Ireland's position in the European Union but also for the role played by official discourse in relating the public to the EU. These factors are analysed in the final chapter, with a specific focus on their likely impact on the future 'imagination' of Ireland in the European context. It is revealed that the relationship between official nationalism and European integration has a significance that extends to a wide range of issues, from specific instances of cross-border partnerships to the broadest questions regarding the 'future of Europe'. This study has positive implications far beyond the Irish example. Revealing the role of official nationalism in the building of an 'agreed Ireland' offers a new perspective on the processes involved in the quest for an 'agreed Europe'.

Notes

1 Differences in theories of nationalism centre upon the explanation for the sense of continuity between past, present and future that is resident in the concept of the 'nation'. Primordial theories of nationalism argue that this feature arises from the actual antiquity of nations as distinct from 'given' entities (e.g. Shils, 1957). Ethnosymbolists identify this continuity as arising from the 'ethnic' origins of nations, with myths, symbols etc. of the ethnic group enduring over centuries to define what developed into a nation (e.g. A. D. Smith, 1995: 59–60). Social constructivists and modernists contend that nations are modern constructions, and a sense of continuity is largely 'factitious', constructed by ruling elites (e.g. Hobsbawm and Ranger, 1983: 1–2, 12–14).

2 For example: 'Many of the candidate countries for EU membership look to Ireland as a model of what they hope to achieve by joining the European Union' (Minister for Foreign Affairs, Brian Cowen, 27 May 2001). 'With great intelligence, application and far-sightedness, you have taken full advantage of Europe's political and economic development. As a result, your country has achieved success and fame as the Celtic Tiger economy' (President of the European Commission, Romano Prodi, 22 June 2001).

3 Sinnott's (1995: 4–5) study shows that 'there is very considerable room for improvement in levels of knowledge' of the European Union, with 65 per cent of the Irish population not well informed about the EU. Yet (with the exception of a period from the early to mid-1980s) the Irish public has generally been positive about the benefits of EU membership. In a *Eurobarometer* survey of 2008, only 7 per cent of those surveyed stated that Ireland had not benefited from EU membership and 82 per cent said Ireland had benefited (European Commission, 2008: EB69).

4 A precedent for the involvement, if not the intervention, of the Irish state in developments in Northern Ireland was de Valera's opposition to the stationing of American troops in Northern Ireland in 1942 without prior consultation with the Irish government: 'it is our duty to make it clearly understood that, no matter what troops occupy the Six Counties, the Irish people's claim for the union of the whole of the national territory and for supreme jurisdiction over it will remain unabated' (de Valera, 28 January 1942).

5 According to the full report on the 2006 Eurobarometer survey, only 2 per cent of Irish respondents said they were not proud to be Irish (the lowest

result in the EU). In a Eurobarometer survey of 2007, Ireland had the highest positive response level (87 per cent) in the EU27 (the average being 58 per cent) to the question of whether Ireland has benefited from EU membership.

6 For further examination of the 'two communities' analysis made by the Haagerup committee regarding Northern Ireland, see Hayward (2006a).

7 Interview with John Hume (former MP, MEP, MLA and SDLP leader) for *EUBorderConf* project, Belfast, 1 June 2004.

2

Nation-state and European Union

The purpose of this chapter is to elaborate in detail the theoretical basis
for the application of the triform model – identity, borders and governance – to the nation-state and the European Union. Theories of nationalism and European integration are examined in three sections. The first
section sets out a constructivist/modernist conception of official nationalism and nation-statehood, which traditionally frames a political system
in a triform model of 'nation', 'territory' and 'state'. Section two considers the significance of national governmental elites and their official
discourse in the process of European integration. It also shows how the
identity, borders and governance of the European Union may be broadly
conceptualised as 'community', 'space' and 'polity'. The final part outlines a symbiotic theory of the relationship between the European Union
and nation-statehood, having considered the two main alternative
conceptions of the EU leading to a replacement or a renewal of the
nation-state. This chapter thus prepares the theoretical groundwork for
the identification of symbiosis between the conceptualisation of the
nation-state and the European Union in official Irish discourse that constitutes the focus of this book.

An emphasis on context, the governmental elite and the role of discourse places this research in a broadly constructivist framework. In the
realm of social science, 'constructivism' holds (following Berger and
Luckmann [1967] and Searle [1995]) that social realities exist only by
human cognitive action and agreement. Hence they are fragile and
changeable – shaped, among other factors, by context, influence and
discourse. Thus, aside from the admittedly broad and even apparently
essentialist use of the terms for the sake of clarity, 'nation-state' and
'European Union' are here assumed to represent *processes* rather than
static institutions or objects. It is crucial to this research to acknowledge
that a nation-state is a construct of imagination and interaction; the
term summarises, and even distorts, a complex combination of theoretical and practical elements that vary according to context. This chapter

illuminates and justifies the constructivist path taken in this research amid a multitude of theories of official nationalism and European integration.

Official nationalism

Nationalism and governmental elites

The very use of the phrase 'official nationalism' implies a theoretical conception of nationalism (and its functioning) that is more allied with modernist than primordial or ethnosymbolist approaches to the subject. For the 'official' element of official nationalism highlights the centrality of the state, and a core point of agreement among the diverse theories constituting the modernist school is that nationalism rose to prominence alongside the modern (generally post-eighteenth-century) development of statecraft in Europe (Özkirimli, 2000: 213–14). Nonetheless, divergent ideas as to the role of governmental elites in this marriage of nationalism and statehood mean that there are various interpretations of the idiom 'official nationalism' itself. The phrase was first used by Seton-Watson (1977) when arguing that educated elites in the modern era used ideology and power to shape the populations of their states into what he termed 'new' nations. Brass (1991: 63) goes further in stressing the 'instrumental' nature of ethnic and national identity, and ultimately defines nationalism as a political movement shaped by elite competition and manipulation. Breuilly (1993: 1, 112) specifically relates nationalism to 'the objectives of obtaining state power', with governmental elites ultimately placing themselves as the 'spokesmen for the nation'. However, this is not to say that the nation is a construct forged entirely on the whims of a political elite for, as Connor (1994: 352) concedes, 'a nation exists only when appeals to national consciousness can effectively trigger a mass response'. Moreover, although nationalism may be seen as the ideology of nation-statehood, the 'nation-state' is conceived daily by those within and outside it as '*material*, lived, tangible' (Sofos, 1996: 251). It is important, therefore, to balance an awareness of the importance of elite players with consideration of the context (political, cultural, historical etc.) within which they operate (Smith, 1991: 79; Calhoun, 1997: 20–3).

Tilley (1997: 511) argues that a constructivist approach addresses this issue by recognising that 'knowledge/value systems are continually reshaped as groups react to changing environmental and social conditions'. Although Tilley is specifically referring to the formation of ethnic groups, the point is equally relevant to nation-states: the meaning and value of the various constituents of nationalism (including symbols and myths) are 'interminably negotiated, revised and redefined' (Özkirimli, 2000: 217). Such negotiations happen within the nation-state itself, yet they are necessarily led, expressed and drawn into a coherent whole by the governmental elite. Official nationalism may be seen, therefore, as the ideology of the nation-state defined by the governmental elite. It incorporates elements of the existing political and social situation into a broader vision that constitutes the ideological justification for the national projects of the governmental elite. Hence, official nationalism appears relevant to the interests of all social groups within the state's jurisdiction; its elaboration by members of the governmental elite serves to both define and legitimate the nation-state.

The difficulties involved in theorising official nationalism are intrinsically related to the key to its enduring success, namely its ability to merge apparently conflicting elements in a cohesive discourse. It is a process that links the internal context to the external sphere, the past with the present and future, reality with ideals, ideology with activity, continuity with change. Paradoxes and tensions are intrinsic to nationalism. However, in order to construct a framework with which to understand these processes, it is helpful to deconstruct nationalism into its core component parts. This may be done by considering nationalism to be, in essence, the ideology of the nation-state.

Triform model: a preliminary elaboration

Although theorists disagree as to whether there are any essential characteristics of a nation-state, let alone what they are and how many, few would dispute the need for a nation-state to have a clearly defined national *identity*, demarcated territorial *borders* and a distinct form of *governance* before it could be described as such. This is similar to Anderson's (1991: 6–7) description of the nation as being imagined as a community ('conceived as a deep, horizontal comradeship'), limited (with 'finite, if elastic, boundaries, beyond which lie other nations'), and sovereign ('the gage and emblem of [national] freedom is the sovereign state'). To relate Anderson's concepts to the triform model of nation-statehood employed here: the 'community' element inspires the conception of a group with a collective identity known as the *nation*. Second, the 'limited' nature of the nation-state is defined by borders that circumscribe its *territory*. Finally, the 'sovereign' nature of the nation-state is embodied in the institutions of governance within the national jurisdiction, ultimately expressed in the form of an independent *state* (see table 2.1). Official nationalism is the glue that binds these core elements of nation-statehood together.

Table 2.1 The traditional triform framework of the nation-state

Official discourse	*Identity*	*Borders*	*Governance*
Traditional framework of the nation-state	Nation	Territory	State

The remainder of this part of the chapter will address the theoretical foundations of each of these tenets. It does this through the further development of the triform model in examining the *framework*, *narrative* and *model* of the concepts concerned. The theoretical logic of these three parts are elucidated in detail in the next chapter; at this point, they may be said to simply depict how official discourse tends to describe or present the usual form (i.e. framework), legitimating story (i.e. narrative) and ideal type (i.e. model) of the concept in hand. It is also worth explaining here that the use of the terms 'traditional' and 'new' when describing discourse on the nation-state and the EU respectively is an admittedly imprecise and yet, again, usefully clear means of comparing and contrasting the themes and images concerned.

To describe concepts as 'traditional' or 'new' is not intended to imply their confinement to particular historical periods – indeed, the core argument of this book is that these conceptions are blended and used interchangeably in contemporary Irish political discourse. Neither does it reify these concepts as 'national' or 'European' as such. Rather, the highlighting of 'traditional' themes in relation to nation-statehood and 'new' themes in relation to European integration is intended to identify general trends in the discursive use of these themes. That is to say, concepts associated with nation-statehood (such as a sovereign state) would be considered the more traditional fare of official nationalism than the newer concepts associated with European integration (such as a transnational polity). This aim of this simplification is to enable the development of such concepts to be traced in the detailed analysis of Irish official discourse contained in the third part of this book. There it is argued that traditional and new concepts of identity, borders and governance have been used strategically to respond to the challenges of the political context of the late twentieth century.

Nation

Of the three elements of nation-statehood, 'nation' is the most difficult to define, it being, according to Tishkov (2000: 625), no more than 'a ghost word escalated to the level of meta-category through historic accident and inertia of intellectual prescription'. The ephemeral nature of the nation as a subject for analysis does not in anyway undermine its value as a concept central to an individual's sense of identity. Indeed, it is the fact that the nation is about *identity*, and is intended to represent a distinct collective identity, that makes it elude definition. For, in line with constructivist analyses, Hall (1990: 222) states that identity is not a 'given' but 'a "production", which is never complete, always in process'. Furthermore, Schlesinger (1992: 16) describes identity as involving two processes: an 'imaginary process of creating traditions and of activating collective memories' and, secondly, an 'active process' of 'inclusion and exclusion'. Both processes are intended to define the 'us' of group identity by placing it in relation to those who preceded us as members of the group and in relation to those who are outside our group. These qualities of collective identity are given a particular significance in the context of nationhood.

The nation, as the embodiment of a collective identity, functions to equip members of a nation-state with 'a sense of belonging and a security in themselves and in each other' (Keane, 1995: 187). To apply Schlesinger's (1992) dual definition of the processes involved in identity formation, national identity involves an imaginary process based on myths, symbols and emblems of the historical nation and drawing a connection between the experience of the contemporary members of the nation and their ancestors. The perception of common historical origins contributes to the second element of identity formation, namely the active process of distinguishing between 'us' and 'them'. For it helps a 'stratified national population [to be] perceived as essentially homogenous' in the face of vast diversity and complexity in the international sphere (Greenfeld, 1992: 7). The narrative of a historical national culture and the ideal model of a distinct, unique national people are epitomised in the features of a nation-state intended to define the collective identity of the nation. For example, the school textbooks on national history, the constitution and the citizenship laws of any nation-state would all have been written with the intention of reiterating national identity. Table 2.2 depicts the traditional elements involved in the conception of the identity of a nation-state. It functions to show that, according to traditional official discourse on the subject, the identity of a nation-state is framed in the nation, supported by a narrative of an historical culture and based on a belief in the essential distinctiveness of the national population.

Territory

Official nationalism's conceptualisation of the territory of the nation-state contains a potent mixture of objective and emotive elements,

Table 2.2 Traditional conception of identity in the nation-state

Traditional official discourse	Identity
Framework of identity	Nation
Narrative of identity	Historical culture
Model of identity	Distinct people

Table 2.3 Traditional conception of borders in the nation-state

Traditional official discourse	Borders
Framework of borders	Territory
Narrative of borders	Homeland
Model of borders	Demarcated boundaries

elevating the jurisdiction of the state to a position of immense ideological significance and literally 'grounding' the identity of the nation in an internationally recognisable framework. The geographical dimension of the nation-state gives it a palpable material existence intrinsically connected to the ideological dimension of nation-statehood (Bassin, 2001). Nationalism functions to connect the geographical and the conceptual in the territory of the nation-state (Murray, 1997). Indeed, continuous attempts to merge material and emotional forms of identity have inspired Penrose (2002) to describe nationalism itself as 'an innovative and powerful form of territoriality'. Even prior to nationalism, geographical space has emotional and material power. Through the activity of official nationalism, this emotional and material power is harnessed in the delineation of territory as the embodiment of, and point of connection between, state and nation (Penrose, 2002). Thus, in a way similar to the processes of identity formation, the territorial borders of a nation-state become associated with an imaginary process of linking present with past (in the historical narrative of the territorial 'homeland') and with an active process of drawing lines of inclusion and exclusion (in the clearly demarcated boundaries of the model nation-state) (see table 2.3).

The narrative and model of territory in the traditional conception of nation-statehood, reflects the 'inclusionary as well as exclusionary' nature of borders (O'Dowd and Wilson, 1996: 14). Indeed, the spatial dimension of nationalism physically embodies the fundamental gesture of ideology in drawing boundaries between the self/familiar and the non-self/unfamiliar (Jameson, 1989: 114–15). As a result of the processes of territorial inclusion, the nation-state has 'a more-or-less concentrated form of settlement in geographical terms' (Van Amersfoort, 1995: 173). Over time, individual members are socialised within the territorial unit of the nation-state and a 'collective consciousness' among diverse groups and experiences is forged within this common delimited space (Herb, 1999: 17). Hence, bounded territories 'are not simply a matter of control or access to resources, or of networks of interaction within fixed geographical limits, rather they denote participation in a collective consciousness' (O'Dowd and Wilson, 1996: 8). The association of common experience, practice and culture with a particular territorial space is epitomised in the notion of the national homeland (Billig, 1995a: 83). The narrative of the homeland supports the intrinsically *spatial* identities of state and nation with an historical and physical context: in the national territory, the ancestral and cultural origins of the nation connect with the contemporary and political activity of the state.

The clear demarcation, and international recognition, of the borders of the nation-state serves to bolster the shared national belief that the homeland is a given, a physical and historical reality, regardless of the actual point at which the state borders were drawn. This blurring of objective/material and subjective/conceptual distinctions is an integral part of the functioning of official nationalism in this arena. An important distinction is made by Smith (1995: 2–3) between two types of geographical boundaries: 'bona fide' (i.e. those which exist independently of human cognitive acts, such as coastlines) and 'fiat' (i.e. those which do not exist independently of human cognitive acts, such as property lines). One of the central roles of official nationalism in relation to territory is to blur the division between these types of boundaries. In this way, the idea that the borders of the nation-state are its natural boundaries, marking the space of the ancient homeland of the nation's people, is affirmed. This point leads to recognition of the difficulties facing official Irish nationalism in conceptualising the territory of the nation-state. The governmental elite of the Irish state has sought to assert the national identity and legitimate governance of the twenty-six-county jurisdiction, with its externally 'imposed' fiat borders, whilst continuing to support the notion that the Irish homeland is defined by the bona fide boundaries of the island of Ireland. Such a notion was made more important by the fact that the discontent behind modern Irish nationalism was territorially based and conceived (Mann, 1995: 52).

The fact that the boundaries of a nation-state are by definition fiat boundaries, determined by agreement between states, and that their correspondence with bona fide boundaries varies according to context, highlights the constructed nature of national territories. The territory of a nation-state, according to the ideal model of nation-statehood, embodies the jurisdiction of both the nation and the state. Yet, for territory to become an important aspect of identity, a 'complex group of other elements' must be seen to comply rather than conflict with its integrity (Paasi, 1996: 52). As Armstrong (1982: 10) illustrates, such elements as economic development, political action, language and folklore can create and define borders between collective groups. The way in which this complexity of elements is perceived to interact with the bordered territory is crucial in deciding the prevalence and potency of the nation-state idea itself (Herb and Kaplan, 1999: 2). Official nationalism focuses, therefore, on legitimating the boundaries of the nation-state in cultural, historical and economic as well as territorial terms. In the early stages of nation-state building, such boundaries give the elite a 'tangible' and distinct platform from which to promote their ideas (Periwal, 1995: 236). As the nation-state is established, its cultural, historical, economic and territorial borders become, according to the ideal type, analogous. In this way, different conceptions of the national territory reflect different notions of nation-statehood (Penrose, 2002).

State

Bassin (2001) notes that national territory is deliberately defined in a way that animates the national priorities of the state. This relates to the fact that the process of state-building in the modern era was directly linked to the creation of territorialised social relations as well as the politicisation of national identity (Hall, 1995: 22). For the economic, social and political factors associated with modernisation reflect increased awareness of territoriality as a significant form of power (Penrose, 2002). The modern conception of political space in 'territorially defined, territorially fixed and mutually exclusive state formations' is intrinsically connected to the role of nationalism (Ruggie, 1993: 144). For nationalism is about 'the construction and contestation of concepts of identity in the social conditions specific to modernity'. It is therefore, Periwal (1995: 229) concludes, 'essentially political', encompassing the rise of modern democracy and the related notion of an active identification of citizens with the institutions of governance. Modern nationalism and modern democracy are 'twin sums' (Barnett, 1996: 162). Nationalism gives rise to a sense of 'common identity that makes it possible for them to conceive of shaping their world together' within the 'multi-layered political and social mosaic' of democracy (Miller, 1989: 184; Keane, 1995: 187). In this way, nationalism is intrinsically related to the spread of the unified administrative reach of the modern state over its territory; and, thus, the nation came to be – or at least ideally conceived as – a 'bordered power container' (Giddens, 1985: 119).

So nationalism is in essence a political principle, holding that 'the political and the national unit should be congruent' (Gellner, 1983: 1). This idea is central to the narrative of national self-determination, which brought together 'the principle that citizens should govern themselves . . . with the principle that nations should determine their own destiny' (Keane, 1995: 185). 'Self-determination (and the claims for it), as a political activity and, ultimately, as a historical change,' Hroch (1995: 65) notes, 'is the final stage of a historical process and of a specific kind of political or social movement which has its roots in the nineteenth century'. However, although the narrative of national self-determination became associated with the proliferation of independent nation-states in the twentieth century, it would be inaccurate to construe 'national goals as the struggle for independence' (Hroch, 1995: 73). This argument is borne out by the case of Ireland, where the quest for national self-determination was pursued by not only republicans but also constitutional nationalists, who could conceive of autonomy for Ireland within the wider framework of the British empire. Nevertheless, as the concept of 'the nation' gained strength in Ireland, so the belief that it could be adequately represented within the imperial context became less popularly acceptable. The subsequent convergence of nationhood with statehood in Irish nationalism reflected the traditional conception of the nation-state as epitomised in official nationalism throughout Europe and beyond.

According to the traditional model of the state, it controls 'the principal means of coercion within a given territory' and is 'differentiated from other organisations operating in the same territory, autonomous, centralized and formally coordinated' (Tilly, 1975: 638). The capacities of governance thus reside in the state as the core political unit of the nation-state and the framework within which the nation is governed (Hirst, 1996: 97). For the reasons outlined above, modern nationalism conceived the nation as being of primary political significance and, indeed, the bearer of sovereignty (Greenfeld, 1992: 7). Whilst the idea of sovereignty, as Cobban (1969: 30) notes, 'emphasise[s] the rights of government', it also stresses the rights of the citizens to be governed in a way that reflects their identity and requirements as a distinct, territorially demarcated nation. If, as nationalism asserts, the nation is a unique, historical, self-contained and self-aware entity, not only should it be represented as such in political terms, it should have as much independence as possible (Breuilly, 1993: 2). Sovereignty, therefore, has two aspects: one dealing with relations between states, the other with the relations of

Table 2.4   Traditional conception of governance in the nation-state

Traditional official discourse	*Governance*
Framework of governance	*State*
Narrative of governance	National self-determination
Model of governance	Sovereignty

the state and its citizens (Kohn, 1965: 20). The ideal model of sovereignty is integrally related to the narrative of national self-determination; both are drawn together in the conceptual framework of statehood (see table 2.4).

To conclude, the traditional conception of the nation-state 'represents the coincidence in [territorial] space of a number of principles of social and economic organisation', all of which are founded in modernity but are continually reimagined for the contemporary context (Keating, 1997: 691). As we have already noted, one of the most significant elements influencing the redefinition of the tenets of Irish nation-statehood in the late twentieth century has been membership of the European Union.

European integration

European integration and governmental elites

The European Union constitutes an entity of utmost significance for the concept and practice of nation-statehood. Important connections between the conceptualisation of the nation-state and the European Union are made in official national discourse. Indeed, national governmental elite members have played a central role in linking the redefinition of the nation-state with the development of the European Union. For governmental elites are not only actively involved in the development and definition of both the nation-state and the EU, they are also positioned 'between' the two in terms of relating one to the other. From this position, the governmental elite of EU member-states have, as Laffan (1996a: 87) argues, 'embraced' the 'European project' as 'a means of strengthening their existing state identities and as an arena within which to project their state identities'. This process, Laffan (1996a: 87) contends, has enabled the development of 'a high degree of compatibility between the national project and European integration' (a development encapsulated in the concept of 'symbiosis'). Governmental elites have then 'sold' European integration 'to domestic audiences as part of the national project' (Laffan, 1996a: 87). The extent to which national

Table 2.5   A triform framework of the European Union

Official discourse	*Identity*	*Borders*	*Governance*
New framework of the European Union	Community	Space	Polity

citizens have 'bought' this notion is integrally related to the degree of 'compatibility' that there appears to be between the national project and the European project – a factor determined by the particular discourse of the nation-state epitomised in official nationalism. All governmental elites present membership of the EU as being in 'national interests' but moreover, I argue, it is specifically presented in accordance with the official conceptualisation of the nation-state, i.e. its identity, borders and governance and its framework, narrative and ideal model.

Another reason why official discourse is a significant source for considering the nation-state–European Union nexus is that the nation-state is far more established as a concept and political entity than the EU. Nevertheless, just as disagreement regarding the history, goals and path of nation-statehood does not undermine its potency as a political and popular entity, so the EU can be a contested entity (lacking, for example, consensus as to its identity or end-goals) without being a failed one. Indeed, part of the success of the construction of the EU to date has in some ways depended on ambiguity as to its development in the future. Such ambiguity has arisen in at least some part from the governmental elite of each member-state conceptualising and presenting the EU in their own nation-centric way. Yet, the EU certainly has enough coherence and history of its own to make it possible to identify its broad characteristics using the triform model (see table 2.5). Such analysis is made all the more pertinent by the fact that the development of the EU is giving it an increasing relevance to and impact on sensitive areas of political identity, borders and governance that were previously the nation-state's preserve (Laffan, 1996a: 83).

Community

The political nature of the European Union, as with that of the nation-state, means that collective identity or, more specifically, identification with the project of European integration is of great significance (Wallace, 1990: 13). A democratic political project requires consensus based on a popular sense of commonality within the group and towards the project (Eder and Giesen, 2001: 8). For a political project or entity to be 'owned' by a group, the group itself must possess some level of collective and cohe-

Table 2.6 New conception of identity in the European Union

New official discourse	*Identity*
Framework for identity	*Community*
Narrative of identity	Unity in diversity
Model of identity	Multidimensional identities

sive identity (Yiangou, 2001: 36). In the area of collective identity, the European Union has been conceived as having a 'community' dimension. As a nation-state is (according to nationalist discourse) the political embodiment of the nation, so the European Union acts on behalf of a European community. The sense of European community is supported by a narrative of European integration that places the European Union as the ideal and even natural outcome of a common European history and experience. The narrative of European community can contain a notion of a European culture, whose most distinctive feature is that it is all-embracing, bringing harmony between different national groups rather than division. This can be summarised under the heading 'unity in diversity'. The origins of this narrative were present in the foundation of the European Coal and Steel Community (ECSC) in 1951, as seen in the following extract from the Paris Treaty (quoted in Gillespie, 1996: 32):

> [The ECSC member-states are] resolved to substitute for age-old rivalries the merging of their essential interests; to create by establishing an economic community the basis for a broader and deeper community among people long-divided by bloody conflicts; and to lay the foundations for institutions which will give direction to a destiny henceforward shared.

The 1992 Maastricht Treaty (Treaty on European Union, or TEU) marked a significant development in the practice and conception of the EU as a political entity. As part of its focus on European citizenship, the TEU also recognised the significance of collective identity and culture. Article 28 of the TEU encapsulates the narrative of the European 'community' in directing the EU to:

> contribute to the flowering of the cultures of the member states, while respecting their national and regional diversity and at the same time bringing the common cultural heritage to the fore.

The fact that this narrative emphasises harmony and not uniformity as such among the member-states of the EU leads to the ideal model of European community being one of multidimensional identities, including regional, national and European, rather than a supranational European identity (Meehan, 1993; see table 2.6).

The conceptualisation of a European identity as one of many rather than an overarching collective identity represents a deliberate distinction being made by official discourse between European and national models of identity. In the model of multidimensional identities, people's (primary) identification with their nation-state can be seen to be compatible with their local and 'ethnic' identities as well as with their identity in the international sphere as 'Europeans'. In this way, the potential for conflict between national and European identities is minimised, by placing them on different planes or levels, rather than competing for dominance in the same identity space (Hayward and Howard, 2002: 4). Hence, Pinder's (1995) suggestion that European identity is 'extra national' rather than 'supra national'. This is borne out by the fact that 'different Europeans experience their Europeanness in different ways' (Laffan, 1996a: 99). European 'community', culture and identity are not experienced or conceptualised by European citizens in the same way that national identity is. This points to the fact that the EU is not an alternative to the nation-state but conceived in national official discourse as a complement to it.

Space

Unlike the theme of identity, it was not until relatively recently that European integration became expressly concerned with the significance of political borders and space. As O'Dowd (2003) notes, the end of the Second World War brought with it a strengthening of national territorial boundaries, as states improved and expanded their infrastructure within their borders. It was the Council of Europe that first projected an alternative view of borders as bridges, through its ideal of regional cross-border co-operation. In contrast, the EEC at this time *strengthened* state borders, with the regulation of national markets enhanced by the Treaty of Rome (1957) – a trend continued with the development of the Single Market in the 1980s and the corresponding role of the state within its own borders (O'Dowd, 2003: 7). This changed with the focus on political co-operation as a part of economic integration within the European Union, and the 1990s saw growth in the ideals of cross-border co-operation, with a significant shift away from the use of borders as symbols of exclusive national power, at both a European and a national level (O'Dowd, 2003: 11). Herb (1999: 9) suggests that this process should be seen in the light of the general international trend of 'globalisation', in which the territoriality of political power is becoming 'discordant' with that of national identity. Harvey's (1995: 283) vision of the postmodern era supports this notion, with its identification of a 'new set

Table 2.7 New conception of borders in the European Union

New official discourse	*Borders*
Framework for borders	*Space*
Narrative of borders	Overcome divisions
Model of borders	Cross-border co-operation

of experiences of time and space'. Yet new understandings of territory continue to draw on material and constitutional powers of space, with sovereignty and governance still associated with bordered territorial jurisdictions (Herb, 1999: 13; Penrose, 2002).

The European Union's development in the arena of 'borders' reflects these competing influences. On the one hand, the EU is founded on a territorially based notion of material and constitutional powers, due to the fact that its conception and practice is confined for the most part within the territorial jurisdiction of its member-states. On the other hand, the EU itself cannot be said to be a territorial entity itself, given that its external borders are flexible due to processes (and expectations) of enlargement. Hence, the concept of 'borders' for the EU produces a framework of 'space' rather than territory. The key point of 'space' (as opposed to 'territory') is that it is to some degree apolitical. Thus, the narrative of the EU in this area enables the political entity of the European Union to be seen to depoliticise *internal* borders for common security and peace. Overcoming internal division and enhancing internal unity is reflected in the ideal model of the EU as one in which internal borders are no barrier to co-operation in the achievement of common interests within the common space of the EU (see table 2.7). It is notable that this conception of the EU does not 'compete' with that of the nation-state, given that it does not presume that the EU has a territorial 'homeland' at all, let alone one that supersedes that of the nation-state.

Polity

The fragmentation of the 'political public sphere . . . into national units' has complicated the task of building democratic processes for governance within the EU (Habermas, quoted in Laffan, 1996b: 21). As a system of governance, the EU is weak in comparison to the national political system, yet it 'generates a formidable corpus of law, develops and implements common programmes, negotiates international agreements and raises revenue' (Laffan *et al.*, 2000: 74). The European and the national systems of governance are different, and fulfil different functions, yet they are 'enmeshed' (to use Laffan *et al.*'s phrase). The way in which the two differ from and relate to each other is epitomised in the conceptualisation of citizenship in the European context. The political project of the EU has centred on the creation of a European polity, which itself has been central to attempts to conceptualise the EU as a community with a common space. Although elements of this 'building' process were there prior to 1992 (as seen in the introduction of direct elections to the European Parliament in 1979), the construction of a European polity received a major boost with the introduction of a European dimension to citizenship. The development of a European level of citizenship has been so important to the building of a European polity because it has marked a significant move away from the exclusive association of nationality with citizenship and, thereby, nation-statehood with governance (Meehan, 1997).

Citizenship can be conceptualised most simply in terms of three aims: to secure individual rights, to enable participation in and responsibility for the democratic processes, and to forge a sense of common membership (Eder and Giesen, 2001: 5–7). The Treaty on European Union (1992) contained a minimalist conception of a European citizenship based on the first of these spheres, i.e. individual rights. The European Union has thus created a civil citizenship, in that it guarantees among and between member-states a wide range of economic and social civil rights that already exist through national citizenship. None of these imply significant changes in the position of national citizens (Geddes, 1995: 203); European citizenship lacks a social dynamic and does not transcend national citizenship, not least because it excludes non-nationals resident in Europe (Pinder, 1995: 112, 121). In addition to this, the EU is too complex and inefficient as a polity; it lacks a demos and possibilities for participation as a focus of citizenship (Dobson, 2001). Low levels of socialisation in the unfamiliar (and generally inaccessible) political system of 'Europe' are reflected in opinion polls regarding European integration (Beetham and Lord, 1998: 53). In recognition of these limitations, the ideal model of the European polity entails a new constitutionalist conception of *multilevel* citizenship, with the coexistence of national citizenship (duties and rights) and European 'new citizenship' (with supranational rights) (Meehan, 1993; Close, 1995; Eder and Giesen, 2001: 9–10). This model is based on a narrative of partnership for mutual prosperity and peace, following the destructive consequences of war on the continent. It reflects, again, an attempt to accommodate the 'national' and the 'European' (see table 2.8).

Table 2.8   New conception of governance in the European Union

New official discourse	*Governance*
Framework for governance	*Polity*
Narrative of governance	Partnership
Model of governance	Multilevel citizenship

The nation-state in the European Union

Differing perceptions of the way in which the tenets of 'nation-state' and those of the 'European Union' are connected at a conceptual as well as practical level by governmental elites (and their 'official discourse') give rise to differing interpretations of the overall process and goals of European integration. The approach taken in this research to the complicated issue of the conceptual relationship between the nation-state and the European Union is elaborated here in distinction from two alternative schools of thought. For purposes of clarity, a complex range of theories have been simplified under two generalised headings. The first has been termed theories of 'replacement', in which the traditional conception of the nation-state is replaced by the new conception of the European Union. The second refers to theories that point to a 'renewal' of the nation-state via the development of the European Union. This book seeks a middle ground between these two schools of thought, with a more holistic conception of the symbiotic relationship of 'nation-state' and 'European Union' in official discourse.

Replacement

Theories about the 'replacement' of the nation-state in the European context are centred on the paradigms of federalism and functionalism/ neofunctionalism, not to mention the assumption of 'replacement' made by forthright critics of European integration such as Laughland (1998: 137). Both federalist and functionalist interpretations of European integration are based on the belief that the framework, model and narrative of the 'nation-state' are heading towards obsolescence in the contemporary context. Both also perceive there to be a fundamental tension, even antagonism, between the processes and aims of nationalism and European integration. The difference between these theoretical approaches lies in their conception of the origins, aims, pattern and progress of European integration. To consider the federalist approach first: Spinelli (1972) and Lipgens (1982) locate the origins of intergovernmental co-operation in Europe in the influence of federal movements in European countries during and following the Second World War. These transnational movements were motivated by political idealism, namely a desire to overcome the divisive and regressive influence of nationalism. This ideal notion was epitomised in the Ventotene Manifesto of 1941 co-written by Spinelli when imprisoned as a member of a Resistance movement:

> The problem which must first be solved is the final abolition of the division of Europe into sovereign national states . . . The manifold problems which bedevil the international affairs of the continent have become insoluble: definition of the boundaries in areas of mixed populations, protection of rights of ethnic minorities . . . Balkan question, Irish question, etc. All of them could most easily be resolved by a European Federation.

Federalist theorists interpret the European Union as an embryonic European Federation, a wholly new entity that is in the process of superseding the nation-state. For example, Wistrich's (1991: 1–2) comment that, in response to the 'outdated' principle of 'total independence and unfettered sovereignty' for nation-states,

> The European Community was founded to deal with the changing political and economic world and has advanced quite far along the federal road towards a European Union, which is its explicit objective.

The failure to create a federal European Union to date is, federalists contend, a consequence of the continuing strength of the nation-state and the parallel weakness of the European Union.[1] Yet, the European Union is gradually replacing the nation-state, Burgess (2000: 28) asserts, by 'offering the means by which the various elements and forces extant in the daily practice of European social, economic and political life could be effectively canalised and coordinated into an organic whole'.

In rhetorical terms at least, the 'founding fathers' of the European Community, including Monnet and Schuman, appear to have been strongly motivated and influenced by the concept of a European entity to replace the divisive nation-state.[2] However, their 'search for salvation' beyond the nation-state, to use Friedman's (1992: 355) phrase, fitted more generally within the functionalist rather than the federalist conception of European integration. Functionalist theorists share with European federalists the perception that the weakening of the nation-state is integrally linked to European integration. Yet they believe this to be – more than a pursuit of normative ideals – a necessary and inevitable consequence of global change (Haas, 1968, 1997). Functionalist theorists of European integration therefore inherit a tradition from functionalist theories of international relations, which view the international system as a community with shared interests and goals (Mitrany, 1965).

Indeed, sociological theories of functionalism are also relevant here, in their view of social structures (and, subsequently, social relations and conceptions) as adjusting to meet the imperatives of the wider system (Durkheim, 1982). The strength of new structural forms is seen to increase as people come to identify with them over time. It is interesting to note that modernist theories of nationalism are also functionalist in that they consider nationalism to have developed in response to the conditions of modernity, such as industrial development (Gellner, 1983) or psychological need (Llobera, 1994). As a consequence, some envisage the changing global system as leading towards the eventual replacement of the nation-state by new forms of governance and ideology (Hobsbawm, 1990: 164, 1995: 427–31).

The vision of the transcendence of the nation-state is related to the functionalist perception that the logic of transferring sovereignty from the nation-state to the European Union is self-sustaining and self-perpetuating (Dedman, 1996: 9). For changes in the economic, political and social spheres will lead, it is argued, to the search for integrationist solutions to common problems. The distinction between functionalism and neofunctionalism is relevant here. The traditional type of functionalism encapsulated in the ideals of Monnet and Schuman, assumes that gradual integration, with a transferral of sovereignty and loyalty from the nation-state to the European Union, would occur as a matter of course once the process was begun. Authority and, thereby, loyalty and identity, would no longer be based on territorial or historical organisations, for example, but would rather be allocated according to the tasks faced. Hence, the EU would ultimately be a functionally specific and entirely unique organisation.

Neofunctionalists also hold that the nation-state would be transcended by the European Union, but they do not envisage the end result as a qualitatively different organisation; in this sense, neofunctionalism may be seen to aim for a federal Europe via functional means. In addition, neofunctionalists emphasise the proactive role of elites (and their interaction) at a national and transnational level in this process (Schmitter, 1970). In the neofunctionalist model, governmental elites increasingly operate at a transnational level, forging co-operative agreements between themselves in response to shared interests (O'Neill, 1996: 42). The belief that governmental elites are in favour of European integration on functional grounds and, therefore, are becoming increasingly cosmopolitan is counterbalanced by the fact that the majority of the population of European member-states retain primary identification with the nation-state and, moreover, that their impression of the EU is still predominantly mediated through national structures of communication and organisation (Beetham and Lord, 1998: 53). The image of the process of European integration led by Europhile governmental elites but slowed down by their citizens who obstinately cling onto their outdated national identities and loyalties is, however, a problematic one. Governmental elites are so central to the process of European integration precisely because they are central to the functioning and maintenance of the nation-state. In order to understand the response of national populations to European integration, it is, therefore, necessary to consider the role of the governmental elite in the EU as representatives of the nation-state.

Renewal

Theories that point to the renewal of the nation-state in the context of European integration focus on two points that the 'replacement' theorists struggle to account for: namely, the weakness of the European Union and the strength of the nation-state as popular political entities and identities. In a similar way to theories of 'replacement', theories of the 'renewal' of the nation-state perceive there to be a fundamental tension between nationalism and European integration. To some degree, both theories have a 'zero-sum' interpretation of the nation-state/ European Union relationship: if one is strong as a political and ideological entity then there must be a corresponding weakness in the other. However, whereas the 'replacement' thesis emphasises the dominant position of the EU over the nation-state in the process of European integration, the 'renewal' thesis argues that the nation-state and the instrumental interests of its governmental elite are central to the process of European integration. Theories that point to a renewal of the nation-state in the European context fall into two categories: intergovernmentalist and confederalist.

A leading exponent of an intergovernmentalist interpretation of the development of the European Union is Milward (1992) who contends that its origins lie in the search not to replace national sovereignty or nation-statehood, but, rather, to 'rescue' it in the post-war context. Milward's statecentric approach views European integration as neither cause nor symptom of a 'crisis of the nation-state', but rather as a course of action chosen by member-states as a means of pursuing national interests. Hoffmann (1966), a realist intergovernmental theorist, also argues that the European Union is the product of governmental elites' awareness of the need for co-operation in order for the nation-state to remain the principal actor in the international system. As a liberal intergovernmentalist, Moravcsik (1999: 674) contends such decisions regarding European integration have occurred as a result of three core state considerations: economic interests, relative power and the need for credible commitments to certain policies. As to why nation-states would commit to 'pooling' sovereignty in the EU as opposed to mere economic interdependence, Milward and Sørensen (1993: 19) suggest that the binding laws and institutionalised patterns of negotiation involved in European integration enable member-states to preserve a balance of power in the EU in favour of nation-statehood. Hence, European integration is moving power beyond the confines of the state, but to increase the influence of the national elite rather than to transfer power elsewhere.

Thus, intergovernmentalist theorists contend, it is simply inaccurate to define the European Union in terms of a decline of the 'nation-state' as idea and institution. Indeed, the success of the European Union can be explained in terms of the success of its member-states (Moravcsik, 1999). The European Union is dependent on its member-states for financial resources whilst the process of integration itself continues to be based on the nation-state (Münch, 1996: 389–90). This is exemplified in the power of the Council in the EU decision-making process, the national basis of European citizenship and the national context of elections to the European Parliament. Indeed, as Billig (1995b: 95) notes, the European Union could be defined as an organisation of nation-states, with the primary criteria for membership being nationhood. Hence, national diversity is reproduced even in the very framework of European integration, with the straightforward implication that the 'European project cannot replace the national project' (Delors, 1992: 22; Milward and Sørensen, 1993: 21).

Critics of the intergovernmentalist interpretation of European integration include confederalist theorists, who concur with the statecentric model yet argue that the complex dynamics of the European Union are not fully accounted for by intergovernmentalist theories (Taylor, 1975; Forsyth, 1981; Wallace, 1982). A confederation is arranged for the mutual advantage of its sovereign member states, yet it goes beyond the pursuit of national interests to develop interests, an identity and even a polity of its own. European confederalism is, therefore, seen as a rational response by nation-states to the new international environment. One such theorist, Taylor (1975), contends that national governmental elites have used European integration as a means of securing their position in an insecure context. Hence, these theories support the notion that European integration ensured the survival of the nation-state, yet they also attempt to acknowledge that it is a two-way process, and that nation-statehood and sovereignty has altered as a consequence. As a thesis, confederalism goes some way towards recognising the flexible and changing nature of the nation-state and its complex relationship with the European Union, as opposed to traditional conceptions of the two as distinct, static entities.

Symbiosis

Theories of the 'replacement' of the nation-state arguably over-emphasise the strength and significance of the new framework, model and narrative of the European Union, whilst theories of the 'renewal' of the nation-state tend to under-state the significant changes occurring in the traditional framework, model and narrative of the nation-state. The approach taken in this book builds on the notion of nationalism and European integration (and, thereby, nation-statehood and European Union) as mutually affective, complex and interlinked processes. The European Union itself has become 'an inescapable frame of reference that both reflects and shapes regional change' (Murphy, 1999: 62). European integration also has a 'transformative impact on the European state system and its constituent units' (Christiansen *et al.*, 1999: 529). Due to the processes occurring in the international arena that the theories in both the 'replacement' and 'renewal' schools seek to address (such as economic 'globalisation', multiple identities and overlapping sovereignties), the nation-state is simultaneously becoming less capable and more active as an international actor (Parker, 1998: 87). As part of this, the European Union does have a significant impact on the nation-state in conceptual as well as practical ways. The empirical research of this book focuses on the way in which official national discourse reflects and portrays the impact of European integration on the changing conceptualisation of the 'nation-state'. Each nation-state in Europe is being redefined in line with the image of the European Union that is propagated in official discourse. Nevertheless, it remains true that the impact of the European Union in conceptual and practical ways remains largely mediated through the *national* institutional, structural and discursive realms.

Through analysis of official national discourse, the research recounted in this book highlights the way in which the EU and European integration is conceived in a manner that reflects the continuing dominance of the nation-state model. As Smith (1992: 76) notes, each of the European Union's member-states understands and seeks to influence European integration along the lines of its national self-image, justifying the development of the EU in accordance with the logic of its own nation-statehood. This is because 'visions of tomorrow's Europe are consciously or subconsciously related to beliefs about the nature of society and country' (Skotnicka-Illasiewicz and Wesolowski, 1995: 209).

Nevertheless, moving beyond the specific focus of this research, it is important to acknowledge that the conceptualisation and the practice of European integration are not confined to the discourse of its member-states. Indeed, a European discourse and identity are arguably becoming more significant and, although their impact and appeal varies within member-states as much as between them, there is a strong case for regional, national, European and other identities to be regarded as compatible rather than competitive (Tonra and Dunne, 1997: 28). It is argued here that the 'two-level game' played by governmental elites in making decisions that are viable in both domestic and European bargaining means that they are actually under pressure to promote compatibility between European and national identities and discourses.

It is worth briefly considering the way in which the approach set out here relates to and differs from social constructivism as an 'ontology' that has become increasingly prominent as an academic approach to EU politics since the late 1990s (Risse and Wiener, 1999: 778).[3] This research shares the social constructivist's emphasis upon the significance of collective discourses (and thus also ideas and identities) in assessing the activity of governmental elites. Social constructivism asserts that these are significant because they delimit governmental elites' choices in the area of policies, interests and strategies, in the sense that policy-making has to be consistent with the discourses they espouse. Collective identities, based on the ideas that define a distinct social group, therefore 'define the realm of legitimate interests in political discourse' (Risse and Wiener, 1999: 779). The means by which actors 'internalise' the norms of a collectivity is 'socialisation', for this exposes the actor to the influence of the norms, rules and procedures of the group. The European Union does possess such qualities, meaning that actors can be influenced by the EU, but whether it has a constitutive or merely a constraining effect on behaviour is still too difficult to deduce (Risse and Wiener, 1999: 778). The final core tenet of social constructivism is that the rationale of collective actors changes according to experience, in order to adjust to a new position regarding other social actors or structures (Offe and Wiesenthal, 1979). Social constructivism tends to view these new positions, in which collective 'embedded' identities become 'contested', as arising from 'critical junctures' of political crisis which lead to change in the underlying discourses (Risse and Wiener, 1999: 789–90).

Regarding social constructivism's key points on discourse, socialisation and change, the perception of symbiosis upheld in this research is slightly different. First, it is necessary to point to the inseparability of discourse and practice. Indeed, official discourse represents the interconnection of ideas and activity. Hence, official discourse is one of the means by which elements of both the internal and the external contexts are interpreted and seen to be relevant. Discourse analysis considers what is being presented and how and thus highlights the logic of the conceptual/ practical link and the way in which it is continually progressing. This relates to the second point: namely, that, although these discourses are linked to an historical development, they are continually changing in relation to their context, both internal and external, and therefore both facilitate and reflect progress. Hence, 'critical junctures' are significant, but should not be regarded as the only points at which the underlying discourse changes. Such a view risks reifying the discourse as a 'given' (with the political elite and collectivity remaining faithful to an essential set of discursive norms and principles until a crisis) rather than a 'construct' (with evolving and varied interpretations of these norms and principles at all levels). The impact of the actors on the definition and changing of discursive norms and principles is clearly as important a consideration as how these factors might influence the actors themselves. Yet, elite actors at levels of political authority admittedly have to be perceived to act in accordance with these norms and principles because they are intended to legitimate the institutions governed by the elite. In trying to stay in control, the national governmental elite has to manage the perception of the nation-state and the EU in the continually fluctuating light of the context in which the two interact. This research focuses on the way in which this conceptual balance is achieved in official discourse, rather than on how the 'nation-state' or the 'European Union' as such constrains or moulds the activity of the governmental elite. For, this book contends, nationalism and European integration are not opposing forces of past and future, or even 'traditional' and 'new' phenomena as such, but, rather, integrally linked processes.

The use of the term 'symbiosis' captures the image of the nation-state and the European Union as two different entities living in close association to their mutual benefit. The discourse of governmental elites of EU member-states brings together elements of the framework, model and narrative of the nation-state and those of the European Union in the development of a new discourse that accommodates and facilitates the evolution of both. This approach does not reduce the nation-state or the EU to mere constructs of official discourse, nor does it see one as naturally dominant over the other. Instead, the nation-state and the EU are brought *together* at a conceptual level in official discourse, the definition of each being shaped by the definition of the other. For both the nation-state and the EU are complex systems (including social, political and economic institutions, structures and relations) that make an impact on the context in which each is conceived and progresses. Official discourse helps to shape conceptions of the nation-state and the EU in a way that reflects and responds to this ever-changing context. The next chapter examines how discourse theory offers an insight into this process and introduces the context for analysing official discourse in Ireland.

Notes

1 'The United States of Europe will never become a full reality until all its inhabitants feel themselves to be its citizens with a sense of belonging and a sense of loyalty towards it that is no weaker than that which they feel towards their nation, region or local community' (Wistrich, 1991: 146).

2 'The moment has come for us to attempt for the first time the experiment of a supranational authority which shall not be simply a combination or con-ciliation of national powers' (Schuman, 1950: 180).

'The every day realities will make it possible to form the political union which is the goal of our Community and to establish the United States of Europe' (Monnet, 1978: 431).

3 Social constructivist analysis of European integration, like functionalism, has received a theoretical inheritance from theories of both international relations and sociology – exemplifying the 'unique' position of the European Union as an international organisation involving issues previously confined to the national level.

3

Official discourse and political change in Ireland

The purpose of this chapter is to elaborate the theoretical and method-ological framework for this research, both in relation to the key tenets of discourse theory and to the empirical content of the analysis. It begins by considering the meaning of 'discourse' as language, practice and context. Its multidimensional meaning and function means that dis-course analysis has particular value in the study of nationalism and polit-ical change. The articulation of discourse in texts, written or spoken, offers a means by which the processes at work in a particular context can be analysed. Given the model of the observer/object relationship that is proposed in discourse theory, it is noted that what is being sought is not an explanation of events but, rather, an understanding of the processes involved. The chapter concludes with an explanation of the criteria applied in the selection of discursive texts and a brief outline of the wider political context in which they were originally presented.

Discourse theory

Discourse theory is an approach based on the 'transcendental turn' in modern philosophy in which focus moves from 'facts' to the conditions in which these facts are made possible (Laclau, 1990: 431). More specif-ically, discourse theory is interested in the *meaning* of facts, rather than their mere existence. In discourse theory, meaning is considered to be relevant at two levels: the interpretation of the facts by actors and, sec-ondly, the way that the social world is consequently constituted. The focus on meaning and interpretation in discourse theory places it in the hermeneutical paradigm of the social sciences. The model of analysis introduced in discourse theory, as a theory deriving from the hermeneu-tical tradition, takes into account the significance of the framework or field within which the observer, concept, and object – and the relation-ship between them – is constituted. As a means of finding a point from which to analyse the observer-concept-object relationship, discourse

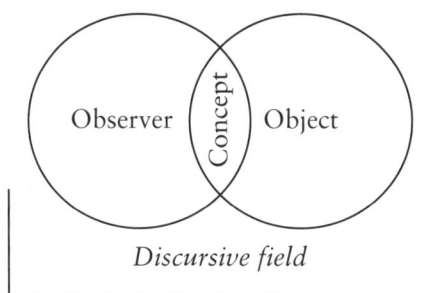

Figure 3.1 A model of analysis according to discourse theory

theory conceptualises it as being shaped within a 'discursive field' (see figure 3.1).

Concepts are never held or used in isolation but in constellations that make up entire schemes or belief systems; discourse theory describes these constellations as 'discursive fields' (Farr, 1989: 33; Laclau and Mouffe, 1987: 85). A discursive field refers to the socially constructed system of rules, practice and relations that form the 'theoretical horizon' for the functioning of discourse (Foucault, 1974: xiv; 1972: 47–8, 72–4; Howarth and Stavrakakis, 2000: 3). Hajer (1995: 44) defines '*discourse*' as:

> an ensemble of ideas, concepts, and categorizations . . . that is produced, reproduced, and transformed in a particular set of practices [i.e. discursive field] and through which meaning is given to physical and social realities.

The term 'discourse', therefore, refers to each of three levels of the social world – language/text, practice/interaction and context – and, importantly, the connections between them (see figure 3.2, source: Fairclough, 2001: 21).

The first element of discourse, and one examined in this research, is discourse as *text*, both written and spoken (Halliday, 1978). A text has two dimensions: (1) a result of the process of production and (2) a resource for the process of interpretation. Both these processes take place in the arena of social *interaction*, which is the second element of discourse. The third aspect of discourse is the social *context*, which determines the processes involved in social interaction. In this arena, discourse involves social conditions that shape the way in which individuals interact and, thereby, their production and interpretation of texts (Fairclough, 2001: 19–21). At all points in this three-dimensional function of discourse, individuals draw upon the 'discursive field' in their interpretation and production of texts. What Fairclough refers to as 'members' resources' arise from the discursive field, given that they

Social conditions of production

Process of production

Text

Interaction   Process of interpretation

Context   Social conditions of interpretation

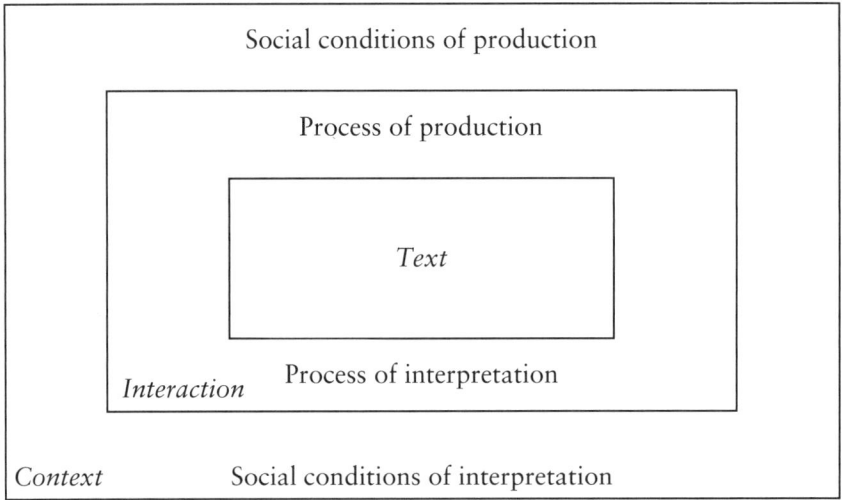

Figure 3.2   Discourse as text, interaction and context

include such factors as values, assumptions, knowledge of language and ideas of the social world. In analysing texts, discourse analysis as a methodological approach seeks to deepen understanding of the relationship between texts, interaction and context (Fairclough, 2001: 19–21).

The second point to be made about the meaning of 'discourse' in discourse theory illuminates the observer/object relationship that was debated in the alternative paradigms outlined above. Because, it is suggested, 'objects of knowledge, situations and social roles as well as identities and interpersonal relations' are all constituted through discourse, discourses function to 'form the identities of subjects [i.e. observers] *and* objects' (Wodak *et al.*, 1999: 8; Howarth and Stavrakakis, 2000: 3, emphasis added). Hence, the role of discourse in the social realm blurs the philosophical distinction between the 'observer' as the conscious mind and the 'object' as the thing external to the mind. This has great significance for social scientific research. For the observer is moulded by discourse through his/her position in the social world. Such a theory of discourse is linked to Althusser's (1971) view of ideology as a 'practice' of constituting individuals as subjects/observers in the social world and thus central to the structure of social relations. Secondly, because the observer cannot view an object outside of a discursive field (i.e. free from 'discourse'), the object is in a sense constituted by discourse, for discourses 'systematically form the objects of which they speak' (Foucault, 1972: 49). This is not to say that the object does not exist independently of a discursive field, but discourse gives the object its *meaning*. This is essentially because an object only has meaning, significance or value in relation to other objects and concepts. Discourse functions to position objects in relation to others, thus giving them meaning.

Applying discourse theory

This conceptualisation of observer and object in discourse theory challenges certain common assumptions in social science and consequently raises issues that need to be addressed before applying the tenets of discourse theory to research in this field. The first such issue arises from the fact that, taken to its logical conclusion, discourse theory emphasises subjectivity over objectivity. According to the model of analysis outlined in figure 3.2, the conduct and conclusions of analytical research would say as much about the observer as about the object of analysis. For the outcome of the research would be affected by the context in which the research is being conducted, the assumptions of the researcher, the context of the object being analysed, etc. However, the contextual nature of observer, concept and object does not lead to a devaluation of the analysis or the contribution it may make to knowledge of the object. Acknowledgement that the subjectivity of the researcher is inescapable means that, according to discourse theorists, to measure the research against the rule of objectivity would be misleading. Instead, the researcher, having shown the validity of his/her analytical perspective, claims to offer *one* explanation rather than *the* explanation for the matter in question.

A second important issue arises from the complex nature of discourse as both a 'term' and 'function', due to its encapsulation of the connection between language and all types of socio-political practice (Fairclough and Wodak, 1997). Awareness of this complexity does not, however, negate the need to be able to distinguish between the various elements of discourse and their role. As Eagleton (1991: 209) notes, the discourse that constitutes 'our practices' should not be entirely conflated with the discourse 'in which we talk about them'. For, Eagleton suggests, there is a risk of neglecting the fact that language does not simply 'constitute reality' but it has specific functions in seeking to, for example, explain, legitimate and conceal it.[1] This point is highly pertinent to the particular focus of this book in its analysis of official discourse. Fairclough's (2001: 23–4) clarification of the 'felicitous ambiguity' between discourse and practice addresses Eagleton's objections and, in doing so, elucidates the approach taken in this research. If discourse and practice are to be distinguished, Fairclough states, '*discourse*' may specifically refer to 'discoursal action', i.e. actual written or spoken texts, of which there are various types (such as 'article' or 'conversation'). An instance of discoursal action can draw upon more than one type of discourse. For example, a published interview with a politician may involve a second discourse type, such as advertisement or propaganda. The ways in which the types and structures of discourse vary is closely related to the types and structures of *practice* in the social realm. The interconnection of discourse and practice is central to the political significance of discourse (Chilton, 2003).

Discourse and politics

Discourse, structures and change

The relationship between politics and discourse emanates from the function of discourse in the social world and, therefore, works in two interconnected ways: politics as a product of discourse and politics as a determinant of discourse. The first arises from the notion that discursive acts are 'socially constitutive' in terms of generating and producing particular social conditions, maintaining, legitimating and reproducing them and, finally, transforming or dismantling these social conditions (Wodak *et al.*, 1999: 8). Such activity is, by definition, political because systems of social relations are inherently 'political constructions' (Laclau and Mouffe, 1985). The semiotic element of discourse (expressed through texts, symbols and signs) is also an important form of politics, as exemplified in the political role of nationalism. Yet discourse does not act in an unconstrained social sphere. Indeed, both discourse and practice are constrained within certain conditions that are determined by interdependent networks of discourse and practice, namely 'orders'. Fairclough (2001: 24) defines social order as 'a structuring of a particular social "space" into various domains associated with various types of practice'. Similarly, an 'order of discourse' determines the way in which the various types of discourse are structured. Both orders of discourse (i.e. the role and functioning of discourse) and social orders are constrained and even determined by political dynamics. For they are moulded by 'changing relationships of power' within social institutions and society in general (Fairclough, 2001: 25). This leads to the second aspect of the relationship between discourse and politics, namely that, 'political practices serve to constitute (and undermine) discourses and the identities [and social conditions] they form' (Howarth, 1998: 275).

The definition of discourse as, to use Foucault's (1972) phrase, 'ongoing conversations' across time and space highlights the need to understand it as a dynamic process, simultaneously embodying and changing concepts and contexts (Brown and Yule, 1983: 11). The relationship between the changing political world and the language used to describe and appraise it, i.e. between conception and action, is close and crucial (Skinner, 1986: 6). On account of this, Ball *et al.* (1989: 2) have designated conceptual change to be 'a species of political innovation'. Because conceptual change attends any reconstitution of the political world, political change and conceptual change must be understood as one complex and interrelated process (Farr, 1989: 30–2). A key element of discourse theory is the notion that actors/agents and systems/structures in the social and political realm 'undergo constant historical and social change' (Howarth and Stavrakakis, 2000: 6). Discourse is central to this process of change and, importantly, to the impression of stability through its role in bringing together concepts, interaction and context. Indeed, perceived continuity and consistency in nation-statehood despite the occurrence of substantial change (a theme central to this research) is, according to discourse theorists, a result of (discursive) communicative networks between various actors and systems (Hajer, 1995: 63). Discourse analysis seeks to 'chart and explain' the role of discourse as a vehicle of both stability and change in relation to political practice and logic (Howarth and Stavrakakis, 2000: 6).

Official discourse

To study official discourse is to identify the dominance of some discourses over others with regard to political change and thus to allow for the significance of institutional arrangements in establishing the preconditions for the process of discourse formation and competition. Members of the governmental elite may be distinguished from other actors in the social order by their credibility (which is necessary for the general acceptance of their discourse) and their accountability for the practice and implication of the discourse they espouse. The premise on which this research relies is that the official discourse of the governmental elite is an integral element of political relations, facilitating the 'constant renewal of hegemonic domination' (Burton and Carlen, 1979: 8; see also Habermas' [1976] definition of the state as the representation of monopolistic discourse). This, however, is necessarily accompanied by the need for official discourse to 'retain the intellectual confidence of the parties, elites and functionaries within state apparatuses' (Burton and Carlen, 1979: 48). Hence, a specific function of official discourse is directed at persuading not only those in the public arena, through the medium of the media, but also other members of the elite. Thus, if discursive practices are those through which actors seeks to persuade others to see 'reality' in the same light as themselves, the discursive practices of governmental elites are particularly significant at all levels of society (Billig, 1987).

It is at this point that a distinction should be made between 'rhetoric' and 'official discourse'. 'Rhetoric' has been defined as language that functions to 'adjust ideas to people and people to ideas'; rhetorical analysis consequently examines political language as 'symbolic inducement' (Bryant, 1953; Simons, 1989: 3). Discourse analysis acknowledges the great importance of this facet of political language; however, its examination of political language occurs in the light of the other dimensions of discourse, namely practice and context. Indeed, it is official discourse's linking of language/concepts, practice and context that makes it of crucial importance to the legitimacy of any political institution or community (Gaffney, 1996: 199). For the influence of official discourse depends not only on the cognitive power of its rhetoric but also on whether the audience considers it to be relevant, realistic, progressive, etc. In this light, discourse analysis is seen as the means by which to investigate the ways in which a particular framing of the discussion makes certain ideas attractive or influential. The purpose of the research recounted in this book is to consider the way in which governmental elites present and 'sell' particular concepts of nationalism and European integration to national audiences through official discourse.

Nationalist discourse

In an illuminating study bringing together the elements of discourse theory highlighted above, Sutherland (2005) demonstrates the value of discourse theory for a study of nationalist ideology. Indeed, one may go further and say that nationalism *is* the discourse of the nation-state, drawing together the conceptual and the material dimensions of nation-statehood. As Schlesinger (1999: 264) notes:

> discourses on the nation are not *just* ideal processes but rather the marking out of the national cultural terrain, in a public domain, materially underpinned by a range of institutions, political, economic, and communicative.

Moreover, nationalism serves to blur the boundary between the two dimensions of concept and practice. Indeed, the strength of this conceptual/material marriage in nationalist discourse lies in the fact that the language of nationalism is essentially a normative language (which 'maps political possibilities and impossibilities') masquerading as a descriptive language (Ball *et al.*, 1989: 2). This paradoxical nature of nationalism is reflected in the conception of the nation-state as a 'discursive landscape' (Häkli, 1999: 123).[2] Its ideational 'narration' not only gives its members a link with the wider world, with 'past and future', but also enables the nation-state to be 'a category of practice' (Gilroy, 1987: 59; Bhabha, 1990; Brubaker, 1996: 7). The conceptual and practical ways in which the multidimensional conception of 'nation-state' is applied show how 'it can come to structure perceptions, to inform thought and experience, to organize discourse [in the communicative sense] and political actions' (Brubaker, 1996: 7). The ability of nationalism to affect and, indeed, effect perception, thought and action at all levels of society is related to the fact that the discourse of the 'nation-state' is ubiquitous and pervasive. This is encapsulated in Billig's (1995a) description of 'banal nationalism' maintaining the nation-state through continual reference to, or even mere assumption of, its existence in everyday types of discourse (including news reports, sports commentaries and parliamentary debates).

It is important to note, therefore, that nationalism is not specifically an official discourse. A distinction needs to be made between official national discourse (the discourse of governmental elite at a national level) and official *nationalist* discourse (articulated with the primary intent and/or effect of moulding the conceptualisation of the 'nation-state'). Yet, the fact that the governmental elite of a self-styled nation-state continually elucidate and support the concept and the practice of the nation-state means that the overlap between official national discourse and official national*ist* discourse is broad and deep. As the communicative texts of the governmental elite, official discourse in general constitutes the most significant element and representation of official nationalism, which may be defined as the nationalism (i.e. discourse legitimating the ideal of nation-statehood) endorsed by the governmental elite. For official discourse plays a key role in continually defining and reimagining the context, meaning and activity of the nation-state. The ideational aspect of nation-statehood is developed within the discourse of the governmental elite (with, according to Kornprobst's [2005] perceptive study, reference to their own epistemic understandings of the world) and perpetuated through its manifestation in the policies and practices of the state. Subsequently, conceptualisations of the 'nation-state' that do not fit in with those represented in official discourse have a significantly limited impact on society in general unless the governmental elite engages with these alternative views. It is with such points in mind that the examination of official Irish nationalism, and changes within it, is conducted in this research primarily through analysis of the official discourse of the Irish governmental elite.

Discourse and European integration

Discourse in the political arena of the European Union takes two main forms: official national discourse and the discourse of the elite operating at a European level. The growing encroachment of the EU on areas of political sensitivity (in areas of identity and governance, for example) has made the development of a 'European' discourse increasingly significant, largely for similar reasons that discourse is so inherently important for nationalism, i.e. uniting concepts/ideology and practice/reality. Indeed, it is the similarity of the roles and nature of nationalist and EU integrationist discourses, plus the way in which they 'coexist', that makes them of such interest (Schlesinger, 1999: 266). A key matter for this research is how the official discourse of nationalism approaches, adapts (to), and presents the discourse of European integration.

As we saw in the preceding chapter, official discourse at the national level, and its conceptualisation of the European Union, plays a central role in moulding the discourse of European integration. For, as one of the few studies to date conducted in this area concluded, the EU is conceived differently by different member-states in line with their official national discourse (Marcussen *et al.,* 1999). A point of interest is that official national discourse on European integration does appear to conceive the European Union as a political entity along the same lines as the nation-state in terms of identity/borders/governance and framework/narrative/model. This is encapsulated in the triform diagrammatic models.

Nevertheless, it is clear that the EU is not generally conceived in official national discourses as ideally following the nation-state model of a homogenous European identity, territorial homeland and independent democratic governance. Indeed, in the promotion of, for example, ideas of multidimensional identities and multilevel governance, the nation-state model may be seen as being reinterpreted for its application to the new European political entity. The task of uncovering such complex processes in order to gain an increased understanding of them is one for which discourse analysis is ideally suited.

Discourse analysis

Analysing discourse

The recognition that language is 'both active and functional in shaping and reproducing social relations, identities and ideas' constitutes the theoretical foundations of discourse analysis as a metholodological practice

(Tonkiss, 1998: 248). The fact that discourse analysis is 'practice' rather than 'method' is important: 'discourse analysis' as a term refers to a range of techniques rather than a specific set of rules. This is essentially for three reasons. First, 'discourse theory' refers to a highly eclectic range of theoretical and historical influences from across disciplines – interpretations of which can be varied and even contradictory. Secondly, discourse analysis can take a 'genealogical' or an 'archaeological' approach to discourse. Foucault (1977) defines the former as analysing the events leading up to a particular discourse; this is largely concerned with political practice, for it involves the clashes or forces that produced certain events or institutions. An archaeological approach, in contrast, is concerned with the actual contents of a discourse and the form it takes in a particular context (Foucault, 1972). Finally, the core point of consensus in discourse theory is that the meaning of a word is context-dependent because every discursive object is constituted in the context of an action (after Wittgenstein, 1953: 43, 116). Consequently, the object of the particular research, its context and the sources used determines the nature of each example of discourse analysis. Nevertheless, all applications of discourse analysis have a common aim: interpretation and critique in order to gain a fuller understanding of the matter in question. Moreover, all discourse analysis focuses on texts as linguistic expressions, whether written or verbal, that organise, constitute and perpetuate the other dimensions of discourse (i.e. practice and context) (Laclau and Mouffe, 1985: 146; Smith, 1990: 162). In this way, discourse analysts seek to gain an insight into the reproduction of the 'systems of meaning' in a particular social or political order.

As noted above, there are a number of techniques that can be applied in the use of discourse analysis. Even critical discourse analysis, the leading paradigm in analysing discursive texts from a theoretical basis in line with the hermeneutical/Foucauldian approach outlined in the first half of this chapter, is far from homogenous.[3] Given its theoretical foundations, critical discourse analysis is 'faced with the twofold task of revealing the relationship between linguistic means, forms and structures and concrete linguistic practice, and making transparent the reciprocal relationship between discursive action and political and institutional structures' (Wodak *et al.*, 1999: 9). Whilst noting the value of both, the approach taken in this research places an emphasis on the second aspect of critical discourse analysis. Indeed, due to the nature of the questions, propositions and sources used in this research, this book makes no claim to represent anything other than a flexible application of critical discourse analysis in a broadly 'archaeological' approach. For, as a result of the exploratory character of this research, it is the research questions, propositions and sources that have ultimately decided the selection of the theoretical and method-ological approach of this book, and not vice versa.

Discursive concepts: nation-statehood and European Union

The way in which conceptual and practical notions of the nation-state are brought together in official nationalism is categorised in the triform model of nation-statehood applied in this research. Nation-statehood is traditionally conceptualised in official discourse as primarily important in the three thematic areas of identity, borders and governance (i.e. the objects of this research). Discourse on the nation-state works at three core levels, each of which serve to build a conceptual context for the practical functioning of the nation-state: framework, narrative and model (see table 3.1). Official discourse presents the *framework* of the nation-state, i.e. its essential supporting structure, as 'nation', 'territory' and 'state'. This framework is both conceptual and institutional given that the essential system of nation-statehood is founded on nation, terri-tory and state. The *narrative* of the nation-state is based on an account in official discourse of historical events and experiences that have shaped the nation-state. However, it also includes normative judgements as to the relevance of such events for the contemporary definition of the nation-state. The narrative thus unites history, culture and politics in legitimising the concept of the nation-state in the present context. In this way, the narrative of the nation-state serves as a 'story-line'. Points in official discourse are often presented as part of a continuum through the use of story-lines. A story-line gives the impression of consistency and continuity in discourse by using symbolic references that uphold the notion of common ground whilst enabling actors to pursue a wide range of political paths, etc. Story-lines, and narratives, are therefore at the heart of nationalism's marriage of continuity and change (Hajer, 1995: 56–61). Finally, official discourse upholds a *model* of the nation-state, namely the nation-state as an ideal. This also traverses the boundaries between past, present and future by linking the ideals of yesterday's patriotic heroes, with the ideal conceptualisation of the nation-state as it is today and the ideal nation-state as it could be tomorrow. Thus, offi-cial discourse conceptualises the nation-state in the three thematic areas of identity, borders and governance and at the three broad levels of framework, narrative and model.

    The strength of nationalist discourse lies in the way in which these levels and areas overlap and complement each other, despite external change and internal shifts in emphasis. The purpose of this research is to examine Irish nation-statehood as it is presented in official discourse in

Table 3.1 Traditional conception of the nation-state: framework, narrative and model

Official discourse	*Identity*	*Borders*	*Governance*
Traditional framework of the nation-state	*Nation*	*Territory*	*State*
Traditional narrative of the nation-state	Historical culture	Homeland	National self-determination
Traditional model of the nation-state	Distinct people	Demarcated boundaries	Sovereignty

Table 3.2 New conception of the European Union: framework, narrative and model

Official discourse	*Identity*	*Borders*	*Governance*
New framework of the EU	*Community*	*Space*	*Polity*
New narrative of the European Union	Unity in diversity	Overcome divisions	Partnership
New model of the European Union	Multidimensional identities	Cross-border co-operation	Multilevel citizenship

each of these three themes and at each of these three levels. Hence, this diagrammatic model of the 'nation-state' represents the thematic approach and structure of this book (see table 3.1).

The application of the triform model to the 'European Union' is arguably more problematic than its application to the 'nation-state', mainly because of the contested nature of the European Union in all three thematic areas. Moreover, as upheld in a core analytical assumption of this book, the conceptualisation of the European Union varies to a large degree according to national bases. The conceptualisation of the EU outlined here is one chosen to be as non-contentious as possible and, importantly, one that Irish official discourse on the whole supports and promotes. The component parts of this model are united here in order to present an overview of the key themes constituting the focus of the empirical chapters (see table 3.2).

The framework refers to the basis supporting system of the EU which, as with the nation-state, is more than the sum of its parts. The narrative of the EU is formed as a legitimating account of events, ideas and factors behind the development of the EU. And the model of the EU is the ideal to be followed, in the recognition that practice is justified by ideals. This diagram serves primarily as a conceptual 'map', showing the framework, narratives and models of the EU that the Irish governmental elite refer to in the process of reimagining the Irish nation-state in relation to internal and external developments. Both the diagrammatic models of the EU and the nation-state are intended to summarise the presentation of these entities as ideal-types in official national discourse and it is these presentations that are analysed in this research rather than, for example, their correspondence to 'actuality'. For the focus of discourse analysis is on discursive strategies as *presentations* of 'reality' rather than the discovery of the factuality of certain texts and narratives.

Analysing Irish official discourse

Official opinion

Most applications of discourse analysis are based on a range of texts strictly delimited either in terms of number (the majority of analyses would use from one to approximately two dozen texts), type of discourse (such as party manifesto) or subject (such as party leaders). The nature of this research, with its broad scope and historical comparisons, means that the selection of sources in this research also needs to be broad. There are four key criteria determining the selection of texts for analysis in this research. The first is that the text represents the official opinion of a member of the Irish political elite. For the most part, this means a minister of the government of the time (on occasion a junior minister), particularly the Taoiseach as the leader of the government and the Minister for Foreign Affairs, who has specific responsibility regarding both the EU and Northern Ireland.

It is acknowledged that many of the texts selected in this way were not actually written by the politician who gave the address or speech or in whose name the article, statement or letter was published. For example, many of the texts analysed here were written by special advisors (for example, Dr Martin Mansergh as special advisor on Northern Ireland to successive Fianna Fáil governments) and by civil servants in relevant government departments (for example, Noel Dorr in the Department of Foreign Affairs). Nevertheless, this does not undermine the key purpose of analysing official discourse, which is not to discover the underlying motivations or actual opinions of governmental elite members but, rather, to analyse the text for the message that it presents to the audience. Hence, in official discourse analysis, it is not the author of the text that is as important as the authority of the person in whose name the text is presented.

Authority of speaker

This leads to the second criterion for the selection of texts, namely, that the text is articulated by or, in the case of written texts, in the name of a particularly significant member of the political elite. The choosing of these individuals has been based on an assessment of their prominent profile and significant contribution in the shaping of official policy and practice in relation to the core themes of this research. The subjects whose discursive texts are most frequently analysed in this research are the men who were Taoisigh during the first thirty years of Ireland's membership of the EU: Cosgrave, Lynch, Haughey, FitzGerald, Reynolds, Bruton and Ahern. Table 3.3 shows the key events that took place in Northern Ireland and the EU whilst they were in office. To summarise the table, the speeches from Lynch and Cosgrave are taken from around the time of the most violent years of the Troubles and accession to the EEC; those from Haughey and FitzGerald are from around the time of 'Eurosclerosis' and the Anglo-Irish Agreement; Reynolds and Bruton are from the time of the Treaty on European Union, the Hume-Adams talks and intergovernmental negotiations; and from Ahern around the time of the Good Friday Agreement and the Treaties of Amsterdam and Nice.

Of these Taoisigh, the discourse of Haughey, FitzGerald and Ahern is analysed the most in this study. This is for three main reasons, aside from the accessibility of sources. First, scope of influence: Haughey and FitzGerald's active profile in Irish national politics reaches into four decades, from the late 1960s to the early 1990s, whilst Ahern was Ireland's longest-serving Taoiseach since de Valera. Secondly, the focus on one Fine Gael and two Fianna Fáil leaders is a balance roughly equivalent to the time spent by both parties in government during the first thirty years of Irish membership of the EU. Thirdly, these three actors have taken a particular interest in developments in Northern Ireland *and* in the European Union, with significant progress being made in Ireland's policy towards both under their administrations.

The importance of these central figures means that public statements they made after (or even prior to) their time in office or in Dáil Éireann may still retain importance and be worth analysing. This allows us to look for contradiction and consistency in the discourse they present over time and, especially, when in government and in opposition. In fact, it is notable that discourse does not tend to differ according to whether the actor is in government. Perhaps somewhat surprisingly, oppositional comments on governmental policy on Northern Ireland and European integration can include criticism of the lack of progress

Table 3.3 Taoisigh of Ireland, 1973–2002, with summary of key events for Irish policy on Northern Ireland and the European Union during their time in office

	Notable positions	*Key events:* *N. Ireland*	*Key events: EU*
Jack Lynch	Government minister 1957–66; leader of Fianna Fáil 1966–79; Taoiseach 1966–73, 1977–79	Start of the Troubles in Northern Ireland 1968–70; direct rule from Westminster introduced 1972; ECHR rules internment 'inhumane' 1978[4]	Referendum/ accession to the EEC 1972–73; ERDF created 1975;[5] Irish Presidency of European Council 1979; joins EMS 1979[6]
Liam Cosgrave	Government minister 1954–57; leader of Fine Gael Dublin and 1965–77; Taoiseach 1973–77	NI Assembly 1973-74; Sunningdale 1973; Monaghan 1975; Council bombs 1974; NI Constitutional Convention 1975–76[7]	Irish Presidency of the European British referendum on staying in EEC 1975
Charles Haughey	Government minister 1961–70, leader of Fianna Fáil 1979–92; Taoiseach 1979–81, 1982, 1987–92 1977–79;	Hunger strikes 1981; Northern Ireland Act and Assembly 1982;[8] Brooke-Mayhew talks 1991-92[9]	Referendum on Single European Act 1987; Irish Presidency of the European Council 1990; negotiations for TEU 1992[10]
Garret FitzGerald	Government minister 1973–77; leader Fine Gael 1977–87; Taoiseach 1981–82, 1982–87	New Ireland Forum 1983-84;[11] Anglo-Irish Agreement 1985; NI Assembly dissolved 1986	Irish Presidency of the European Council 1984; Dooge Report 1985;[12] negotiations for SEA 1986[13]
Albert Reynolds	Government minister 1979-81, 1982, 1987-91;	Brooke/Mayhew talks 1992; talks with UUP 1992;	Referendum on Maastricht Treaty 1992; Single

	Notable positions	Key events: N. Ireland	Key events: EU
	leader of Fianna Fáil 1992-94; Taoiseach 1992-94	Downing St Declaration 1993; negotiated US visa for Gerry Adams 1994	European Market enters into force 1993
John Bruton	Minister 1981-82; 1982-87; leader Fine Gael 1990-2001; Taoiseach 1994-97	IRA ceasefire 1994-96; first formal meeting with Sinn Féin 1995; Framework Documents and 'twin track initiative' 1995[14]	Opt-out of Schengen Agreement 1995;[15] Irish Presidency of the Council of the EU 1996
Bertie Ahern	Government. minister 1987–94; leader Fianna Fáil 1994–2008; Taoiseach June 1997– May 2008	Ceasefires 1997; Multi-party talks; GFA and referendum 1998;[16] St Andrews Agreement 2006;[17] devolved power-sharing restored 2007	Referendums on the Amsterdam Treaty[18] 1998 and Nice Treaty 2001, 2002;[19] Euro 1999 (currency 2002); European Convention 2001-03;[20] EU Council Presidency 2004

in these areas as well as apparent defence of traditional nationalist principles.

A final note in relation to the matter of these texts being the official voice of the Irish state should address the consequences of the *McKenna* judgment. Raymond Crotty brought a case to the Irish Supreme Court in 1987 (*Crotty v. An Taoiseach*) in which he successfully argued that European treaties had to be ratified in Ireland via a referendum because they entailed constitutional amendment. In a similar vein, the Green Party's Patricia McKenna took a successful case to the Supreme Court in 1995 (*McKenna v. An Taoiseach*) in which it was ruled unconstitutional for sitting governments to use public money to fund a campaign towards one result or another in a constitutional referendum. The subsequent 1998 Referendum Act led to the creation of the Referendum

Commission whose role it is to provide factual information on the subject of the referendum and to allocate equal expenditure and space for the articulation of the cases for 'yes' and 'no'. This means that official discourse is relieved of the responsibility of public information about EU treaties in the run-up to referendums. What is more, government ministers are acting more with regard to party political or even local constituency pressures than in an official capacity when they present speeches and write articles etc. at such times. This perhaps explains some of the divergence from the script around the first referendum on the Treaty of Nice in 2001, in which several Fianna Fáil government ministers were more frank than ever before in expressing concern about the direction of European integration (Hayward, 2002). Regardless of whether the 'yes' campaigning of government ministers is done whilst wearing an official hat, official discourse becomes no less important or revealing around referendums on EU treaties. The use of the 'national interest' card remains as frequent as ever in pro-European political elite discourse. Moreover, perhaps the fact that the funds for such campaigns are coming from parties rather than taxpayers makes the arguments all the more credible.

Public domain

The third criterion is that the text is articulated in the public domain. The audience to whom the text is addressed has a defining effect on the tone and content of the text itself, and this is borne in mind when the text is analysed. For the most part, the 'audience' is the national population; yet, some of the most significant examples of official discourse on the identity etc. of the Irish nation-state have been made to non-national audiences. Nevertheless, the texts presented to an audience outside the nation-state are also generally placed in the national public domain, particularly in recent times with the use of the internet to post press releases on the date of delivery. The type and form of discourse also affects the content and tone of a text. The following types/forms of discourse are analysed in this research, all presented by members of the governmental elite:

- statements (e.g. to Dáil Éireann);
- addresses (e.g. an opening address to a conference);
- speeches (e.g. to an Ardfheis [party convention]);
- written publications (such as articles, books and letters);
- interviews (the transcripts of which have been published);
- pamphlets and information leaflets (published by the government or by a political party);
- official or legal documents (e.g. an intergovernmental agreement).

Due to the importance of the public accessibility and influence of these texts, analysis of speeches/statements presented in the Oireachtas has been deliberately restricted because their audience can be limited (not just in terms of being other politicians but also, disappointingly, in numerical terms). Also, I have chosen to include a wide range of texts instead of focusing on some of the more famous speeches in order again to get a fair representation of what is consistently presented in Irish official discourse rather than that presented at 'critical junctures'.

Thematic and historical relevance

Together, the sources selected in this research are intended to provide a sound basis for analysing the processes of conceptual change that have accompanied political development in Ireland in the first thirty years of EU membership. This conceptual change is mapped out according to the triform model we have developed. Thus, the final criterion for selecting a text is that it explicitly addresses a theme relating to the objects of this research, i.e. identity, borders and governance. Due to the nature of these themes, there are points in time in which there is a concentration on such themes in texts of official discourse: for example, during a referendum on ratifying a treaty of the EU or surrounding an intergovernmental agreement on Northern Ireland. This is reflected in the sources used in this research, not least because at times of significant developments the governmental elite rely particularly heavily on official discourse to guide the population.

The last and most obvious element in the selection of sources for this study is their presentation within the first thirty years of Irish member-ship of the EEC/EU, i.e. 1973–2002. There are a few texts that predate this time period in the main empirical study in order to encompass the official reasoning behind the membership applications and also to include some of the responses of the Lynch government to the volatile situation in Northern Ireland. Figure 3.3 puts the key events in Northern Ireland and the EEC/EU in parallel timelines whilst also showing the Taoiseach and government in power at the time. It is intended to give a broad impression of the type of pressures towards change that were faced by these governments from the north and from Europe.

As noted above, the relationship between language, practice and context means that discourse analysis provides one means by which processes of political change can be analysed. Chapters 6, 7 and 8 examine Irish official discourse in the last decades of the twentieth century and show the links between the political elite's response to devel-opments at home and abroad. In setting the context for this analysis, the

N. Ireland		Irish Govt		EEC/EU
Sunningdale		Lynch [FF]		
Assembly	1973	Cosgrave [FG/L]		Ireland accession
UWC strike			1974	Oil crisis
Constitutional	1975			
Convention			1976	
	1977	Lynch [FF]		
			1978	
				EMS
	1979	(Haughey)		Elections to EP
			1980	
Hunger strike	1981	FitzGerald [FG/L]		
NI Act, Assembly		Haughey [FF]	1982	
		FitzGerald [FG/L]		
New Ireland	1983			'Eurosclerosis'
Forum and			1984	
Report				
	1985			
AIA			1986	
	1987	Haughey [FF]		SEA
			1988	
	1989			
			1990	
Brooke/Mayhew	1991			
		(Reynolds)	1992	TEU
	1993	Reynolds [FF/L]		
Joint Declaration			1994	
Ceasefires	1995	Bruton		
Framework docs		[FG/L/DL]	1996	Irish presidency
	1997	Ahern [FF/PD]		Amsterdam Treaty
Renewed ceasefire			1998	
GFA				
	1999			Euro
Devolution			2000	Convention
(suspended Oct.		Ahern		
2002–May 2007)	2001	[FF/PD]		Nice Treaty
			2002	

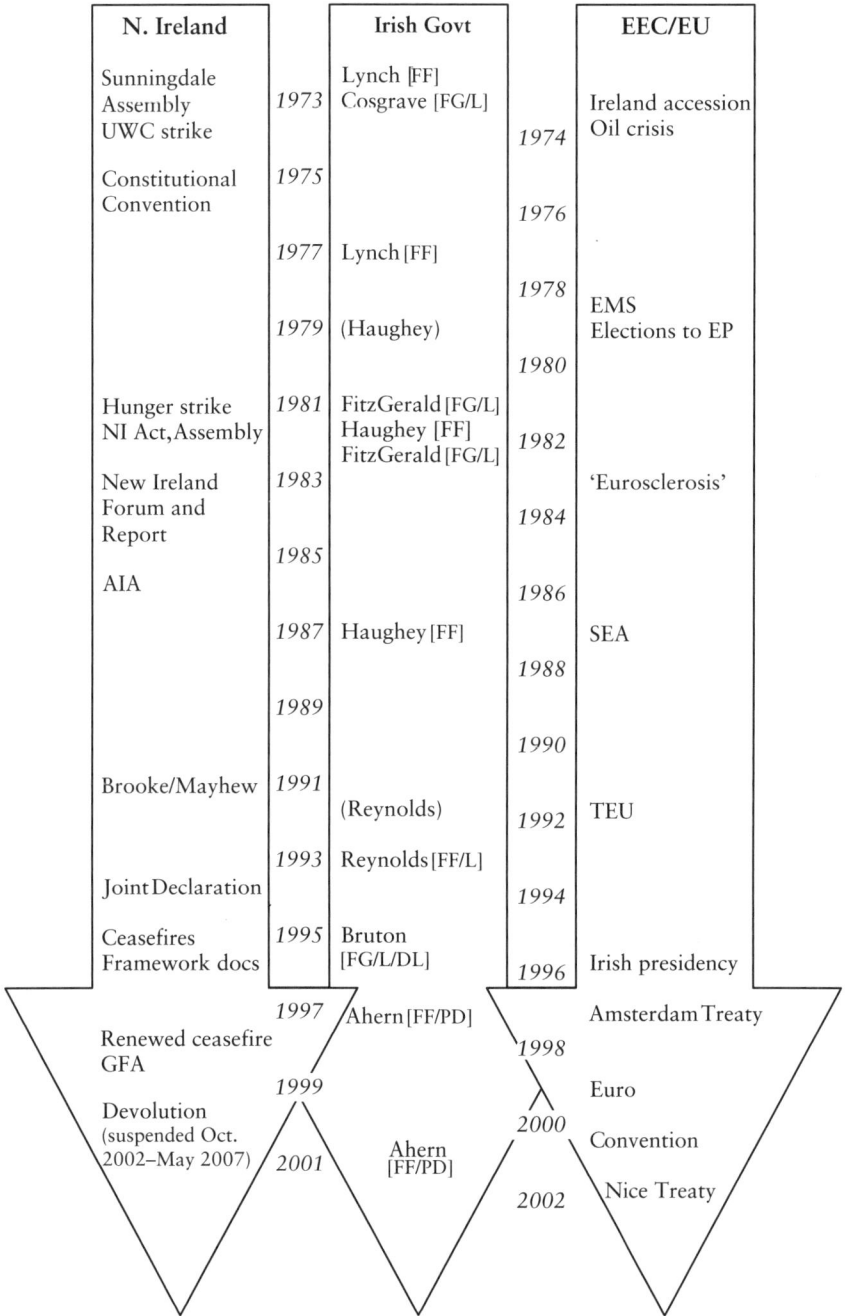

Figure 3.3 Parallel timelines of key events in Ireland, Northern Ireland and the EU, 1973–2002[21]

next two chapters provide an overview of the political and ideological dynamics that contributed to the development of Irish official nationalism since the early twentieth century. One thing that is revealed in such analysis is the early and continued dependence of official discourse on the language of nationalism. The ideal of the nation-state is the centripetal point throughout this period of social, economic and political upheaval.

Notes

1 Eagleton's points are made in criticism of Hindess and Hirst's (1975) 'anti-epistemological' thesis which, Eagleton asserts, rightly points out that the 'signifier' (as the linguistic concept) is not neutral but then goes too far in implying that the signifier 'simply conjures the "real" into being' (Eagleton, 1991: 203–13). Eagleton's comments correspond with Austin's (1962) thesis that words are primarily tools, and not objects or facts.

2 Many of the theorists of nationalism referred to in this section and, indeed, in the book in general, are analysing the use of the term 'nation' rather than that of 'nation-state'. For purposes of clarity and consistency, and in order to avoid giving the impression that 'nation-state' is less of an ideologically-weighted term than 'nation', the term 'nation-state' is occasionally substituted for theorists' use of the term 'nation'. Yet, this is not to say that the terms are interchangeable, as the model of nation-statehood elaborated in chapter 2 and applied in this book makes clear.

3 There are, for example, various schools of critical discourse analysis. These include the British school, which draws upon both Foucault's theory of discourse and linguistic theories such as Halliday's (e.g. Fairclough). More strongly influenced by Foucauldian theory is the German school (as practised by Maas). There is also the cognitive-oriented Dutch school (e.g. van Dijk) and the Vienna school (e.g. Menz) (see Wodak *et al.*, 1999: 7).

4 The Irish government had taken the British government to the European Commission of Human Rights in 1976 in protest at the use of internment in the early 1970s. The European Court of Human Rights (ECHR) ruled in January 1978 that there had been 'inhumane and degrading' treatment of detainees.

5 The decision to found the European Regional Development Fund in December 1974 was one of the most significant developments in the EEC from the Irish point of view. In agreeing to address regional disparities within the Community through the use of direct economic intervention, the EEC showed recognition of the particular vulnerabilities of the Irish member-state. The ERDF has benefited Ireland in a large range of direct and indirect ways, including the growth of subnational governance and cross-border partnerships (Loughlin, 2001; McCall, 2007).

6 The European Monetary System (EMS) was an attempt to create more monetary stability among the nine member-states. It included the Exchange Rate Mechanism (ERM) whereby the currencies of member-states were linked in

an attempt to avoid the fluctuation that troubled the start of the decade. Because Britain did not join the ERM, this move meant that the Irish pound broke parity with sterling for the first time and an exchange rate between the two was introduced. This had political as well as economic consequences for British-Irish relations (see Clery, 1979).

7   The Northern Ireland Constitutional Convention was formed following direct elections in May 1975. The aim (according to the Northern Ireland Office [NIO] white paper of July 1974) was for the consultative forum to agree a political settlement, eventually allowing for the devolution of executive powers. However, the anti-Sunningdale coalition of the United Ulster Unionist Council was revived to contest the election and won over half the seats available. These representatives were opposed to the very idea of the Convention and therefore its official report recommended the return of majority rule to Northern Ireland. Despite attempts by then-Secretary of State, Mervyn Rees, to achieve a different outcome, the Convention was dissolved in March 1976.

8   The Northern Ireland Act of July 1982 arose from the white paper the previous April setting out a framework for 'rolling devolution' in which the Assembly would begin with having a deliberative and consultative role (also known as the 'Prior initiative' after the then Secretary of State, James Prior). It led to elections to a Northern Ireland Assembly in which Sinn Féin contested for the first time, although both Sinn Féin and the SDLP abstained from the Assembly. Direct rule remained in place and the Assembly was dissolved (and some members removed by force) in June 1986 following the Anglo-Irish Agreement.

9   The Brooke-Mayhew talks of April 1991-November 1992, named after the Secretaries of State for Northern Ireland at the time, were between all the main parties with the exception of Sinn Féin for the purpose of agreeing the basis for formal talks in the future. These talks were particularly important for north-south relations in that representatives of the Irish government were accepted at discussions in Northern Ireland and delegates from the Ulster Unionist Party (UUP) travelled to Dublin for the first time for meetings with Reynolds' government.

10   The Treaty on European Union (Maastricht) (signed 1992, enacted 1993) created the European Union and its three pillars (Common Foreign and Security Policy, Justice and Home Affairs, European Communities).

11   The New Ireland Forum was established by Taoiseach FitzGerald (with the original proposals having been approved by Haughey as leader of the opposition) in May 1983. It was open to all parties on the island, together with external contributors, to discuss possible solutions to the future of Northern Ireland, but only four parties participated (FF, FG, Labour and the SDLP). The Forum report, published a year later, set out three alternative means of resolution – a unitary thirty-two-county state, a federal state between north and south, or joint British and Irish authority – all of which were dismissed by Prime Minister Thatcher in her infamous 'out, out, out' speech.

12 The Dooge Report was the report of the Ad Hoc Committee on Institutional Affairs set Cathaoirleach (chair) of Seanad Éireann and Minister for Foreign Affairs, Jim Dooge. The report recommended the creation of a European Union, further development of EMS, and strengthening the powers of the European Commission and European Parliament.

13 The Single European Act (signed 1986, enacted 1987) reformed the Treaty of Rome to establish the Single European Market and introduce the concept of European political co-operation.

14 The 'twin-track initiative' was formally set out as joint government policy in the Joint Communiqué of November 1995, which stated that parallel progress needed to be made regarding decommissioning of arms and all-party negotiations.

15 The Schengen Agreement of 1985 formalised the erosion of border controls between member-states. In order to preserve the particular arrangements on freedom of movement between Ireland and the United Kingdom (i.e. Common Travel Area), Ireland followed the UK in opting-out of this Agreement, its development in the Schengen Convention (1990) and its implementation from 1995.

16 The referendum on the Agreement held on 22 May 1998 in Northern Ireland was passed by 71 per cent (turnout 81 per cent).

17 The St Andrews Agreement (October 2006) between the two governments and Northern Ireland, crucially saw the DUP agree to power-sharing with Sinn Féin. It enabled an executive to be formed on 26 March 2007, with Ian Paisley and Martin McGuinness at the helm, and devolution to be restored.

18 The Treaty of Amsterdam (signed 1997, enacted 1999) allowed for the creation of a Common Foreign and Security Policy and furthered the EU's provisions for citizenship and employment rights.

19 The Treaty of Nice (signed 2001, enacted 2003) served to reform the institutions of the EU in order to facilitate its enlargement to twenty-seven members.

20 The Convention on the Future of Europe produced the draft treaty establishing a Constitution for Europe.

21 Note: Taoisigh named in brackets in figure 3.3 indicate their ascension to leadership on resignation of sitting Taoiseach and without a general election.

4

The origins of official Irish nationalism

The establishment of an independent Irish state was severely complicated by the fact that there was not *an* Irish nationalism seeking *an* Irish nation-state as such but rather a range of nationalisms competing for political space and influence in Ireland. The three core versions of nationalism – unionist, constitutional and republican – fostered different conceptions of the meaning and implications of Ireland's identity, borders and governance and consequently occupied conflicting positions regarding the ideal notion of Irish nation-statehood. In relation to their opposing views on Britain's role in Ireland, these competing nationalisms also fostered different opinions regarding the relevance of developments in the international context for Ireland. Events in the international (particularly European) arena also provided examples that were followed by, and forces that impinged upon, the direction and popularity of differing nationalist movements. Together, these factors led to a narrowing of the centre ground upon which the official nationalism of the Irish state would be founded. This had significant consequences, as will be elaborated in the next chapter, for the nature and development of official nationalism during the state's first fifty years.

Competing nationalisms

The general election of 1885 had a decisive impact on the form that mass parliamentary politics was to take in modern Ireland. In a pattern made inevitable by the 1884 Representation of the People Act and later reinforced by the 1892 election, parliamentary seats were redistributed so that the Protestant majority in the north-east was represented by unionist political parties and the Catholic majority in the south was represented by political parties defining themselves as nationalist (Coakley, 1999: 4, 10). A sweeping image of a Protestant unionist north versus a Catholic nationalist south was to become reified by the official discourse that emerged after the establishment of Northern Ireland and the Free State.

Yet, this image is not merely a consequence of the differences between nationalist and unionist outlooks; it actually obscures a number of other significant differences between versions of pro-independence nationalisms at the time. Such differences, as well as similarities, between constitutional and republican nationalisms (to categorise them broadly) are argued here to be in relation to contrasting interpretations of the meaning of Irish identity, borders and governance. They were embedded in the new Irish nation-state in such a way as to cause tensions and problems for Irish official national discourse long after independence. Such contradictions were most acutely felt with regard to the status of Northern Ireland and to Ireland's position on the international stage. For this reason, it is worth examining such points of convergence and divergence between the competing versions of Irish nationalism before looking at the approach of Irish official nationalism to these topics after independence.

Whilst acknowledging the great diversity and even conflicts that existed *within* these movements, the three dominant versions of nationalism in Ireland in the late nineteenth and early twentieth centuries may be classified under the headings of 'unionist', 'constitutional' and 'republican'. The application of the triform model facilitates an examination of the core ideological and political positions of the elite in contemporary Ireland as they stood in relation to issues of identity, borders and governance (see table 4.1). Each version of nationalism is elaborated in more detail here, beginning with unionism.

Unionist nationalism

Prior to Irish independence, many unionists, particularly those based outside the nine counties of Ulster, argued against the establishment of a separate Irish parliament not on the strength of their 'British' identity but, on the contrary, because of a fervent sense of their *Irish* identity; as a contributor to the 1892 Unionist Convention in Dublin exclaimed, 'we are the true united Irishmen' (Prenter, 1892: 126). If religion, cultural background or political affiliation was seen as no barrier to identification with Ireland, the question arises as to how unionists defined their Irishness. It appears that, similarly to nationalists, unionists considered the territorial ('bona fide') borders of Ireland as defining the grounds for an Irish identity. This is reflected in a comment made by Lord Castletown[1] (1892: 152), also at the Unionist Convention, who notably did not define Irish identity in terms of 'nationality' but as a 'race' made up of other nationalities, 'Celt and Norman, Dane and Cromwellian'. According to this interpretation, therefore, to claim membership of the Irish race is to associate one's self and ancestors with settlement on the

Table 4.1 Divergent forms of nationalism in pre-independence Ireland

Version of Nationalism	Unionist	Constitutional	Republican
Adherents in Ireland	Unionists, Ulster and southern. As led by Saunderson, Carson, Craig	Home Rule movement; Irish Parliamentary Party.[2] As led by Butt, Parnell, Redmond, Dillon, Devlin, Healy	Gaelic League;[3] Sinn Féin;[4] Irish Volunteers;[5] Irish Republican Brotherhood.[6] As led by Hyde, Griffith, Pearse, de Valera
Identity (nation)	Irish 'race' constituted of various nationalities. Separate from governmental structures	National culture legitimates nationalism. Requires own structures of political representation	*Primarily important.* Nation is political entity. National culture is driving force for own state
Borders (territory)	May demarcate identity. Irish identity is territorially defined	*Primarily important.* Defines both state and nation, which are distinct but may overlap	Ancient ancestral homeland should decide borders of state
Governance (state)	*Primarily important.* Supersedes the nation. Self-determination weakens nation	Can be multilevel, i.e. national and imperial, or federal. Self-determination to represent nation	State must be independent to reflect and be determined by nationhood

territory of Ireland, whereas 'nationality' is a far less permanent phenomenon, arising from the political and military trends of the day. This argument is particularly interesting due to its resonance with points that have been made in more recent times by members of the Irish governmental elite in attempting to move away from an 'ethnic' or culturally exclusive definition of Irish identity (as will be examined in chapter 6).

The key point on which unionists' Irish identity conflicts with that of constitutional and republican nationalists is in their interpretation of the political significance of this identity. Unionists viewed their Irish identity as apolitical in the sense that it was not associated with any particular political demands for representation – membership of 'Ireland' was not a politically live issue, rather, a geographical fact. Hence, unionists perceived British institutions of governance and Irish bonds of identity to be fully compatible. Unionists argued against the diminution of the Union between Britain and Ireland on the grounds that it would *damage* Ireland's interests. Unionists contended that Home Rule would reduce the status of Ireland from being an integral part of one of the most powerful empires of the time to that of a dominion or colony. This, they argued, would undermine Ireland's national and, moreover, international position. Ireland's crucial role in Britain's imperial strength was epitomised, many suggested, by the contribution of their forefathers to the British empire. Indeed, it was claimed within the forum of the Unionist Convention (Castletown, 1892: 613) that Irishmen were 'those to whom the Empire owes its prosperity and fame'. As a result of the unique position of Ireland in relation to Britain, unionists did not perceive there to be necessary conflict between pride in Irish identity and civic loyalty to the United Kingdom.

Constitutional nationalism

Constitutional nationalists differed from unionists in their conviction that membership of the United Kingdom did not strengthen Ireland's distinctiveness but, rather, subsumed it under Britain or, to be more precise, England. Indeed, constitutional nationalism in the late nineteenth century was, as Boyce (1991: 222) notes, 'not constitutional merely, but anti-British as well'. The question of how to achieve the aspired end of autonomy from Britain through constitutional means was a source of debate that defined the shape of constitutional nationalism during this period. Parnell himself moved from an 'obstructionist' policy as a Home Rule MP, to popular agitation through the Irish National Land League, to co-operation between his Irish Parliamentary Party[7] and Gladstone's Liberal Party in support of the 1886 Home Rule Bill, and finally to pre-1886 militant 'Parnellite' opposition to such a Liberal alliance after 1890. The legacy of Parnell's indecision as to how to balance separatist aspirations with constitutional claims emerged after his death in 1891 in the form of disagreement among leading constitutional nationalists. The Irish Parliamentary Party was divided into Parnellite (led by Redmond in opposition to the second Home Rule Bill of 1893) and anti-Parnellite (led by McCarthy and Dillon) factions.[8] Yet in 1900, leading political figures such as Redmond, Dillon and Healy came together to reunite the Irish Parliamentary Party in support of the tenets of constitutional nationalism that were under increasing pressure from both its unionist and republican counterparts.

The principles of constitutional nationalism as set out by the Irish Parliamentary Party at this time were based on a conception of the Irish nation as a territorial unit with its own identity. Irish national identity was, according to constitutional nationalists, not based on religious or cultural homogeneity, but, rather, on common history and experience arising from residence on the island of Ireland. Unlike the unionist conception of Irish identity, this commonality was perceived by constitutional nationalists as being necessarily distinct from British experience and identity, not least because Britain was seen as the source of much of the discontent and disunity in Irish history. Constitutional nationalists' conception of national identity, therefore, had fundamentally political implications, at the root of which was the quest for institutions of governance for Ireland that were distinct from those of Britain. The notion of national self-determination in this quest did not translate into independent statehood but, rather, separate political representation for Ireland's distinct nationhood. 'Home Rule' acted more as an umbrella term for constitutional nationalist aims than as a specific demand. The interpretation of Home Rule that was held by the Irish Parliamentary Party in the early twentieth century was premised on Ireland's equality with England. This did not imply a severing of all connection with the British empire, but, rather, a new vision of the United Kingdom (O'Leary, 2000).[9] Perhaps the most crucial point about the quest for Home Rule, however, was that it distinguished constitutional nationalists from unionists and republicans, both of which rejected Home Rule for opposing reasons.

Republican nationalism

Constitutional nationalism under Parnell had gained popular support and a revolutionary character through its politicisation of social discontent. Things changed, however, in the twenty years following the 1890s, as Ireland became more developed and more democratic (Hurst, 1987: 33–59). Spender (1912: 19) describes there being at the time a significant growth 'of self-confidence, of prosperity, of hope' in Ireland. Rather than 'killing home rule with kindness', as the Conservative government had hoped, such development contributed to the growth of nationalist sentiment in Ireland, particularly among the intellectual elite (Boyce, 1991: 262). Republican nationalism, particularly, benefited from this growth in self-confidence, not least because constitutional nationalism appeared unable to consolidate its position in this new dispensation. As with unionism and constitutional nationalism, the elements of republican nationalism at this time were highly diverse; nevertheless, a particular conception of the political implications of Irish nationhood united it. The 'nation' was conceived in republican nationalism as a *political* as much as a cultural entity – sovereignty resided in the nation itself. National identity, history and culture, united in a territorial homeland, necessitated the granting of political independence, so that the nation was free to govern itself. Nationhood was, therefore, of primary importance to republican nationalism; it was a 'given' and an 'absolute', and integration within a supra- or extra-national political framework was anathema to the very principle of nationhood. As the republican poet Ó hAodha commented in the *Irish Volunteer*, the nationalist newspaper for its namesake organisation, in October 1914: 'God made Nationalities; men and women, mostly bad men and women, made Empires, not by improving God's plan but by assailing it.'[10]

The centrality of the 'nation' in republican nationalism was reflected in an emphasis on the cultural elements of nationhood and the need to revive these in order for the nation to be able to achieve its destiny. Hence, the revival of cultural nationalism that fed into the republican movement was intrinsically related to the establishment of educational and cultural movements that had overtly political resonance, such as the Gaelic Athletic Association (established 1884), the Gaelic League (1893) and Pearse's Saint Enda's school (1908). The Gaelic movement had for its aim 'the intensifying of Irish sentiment, the preservation of Irish ideals', inciting enthusiasm 'by awakening memories hot with hate and fierce with desire of vengeance on the foreigner' (Henry, 1920: 59). Lynd[11] (1919: 184) describes Pearse as 'bent upon the making of an Irish civilisation, which would be as unlike English civilisation as is the civilisation of France or Bohemia'. The leaders of such movements were generally characterised by their idealism and intellectual motivation rather than by political influence. Nonetheless, belief in the intrinsic connection between culture and politics was reflected in the revolutionary tone of these movements. For example, the Gaelic League was developed by its leaders along the lines of an ideology of insurrection, allowing it to become the central institution in the development of a revolutionary elite in the post-1916 era (Hennessey, 1998: 29). The events following the Easter Rising, including the 'martyrdom' of its leaders, gave the cultural movements of republican nationalism a political significance in the public consciousness that made the 'liberation' of Ireland appear all the more urgent.

In order to understand the development of official nationalism in Ireland following the establishment of the Irish state, it is necessary to examine the points of convergence and divergence between constitutional and republican Irish nationalism prior to this event. The key points on which constitutional and republican nationalism converged are considered first, not least because all these elements continue as core tenets of official nationalism after independence.

Convergence among Irish nationalisms

The centrality of elites

It is perhaps unsurprising, given models drawn by modernist theorists, that members of the intellectual and cultural elite were prominent in each of the movements. Even unionism was given some historical and intellectual grounding by the contribution of scholars such as Lecky[12] of Trinity College Dublin (Jackson, 1996: 122–5). This was particularly valuable for unionism in the late nineteenth and early twentieth centuries – a period marked by a profusion of publications emanating from an emerging intelligentsia in support of Irish cultural nationalism and its interpretation of Irish history. These publications included pamphlets, newspapers, periodicals and fictional writing that reflected the activity of Irish nationalism's 'political-cultural entrepreneurs' (O'Mahony and Delanty, 1998: 111). Such a use of instruments of mass communication represented an attempt by the leaders of Irish (mostly republican) nationalist movements to stimulate wide-ranging public support for their cause. Constitutional nationalists had one significant advantage over republican nationalists in that they had a strong power base from which to present their message, with the Irish Parliamentary Party's command of electoral and local government politics. Yet, the Irish Parliamentary Party also had the effect of delimiting the appeal of constitutional nationalism, with the result that it did not widely infiltrate the lower middle classes.

The most significant factors in determining the appeal of the tenets of Irish nationalism in general, however, were beyond the control of the intellectual elite who presented them. As Garvin (1987: 43–9) notes, rapid modernisation, increased prosperity and higher levels of education contributed to disaffection among the Catholic middle classes. Hence, well-educated young Catholics constituted at this time a growing proportion of the active supporters of Irish nationalism (Hutchinson, 1987: 179). The 'revival' of cultural elements of Irish nationality, such as the Gaelic language and myths, fitted in with their search for a new vision of social order in Ireland.

Narratives of nationhood

The way in which tenets of Irish nationalism appeared to address social discontents was inseparable from the manner in which they were presented, such as in the use of historical story-lines to draw parallels between past and present. It is interesting to note that, despite their different ideal models, constitutional and republican nationalism presented (to a substantial degree) a shared narrative of the Irish nation. This narrative was based on the conception that the Irish nation was distinct and its members were 'uniquely Irish, and in every fundamental aspect distinct from and alien to English patriotism' (Hobson, 1912: 222). The uniqueness of the Irish nation was seen as a 'given', an historical fact enduring through centuries of change – a view that reflects the primordial assumptions of constitutional as well as republican nationalists such as Alice Stopford Green:[13]

> The Teutonic invaders stopped at the Irish Sea. At the fall of the Empire, therefore, Ireland did not share in the ruin of its civilisation. And while all continental roads were interrupted, traffic from Irish ports still passed safely to Gaul over the ocean routes. Ireland therefore . . . preserved her culture unharmed. (Green, 1911: 42–3)

This image of the irrepressible national spirit of the island of Ireland is intended to signify the historical precedence of Irish independence. In this vein, events on the continent of Europe are presented as influencing developments in Ireland only to an extent determined by leaders within Ireland itself.

The quest for the political recognition of Irish nationhood, whatever its form, was supported with a narrative that placed Ireland in an international sphere, i.e. outside the realm of the British empire and prior to the 'Anglicisation' of Ireland. One of the most common myths used to emphasise both Ireland's historical role in Europe and the 'civilised' nature of Irish culture was that of Ireland's role in dispelling the 'Dark Ages' in Europe:

> Erin was a veritable hive of learning, European scholars flocking to her shores to receive food, education, shelter – all gratis. Learning, which had been exiled from Europe by the din and tumult of war and the invading hosts of illiterate barbarians, found a safe asylum in the peaceful valleys of Erin. (West, 1926: 23)

The image of Ireland projected in this myth is one of a nation comfortable with its own culture and willing to share it, the implications of this being that Ireland has a contribution to make to the international arena as a distinct nation.

The motivating power of cultural identity

Constitutional and republican nationalists also agreed that the distinctiveness of the Irish nation was displayed throughout history and is more than a product of environmental factors. Moreover, both viewed Irish cultural identity as a motivation for independence. Whilst constitutional nationalists may have admitted the defining influence of 'settled' ethnic groups in Ireland more readily than republicans, they did argue strongly for the distinctiveness of Irish identity; see, for example, the retort of Hobson (as a constitutional proponent of Home Rule) to the contention that 'Irish political history would be much what it is whatever the race inhabiting the island':

> the Irish temperament is on the whole more *spirituel* [sic], more alert and vivacious, quicker-witted, more imaginative than the Anglo-Saxon . . . The Gael still persists in the Irish character; so also the Celt; Norman ancestry and Norman types are not uncommon . . . Anglicisation has played no inconsiderable part. In the sum-total a type (endlessly varied) is produced, and we know him as the Irishman. (Hobson, 1912: 26–7)

It is interesting to note that, unlike Green, Hobson readily admits the defining influence of cultures that 'settled' and became established in Ireland. This, however, is not seen to weaken his main argument, namely that the Irish 'race' is inherently different from that of England, the latter being the 'temperamental opposite' to the 'imaginative and quick-witted' Irishman (Hobson, 1912: 27–8). The 'fight' that Hobson identified between the England and Ireland, therefore, was as much a cultural as a political matter. It is not surprising, therefore, that constitutional nationalists also sought to capture and engage the power of identity in their drive for distinction from Britain.

Popular cultural movements at this time, particularly those with an exclusive notion of Irish culture (such as those based on the Irish language or Roman Catholicism), tended to be motivated and dominated by an Irish republican ideology. Nevertheless, the Irish Parliamentary party pursued a policy of 'nationalisation' in the period 1875–1921 that utilised the notion of a distinct Irish culture or cause in order to support their arguments for a distinct Irish parliament and to reclaim ground from the republican movement.[14] Hence, by the turn of the century, Ireland 'possessed the entire series of symbols which were to be found in all European nation-states' (Alter, 1987: 10). The political importance of cultural elements of nationhood was thus recognised by both constitutional and republican nationalists, although national culture was a driving force in the republican tradition and more of a supporting element for constitutional nationalists.

The common ground between constitutional and republican nationalism was deep as well as broad, therefore, and occasional crossover between the two broad groupings of nationalism was to be expected. For example, Sinn Féin originally benefited to a small degree from the disaffection of members of the Irish Parliamentary Party, who viewed the organisation as a possible form of new constitutional politics appealing to those beyond the reach of the Party, specifically the young and lower middle classes (Foster, 1989: 458). Many of the differences between constitutional and republican nationalism were, however, made starker in the context of the growing radicalisation of Irish politics after 1900 and the impact of international and national events after 1914, at which point the centre ground began to disintegrate rapidly.

Divergence among Irish nationalisms

Models of nationalism

Despite convergence on some of the core tenets of their versions of nationalism, republican and constitutional national ideologies in Ireland diverged in four main areas: the ideal model of the nation-state, the methods of realising that model, the significance of the international context for those models and methods, and the response to the European crisis. Central to these differences was their interpretation of the functions of a state in relation to a nation. The aims of republican nationalists, as expressed by Sinn Féin, were 'the complete political, the complete economical and the complete moral and intellectual independence of Ireland' (Henry, 1920: 283). In contrast, constitutional nationalists could conceive of a flourishing of a unique culture within political structures that were based on a British model and not entirely free from British influence. Hence, whereas constitutional nationalists had a dynamic, even flexible, conception of the nation (viewing cultural elements as the signifiers rather than the substance of the nation), Irish republican nationalism had a more static interpretation of culture (the role of the state is to preserve and reflect the nation).

These contrasting interpretations of the functions of a state in relation to a nation were shaped by historical and external influences. The Irish republican movement was inspired by the American and French models of revolution, yet merged this with a goal of absolute separation from British (specifically English) influence and, in relation to this, a romantic Roman Catholicism (Garvin, 1996: 11–12). Republican rhetoric emphasised the primacy of the Irish people over the state, i.e. that the forms of governance were to be uniquely Irish. Republican nationalists thus asserted that loyalty to the Irish state would be a demonstration of membership of and loyalty to the Irish nation itself.[15] In contrast, Irish constitutional nationalists could conceive of an acceptable level of independence for the Irish nation within a supranational state structure. This is in part because they had conceptualised the Irish nation in a pre-First World War era in which 'the tendency of the world [was] all towards great empires and away from little states' (Spender, 1912: 133). The legacy of these notions of identity in Irish official discourse on Ireland's place within the European Union is noteworthy and is considered in detail in chapter 8.

Methods of nationalism

These two very different models of nation-statehood were reflected in the methods that were applied by republican and constitutional nationalists. Both movements sought to raise public consciousness of a distinct Irish identity, yet they had different conceptions as to the way in which cultural identity related to their ultimate aims. Whereas constitutional nationalists viewed the ideal model as being one in which the structures of governance would be shaped to *represent* the particular needs of the governed, republican nationalists contended that structures of governance should be *derived from* and determined by the nation, its identity and requirements. This was reflected in the activity of both movements that was intended to directly contribute towards the realisation of their ideals. Constitutional nationalists concentrated on political activity that 'proved' the competence and trustworthiness of Irish politicians and officials for greater responsibility in governance. Republican nationalists instead focused on preparing 'the nation' for the achievement of the goal of sovereign statehood by strengthening the distinctiveness of its culture (as seen in Hyde's de-Anglicisation campaign) and public consciousness of the political implications of this nationhood. However, there was significant disagreement even amongst republican nationalists as to the means by which the goal of complete independence would be achieved.[16]

However, events soon surpassed the conjecturing of nationalist leaders, and all had to adjust to the new environment created in Ireland by events within and beyond it. One of the most significant of these events, alongside the First World War and the passing and subsequent suspension of the third Home Rule Bill in 1914, was the Easter Rising of 1916. It was organised by republicans who believed that the rest of Europe would not seriously regard claims to Irish sovereign nationhood unless the Irish people had strongly demonstrated their independence from Britain in political and military action, not just in cultural terms. The Rising contributed to a situation in which nationalist sympathies were polarised into more distinct 'constitutional' and 'republican' camps, for it signified the clear differences in the models and methods of these two versions of nationalism. The main aims of the Rising – to raise the cause of Ireland from a domestic issue in the United Kingdom to an international concern and to prevent the demise of the separatist ideal – were in conspicuous contrast to the principles of the Home Rule movement (Hennessey, 1998: 158). It is no surprise, therefore, that Redmond and the Irish Parliamentary Party (which he had led since 1900) viewed the Easter Rising as treason to Home Rule (Hennessey 1998: 140). For the Rising epitomised a form of nationalism that was antithetical to Redmond's efforts to gain national independence in a reworking of the Union through reconciliation between Britain and Ireland. The constitutional nationalists held a view of Britain and of the future shape of European power politics that was entirely different to that assumed by the instigators of the Easter Rising. Indeed, this 'worldview' of constitutional nationalism appeared to become increasingly discredited by events not only within but also beyond Ireland as the First World War continued on its course. The way in which the different types of nationalism conceptualised Ireland's position in relation to the international context is outlined below.

Conceptualisation of international context

Republican ideology is often associated with an isolationist attitude towards international affairs, in contrast to the 'cosmopolitanism' of constitutional nationalism. This is because republican nationalism conceived the nation as the foundation of civilisation and held the view that the Irish nation treads a unique path in the course of civilisation. Constitutional nationalism, on the other hand, saw the nation as being an instrument of civilisation and argued that the path of nationhood is part of the road to progress trodden by humanity in general. The precept that nationhood is part of and not distinct from the wider interests of an international community was a fundamental element in constitutional nationalism. Such different conceptions of the nation's position in the international context gave rise to different approaches to the international context as both influence and example.

Due to the indirect impact of Ireland's position in relation to Britain, the Irish population had relatively high levels of awareness of the international context. On the opposite side of the coin to the historical diaspora of Irish misfortune and exploitation, members of the Irish elite participated in Britain's policy of cultural imperialism abroad. Added to this, although economic-related factors such as infant mortality rates and gross domestic product rates per capita were significantly worse than its European contemporaries, Ireland had good levels of literacy, freedom of expression and political participation (Kennedy, 1992: 110–11). These factors were arguably central to the development of all types of nationalism in Ireland and to their different conceptualisation of Ireland's international position.

By setting Irish nationalism in an imperial context, the proponents of constitutional Home Rule were responding to the need for change in the international order as they saw it, whilst avoiding the stark contrast between nation and empire. Thus, Redmond advocated Home Rule in terms of a reinstatement of what Ireland had lost in 1800 but without proposing to undermine the supremacy of the British imperial parliament.[17] Redmond's arguments for Irish autonomy were subsequently framed in terms of a request for 'what has already been given in twenty-eight different portions of the Empire' (1911, quoted in Amery, 1912: 130). However, unionists dismissed the constitutional nationalist demand for national autonomy within the imperial framework as a confusion of terms. Amery (1912: 130), for example, requested clarification from Redmond and other proponents of Home Rule as to whether 'the supremacy of the Imperial Parliament to be retained [would be] like that of Canada over Ontario or of the UK over the Dominions'. Without such assurance, unionists viewed the imperial framework of the Home Rule movement as merely sugar-coating the quest for Irish independence from Britain.

Whilst unionist battled with constitutional nationalist in Westminster, republican nationalists were looking elsewhere for support in their search for Irish sovereignty. Whereas constitutional nationalists cited dominions in the British empire as examples for Irish nationalism to follow, republican nationalists based their conception of Irish nation-statehood on European experience (such as Griffith's formula for Ireland based on the 'dual monarchy' example of Austria-Hungary) (Colum, 1959: 65–6; Davis, 1974: 113–18; Maye, 1997: 94–111). Activity that was more typical within republican nationalist circles, however, was Griffith's leading role in the 'Irish Transvaal Committee', whose purpose was to enlist public sympathy for the Boers and dissuade young Irishmen from joining the British Army in its war against them (Younger, 1981: 11–12). The Boer War was an international event that stimulated an interest among Irish republicans, many of whom used the opportunity to express Ireland's alignment with the majority of European states in disapproval of Britain's actions.

Response to the European crisis

The context of Europe was a crucial element in Ireland's development and self-awareness. For, as Kennedy (1992: 115–16) notes, social, political and economic processes that were at work in Europe as a whole in the eighteenth and nineteenth centuries had a significant impact of change on British-Irish relations. By the end of the nineteenth century, political Romanticism, cults of youth and violence, and general disillusionment with the existing order were spreading throughout Europe (English, 1998: 77). The events that occurred in Europe in the following decades would provide opportunities for the influence of these movements on the Irish nationalist elite to come to the forefront of Irish politics. In the period 1914–19, a crucial time of transformation in state orders in Europe, nationalist intellectuals in Ireland 'consciously embraced' a project of 'imagining' Ireland as an historic cultural nation requiring a modern, European-style state (O'Dowd, 1996: 16). As the various sections of the intellectual and political elite in Ireland formed their own response to the crisis in Europe, the issue of Ireland's relationship to Britain following independence (in some shape or form) became established as the dominant national question. For the First World War, with its implications for Home Rule and conscription in Ireland, ignited real interest in the question of Ireland's position regarding other states and polarised political opinion among the Irish population in general (Andrews, 1979: 305).[18] In the context of Britain's drive to recruit Irish men as British soldiers, the politics and rhetoric of the elite in Ireland explicitly connected the 'national question' with individuals' political, social economic and religious ideological positions.

The European crisis of 1914–19 heightened the prominence of Irish Parliamentary Party MPs due to the increased urgency placed on the need for the British government to defuse the 'Irish Question'. In an effort to avoid civil war in Ireland, the British government led moderate Irish parliamentarians to believe in the inevitability of Home Rule whilst emphasising Ireland's vital role in hastening the end of the war. In this way, the British government sought to address two of its major problems – unrest in Ireland and too few soldiers on the battlefields – through convincing moderates on both sides in Ireland of its intentions for an Irish settlement and its prospects for success in Europe. However, unionist and nationalist MPs were led to deduce different conclusions from the same assurances. Hence, Ireland's role in the First World War was seen by unionists as delaying the implementation of Home Rule and by nationalists as securing and even hastening it. However, the British negotiators had underestimated the strength of the extreme elements in Ireland and the fact that the war would actually highlight the divisions not only between unionists and nationalists within Ireland but also between Ireland and Britain.

The Irish Parliamentary Party's support for the British forces in the First World War was to some extent a reflection of its belief that Ireland's interests lay in reconciliation between Britain and Ireland. Yet, it would be wrong to view Irish constitutional nationalists' position regarding the war entirely in the sphere of British–Irish relations. The rhetoric of elite members of this group, including those dedicated to a 'cultural' regeneration of Ireland, indicates the links between support for the war and their vision of Ireland's place in modern Europe. The image of a 'liberal and democratised Europe' was a motivating one for many Irish constitutional nationalists (Paseta, 2000: 18–19). The war threatened the very core of this ideal, and the involvement of Irish soldiers in an effort to support the rights of small nations was seen as a moral duty and, indeed, necessary for the future of Irish nationalism.

> the truth is that this war is Ireland's war, and that Ireland for the first time in the passage of long centuries sends out her sons fully accredited to fight for the sake of Ireland and for Ireland's cause.[19]

Constitutional nationalist discourse brought together the rhetoric of the Allied powers with that of national self-determination. For example, attempts by Britain to recruit Irish men into the army using descriptions of 'gallant little Belgium' echoed in the declaration of Ireland's right to self-determination and freedom as a small European nation with a powerful and dominant neighbour (De Paor, 1997: 58).

In contrast, for most unionist groups, the 'Irish Question' simply no longer existed 'in the face of the European difficulty';[20] such an underestimation of the impact of the divisions in Ireland and Europe was to have damaging consequences for their post-war political survival. Unionists in Ireland, north and south, saw the First World War as the most important issue of the time. Indeed, even before war was declared, many unionists had foreseen 'the critical situation in Europe' as necessitating that Ireland not 'be regarded as a potentially hostile country' (Percy, 1912: 197; Beresford, 1912: 182). However, the 'Irish Question' persisted and the European crisis actually diminished the influence unionists had in British politics. Unionists were thus forced into a position of accepting Home Rule as ultimately inevitable, as a means of keeping Ireland off the British agenda (Hennessey, 1998: 71). In the debate over the granting of Home Rule to Ireland during this period, a rift became established between unionists in Ulster and those in the south of Ireland (Hennessey, 1998: 19).

Republicans advocated a policy of neutrality towards the war on the grounds that national loyalty was indivisible and Ireland had 'no quarrel with any Continental power' (Griffith in *Sinn Féin*, August 1914, quoted in Hennessey, 1998: 64). The nation-focused opportunism of republican nationalism in the context of European upheaval was epitomised during the Easter Rising itself. By 1916, it had become clear that the war would endure for longer than had been anticipated and, prior to the involvement of the United States of America, the outcome of the war looked uncertain. The discourse of the extreme Irish nationalist elite at this time turned significantly towards Europe, not as a point of crisis but a source of hope, an alternative to British rule. Arthur Griffith claimed that because of the war 'Ireland was no longer an island lying behind England but was again, politically, as well as geographically, part of Europe' (Hennessey, 1998: 163).[21] Ireland's engagement with European states was presented by republican nationalists as continuing the tradition of Irish patriotism:

> Wolfe Tone and the United Irishmen raised in Ireland the banner of the French Revolution. They were European as well as Nationalist in their ideas, and none the less Nationalist for being European. (Lynd, 1934 [1916]: vi)

The Declaration of Independence epitomised the attempt by Irish nationalists to justify their cause both within Ireland and in the wider European and international context.

Poblacht na hÉireann, the republican proclamation of Ireland's independence in 1916, claimed that Irish independence was supported by 'allies in Europe'.[22] In this way, Ireland's equality with other European nations was being declared for, as Hennessey (1998: 166) notes, an 'alliance' is a union of sovereign states. The 'gallant allies' referred to in the Declaration were in actual fact Germans, whose support (exemplified in Chancellor Bethmann Hollweg's agreement to send arms to Ireland) was seen by the leaders of Clan na Gael, the Irish Republican Brotherhood and the Irish Volunteers as a means to an end (De Paor, 1997: 59). However, Germany's support for the Irish 'cause' was less a product of ideological sympathies than a by-product of its anti-Allied stance. Germany, an imperial power, did not seek to assert nationalist principles yet it saw an opportunity to exploit Britain's vulnerability (De Paor, 1997: 59). Hence, the phrase acknowledging the republicans' reliance on outside support was sufficiently veiled for Germany to take advantage of the opportunity the Rising was intended to provide for the weakening of Britain (De Paor, 1997: 59).

The unsteady origins of Irish independence

Irish vulnerability in post-war Europe

The failure of Germany's planned support of the Rising contributed to the overall failure of the attempt to place the Irish question on the

international stage. This was most clearly shown in the rejection of Sinn
Féin's claim for Ireland's consideration at the post-war peace conference.
Hennessey (1998: 163) contends that, particularly after the suppression
of armed rebellion, Sinn Féin had looked to the peace conference as an
alternative forum for achieving self-government. Sinn Féin's assertion
that Ireland's case should be heard by the peace conference relied on the
claim that Ireland was one of the four ancient and sovereign European
states, as recognised by the Council of Constance in 1417 (Hennessey,
1998: 164). However, the key decision-makers at the peace conference
worked with more recent templates of Europe than did the Irish peti-
tioners. President Woodrow Wilson informed delegates of the Irish Race
Convention in Paris that Ireland, as a small non-sovereign nation, would
not have its case heard by the conference without the unanimous
approval of the four Great Powers, including Great Britain (Andrews,
1979: 133).

Nevertheless, somewhat ironically, the map of Europe that was drawn
by the great powers made the Irish republican search for a solution
outside the imperial framework increasingly plausible. In the wake of the
First World War came the beginning of the 'end of empires' in Europe
and the flourishing of national self-determination as a 'right' and a principle of political organisation. Within Ireland, this contributed significantly to the alienation of those who supported the British imperial
framework on a world stage, if not on the territory of Ireland. The First
World War had brutally altered the political and social landscape of
Europe and the change in the political and social landscape of Ireland at
this time can only be understood in this context. The dominant political
parties and elite members in Ireland before 1914 were products of their
time and context and traversed with difficulty the transition to the post-
war era. The Irish Parliamentary Party, for example, was established and
acted, as previously noted, in the context of British imperialism. It did
not perceive the possibility of Ireland being an independent nation-state
on the international stage, but limited its claim to Home Rule within the
British imperial structure. The disillusionment felt by many Irish nationalists towards the British government's earlier assurances contributed to
the popular movement away from support of the Union or the empire by
the end of the war. As Joseph Devlin questioned in a House of Commons
debate, April 1918:

> what guarantee have we that when the War is over, when the fields of
> Europe . . . are red with Irish blood, that your declaration of devotion to
> small nationalities is anything more than a scrap of paper . . . We believe
> it a War for small nations in every part of Europe, except that small nation
> that you control. (quoted in Hennessey, 1998: 225)

After the war, two of the victorious powers, who prided themselves as world empires, oversaw the dismantling of other European empires into smaller nation-states. The prime motivation of such action in the post-war treaties was to emasculate the enemy, yet it had posited nations versus empires on the world stage and given nations the prize. National self-determination was too utopian, too rare a principle for it to remain a tool of the treaty-cartographers; Britain bore much responsibility for the way in which this ideal would change not only the map of Europe but the conception of political identity within it. By 1919, a policy of Irish self-determination within the British empire was simply unacceptable to a new generation of Irish political elite members, not least because its very frame of reference was made untenable by the way in which Europe was redefined by the post-war treaties. Indeed, the idea of the compatibility of imperialism and nationalism (encapsulated in Seymour's [1888: 44] vision of an Irish national flag depicting 'the Irish harp surmounted by the British crown') was shown to be 'unnatural' according to the very principles on which Europe was reconceptualised in 1919. Thus, 'Europe' as both context and example at the time of the Irish War of Independence lent itself to the success of republicanism and the demise of nationalist parties that had seen national self-determination as possible within an imperial framework.

Nationalism's dissipating centre ground

As stability and order declined in Europe, there was increased polarisation between unionist, constitutional and republican nationalism within Ireland. In this context, new forms of constitutional Irish nationalism competed to fill the vacuum in a period of transition before 1921. The unsuccessful Irish Centre party founded by Stephen Gwynn continued to hold many of the same principles as Redmond, including the achievement of Irish self-government within the British empire (Paseta, 2000: 21). Gwynn and his colleagues, frustrated by the proliferation of cultural idealism and provincialism in Ireland after 1918, advocated a constitutional solution to the divisions in Ireland along the lines of the European nation-state model:

> We do need in Ireland to get a civilised State, and we can only do that by adopting the patterns which are established in Europe, to which we belong. It is a great deal more important to be civilized than to be Gaelic.[23]

An alternative was put forward by Plunkett's Irish Dominion League (IDL) in its manifesto of June 1919 (signed by Unionist MPs as well as members of the Irish Convention and nationalist non-politicians), which advocated self-government for Ireland within the empire but with dominion status.[24] The IDL aimed to win the support of the middle class in Ireland, in the context of worsening British-Irish and nationalist-unionist relations, by proposing that dominion status would defuse these tensions. The Irish Dominion League 'self-consciously presented itself as moderate alternative to both [u]nionism and extreme nationalism' (Paseta, 2000: 24) and sought to persuade moderate Sinn Féin leaders as well as moderate public opinion as to the advantages of compromise. The short-lived co-operative agreement between Gwynn and Plunkett disintegrated in 1922 over the latter's willingness to accept partition (Paseta, 2000: 25). Yet, although partition was an issue over which elites within the various nationalist organisations were divided amongst themselves, the matter of whether Irish self-government within the British imperial structure was acceptable was the main line of division between nationalist and republican in post-Treaty Ireland.

The 1916 Rising and the First World War had also weakened the centre ground within republican nationalism. In 1917, under the new presidency of de Valera, Sinn Féin changed its constitution to reflect a demand for an independent republic – 'the separatist option had apparently replaced the home rule compromise' (Foster, 1989: 489). The popularity of constitutional nationalism took a further blow following the enactment of the Military Service Bill in April 1918 (seen as the ultimate act of betrayal by the British government), despite the fact that the active anti-conscription campaign was led by an inter-party committee that included Dillon and Devlin of the IPP, and Healy of the All-for-Ireland League, as well as Griffith and de Valera of Sinn Féin. The general election of December 1918 consequently epitomised the increasing polarisation in Irish politics with a dramatic victory for Sinn Féin, which won seventy-three parliamentary seats compared to the Irish Parliamentary Party's six seats. Sinn Féin's success in this election epitomised the disaffection of the general electorate (substantially larger since the 1918 Representation of the People Act) with the British government and the related demise of the Irish Parliamentary Party. As Professor R. M. Henry (1920: 227) of Queen's University Belfast asserts in his somewhat sympathetic contemporary account of the evolution of Sinn Féin:

> It was now plain to the average Nationalist that the parliamentary prospect held no promise: that the Irish Parliamentary Party were no longer listened to, and that the sworn enemies of Irish nationality were in the seats of power both in Ireland and in England.

In January 1919, in a climate of increasing confidence and determination among republican nationalists, Sinn Féin established the first Dáil

Éireann. This Dáil ratified the 1916 *Poblacht na hÉireann* and set up its own government under the presidency of de Valera. It also established its own Constitution (1919), which was primarily an attempt to replace the British administration, although it did not purport to establish an Irish republic and, indeed, it 'presented the most basic rules of the British model of government' (Ward, 1994: 156). Despite the fact that the Dáil was banned in September 1919, that it had an extremely small civil service that had to operate in secrecy, and that the British state still controlled official government agencies, 223 public bodies pledged allegiance to the Dáil (O'Malley, 1979: 167; Coakley, 1999: 14). One of the first laws passed by this Dáil was the prohibition of emigration in 1919 – an act that reflected Sinn Féin's protectionist view of the 'nation' as a people (O'Malley, 1979: 167). Clarification of the ideal of the 'nation' was arguably made all the more necessary by the severe lines of internal division that existed within Ireland, including among republicans themselves. The continuing tensions *within* Irish nationalism were epitomised in the Civil War that followed the 1921 Anglo-Irish Treaty.

The Treaty was negotiated with the British government by leading republican nationalists from all traditions, including Griffith, who had been 'heart and soul with the Volunteers but against the Rising', Collins (commander of the Irish Republican Army) and Gavan Duffy (Sinn Féin representative at the Paris Peace Conference) (O'Hegarty, 1998: 31). The negotiations centred on the reconciliation of Irish aspirations for a united independent state with the British requirement that Ireland remain within the empire. The Irish negotiators were prepared to accept the inclusion of a British monarch into the Irish constitution for the sake of unity within Ireland; hence, the agreement to follow the example of Canada, in which the Crown was excluded 'by fact if not by law' (Colum, 1959: 284, 290–4).[25] However, there were significant differences between Canada and Ireland, not least in terms of size, history, proximity to Britain and the existence of a significant 'loyalist' population. The fact that Ireland had been effectively given dominion status within the British imperial framework did not fit well with the version of nationalism that had stimulated the War of Independence in the first place. Although passed in the Dáil by a small minority, the Treaty was rejected by nationalists (such as de Valera) who believed that Ireland should accept nothing less than the status of a republic.

Unionist/nationalist and north/south polarisation

The inclusion of partition in the Treaty added to the difficulty of the Provisional Government's task of presenting the new state as the legitimate representation of the Irish nation. This was the case even though the issue of partition was arguably considered much more urgent by those resident in the north, unionist as well as nationalist. For example, it was the Bishop of Derry, Charles McHugh, who established the Anti-Partition League, which later became the Irish National League, in 1916 (Hennessey, 1998: 148). By the time of British cabinet discussions of a Partition Act in 1919, Anglo-Irish relations generally took precedence over intra-Irish ones in the priorities of southern nationalists (O'Halloran, 1987: 72). The terms of partition put forward in 1919 stimulated riots not in the south but in the north, partly because the acceptance of partition implied the dissolution of the Ulster Covenant, which rejected any form of Home Rule in Ireland (Hennessey, 1998: 154). These riots were portrayed in the southern press as anti-Catholic pogroms, and the first Dáil responded by imposing a boycott on Belfast firms (Andrews, 1979: 224; O'Malley, 1979: 167, 324). Thus, the north-south, nationalist-unionist division was reinforced by the political actions of southern nationalists even prior to the legal establishment of partition. The Government of Ireland Act of 1920 (with provisions for parallel governing institutions in Dublin and Belfast) was the first to make the partition of Ireland official. Yet, as Coakley (1999: 15, 19) notes, the Government of Ireland Act did provide for all-Irish institutions, including the office of the Lord Lieutenant and an interparliamentary Council of Ireland, but this aspect of the Act was virtually ignored in the south.

Although the Civil War of 1922–23 was not specifically fought over the issue of partition, the division of Ireland between the twenty-six counties and the six counties was strengthened through its conduct. For, as O'Halloran (1987: 66, 157) points out, the Provisional Government's prioritising of winning the Civil War led to increased isolationism in the south and a growing impatience there with the nationalist minority in the north. The Anglo-Irish Treaty itself was not only disliked by militant republican nationalists, the unionist population in the north was further alienated from the south by the granting of what it considered to be too much independence to the new Irish state. The Northern Ireland parliament (established by the Government of Ireland Act) subsequently used its powers under Article 12 of the Anglo-Irish Treaty to reject the extension of the powers of the Free State to Northern Ireland that was provided for in Article 44 of the 1922 Constitution (Ward, 1994: 179). Thus, the War of Independence, the Government of Ireland Act, the Civil War and the establishment of the Free State all contributed to a polarisation of Irish politics along nationalist versus unionist lines, with the division between nationalists and unionists becoming increasingly

Dec. 1918 General election	
Jan. 1919 1st Dáil Éireann [SF boycott of Westminster; 1st ministry under Brugha; 2nd ministry under de Valera]	**Jan. 1919 –** **July 1921** War of Independence
	Dec. 1920 Government of Ireland Act [partition]
May 1921 Election Southern Ireland [all candidates return unopposed, officially to House of Commons of S. Ireland but in practice for 124 SF (of 128) TDs to 2nd Dáil Éireann]	**Aug. 1921** 2nd Dáil Éireann [3rd ministry ('of the Irish Republic') under de Valera]
	Dec. 1921 Anglo-Irish Treaty [Irish Free State]
Jan. 1922 Dáil ratifies Treaty [de Valera resigns; 4th ministry formed under Griffith]	**Jan. 1922** 1st Provisional Government [Collins-led interim administration]
June 1922 General election [pro- and anti-Treaty SF pact]	**June 1922 –** **May 1923** Civil War
Sept. 1922 3rd Dáil Éireann [inc. provisional parliament (prev. HoC S. Ireland); 2nd Provisional Government (inc. 5th ministry) of Collins, Cosgrave]	**Dec. 1922** Constitution of the Irish Free State **Dec. 1922** 1st Executive Council of Free State [led by Cosgrave, replaces Prov. Govt]
Apr. 1923 SF split; Cumann na nGaedheal	
Sept. 1923 4th Dáil Éireann [Cumann na nGaedheal-led 2nd Executive Council, under Cosgrave]	**Aug. 1923** General election [Cumann na nGaedheal majority]

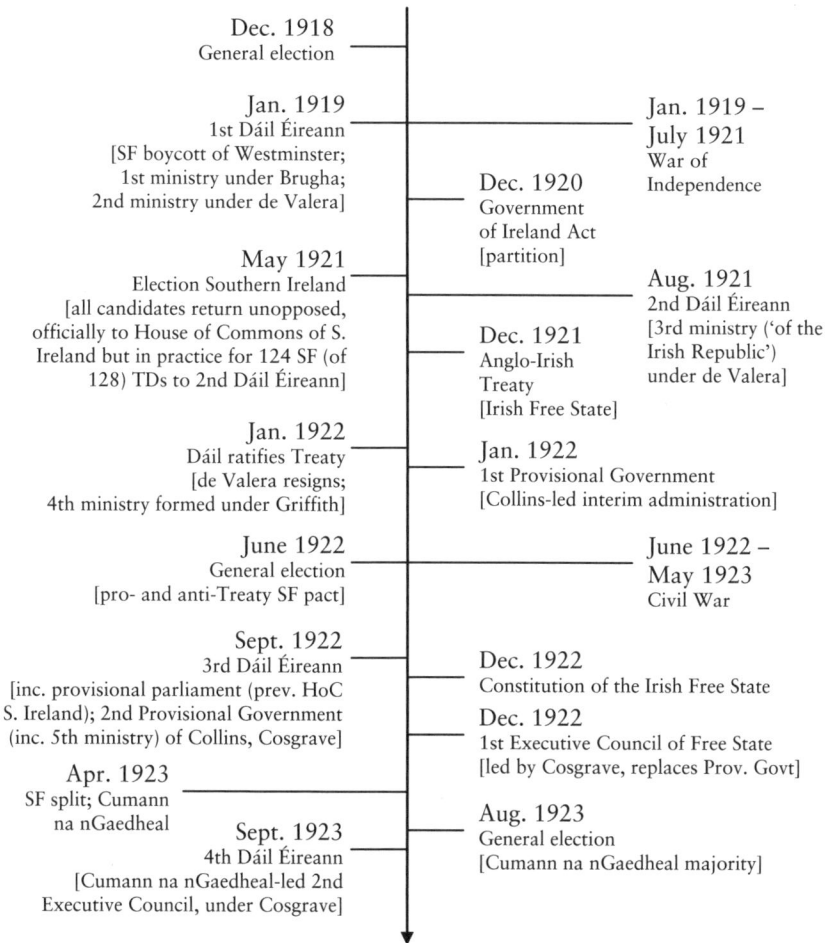

Figure 4.1   Summary of key political developments in Ireland, December 1918–September 1923

defined in territorial as well as political terms. An overview of the key political events contributing to such divisions in this turbulent period are summarised in figure 4.1.

Official nationalism: co-ordination, mobilisation, legitimisation

The democracy that was established in Ireland after 1922 emerged, Garvin (1996: 1, 9) notes, in the context of a 'general wave of European democratisation'. The Constitution of the Irish Free State Act went into effect in December 1922, six months after a draft constitution had been published (on election day in June 1922). The adoption of concepts from European (particularly French) models enabled the modification of British influence and added credibility to the Free State (Macmillan, 1993: 186). Indeed, the Constitution shared a number of features with the written constitutions of newly established democratic states in post-1919 Europe. However, as Macmillan (1993: 194–5) notes, the Free State 'was distinguished from its European counterparts by the nature of the political culture and socialisation process in which the constitutions were expected to function'. As a constitution, it contained many internal tensions, reflecting the fact that it was structured for the continuation of British political institutions and practices and worded for the develop-ment of an independent Irish polity. In essence, it was an attempt to merge British constitutional theory with republican ideas of popular sov-ereignty.[26] Although the Constitution of 1922 recognised the Free State as a constitutional equal of the United Kingdom (Article 1), Article 2 provided that the Anglo-Irish Treaty would become part of constitu-tional law, thus sealing Ireland's dominion status under the Crown (Ward, 1994: 180, 187). Yet, despite attempts to recognise all interests, the Constitution was not enough to convince either unionists in the north or republicans in the south that the Free State was a plausible state or polity.

The Free State government led by Cosgrave from September 1922 recognised that the new state faced a crisis of legitimacy that would endure without some significant degree of accommodation for republi-can ideals in the official nationalism of the state. Hence, the official nationalism that emerged was not party-specific but nation-building, i.e. focused on unifying the nation behind the state. This was important not least because the cleavage of the Civil War was replicated in the par-liamentary system of the Free State and many of the elite of the new political system had their roots in Sinn Féin. Yet, arguably more sig-nificant for the consolidation of the Free State was the change in public opinion of the rebels, towards a marginalisation of them in political terms (aided by the response of the Irish Catholic hierarchy)[27] which enabled the parliamentary elite to portray themselves as the true inher-itors of the nationalist cause. Also, by 1923 there was increasing disaf-fection with the more romantic notions of national identity even within the anti-Treaty republican movement. Andrews (1979: 296), an IRA prisoner in Newbridge Internment Camp at the time of the Truce, noted that:

> The will to escape had gone. Interest in the Irish language was at a dis-count; nobody spoke it and nobody learned it. Cathleen Ní Houlihan was something of a joke.

The general election of autumn 1923 was conducted with a larger electorate than previously (following the 1923 Electoral Act) and using Proportional Representation (as endorsed by the 1922 Constitution). In this election, Cumann na nGaedheal[28] (led by pro-Treaty former Sinn Féin members) gained 39 per cent and anti-Treaty Sinn Féin gained 27.6 per cent of the vote (Andrews, 1979: 300; Coakley, 1999: 5, 18; Sinnott, 1999: 101).

Conclusion

A primary difficulty facing members of the nationalist political elite in Ireland in the wake of the First World War had been the absence of political unity – the roots of which lay in the diversity of nationalist ideologies and movements prior to 1914. As this chapter has shown, the situation deteriorated before it improved, as holders of different versions of Irish nationalism competed for the right and the power to define the new nation-state in their own image. Yet, once the state was established, nationalism played a crucial role in the stabilisation and consolidation of the state. To this end, the threefold function of nationalist ideas identified by Breuilly (1996: 166–7) continued beyond the quest for independence: nationalism co-ordinated the interests of elites; it mobilised support for the state from a wide range of previously excluded groups; and it was used to justify the goals of the political movement to the general population, to the British state and to foreign states. The next chapter analyses the development of official nationalism in fulfilling these roles during the first fifty years of the Irish state.

Notes

1 Lord Castletown, also Bernard Fitzpatrick (1849–1937): Conservative MP for Portarlington (Queen's County/Co. Laois).
2 The Irish Parliamentary Party, formed in 1882 by Parnell, brought cohesion to the loose group of Irish nationalist/Home Rule MPs in Westminster.
3 The Gaelic League was founded 1893 by Douglas Hyde, for the express purpose of supporting a Gaelic revival to keep the Irish language spoken in Ireland.
4 Sinn Féin was founded as a political party in 1905 by Arthur Griffith and Edward Martyn. Griffith's Sinn Féin movement originally advocated a dual monarchy solution (whereby the only link between a separately-governed Ireland and Britain would be a shared monarch) to the status of Ireland and linked itself with proponents of the Gaelic revival as a self-conscious alternative to the mainstream nationalism offered by Redmond's Irish Party. After the 1916 Rising, the party gained new momentum, identity and even

ideology as republicans saw it as a possible vehicle for a political campaign. Soon after joining Sinn Féin, de Valera took Griffith's place as president and led it to accept the aim of an independent republic (put forward as a motion in the 1917 Ardfheis). Sinn Féin then gained from growing sympathy for republicanism and disenchantment with constitutional nationalism and won landslide victories in the 1918 general election and the city and county council elections of 1920. In 1919, Sinn Féin declared itself to be parliament of Ireland (Dáil Éireann) under the government of Cathal Brugha and then de Valera. British rejection of the Dáil as illegal led to the War of Independence, during which time governance of the Dáil was left in the hands of Michael Collins, designated Minister for Finance. Following the truce of 1921, Collins and fellow representatives of the Irish Executive subsequently engaged in negotiations with the British government over the status of Ireland. The signing of the resultant Anglo-Irish Treaty in late 1921 was narrowly approved by Dáil Éireann and saw the creation of the Irish Free State (from which Northern Ireland, created by the 1920 Government of Ireland Act, opted out). But pro- and anti-Treaty division led to the first of many splits in the party (forming Cumann na nGaedheal) and to a Civil War (1922–23). Later splits led to the creation of Fianna Fáil (1932), and Official Sinn Féin/the Workers Party (1970).

5 The Irish Volunteers was founded in 1913 as a combined nationalist response (including organisations such as the Ancient Order of Hibernians, Gaelic League and Sinn Féin) to the Ulster Volunteers, which was formed the previous year by northern unionists to oppose the third Home Rule Bill. As the latter developed into the Ulster Volunteer Force, with military capacity and weighty threats, arming the Irish Volunteers became a priority for its leaders. The Volunteers split in 1914 between the Redmondite National Volunteers, who joined the British Army, and a minority led by Eoin MacNeill who retained the name of the Irish Volunteers. It was this relatively small group that was involved in the Easter Rising (due to the carefully orchestrated plans of the IRB and contrary to MacNeill's intentions). In 1919, the Irish Volunteers was designated the Irish Republican Army with allegiance to the first Dáil Éireann.

6 The Irish Republican Brotherhood (IRB) was founded some ten years after the 1848 Revolt as a secret organisation operating to incite revolt against British rule in Ireland. It was involved in the failed revolt of 1867 as well as the Land Wars of the 1870s and 1880s. It sought to build links with similar organisations, including the Fenian Brotherhood in the United States, the Irish Land League and the Gaelic League. Such strategies of coalition-building (or infiltration) led to its role in the growth of the Irish Volunteers and its central, motivating role in the 1916 Rising. Although, under Collins and Richard Mulcahy (1886–1971), it was militarily active during the War of Independence and Civil War, the difficulty of integrating the revolutionary organisation in the post-conflict Free State led to its dissolution in 1924.

 7 The Irish Parliamentary Party, or the Irish Party, was honed by Parnell to be
    the official party of pro-Home Rule Irish MPs in Westminster.

 8 Indeed, these factions were themselves divided, as seen in the disapproval of
    Healy's clericalist People's Rights Association that existed among fellow
    anti-Parnellites (Foster, 1989: 400–35).

 9 One such vision entailed a federal solution to the problem of national rep-
    resentation in the British Isles – a proposal that had its roots in seventeenth-
    century Jacobinism and had been revived in the late nineteenth century by
    Isaac Butt (Ward, 1994). The federal solution was posed by some as a means
    of redeeming the Union through 'effect[ing] that reconciliation without
    which there can be no real union' and recognising equality between Britain
    and Ireland (Grey, 1912: vi).

10 Séamus Ó hAodha (1886–1967): poet and playwright in the Irish language.
    Extract source: Hennessey (1998: 94).

11 Robert Lynd (1879–1949): Belfast-born Protestant, prolific essayist and
    writer for the Irish nationalist cause. Member of the Gaelic League and Sinn
    Féin.

12 W. E. H. Lecky (1838–1903): historian and political essayist.

13 Historian and political writer Alice Stopford Green (1847–1929) (a.k.a. Mrs
    J. R. Green), has been described by Foster (1989: 447) as a 'zealot' of the
    Gaelic movement. She is more kindly credited by Lynd (1919: 196) with
    'rehabilitat[ing] Ireland as a civilised European country'. Like Lynd, Green
    was born into a Protestant family in Ireland but spent most of her adult life
    in Britain, from where she played a significant role in enabling links between
    Irish nationalists, intellectuals and literary persons and propagating the
    nationalist cause (Sawyer, 1993: 63).

14 This included such actions as the teaching of the Irish (Gaelic) language in
    schools from 1908 and the reclaiming of Daniel O'Connell as a symbol for
    Irish aspirations for autonomy. In 1882–84, Dublin Corporation oversaw
    the building of the O'Connell monument and the renaming of Sackville
    Street and Carlisle Bridge in his honour (Alter, 1987: 10–17). Moreover, the
    Irish Parliamentary Party was involved in the promotion of a distinct flag for
    Ireland (green, with or without a golden harp – as originally conceived in the
    late eighteenth century), national festivals and a national anthem ('God save
    Ireland').

15 Ernie O'Malley, the so-called 'IRA Intellectual' (English, 1998), described
    the sentiment of republican nationalists regarding Irish statehood: 'The
    people of this country would have to give allegiance to it or if they wanted
    to support the Empire they would have to clear out and support the Empire
    elsewhere. Race did not matter; it was a question of allegiance to Ireland
    that separated Celt, Viking, Norman, English and their intermixture there'
    (O'Malley, 1979: 332).

16 For example, Griffith, the founder of Sinn Féin in 1906, was known to
    argue that physical-force nationalism was moribund (Miller, 1973: 136).
    However, Griffith's proposals were conceived as an alternative to physical

force, and only '*so long as* [Ireland's] people are unable to meet and defeat England on the battlefield' (quoted in Colum, 1959: 65, emphasis added).

17 Many advocated a return to the situation prior to the Act of Union of 1800, in which Ireland had a modern parliament of its own. However, as both unionists and republicans were quick to point out, Grattan's parliament was neither autonomous nor representative (dominated as it was by a Protestant elite) and lasted for less than twenty years (1783–1800).

18 C. S. 'Todd' Andrews (1901–85): active republican from the age of fifteen, when he joined the Irish Volunteers, he was an IRA member during the Irish War of Independence and Civil War, for which he was interned until 1924. He later had a career as a notable civil servant.

19 S. Gwynn and T. M. Kettle, *Battle Songs for the Irish*, 1915 (quoted in Paseta, 2000: 19).

20 This quotation is taken from the *Leitrim Advertiser*, a southern unionist newspaper, August 1914 (Hennessey, 1998: 51).

21 Count Plunkett's defeat of a Home Rule candidate in the Roscommon North by-election of February 1917 marked general disaffection with the Irish Party and a move away from the belief that the Irish question could be solved within the British framework. Sinn Féin's policy of abstentionism meant that, Griffith argued, Ireland had elected a representative to Europe rather than to the British Parliament (Hennessey, 1998: 159, 163).

22 It is also significant that the preceding phrase in *Poblacht na hÉireann* was in direct recognition of the moral and material support that Irish Republicans had received from Irish-Americans. As De Paor (1997: 58) notes, several of the signatories of the Proclamation had direct experience of America. By claiming an ally in America, which at that time held a neutral stance towards the First World War, Irish Republicans were making a direct statement about the complexity of the situation, namely that the conflict was not merely a matter of coloniser versus colony. Moreover, this sentence was implying that Great Britain was in a minority not only in the Irish conflict but also in the war in which it was engaged in Europe.

23 S. Gwynn in the *Observer*, 13 May 1923 (quoted in Paseta, 2000: 21).

24 Source: 'Irish Dominion Plan', *New York Times*, 28 June 1919.

25 Articles 1 and 2 of the Anglo-Irish Treaty, 6 December 1921, read as follows: 'Ireland shall have the same constitutional status in the Community of Nations known as the British Empire as the Dominion of Canada, the Commonwealth of Australia, the Dominion of New Zealand, and the Union of South Africa, with a Parliament having powers to make laws for the peace order and good government of Ireland and an Executive responsible to that Parliament, and shall be styled and known as the Irish Free State.

'(2) . . . the position of the Irish Free State in relation to the Imperial Parliament and Government and otherwise shall be that of the Dominion of Canada, and the law, practice and constitutional, usage governing the relationship of the Crown or the representative of the Crown and of the Imperial

Parliament to the Dominion of Canada shall govern their relationship to the Irish Free State.'

26 The author is grateful to Muiris MacCárthaigh for this insight.

27 In 1923, Cardinal Logue sent a Pastoral Letter, signed by Archbishops and Bishops in Ireland, condemning the rebels and denying them the Sacrament of Penance (Andrews, 1979: 248).

28 Cumann na nGaedheal: political party formed just before the end of the Civil War by pro-Treaty members of Sinn Féin. The party is inextricably associated with W. T. Cosgrave, who was its founding leader, who led it for the ten years it governed the Irish Free State, and who oversaw its dissolution in the creation of Fine Gael. Despite its position of power, Cumann na nGaedheal was never that successful at elections (winning a maximum of 39 per cent), and the length of time it was in power was due in part to Sinn Féin and, until late 1927, Fianna Fáil's policy of abstention from the Free State parliament.

5

Building the Irish nation-state, 1922–72

The initial focus of official nationalism in the Irish Free State was on the activity of *nation-building*. 'Nation-building' refers here to the process by which the governmental elite seek to construct a sense of popular affinity and collective identification with the state as the representation of the identity of the historical and cultural nation. The core purpose of this process was to unite the nation behind the new state. This necessarily involved the establishment of common ground between the republican and constitutional nationalisms that competed for political space long before and after 1922. Consequently, the Irish official nationalism that developed emphasised the points of convergence between republican and constitutional nationalism. These, as discussed in chapter 4, included the roles of intellectual and political elites and a shared conception of the importance of the narrative and cultural identity of the nation. This chapter examines the way in which official nationalism developed from this basis, noting in particular the implications of the subsequent conception of the Irish nation for its relations with Northern Ireland, Great Britain and the wider international community.

The second part of this chapter identifies the processes of *state-building* that occurred after 1937, and the complexity of influences and nationalist ideologies involved in determining the path of the Irish state. 'State-building' refers here to the process by which the governmental elite seek to strengthen the cohesion and integrity of the state structures, institutions and governance in the internal and international spheres. Again, Northern Ireland and the international context, particularly Europe, were of immense importance in this process. The way in which the internal and external pressures arising were addressed by successive Irish governments is also elaborated. This leads into a concluding analysis of the approach, and motivating assumptions, of the Irish government towards Northern Ireland and European integration in the late 1960s and early 1970s. The use of time periods to categorise broad phases in the development of Irish official nationalism is meant to be indicative rather than definitive.

Nation-building in the new context, *c.*1922–26

The 1922 Constitution of the Free State positioned the Irish governmental elite in a tenuous position. On the one hand, the republican nationalist concept of the centrality of nationhood in legitimating structures of governance was upheld:

> All powers of government and all authority, legislative, executive and judicial, in Ireland are *derived from* the people of Ireland. (Article 2, emphasis added)

On the other hand, the state was confined within the framework of the British Commonwealth of Nations (Art. 1), its executive authority 'vested in the King' (Art. 51) and the bills of the Oireachtas subject to signification of the Governor General (as the Crown's representative) (Arts 41, 60). In the light of this complex position, the official nationalism of the Free State needed to affirm the integrity of the state in relation to the Irish nation and to build upon the independence that had already been achieved. The Irish governmental elite responded to this challenge by prioritising and strengthening the *national* elements of the state. Indeed, the Preamble of the 1922 Constitution (emphasis added) expressed 'confidence that *the National life and unity of Ireland* shall . . . be restored' through the establishment of the Free State. This resonated with the core principles of the Cumann na nGaedheal government, whose brief had been defined as one 'for the common people of Ireland' in wanting 'to abolish ascendancy, to undo the Conquest and *resume the course of their national life* as masters in their own land'.

The impact of nation-building by the Free State was dependent on a credible connection between the structures of governance and the features of nationhood. Having gained self-government (albeit contested) it was believed that those who governed the state should be different, i.e. 'more Irish', than those who governed colonial Ireland. This notion underlies vice-president Kevin O'Higgins' comment that unpopular officials should be dismissed 'because they had not an Irish outlook'.[2] The actual substance and meaning of a 'national view' or 'national life' were integrally related to the official conceptualisation of the Irish nation, territory and state. This part of the chapter considers the link between the political development of the Irish state in the period 1922–26 and the tenets of official nationalism as presented in official discourse during this period. These are summarised in table 5.1.

Table 5.1   The core tenets of Irish official nationalism, c.1922–26

Nation	Territory	State
Thirty-two county. Culturally and religiously mixed	Anticipated dissolution of border, yet indirect reinforcement	Secular. Citizenship territorially based on twenty-six counties

Nation

The official nationalism of the early Free State held an essentially 'civic' conception of nationhood. The 'nation' was not defined in ethno-cultural or religious terms, for the Constitution of 1922 was deliberately secular and acknowledged the variety of religious affinities within the population in the Free State.[3] For similar reasons, the Irish and English languages were given equal status, the former as the 'National language' and the latter as an 'official language' (Article 4). Thus, officially neutral in terms of religious and cultural tenets,[4] the definition of the Irish nation was territorially based, i.e. its membership consisted of all the people on the island of Ireland. Official discourse at this time encapsulates the conceptualisation of the Irish nation on an all-island basis. Cosgrave, as President of the Free State, regularly used such rhetoric, as shown in this quotation from 1923:

> And of course, as a nation Ireland has no land frontier at all . . . The present frontier is thus clearly seen as a political contrivance which cannot endure, for it ignores historical, territorial and economic realities. (quoted in O'Halloran, 1987: 158)

The rhetorical usage of *a thirty-two county definition of the Irish nation was a point of political unity within the twenty-six counties of the Irish state.* For, O'Halloran (1987: xi) contends, the issue of partition went a long way towards unifying the polity of the southern state, not least because it made the issue of sovereignty in the south 'all the more urgent'. This reflects the fact that nationalist official discourse was aimed at the citizens of the Free State rather than those beyond its border. Hennessey (1998: 155) contends that, due mainly to their minority status in the twenty-six counties, unionists in the south were more overt in their opposition to partition than their nationalist neighbours. Thus, it is possible to view the all-island vision of official nationalism of the Irish state as an attempt to assuage the concerns not only of republican nationalists but southern unionists. It is important not to overlook, however, the wider implications of a territorial definition of Irish nationhood. Such a 'civic' or 'territorial' conception of membership of the Irish nation, it may be argued, exacerbated the virulence of the unionist-nationalist divide through its *non-recognition* of distinction between the two.[5]

Territory

Discrepancy between the visions put forward in official nationalist discourse of the Irish governmental elite and the reality of the state's jurisdiction and powers was significant. The depiction of the territory of Ireland exemplified this. The governmental elite of the Free State viewed the border between north and south as 'artificial' and official discourse reflected anticipation of its dissolution. For example, the propaganda of the North-Eastern Boundary Bureau campaign represented the border as 'a purely fictitious one' (quoted in O'Halloran, 1987: 158). However, this discourse ignored the practical reality of partition and covered over the activity of the state elite that served to reinforce it. Ultimately, Cosgrave's Cumann na nGaedheal government (Executive Council) perceived that it had more to gain than to lose from agreements that accepted the existence of partition. Thus, the six counties were excluded from the practice, if not the rhetoric, of Irish nation-statehood in the interests of internal cohesion, development and stability. For example, the Free State was relieved of its share of the British national debt in return for sacrificing its right (bestowed by Article 12 of the Anglo-Irish Treaty) to demand a readjustment of the border (O'Halloran, 1987: 60). The official Report of the Boundary Commission, presented in November 1925, also made the significant assertion that the Free State would be disadvantaged by an increase in the size of its territory (see O'Halloran, 1987: xiii). With this in mind, the Irish Executive Council signed the Boundary Agreement with the British government in December 1925. A policy of 'non-intervention' regarding northern affairs was maintained by the Irish state from this point, and partition was cemented as a ideological rather than practical issue for Irish official nationalism (O'Halloran, 1987: 3).

Nation-building in an independent context, c.1927–37

Citizenship

The definition of citizenship reflects the conceptualisation of the nation, territory and state and, therefore, provides a particular insight into the official nationalism of a particular period. The qualifications of citizenship enshrined in the 1922 Constitution (Article 3) also reflect the curious tension between the ideal and the practical definition of the relationship between the Irish nation, territory and state. Citizenship of the Free State was granted automatically to all those domiciled in the jurisdiction of the Free State (i.e. twenty-six counties) at the coming into operation of the Constitution who met at least one of the following criteria:

- birth in Ireland (thirty-two counties);
- birth of a parent in Ireland (thirty-two counties);
- ordinary residence in the jurisdiction of the Free State (twenty-six counties) for at least seven years.

The fact that the key point of citizenship of the Irish state was at this point residence in the twenty-six counties suggests to some degree a civic conception of Irish nationhood. However, the additional conditions point to notions of an all-island territorial definition and an ancestral or 'ethnic' definition of the nation that were to become increasingly significant as the state developed. The way in which the tenets of the Irish Nationality and Citizenship Act of 1935 differed from those of the 1922 Constitution reflects the process of change that was at work in the official conception of the Irish nation and state.

The 1935 Act clarified the definition of Irish citizens laid out in the 1922 Constitution; its conception of 'natural-born citizens' represented an interesting emphasis on the jurisdiction of the state. This was reflected in the granting of natural-born citizenship not only to those born in the twenty-six counties but also to those born on a ship registered in the Free State and to those whose fathers were (natural-born or naturalised) citizens of the Free State. These state-specific and gender-specific conditions stand in contrast to the 1922 Constitution's allowance of citizenship on the basis of the Irish birth (in the six or twenty-six counties) of 'either' parent. The state-centred focus of the 1935 Act is also reflected in the fact that those born in Northern Ireland after 6 December 1922 are considered in fundamentally the same way as any other person born outside the state's jurisdiction, i.e. their birth has to be registered within one year. Natural-born citizenship granted through registration in the Northern Ireland register or foreign births register was not considered equal to that granted by birth within the jurisdiction of the state, for it expired within a year of the citizen reaching the age of twenty-one unless (s)he registered with the Minister for Justice as a citizen within that year. Both the 1922 and 1935 conditions of citizenship share a strictly individualised notion of citizenship allocation (with the exception of parental ties). For neither allows for marriage to have an effect on citizenship nor for the possibility of dual citizenship – Irish citizenship is lost with the acquisition of citizenship in another country. This sense of *exclusivity* regarding the membership of the nation-state was reflected in the definition of the nation-state itself, as defined two years later in the new Constitution of Ireland (1937).

State

It is necessary to place the Irish Nationality and Citizenship Act in context, particularly in terms of the political elite in Ireland and Europe at the time. Fianna Fáil, established in 1926 as a result of a split in Sinn Fein over the issue of abstention from the Dáil, grew rapidly and became the largest party in Dáil Éireann following the election of 1932. Although it shared governmental power with the Labour Party, the strength of Fianna Fáil was of great consequence to the development of official nationalist discourse in the 1930s. Fianna Fáil itself (and its origins) reflected de Valera's determination to change the structure and rationale of the Free State through active participation and the acquisition of power from within. This was in line with a core tenet of Irish republican nationalism, namely the necessity of having a state elite and structures that uniquely represent the 'nation' as a polity. The accumulation of state power and consolidation of strong state leadership in Ireland also reflected developments in contemporary Europe. De Valera shared with other European leaders the desire to use his power to shape the state in accordance with his party's vision of the nation, although he chose to do this primarily through constitutional change rather than dictatorial power. Nevertheless, the abolition of the Seanad and the non-requirement of effective judicial review or popular referendum (made possible by the Public Safety Act of 1931) meant that little stood in the way of de Valera accomplishing his objectives (Farrell, 1988: 30). By 1936, all remnants of the predominance of the British imperial structure had been removed. These included the oath of allegiance (to the British monarch), the right of appeal to the Privy Council, the office of Governor General and all remaining references to the Crown with regard to domestic arrangements (Farrell, 1988: 29–30).

The pinnacle of this process was Bunreacht na hÉireann, the Irish Constitution of 1937, which substituted a constitution originally framed within the terms and logic of British imperialism with one that based the legitimacy of the Irish state on the integrity of the Irish nation. As Article 1 of the 1937 Constitution states:

> The Irish nation hereby affirms its . . . sovereign right to choose its own form of Government.

The declaration of national sovereign independence encapsulated in the 1937 Constitution was primarily directed at the citizens of Ireland, although very much also with an eye to the British government and, less successfully, to international powers. De Valera believed that by 're-patriating' the constitution and, therefore, the state in Ireland, the ambivalence and divisions within Irish nationalism with regard to the Irish state would be resolved in the interests of the nation-state (FitzGerald, 1998: 32). Nonetheless, the implementation of this change was restricted to official discourse rather than practice. Although the 1937 Constitution used republican rhetoric, ideas and style, the international status of the state it represented remained that of a dominion within the British Commonwealth (FitzGerald, 1998: 33). It was for these reasons that the 1937 Constitution had its greatest impact in terms of domestic politics, i.e. the consolidation of state and nation.

The version of nationalism that the 1937 Constitution reified encapsulates a specific approach to Northern Ireland that defined a conception of the 'nation' that was essentially ideological. To elaborate, the definition of the 'nation' as the 'whole island of Ireland' (Article 2) was followed by the acceptance that the laws of the national parliament and government were effective only within the jurisdiction of the Free State, i.e. the twenty-six counties (Article 3). The naming of the *state* as 'Ireland' (Éire) in Article 4 epitomised the delineation of the twenty-six counties as a nation state, with the implication that the six counties outside the state's jurisdiction were not part of Ireland. This was an important point in the definition of official nationalist discourse in Ireland, for it affirmed the distinction (begun in the first years of statehood) between the defining *ideology* of the nation-state and the *practice* of the state as the representative of the nation. For the 1937 Constitution did not undermine the viability of the Government of Ireland Act of 1920, which had established the Northern Ireland Parliament and enabled it to remain under the auspices of the United Kingdom. Indeed, it has often been argued that the claim for territorial 're-integration' made by Ireland in the 1937 Constitution made unification less likely than ever, given its reception in the six counties as a threat to unionists. The inclusion of the controversial reference to the 'special position' of the Roman Catholic church as the guardian of the faith of the 'great majority' of Irish citizens (Article 44) in another attempt to legitimate the Irish nation-state also had the side-effect of alienating Northern Ireland. It may be concluded that the 1937 Constitution represents a deliberate move away from nationalist ambiguity towards an affirmation of the Irish state on the basis of the homogenous identity and interests of its citizens (see table 5.2).

Table 5.2   The core tenets of Irish official nationalism, c.1927–37

Nation	Territory	State
Culturally homogenous twenty-six counties. Catholic	Partition 'chosen' by N. Ireland. The island defines the national boundaries	Exclusively Irish. Citizenship based on twenty-six county birth/ancestry

Nation

These measures reflect the culmination of a nation-building process that had intensified after 1926. Following its acceptance of the Boundary Agreement, the Irish governmental elite could no longer present the border as a temporary and insignificant line across the Irish nation. As a result, official Irish nationalism had to build a concept of Irish nation-hood that was not merely territorially based. The ethno-cultural nation that was subsequently fostered by the governmental elite drew upon narratives and concepts that were generally shared by constitutional and republican nationalists (see chapter 4). This process did not represent a move from a 'civic' to an 'ethnic' conception of nationhood; neverthe-less, it did worsen the period of polarisation between Northern Ireland and the Irish state. The affirmation of the national identity of the twenty-six-county state had significant implications for its relationship with the six counties of Northern Ireland. For the association of 'civic' qualities with a distinct identity in Irish official nationalism had the effect of excluding those on the island who were not 'Irish' in political conviction, state jurisdiction or cultural ascription. The stronger the assertion of the unique characteristics of the Irish nation, the clearer their distinction from those of others; thus, as the Irish state became 'more Irish', so those outside its jurisdiction, including Northern Ireland, became automatically less so. With the galvanisation of the sense of 'us' through the process of nation-building in the twenty-six counties came a stronger perception of the 'otherness' of Northern Ireland. Indeed, the six counties in some ways became the opposite side of the Irish coin; as the more virulently Ireland was identified as Gaelic, Catholic and rural, so almost by default, Northern Ireland was seen as a land of the planter, Protestant and industrialised. The casual use of such indiscriminate markers gave a new political boundary the status of an ethnic divide. Although contemporary official Irish nationalism did not sway from the assertion of the thirty-two-county 'whole' of Ireland, in affirming the legitimacy of their own states, official discourse on both sides of the border contributed to the galvanisation of such overstated differences and examples that transcended them were less frequently acknowledged.

Territory

The fact that Northern Ireland was part of the United Kingdom, combined with the consolidation of devolved governance within Northern Ireland during the same period, meant that its very existence was frequently presented in official Irish discourse as the obstacle to the fulfilment of Irish nation-statehood. This was evident in the presentation of the decision made by the unionist-dominated Northern Ireland parliament to reject the extension of the powers of the Free State to the province (in accordance with the 1921 Treaty, Articles 11–14) as the cause of partition. Hence, de Valera's (emphasis added) comment:

> Those elements in the North which have wilfully assisted in mutilating their motherland can justly be made to suffer for their crime and I do not think they should continue to receive the favoured treatment which they now enjoy in the Free State. *They have chosen separation*, let them feel what separation means.[6]

In depicting partition in terms of a *choice* of those resident in Northern Ireland, official discourse in the Free State sought to avoid undermining its own constitutional legitimacy, which it would have done if it had portrayed the foundation of Northern Ireland as democratically illegitimate. As the myths associated with nation-building took hold, an explanation for the reasons behind this 'choice' tended to be framed in terms of a more fundamental (i.e. 'ethnic') difference between the British citizens of the north and Irish citizens.

International profile

It is important to note that the process of nation-building was not confined to activity within the jurisdiction of the state. One of the most significant elements of the early years of the Irish state was its membership of the League of Nations. The League of Nations (Guarantee) Act, passed in 1923, allowed the Free State, as a 'fully self-governing State', to be admitted to the League of Nations. As a consequence, the Irish Executive Council was bound to give guarantees to and accept regulations (in regard to military, naval and air forces and armaments) from the League. From the point of accession, the League was an important platform for Ireland's 'carefully cultivated' neutral status. Foster (1989: 533, 559) describes Ireland's 'self-consciously high profile' membership of the League as part of a 'deliberate decision to follow a policy that would keep it aloof from the strategic designs of the larger powers'.

De Valera's presidency of the Council and the Assembly of the League in the 1930s encapsulated the fusion of external and internal issues in the government's approach to international relations. The independence of the Free State in its relations with other states was boosted in 1936 by the External Relations Act, which granted it treaty-making power and the right to appoint diplomatic and consular representatives (albeit in the context of Commonwealth membership).[7] Such international activity was highly important for the new Irish state, not least because it signified international recognition of its independent status and its distinction from Britain (with whom it had been engaged in a trade war since 1932). This had long been a goal of Irish nationalists. However, things were soon to change. At the same time as the Irish governmental elite was becoming more established on the international stage, the League of Nations was proving to be disappointingly fragile and ineffective. Events in Europe were to put the Irish state's self-conceived independent international role to the test.

State-building in an international context, c.1938–57

International legitimacy

The central focus of Irish state-building in the period 1938 to 1957 was the development of its international legitimacy. This goal was approached through policies of building the state in internal and external terms. Table 5.3 summarises the main features and implications of these policies during this period.

Just as the First World War had changed the internal and external context of Irish nationalism, so the Second World War was a substantial event in the development of the internal and external image of the Irish state (led by nationalists who had been prominent during the previous war). As part of the 1938 settlement of the six-year trade war between Britain and Ireland, Britain ceded control of naval facilities under Irish jurisdiction – a retraction that aided facilitation of Ireland's declaration of a position of neutrality in 1939 (Coakley, 1999: 21; Keatinge and Laffan, 1999: 322). According to the 1922 Constitution, Ireland was not under an obligation to enter the war alongside Britain, although it was generally expected that members of the British Commonwealth would do so.[8] The 1937 Constitution did not substantially alter Ireland's international position (given that it still remained within the Commonwealth), yet it did enshrine the principle of neutrality.[9]

Table 5.3   The core tenets of Irish official nationalism, 1938–57

Nation	*Territory*	*State*
Cultural richness of twenty-six counties	Claim involvement in N. Ireland's position during war. Anti-partition movements	Neutrality as expression of sovereignty. Republic status. International role

Although neutrality was primarily a nationalist (as an assertion and application of Irish sovereignty) rather than strategic or even principled stance, its impact was felt particularly acutely (albeit mainly psychologically rather than militarily) between 1939 and 1945. The fact that this period was referred to in Irish official discourse as the 'National Emergency' epitomises the nation-centric focus of Ireland's response to international events.[10] However, as with many other policies that had attempted to assert the independence of the Irish state, Ireland's policy of neutrality during the war had the effect of further deepening the divisions between north and south.

Nation

The internal (as opposed to external) logic of Irish neutrality was reflected in de Valera's opposition to the inclusion of Northern Ireland in Britain's military policy during the war. Signs of this were evident even prior to the war, when de Valera objected to a clause enabling the extension of the Compulsory Military Training Bill, passed in the British Parliament in April 1939, to Northern Ireland (Harkness, 1996: 66). Such 'interference' was rejected by northern Prime Minister, Craig, in terms that resonated with the arguments of unionists posed in the previous war. First, Craig asserted, Northern Ireland should be treated the same as any other part of the United Kingdom; secondly, the principle of neutrality itself was renounced. However, on this occasion the British Prime Minister Chamberlain decided not to implement the clause and in 1940 his successor, Churchill, also decided against conscription in Northern Ireland, thinking it 'more trouble than it's worth' due to de Valera's continued opposition (Harkness, 1996: 68).[11] These events contributed to the perception among unionists in Northern Ireland that the Irish government had a more influential relationship with the British government than its government had with either – a factor which contributed to suspicion in Northern Ireland regarding future relationships between the three governments.

In its negotiations with the British government at this time, the Irish government employed absolutist nationalist terms, determined to assert the independence of Ireland and to seek re-unification of Ireland only in the framework of uncompromising Irish sovereignty. Indeed, the fact that neutrality was viewed as a key demonstration of Irish state sovereignty led the Irish government to reject purported offers of reunification on the condition of waving Ireland's neutral status.[12] Nationalists in Ireland shared bitter memories of Britain's disingenuous promise of Home Rule in return for military service during the First World War and few were prepared to sacrifice Irish neutrality (and thereby sovereignty) on the grounds of another promise made by the British government in time of war. Consequently, although Ireland did give assistance to Belfast in the wake of the bombing 'blitz' and opposed the presence of American troops in Northern Ireland, official discourse and policy during the war did little to counteract (indeed it exacerbated) increasing alienation between north and south (Harkness, 1996: 71–4).

Territory

In the late 1940s, it was believed that Irish sovereignty remained fatally flawed in two core areas: partition and foreign relations; the connection between these areas had been highlighted by relations between Britain, Ireland and Northern Ireland during the course of the Second World War. The Anti-Partition League was established soon after the end of the war, in November 1945. It provided a clear and unifying focus for the Irish public and elite alike in a context of rationing, trade union discontent, continued emigration, and disagreements between church and state on social issues (Harkness, 1996: 77). The significance of the anti-partition movement in Ireland's foreign relations was evident not only in the tensions it produced in relations with Britain but also (after Fianna Fáil's defeat in the 1948 election) in de Valera's promotion of anti-partitionism in his visits to the United States and Australia (Harkness, 1996: 81). Moreover, there was a proposal to hold a 'World Congress' of the Mansion House All-Party Anti-Partition Committee (Williams, 1979: 138). Such attempts to bring partition onto the international stage were motivated by the belief that Irish sovereignty could be fulfilled through external recognition of the integrity of Ireland as nation *and* state (Williams, 1979: 141). Hence, the opening statement of the All-Party Anti-Partition Conference, established in January 1949, which was aimed at Britain and other international actors:

> We assert the right of the Irish people to the ownership and control of all
> the national territory and we repudiate the right of Britain to carve up the
> Irish nation or to occupy any portion of it. (quoted in O'Halloran, 1987:
> 183)

However, O'Halloran (1987: 186) contends that, in reality, the anti-
partition campaign 'marked an advance only in terms of organisation
and resources expended in the full frontal irredentist approach' and
ultimately merely 'reinforced established patterns of southern self-
deception'. This was reflected in the subsequent move towards attempts
by those such as Ernest Blythe to stimulate a cultural revival in the south,
such as in the area of the Irish language, so as to prove the cultural richness of the Irish state.[13] For obvious reasons, however, such efforts by
Irish nationalists did not so much stimulate a desire among northern
unionists to be involved in Ireland's cultural life as a stronger determination to emphasise Northern Ireland's separation from it.[14]

State

In the meantime, the Irish governmental elite concentrated on building
the sovereign status of Ireland through internal means, namely by
expanding upon the successful project of nation-building with a process
of state-building within the twenty-six counties. A key point in this
process was the Republic of Ireland Act of 1948. The Act was conceived
as a means of removing ambiguity about the sovereignty and independence of the Irish state by severing Ireland's 'long and tragic association
with the institution of the British Crown'.[15] It is notable that the Act was
passed during the tenure of a Fine Gael government, led by John A.
Costello, whose traditional sympathies lay with constitutional rather
than republican nationalism. All-party support for the declaration of
Ireland's status as a republic reflects the unity of Irish nationalisms that
official nationalist discourse represented. This unity had been built on
the common ground of constitutional and republican nationalisms – i.e.
the centrality of the nation to the state – and had involved a growing distinction from Britain and British identity and, in relation to this, from
Northern Ireland and unionism.

The Republic of Ireland Act had significant implications for Ireland's
position in international affairs due to its revocation of the External
Relations Act (the Irish President was now endowed with powers and
functions in this area previously held by the British monarch). Even prior
to the implementation of the Act, talks had been held between government ministers from Britain, Ireland and Commonwealth nations
regarding Ireland's future external relations. It was clear from the con-

clusion of these discussions that in practice Ireland would not be entirely disassociated from the Commonwealth. Ireland's links with the United Kingdom, by far the largest of its trading partners, would remain of particular significance. The question of Northern Ireland's position was also (and again) intrinsically affected by the Irish governmental elite's working out of the Irish state's sovereignty regarding its external relations. The Ireland Act passed in Westminster in 1949 was a response by the British government to the situation created by the Republic of Ireland Act. It guaranteed Northern Ireland's position within the United Kingdom (unless the Northern Ireland Parliament decreed otherwise).[16] It also allowed Irish citizens to retain the benefits of Commonwealth membership.

Notwithstanding these continuing connections with the Commonwealth, the primary aim of the foreign policy of the Irish government during this period remained the affirmation of its *independence* from Britain in international affairs. This continued to be expressed in a policy of neutrality, as was evident in Ireland's refusal to sign the North Atlantic Treaty in 1949. The importance of neutrality for official Irish nationalism was apparent in its preservation by successive Irish governments despite the fact that Britain was not the only state to view it in a less than favourable light. Indeed, Ireland's neutrality was viewed by some as implying non-western sympathies in the Cold War, and thus contributed to the nine-year delay in Irish accession to the United Nations (Keatinge and Laffan, 1999: 323). Aside from this, Ireland continued to develop an approach to international affairs that it had begun with its role in the League of Nations, namely one that sought engagement in international organisations focused on economic development and non-military inter-state co-operation. For example, it was a founding member of the Organisation for European Economic Co-operation (1948) and the Council of Europe (1949), and played an active role in the United Nations (when admitted in 1955), the World Bank and the International Monetary Fund (1957). Ireland's accession to the latter two organisations marked the beginning of a new approach to economic policies that was to have great significance for Ireland's relations with Northern Ireland, Britain and Europe as well as for its internal development.

State-building in a modernising context, c.1958–66

State

In 1958, the Irish governmental elite were facing new challenges regarding the development of the Irish nation-state. The success of the policies

Table 5.4   The core tenets of Irish official nationalism, c.1958–66

Nation	Territory	State
Modernisation and development of twenty-six counties	North-south co-operation on practical matters. Public meetings of politicians begun	Secular elite. Better relations with Britain, restoration of free trade

of the previous twenty years intended to enhance Irish sovereignty in the international sphere brought with it increased connection to other states and awareness of Ireland's relative inequality in relation to them. The policies of the government from this point were focused on rectifying the inadequacies of the Irish state-building project, increasing the legitimacy of the Irish state not only in terms of its status or profile but also in practical terms of its prosperity and material development. The period of 1958 to 1966 consequently saw the discourse and practice of the Irish governmental elite gradually move away from previously-held elements of official Irish nationalism that were now viewed as possibly inhibiting the progress of Irish nation-statehood. Table 5.4 summarises the results of this move.

The economic depression suffered by Ireland in the early 1950s was compounded by four changes of government in a short period (1948–57) and inappropriate policy responses to external events (Walsh, 1979: 27). The election of 1957 gave Fianna Fáil a large majority, replacing Costello's coalition government, and the responsibility of improving this poor economic performance. The subsequent re-evaluation of Irish economic policy away from protectionism, epitomised by the Programme for Economic Expansion announced in 1958, was influenced by both domestic and international factors. Indeed, Laffan and O'Donnell (1998: 157) contend that the developments in Irish 'economy, policy and society' at this time 'can be seen as a process of learning how to manage internationalisation and the emergence of international governance'. The new 'outward orientation' of the Irish governmental elite was fostered under the leadership of Lemass. The length of time for which Lemass was leader of Fianna Fáil and Taoiseach was relatively short (1959–66), considering the significant and positive impact that he is widely credited with having made in Irish politics.[17] It may be said that the main achievement of the Lemass era lay in allowing the modernisation of the Irish state, which had been steadily developing since the postwar era, to bear fruit. The modernisation of the cultural climate, political apparatus, economy and educational system of the Republic was accompanied by the maturation of the new secular elite at the core of the state apparatus, of which Lemass was a member (O'Dowd, 1991: 128–34). The new shape of the civil service made a positive contribution to the modern socio-economic policies that moved domestic politics beyond the impasse that the interrelation of the structures of culture and politics (or church and state) had produced. In 1945, the search for markets for Irish products had been hampered by ideological and economic uncertainty regarding moving beyond the framework of the United Kingdom (Hederman O'Brien, 2000: 9). Twenty years later, progress in foreign relations, in relations with Britain and Northern Ireland and in domestic structures prepared Ireland in ideological and economic terms to make the decisive moves.

The Anglo-Irish Free Trade Agreement of 1965 reflected the progress that had been made in economic and political terms regarding Ireland's relationship with Britain, yet it also signalled the continuing dominance of Britain in Irish trade patterns. Trade between Britain and Ireland at that time virtually represented a common labour, trade and agricultural market (Hederman O'Brien, 2000: 11). Hence, Ireland's application for membership of the European Economic Community (EEC) in 1961 was viewed as necessary on two levels. First, because Britain was joining, Ireland had little choice but to do likewise.[18] Secondly, membership of the EEC was viewed as a vital means of weakening the economic hold of Britain over Ireland; as Nöel noted, European membership could 'look like a second declaration of independence'.[19] Lemass was committed to membership of the EEC on the basis of economic principles and the opportunities it presented to improve the performance of Irish business, labour, agriculture and the public service (Hederman O'Brien, 2000: 7). In addition, Lemass' support for market-led policies, focused on free trade, brought Ireland more directly into European politics as an independent player (O'Dowd, 1991: 128).[20] Such important changes in British-Irish and European affairs were of great consequence for the nationalist conceptualisation of the Republic of Ireland and, more specifically, its relation to Northern Ireland.

Nation

FitzGerald (22 February 1980: 2) has identified the roots of the Sunningdale Agreement (1973) in the emergence of an 'alternative moderate nationalist concept' in the Republic in the mid-1950s. Although Lemass was not necessarily a visionary moderniser regarding Irish nationalism,[21] his attempt to break the 'confrontational pattern of de Valera's northern policy' marked a significant development in the approach of the Irish governmental elite towards the north (Collins, 2000: 7). The point on which Lemass differed from his predecessors, and on which his reputation was built, was his pragmatic policies for economic development that were based on the belief that unification of Ireland would not occur as long as the Republic was economically weak and politically unstable. The assertion that the appeal of unification would increase by improving the economic situation in the Republic, similar to that made in the 1930s, reflects the way that traditional terms of nationalism were used in official discourse to justify state policies (O'Dowd, 1991: 128; Harkness, 1996: 91). There was therefore, O'Halloran (1987: xviii, 186–7) suggests, 'no proper reassessment of nationalist attitudes' during the Lemass era. Lemass did not directly challenge the nationalist conception of Ireland, but the policies his government implemented steadily altered its frame of reference.

Territory

In the first news conference that Lemass gave as Taoiseach, he announced 'an end to the term "anti-Partition" in official statements about Northern Ireland' (Hederman, 1983: 62). The government of Lemass was the first to pursue policies that were unapologetically aimed at the development of the twenty-six-county Irish nation-state. The difference between the path taken by Lemass and that of de Valera was exemplified in 1966, on the fiftieth anniversary of the Rising. Although a veteran of the Easter Rising himself, Lemass represented the new political elite who accepted the twenty-six-county republic as a nation-state, and wanted to move Irish politics on from what he viewed as the debilitating predominance of a cultural and mythical self-conception of the nation since 1916.[22] However, neither did Lemass consider it necessary to engage with controversial issues in order to address the more complex dynamics of Irish history. This was epitomised by Lemass' rejection of the suggestion by the Office of Public Works in 1966 that a bridge be built to connect the Phoenix Park with the War Memorial Park, on the grounds that 'it was too late to do anything in recognition of the British soldiers' part of the historical tradition of the Irish nation' (Andrews, 1979: 75–9).

Lemass' pragmatic view of the tenets of nationalism arguably made his two meetings with O'Neill (Prime Minister of Northern Ireland) possible in 1965. Their encounter in Belfast in January 1965 was the first time that leaders of the two states had met publicly for discussions since the early 1920s. The essential subject and outcome of the meetings was improving north-south trade, but the elite and populations of Northern Ireland and the Republic alike noted their wider significance. 'Things can never be the same again', Lemass remarked to journalists in Dublin on his return from his first meeting with O'Neill (Kennedy, 2000: 231).

The nation-state under pressure, c.1967–72

Internal pressures: Northern Ireland

Lemass' pragmatic approach to Northern Ireland laid 'a solid foundation to the growing North-South relationship', particularly at the level of official, publicly-visible co-operation (Kennedy, 2000: 279). However, this was soon put under pressure by the political events in both jurisdictions. O'Neill's position as Prime Minister was under fire from both violent unrest on the streets (including killings by the Ulster Volunteer Force and the 'Paisleyite' riots) and from his own Unionist Party colleagues. At around the same time, in late 1966, Lynch became Taoiseach following the resignation of Lemass. Yet, although slowed for practical reasons and no longer a high-profile priority for either, neither government withdrew from its intention to maintain north-south contact. Lynch pledged to continue the Lemass policy of 'the maximum possible measure of co-operation . . . without the sacrifice of principle on political or constitutional positions' (quoted in Kennedy, 2000: 280). The meetings between Lynch and O'Neill in 1967 and 1968 reflected the determination of each to develop north-south co-operation for the benefit of both. However, by the end of 1968, 'the cross-border co-operation process was at a standstill' (Kennedy, 2000: 315). North-south collaboration on electricity supplies, agricultural policies and trade reform rapidly became low priorities for both governments as each responded to developments internal to their jurisdictions. Civil rights marches and demands (for equal housing allocation, local government reform, etc.), the Nationalist Party's campaign of non-violent civil disobedience, riots in Derry and Belfast and unrestrained criticism of O'Neill among his cabinet colleagues led to the birth of the Troubles in Northern Ireland. The progress made in north-south relations in the previous few years heightened the significance of the response of the Irish government to these developments.

Although Lynch had reiterated Lemass' policy of prioritisation of practical issues in north-south relations, his speeches from the time of his accession to the position of Taoiseach had been more explicitly anti-partitionist than Lemass. In the context of the Troubles, it was this element of Lynch's approach to Northern Ireland, and not the pragmatism, which came to the fore. Faced with demands from nationalists in Northern Ireland and the Republic to urge for necessary reforms in the north, Lynch employed rhetoric of anti-partitionism associated more with de Valera than Lemass. For example, in his speech to the Fianna Fáil Ardfheis of January 1969, Lynch called for the 're-unification of the Irish people as one nation'. The fact that he acknowledged the need for 'the unification of the national territory' to occur '*by agreement*' did not in any way calm the fears of his unionist counterparts (28 January 1969, emphasis added). The purpose of such language was to a large degree an attempt to compensate for the lack of practical action that the Irish government was able to take in the circumstances. Lynch's position thus epitomised the tenuous balancing act played by Irish official nationalism between upholding the principles that had helped to ideologically define the Irish nation-state since independence and the reconsideration of these principles in order to facilitate the practical development of the nation-state. The pressures of events in Northern Ireland were interpreted in official discourse of the Irish governmental elite as necessitating an affirmation of the traditional tenets of nation-statehood. These were, in their simplest form, as follows: an exclusive and distinct national identity, territorial integrity and independent and sovereign structures of state governance.

Garvin (1982: 33–4) perceives the Irish population to have followed the lead of the Irish government during the early 1970s in developing slightly 'harder' views on the issue of Irish unity. This strengthening of traditional desire for unity contributed to the government's response to the increasing problems within Northern Ireland, which was one of closer involvement rather than isolation. In 1972, the reaffirmation of the sovereign integrity of the Republic was focused on its 'right' to be at the centre of political progress regarding the position of Northern Ireland rather than on its distinction from the province.

External pressures: European Union

The era of approximately 1967 to 1972 was also a significant one in terms of Ireland's involvement in external affairs. Ireland had applied for membership of the EEC in 1961 as part of the move towards modernisation that had occurred under Lemass' leadership. However, just as Ireland's close relationship with Britain had contributed to the decision to apply, it also meant that Ireland's accession was delayed as a consequence of the reluctance of some European leaders (notably de Gaulle) to admit the United Kingdom into the EEC. The Irish government elite approached (and presented) the negotiations for accession, which finally got underway in 1969, in both pragmatic and ideological terms – all of which were inherent to the definition of Ireland's nation-statehood. The

new conception of Irish nation-statehood that was present in Irish official discourse on European integration reflected the different types of
pressures that nation-statehood itself was under in the new international
context. National identity, according to this discourse, needed to be
broadly interpreted, with an inclusive approach, particularly towards
'Europe'. Territorial borders were, in this context, seen as barriers to free
trade unless they were used as points of integration and co-operation
between states. This related to the new conceptualisation of states as
interdependent rather than independent – a fact to be reflected in the
operation of structures of governance.

In practical terms, Ireland needed to address the problems caused by
its high rates of emigration, limited markets for its exports and declining
incomes of its farmers, who were central to the highly agricultural
economy of Ireland. These factors were among those noted in official
publications and official discourse in Ireland in the lead-up to the referendum on Ireland's accession to the EEC. For example, membership of
the EEC was presented as being the means by which emigration from
Ireland would be reduced, through its positive impact on job creation
(Department of Foreign Affairs [DFA], 1972a: 4). The market of 250
million people offered by EEC membership was emphasised as an opportunity for Irish exporters to increase their exports and, thereby, their production and employment (DFA 1971a). EEC membership was presented
as the solution to the need for farmers to get higher prices for their main
products, with the alternative being subsidisation of farmers' incomes by
the Irish state (DFA 1972b). With all these factors in mind, negotiations
on Ireland's entry to the EEC centred on:

> industry and agriculture, fisheries, contribution to Community budget,
> Anglo-Irish trading relations during the transitional period, economic and
> monetary union, regional and structural policies, [and] the Irish language.
> (Hillery, 1999: 22)

The reverberation of the Cold War was also among the external factors
that placed pressure for change on the traditional interpretation of Irish
nation-statehood. The significance of the Cold War context was epitomised in a speech given by James Dillon, leader of Fine Gael, at the
Council of Europe Consultative Assembly in 1963. Dillon urged the
expediting of negotiations on membership of the EEC 'as the first and
most essential step to restore economic vigour' but also to draw western
Europe closer together to defend 'free societies' against Khruschev who
'intends to bury us'. 'If we oblige him by engaging in mutual economic
strangulations', Dillon asserted, 'our subsequent internment by Mr
Khrushchev will be made that much easier' (*Irish Times,* 17 October

1963). In relation to this, Hederman (1983: 14–15) notes that the prevailing 'nostalgic, warm and idealised' attitude of the Irish people towards 'Europe' excluded both Britain and the USSR, which was, for the majority, 'a world apart: communist, vast, terrible and largely unknown'. Popular wariness of the USSR and favourable attitudes towards European integration were also encouraged in Ireland by 'US insistence on European co-operation' (Hederman, 1983: 150).

The close bonds between economic/practical and ideological concerns were, therefore, as evident in Irish official discourse on European integration as on the subject of Northern Ireland. Indeed, this was exemplified in the points at which these discourses were drawn together, i.e. in discussion regarding the implications of EEC membership for Ireland's relationship with Northern Ireland. For example, in a Dáil debate on the constitutional amendment to enable Irish accession, Deputy Fitzpatrick of Fine Gael stated:

> Apart from the economic reasons for entry, we have a national incentive in believing that entry into Europe will do away with the Border and make the artificial line between north and south of our country meaningless. (Dáil Debate, 9 December 1971, quoted in Foley and Lalor, 1995: 195)

This particular subject will be examined in more detail in the next part of this book. In essence, the Irish government's approach to European integration and to Northern Ireland reflected the determination that had permeated governmental policy since 1922, namely to assert the sovereignty and integrity of the Irish nation-state. Just as Ireland's approach to Northern Ireland was always presented as a product of nationalist principles, so 'loyalty to an integrated Europe was always put forward by those in favour as an extension rather than diminution' of loyalty to the nation-state (Hederman, 1983: 146).

Conclusion

This chapter's overview of the official nationalism of the Irish governmental elite in the first fifty years of Irish statehood shows how Irish official discourse upheld the three tenets of nationalism – nation, territory and state – whilst adapting their definition to the contemporary context. The 'internal' context and the 'external' context are inseparable in nationalist discourse. This is particularly evident in Ireland's unusual position on the international stage as its status moved from that of colony, to dominion, to republic. Hence, when pressures were placed on the Irish nation-state in 1966–72 by events in Northern Ireland and European relations, the contradictions in Irish nation-statehood came to the fore. Dominant among these contradictions is the fact that whilst Irish official nationalism is self-consciously thirty-two-county oriented in ideal terms, it is *de facto* a twenty-six-county nationalism. The lesson to be learnt by the early 1970s was that the building of the twenty-six-county nation-state upon the vision of a thirty-two-county nation in actual fact decreased the likelihood of a thirty-two-county nation-state, not least because it exacerbated the alienation of northern unionists and did nothing to address the economic and political differentiation between north and south.

A recurrent theme in this chapter has been the fact that relations between north and south in Ireland have been primarily determined by the Irish government's attempts to consolidate twenty-six-county Irish nation-statehood. For this reason, Williams (1979: 138) suggests that in the Irish case 'all policy is internal policy'. Regarding the external context, Ireland's participation in the EEC was directly linked its national project of modernisation (Laffan and O'Donnell, 1998: 156). The official approach of the Irish government to Northern Ireland has employed concepts of identity (e.g. multidimensional), borders (e.g. bridges not barriers) and governance (e.g. not based on exclusive state sovereignty) that are central to the processes of European integration. At the same time, official Irish discourse on Ireland's membership of the European Union has emphasised the way in which it enables Ireland to realise ideal nationalist principles of identity (e.g. distinctiveness), borders (e.g. internal Irish border less significant) and governance (e.g. 'true sovereignty'). Changes in Northern Ireland and Europe have stimulated different pressures on the conceptualisation of Irish nation-statehood. Ambiguity in the definition of the tenets of official Irish nationalism has been used to enable the Irish government to adapt to changes in both arenas in a way that appears to be contiguous with the integrity of Irish nation-statehood. The next part of this book examines official Irish discourse in the period 1973 to 2002 and shows how it has balanced such differing conceptions of Irish nation-statehood in each of its three core tenets.

Notes

1 Extract from *Statement of Views of Coiste Gnotha* [Standing Committee of Cumann na nGaedheal] *Relative to the Political Aspect of the Present Situation*, 10 October 1924 (quoted in Regan, 2000: 47, emphasis added).
2 An extract from *Minutes of Cumann na nGaedheal standing committee*, 10 October 1924 (quoted in Regan, 2000: 49).
3 The 1922 Constitution (echoing Article 16 of the 1921 Anglo-Irish Treaty) stated that the parliaments of the Free State and Northern Ireland were not

to: 'endow any religion or prohibit or restrict the free exercise thereof or give any preference or impose any disability on account of religious belief or religious status' (Article 8). The concern to accommodate religious diversity was also reflected in the fact that the Seanad was intended to 'give strong representation to the Protestant minority' in the south (Gallagher, 1999: 72).

4 Whyte (1971: 34) argued that the acts of censorship (1923, 1929) and effective prohibition of divorce (1925) were not so much demonstrations of the influence of religion in Irish politics as reflections of the traditional conservatism that predominated outside the Irish state at this time as well as within it.

5 An extreme example of the ramifications of this logic is assertion by the republican journalist and Sinn Féin propagandist Aodh de Blácam (1890–1951, born in London to Ulster Protestant parents) that 'the Orangeman is a perverted Irishman' (de Blácam, *What Sinn Fein Stands For*, 1921, quoted in O'Halloran, 1987: 37).

6 De Valera, *The Nation*, 9 July 1927 (quoted in O'Halloran, 1987: 168).

7 The External Relations Act (1936) also abolished the much-resented office of Governor General (Foley and Lalor, 1995: 8).

8 Article 49 of the 1922 Constitution reads: 'Save in the case of actual invasion, the Irish Free State shall not be committed to active participation in any war without the assent of the Oireachtas.'

9 Article 28.iii of the 1937 Constitution provides that Ireland won't participate in any war save with the assent of Dáil Éireann. Article 29.ii states that: 'Ireland affirms its adherence to the principle of pacific settlement of international disputes by international arbitration or judicial determination.'

10 The justification for the use of this phrase lay in the Emergency Powers Act, which became the First Amendment to the 1937 Constitution in September 1939. It was explained to the Dáil by de Valera in the following way: 'some doubt was expressed by legal officers as to whether "time of war" might not be narrowly interpreted by courts to mean a time in which the State was actually a participant, a belligerent' (quoted in Foley and Lalor, 1995: 163).

11 Harkness (1996: 68) reveals that de Valera's arguments against conscription in Northern Ireland in 1940 included the assertion that it could enhance the position of the IRA in popular Irish opinion and that it might provoke a German invasion of Ireland.

12 Both Chamberlain and Churchill proposed the abolition of partition to de Valera in return for Irish defence co-operation with British forces. For example, after the bombing of Pearl Harbor, Churchill sent a message to de Valera: 'Now is your chance. Now or never. A nation once again' (quoted in Harkness, 1996: 71).

13 Ernest Blythe (1889–1975): Ulster Protestant, active member of the Gaelic League and Irish Volunteers, pro-Treaty TD, succeeded O'Higgins as vice-president of the Executive Council (1927–32). In a quotation redolent of the political importance of his cultural ambitions for Ireland, Blythe stated: 'It will be impossible to win over a large number of Northern Protestants to the

side of the Republic in the future without making a sufficient revival of our cultural nationalism, to make it not only clear but incontrovertible, even to the doubters, that the nationalists of the country have a wider aim than to turn Ireland into an independent West Britain with nothing distinguishing its people from those in England but religious affairs' (*Briseadh na Teorann* [*The Smashing of the Border*], 1955, quoted in O'Halloran, 1987: 172).

14 This notion was perhaps present in the passing of the Flags and Emblems Act by the Northern Ireland Parliament in 1954, which effectively prohibited the flying of the Irish Tricolour.

15 Extract from a statement made by Taoiseach John Costello (quoted in Ward, 1994: 251).

16 It is interesting to note that the Bipartisan Declaration on partition (10 May 1949) signed by Costello and de Valera and unanimously adopted by Dáil Éireann responded to the Ireland Act in Westminster by recording its 'indignant protest' at the legislation 'purporting to endorse and continue the existing Partition of Ireland'. In what was to be the only Declaration of policy on the subject of partition adopted by the Dáil since 1937, the Dáil repudiated British 'violation' of Ireland's right to territorial integrity. It therefore called on 'the British Government and people to end the present occupation of our Six North-eastern Counties [*sic*], and thereby enable the unity of Ireland to be restored and the age-long differences between the two nations brought to an end'. This declaration was, at the order of the Dáil, 'transmitted to the governments and parliaments of all countries with whom Ireland had diplomatic relations'.

17 For example, see Bew and Patterson (1982), Brown (1981: 241–66) and Girvin and Murphy (2005). For a differing opinion, see Crotty (1986).

18 As the white paper that announced Ireland's decision to apply for membership of the EEC stated: 'the national interest would not be served by our seeking to join the EEC, unless and until Britain decided to do so' (*Dáil Debates*, 5 July 1961, 191, 205).

19 Emile Nöel (first Executive Secretary to the Commission of the European Economic Community, later Secretary General of the combined European Communities and, on retirement, President of the European University Institute) lecture to the Institute of European Affairs, Dublin, 1993, quoted in Hillery (1999: 18).

20 The possibility of seeking associate status of the EEC and membership of the European Free Trade Area had been mooted in Ireland as far back as 1957. (Source: Irish Statute Book Database 1922–98, Office of the Attorney General and Houses of the Oireachtas.)

21 Bew and Patterson (1982: 11) contend: 'Lemass contributed absolutely no new ideas in the Republic to the "debate" about the North.'

22 Lemass' nationalist 'credentials' may actually be seen as a facilitating factor in his efforts to move official nationalism beyond a preoccupation with being 'true' to Ireland's nationalist past.

6

Identity, nation and community

This chapter examines the conceptualisation of identity in Irish official discourse in relation to the definition of the Irish 'nation' and the European 'community'. As discussed in the first part of this book, 'nation' and 'community' constitute the broad conceptual frameworks for identity in nation-statehood and European Union respectively. These frameworks are legitimated and strengthened through the use of narratives, including story-lines regarding significant historical events and normative judgements as to their contemporary relevance. The traditional narrative of the nation is of a singular culture preserved and respected throughout the ages. The new narrative of the European community is of a diverse but harmonious European culture. These narratives feed into the conceptualisation of the final element of the construction of the nation-state/European Union in official discourse, i.e. the ideal model. The traditional model of the nation in the nationalist ideal is, we have seen, of a distinct people group with a shared collective identity. The new model of the European community conceives identity in terms of multidimensional forms, from local to European.

This chapter explores the way in which the traditional and new frameworks, narratives and models of the nation and the European community have been brought together in Irish official discourse since the 1970s. After a summary of the traditional conception of the Irish nation, we consider the way in which this conception has been upheld in Ireland's approach to the EU. This then leads into an analysis of the way in which Irish official discourse has utilised the European conception of community in developing an 'agreed' approach to Northern Ireland.

Identity in Ireland

Framework: nation

Although the points of emphasis in the official definition of Irish identity changed over the course of the first fifty years of Irish statehood, the central features of Irish identity remained essentially the same. This is primarily because the framework, narrative and model of Irish identity did not significantly alter: Irish identity was framed in the Irish nation, it was based on an historical culture and it defined a distinctive Irish people. Chapter 5 showed that the points of convergence between constitutional and republican nationalism prior to the establishment of the Free State were deliberately built upon in official discourse as a means of legitimising the state in a context of internal and external uncertainty. Hence, the sense of continuity and integrity in Irish national identity is related to the ability of the governing elite to *reiterate* core signifiers and rudiments of Irish identity whilst *reinterpreting* them in the light of an ever-changing internal and external context. This first part of the chapter constitutes an overview of the core signifiers and rudiments of Irish identity in traditional official discourse.

The delineation of the nation is a political activity occurring within the territorial boundaries of the jurisdiction of the state. The political nature of the nation is a central tenet of traditional Irish republican nationalism. Speaking at the annual Fianna Fáil commemoration at Arbour Hill (the burial place of the executed leaders of the 1916 Rising), Bertie Ahern (26 April 1998) defined a nation as: 'a political entity that seeks to become a State'. This implies three fundamental points: (1) the nation pre-dates the state, (2) the nation has a political identity and political will of its own, and (3) the state is derived from the nation. It has become increasingly rare for Irish official discourse to set out a relatively unmodified republican view of the nation. Although Ahern could include it in a speech to a republican audience in commemoration of 1916, it came just a fortnight after the conclusion of the Good Friday Agreement which required the Irish government to concede that the political identity and will of the majority in Northern Ireland differs from that of the majority in the Republic.

The question of whether the nation consists of thirty-two or twenty-six counties has been a perpetual concern of Irish official nationalism. The necessity of nation-state building within the twenty-six counties has meant that the Irish nation has come to be epitomised in the Republic whilst still being ideologically associated with the whole island. In this way, the *institutional* nature of the framework of the nation is identified with the twenty-six counties whilst its *conceptual* nature incorporates the counties of Northern Ireland. This is reflected in another speech given by Ahern at the Arbour Hill commemoration, three years after the one mentioned above, in which he clarifies the significance of the state in relation to the Irish nation. Ahern (22 April 2001, emphasis added) asserts that the state plays an active role in 'lay[ing] the foundations of a united country whilst *developing a national life* and economic stability of its own'. Thus, Ahern seeks to affirm the legitimacy of the state in nationalist terms by emphasising the efforts of the state to bring about unification in the (island) 'country'. Yet, he stresses, this is done through concentrating on the development of the twenty-six counties in both in national (i.e. cultural, political) and economic terms. The 'nation in search of a state' idea has been replaced with the notion that the twenty-six-county state can have a 'national life' of its own, notwithstanding efforts towards forging closer ties with Northern Ireland. Although the legitimacy of Northern Ireland is a tenet of Bunreacht na hÉireann, Irish official nationalism still holds that the state should be facilitating eventual unity.

Ahern's 2001 speech at Arbour Hill, and even the above extracted quotation, reflects three concepts of reunification emphasised in Irish official discourse during the twentieth century. First there is the assumption of the fundamental unity of north and south (which dominated Irish policy towards Northern Ireland in the administrations of 1922–26 and 1938–57). Secondly, nation-building in the twenty-six-county state is necessary to give it cultural legitimacy (prevalent practice in 1926–37). Finally, there is the belief that the economic development of the state will make unification more feasible (a stated goal of Irish economic policy even after the embracing of liberal interdependence in the late 1950s). Together these three approaches highlight the janus-faced nature of nationhood in Ireland as it bridges the gap between past and future, north and south, preservation and modernisation. The narrative of the nation plays a crucial role in legitimating the nation in the midst of such apparent paradoxes.

Narrative: historical culture

The narrative of the historical culture of the Irish nation supports the integrity of Irish nationhood with assertions of its ancient roots, Celtic and/or Gaelic ancestry, Christian ethics, endurance through colonial oppression, and influence as a (pre-colonial) independent European nation. These points are brought together in the collective myth-memory of Ireland's role in dispelling the 'Dark Ages' in Europe or, as Lynd (1919: 26) puts it, 'how Ireland helped to civilise Europe'. As seen in chapter 4, this myth was employed in the processes of 'nationalisation' begun prior to the establishment of the independent state in order to emphasise the integrity of Irish culture. The image of Ireland projected in this myth is one of a nation comfortable with its own culture and willing to share it. It is because of this assuring image that the myth has been revived in the new context of European integration, for it links Ireland's historical legacy with contemporary opportunities to make a positive contribution to the development of Europe. For example, see Ahern's (1 March 2001a) comments, which contain clear echoes of Alice Stopford Green's sentiments written some eighty years before (as cited in chapter 4):

> In the early centuries of the Christian era, the wisdom and learning of our peoples were generously and readily shared. Our mutual love of learning served as a beacon to many other lands, including mainland Europe . . . The history of Ireland over the past 2,000 years indicates that we are an adventurous and outward looking people, seeking not to conquer, but to carry a message of hope and solidarity.

It is significant that these comments were made in a speech given by the Taoiseach to the National Assembly of Wales, for texts of Irish official discourse presented to audiences in Wales or Scotland often emphasise the pre-colonial links and cultural similarities between these nations and the Irish nation. Indeed, each of the main features of the narrative of the Irish nation is brought out in relation to these two nations, not least in the myths of 'the great historical and cultural legacy of the Celts' (Ahern, 11 February 2002).[1] Such commonality between Ireland and Wales and Scotland is classified in terms of 'kindred spirits', 'common stock', 'common culture', shared 'political passions' (Ahern, 1 March 2001a), 'linguistic affinity', and 'countless family links' produced by generations of emigration flows (Ahern, 20 June 2001). Such images serve to both reiterate the concept of an immutable Irish nation and to give weight to contemporary diplomatic and political intentions.

Model: distinctive people

The elements of the narrative of the Irish nation are uniquely drawn together and embodied in the ideal model of the Irish nation. To refer to a phrase used frequently by Taoisigh from both Fianna Fáil and Fine Gael, there is seen to be continuity between the 'ancient nation [and the] modern state' (e.g. FitzGerald, 15 March 1984; Haughey 17 March 1982). Even if the Irish state is facing challenges in the modern world, according to this discourse, Ireland's nationhood is not in question. On the contrary, Haughey (speaking to an Irish–American audience, perhaps the most receptive to discourse on the resilience of Irish identity) argues that the Irish nation's response to external change actually proves its calibre:

> Ireland is an ancient nation whose roots and culture go away back into the
> mists of time beyond the boundaries of recorded history . . . She is an
> ancient nation struggling to establish herself in the modern world, to reaf-
> firm the integrity of her nationhood. (1 March 1985)

The claim that Ireland has a primordial identity, that 'we Irish are a distinct nation', constitutes the foundation of Irish nationalism and, according to Lynch (20 February 1971), has been 'expressed throughout our
history'. This notion of Irish distinctiveness is significant for two reasons.
First, it implies that Ireland's experience of colonialism did not affect its
national integrity. In the same speech, Lynch argues that this Irish identity is 'irrespective of ancient origin or later migration'. This model has
particular implications for relationships between north and south. When
addressing the SDLP conference in Belfast, FitzGerald (5 June 1982) is
unambiguous regarding the essentialism of the Irish culture of the island:

> Ireland has gone through many transitions even within the historical
> period . . . complicated by the arrival of others on our shores. It has seen
> the arrival of Norwegians and Danes, of Normans and English and of
> Scots, many of who became largely assimilated to Gaelic culture and
> became integrally Irish.

Although FitzGerald is acknowledging the mixed origins of the Irish
population, he assumes that the Gaelic culture of Ireland has survived,
and outlasted, repeated attempts at colonisation. The notion that Ireland
is 'Gaelic' is reiterated frequently in Irish nationalism, from the call by
republican nationalists for a 'Free and Gaelic Ireland' (de Valera, 1922:
14) to the proposition that nationalist principles are inherited from 'the
Gaelic past' (Haughey, 7 January 1982). However, Ireland is just as frequently referred to as 'Celtic'. Indeed, the two are generally used as interchangeable signifiers in Irish official discourse, for example: 'Why should
we, the Celts and the English, go on misunderstanding each other?'
(Lynch, 11 July 1970). In this public address over RTÉ, Lynch makes no
allowance for cultural diversity within Britain or Ireland, referring to the
British government and people as 'the English' and the population of
Ireland as 'the Celts'. This leads into the second implication of seeing the
island and the identity of the people on it as uniformly Irish, namely, its
exclusion of those who don't share the cultural or political definitions of
Irishness put forward by the Irish state.

The unionist 'other'

The cultural identity of unionists in Northern Ireland has been traditionally excluded from the ideal model of the Irish nation as a consequence
of nation-state building in the twenty-six counties. This is despite the fact

that since the 1960s there have been notable attempts among the Irish governmental elite to recognise the existence and the strength of unionist identity. The Lemass-O'Neill meetings were a step in this direction, for example, although Patterson (1999) rightly notes the ambiguities in Lemass' policy towards the north – many of which, we see herein, have persisted in Irish official nationalism. Unionists were regularly portrayed as either misguided Irish people or misplaced British people in Irish official discourse throughout (and beyond) the twentieth century. This perception is evident even in examples of official discourse that purport to be attempting reconciliation between unionism and nationalism. In relation to this, as expressed in an open letter to 'the northern unionists' in the *Belfast Telegraph* (29 June 1984), FitzGerald laments the fact that:

> Irish nationalist attitudes have hitherto in their public expression tended to underestimate the full dimension of the unionist identity and ethos. On the other hand, unionist attitudes and practices have denied the right of nationalists to meaningful political expression of their identity and ethos.

The way in which FitzGerald defines the 'identity and ethos' of nationalism and unionism is revealing. The 'nationalist identity and ethos' is defined as a wish to have an Irish identity 'institutionalised in a sovereign Ireland united by consent'. In contrast, the 'unionist identity and ethos' is de-politicised in this text, associated merely with Protestant values and '*a sense of* Britishness, allied to their *particular sense of* Irishness' (FitzGerald, 29 June 1984, emphasis added). The notion of unionist identity as ungrounded and uncertain is also reiterated in FitzGerald's distinction between unionists' 'sense of Britishness', as 'Protestant[s]' who 'settled from Britain', and the tradition of those who are historically ('several millennia'), culturally ('Gaelic'), ancestrally ('roots'), religiously ('Catholic') and territorially ('in this island') Irish:

> Locked into a corner of our small island, in a piece of territory a hundred miles long and sixty miles across, live one-and-a-half million people drawn from two different Irish traditions: the ancient Gaelic, Catholic tradition stretching back through several millennia, and the Protestant tradition of those who settled from Britain in much of the north-eastern corner of our island (FitzGerald, speech to joint Houses of Congress, 15 March 1984)
>
> We agreed that the two traditions there both held their validity. We agreed that the Protestant tradition, the sense of Britishness of the Unionists, was something that had to be given consideration on a par with the Irishness of people with Gaelic roots in this island. (FitzGerald, Dáil Éireann, 11 July 1985: 1455)

The idea that unionists stand between the clear divide of British and Irish nationhood underpins the notion that they may be 'persuaded' into a united Ireland. See, for example, Haughey's reply to the 'Unionist Case' as set forth by Robert McCartney in 1981:

> You say that the Northern Unionist is psychologically bound to Britain by bonds of blood, history and common adversity. But are there not also bonds of blood, history and common adversity between Irishmen of all traditions, and will these not ultimately exert a stronger pull? (Haughey, 15 January 1982)

Not only are the ties of common experience and history emphasised in an attempt to unite unionist and nationalist, Haughey (30 May 1983) also makes a link between the ancestors of unionists and patriotic figureheads of Irish nationalism:

> The people of the North, as part of the people of Ireland, have a long tradition of resilience and courage, which in the past has been put to the service of Ireland. The descendants of those that led this nation in the past, the United Irishmen of the North who made the mental break with the British connection and who thereby altered the whole mould of Irish history, not merely have a future on this island, but are in a position to help guide its destinies.

According to this speech, which was presented at the opening of the New Ireland Forum (a notable venture by the Irish political elite to find accommodation with northern parties), Northern Ireland unionism represents an *Irish tradition*, and unionists could therefore become active members of the Irish nation:

> [Northern unionists] have now, as they had before, an opportunity to help lead a country of 5 million people, and to take a place of honour, in its government. This surely is preferable to being a neglected offshore annex of the island of Great Britain. (Haughey, 30 May 1983)

In a way that echoes strongly the speeches of previous Irish leaders, Haughey portrays Northern Ireland as tenuously placed (by, it is implied, the stubborn will of northern unionists) between 'honour' in a united Ireland and 'neglect' in the United Kingdom.

Reclaiming the Irish diaspora

Another key indicator of the conceptualisation of Irish identity is official discourse on the Irish diaspora. As Howard (2007) convincingly shows, changing discourse on the Irish diaspora is closely connected to new approaches towards Northern Ireland, specifically the position of northern nationalists. Previously surrounded by a 'politicised silence' due to the perception that emigration represented a failure on the part of the Irish state (as with the shame of partition), the issue of the Irish diaspora became redefined in the late 1980s as a point of connection between Ireland and other nations. For example, the Irish government's White Paper on Foreign Policy (1996) describes the Irish diaspora (alleged to include some 70 million individuals) as a resource of 'immense global goodwill' towards the Irish nation. In addresses made in such important 'host countries' as Scotland and the United States, Ahern describes the diaspora as 'a rich source of international influence and goodwill towards Ireland' and 'a constant source of pride and support to us in Ireland' (20 June 2001; 17 March 2001). Official discourse on the Irish diaspora brings together narratives of Ireland's colonial past and claims for a radically different future:

> the tragedy and pain of enforced emigration has in the long run made us the people we are, extended our horizons far beyond a small island off Europe, and given us today's *global Irish family* . . . the broader view which interaction with other cultures through our emigrant communities abroad has given us, has been crucial. Ireland has become a more open, tolerant and self-confident place. (Ahern, 15 May 1999, emphasis added)

The development of a positive public conception of the Irish diaspora was a priority of Mary Robinson's Presidency (1990–97). In a speech to the Oireachtas titled 'Cherishing the Irish Diaspora', President Robinson (2 February 1995) argues for a reconceptualisation of Irish identity, claiming that 'Irishness' is shared by 'an array of people outside Ireland for whom this island is a place of origin'. However, the extent to which this concept represents a new direction for Irish official nationalism is debatable: Irish cultural identity is still linked ultimately (albeit less immediately) to the territory of the island of Ireland and the different identity of northern unionist emigrants is generally rendered invisible in this discourse. The narrative of Ireland as a 'mother country' with 'tens of millions of children scattered throughout the world, keeping fresh the memory of their homeland' endures despite enormous changes in the international and domestic spheres (FitzGerald, 15 March 1984). The next section of this chapter shows how official discourse has managed to harmonise such traditional images of the Irish nation with the new context of European integration.

European integration and the Irish nation

Framework: 'The great community of nations'[2]

Membership of the European Union has been presented in Irish official discourse as a *new* means of reaffirming the *traditional* tenets of Irish national identity. The lengthy extract below from a speech by Bertie

Ahern to the prospective member-state of Cyprus (9 January 2001, emphasis added) illustrates the virility of this concept forty years after Ireland's first application for EEC membership:

> *Culturally and psychologically*, too, EU membership has *broadened our horizons* and encouraged us to look outwards. A fear which existed at the time of our accession in 1973 was that Ireland, as a small and peripheral nation, would be swallowed up by a huge European entity in which our interests and identity would hardly be noticed. The reverse has happened. *Our cultural life is now richer and more diverse* than ever. I also believe that we are now *more confident as a people*, and *more open and generous in defining who we are*, than ever before. Our national identity is if anything stronger, not weaker, than thirty years ago.

Ahern's comments represent the culmination of the tactic of the Irish governmental elite to present European co-operation as a framework for not just the preservation of Irish national identity but its fulfilment. In response to opponents of EEC membership who portrayed European integration as a reversal of the national policies of independence, the Irish governmental elite portrayed a pro-EEC stance as a sign of national confidence. This is demonstrated in an address given by Haughey (15 September 1967) some five years prior to EEC accession to a sceptical audience, the Irish Folk School Movement (a society, after all, dedicated to the maintenance of traditional Irish national identity):

> too many of us have an inferiority complex about our cultural heritage and feel that we must follow a protectionist and isolationist policy if we are to keep it alive. This negative attitude is, I think, responsible for the view held by some that membership of the EEC will in time mean the loss of our national identity.

The European Union has, therefore, long been presented in Irish official discourse as 'a totally new form of political institution' that 'cherish[es] cultural and national identities' (Ahern, 30 April 1998). Allied to this line of reasoning, official discourse has presented European integration as affirming the 'traditional' characteristics of the 'Irish people'. Such characteristics of the Irish population include 'resilience', 'determination', 'self-confidence', 'steady nerves and strong will', 'creative imagination', 'political imagination', 'maturity', 'patriotism', 'generosity', 'pride' and 'integrity'.[3] Many of these characteristics resonate with images of Ireland's oppression under colonialism and the campaign for Irish independence. The implicit logic of this discourse is to draw a distinction between Ireland's experience of colonialism and membership of the EU, which is 'based on the recognition rather than the suppression of individual national identity and culture' (Haughey, 2 December 1981).

Contrast with colonialism

The contrast between images of colonialism and those of the European *community* has constituted a crucial element of Irish official discourse on the framework and logic of the European Union regarding identity. For, although the Irish governmental elite were attempting to steer Ireland away from simple anti-British isolationism on the path of EU membership, the extent to which the collective myth-memory of colonial experience influenced official discourse on European integration should not be underestimated. This is complicated by the fact that the leading member-states of the EU include powerful former colonial states; Irish discourse has therefore focused less on the constituent parts of the EU and more on the ideal European 'project'. For Ireland, this ideal represents an antidote and an alternative to both its colonial experience and post-colonial underdevelopment; Ahern (29 October 1998) sums it up thus:

> Ireland joined the EU principally in the hope that it would help us overcome decades and indeed centuries of underdevelopment that had not been cured by political independence.

The assertion by Commissioner Peter Sutherland (1988: 4) that 'Ireland's trust in Europe has not been misplaced' resounds in much official discourse on Irish membership of the EU, contrasting starkly with the narrative of Ireland's historical relationship with Britain. Official discourse favourably comparing Ireland's experience of EU membership with that of the British empire has not only been directed towards national audiences. It has been used, for example, to strengthen connections between Ireland and its future European partners in support of EU enlargement. Ahern's (8 January 2001) speech to the then-applicant state of Malta illustrates this process at work:

> As island peoples, the Irish and the Maltese are both proud of our rich historical inheritances and our distinctive traditions. We cherish our independence ... We have both had long, complex, at times difficult relationships with Britain – on the positive aspects of which we are now building ... However, both Ireland and Malta have shown through past adversity and present challenge that our people are capable of using their natural talents to achieve a success and influence greater than their numbers alone would suggest.

The above extract epitomises the use of images of Ireland's historical difficulties and disadvantages (as an island with a small population and few natural resources, vulnerable to British domination) within a text that has a wholly positive tone and message (the traditions, characteristics and talents of the Irish people have found the freedom to develop within the EU).

[Ireland] has a sense of solidarity with the many countries which also
achieved independence only in the last century. (DFA, 2001: 1)

This theme – from postcolonial weakness to national vitality as an EU
member – has characterised Irish official discourse on European enlargement in general, with the assertion that it would bring to other nations
the opportunities for 'prosperity', 'self-confidence' and 'influence' that
Ireland was given with EU membership.[4] Nowhere is this new-found
prosperity and confidence more evident than in Ireland's approach to
global trading relationships. Indeed, as the Celtic Tiger has sought to
leap beyond Europe, Ireland's colonial experience has been re-imagined
alongside contemporary images of a growing and dynamic European
nation. For instance, Ireland's position as a former colonised country has
been emphasised to audiences from post-colonial and developing countries. This narrative has been employed in Asia to distinguish Ireland
from its European neighbours, who are in this context Ireland's com-
petitors. See, for example, the extract below from Cowen's speech, as
Minister of Foreign Affairs, to the fourth Asia Europe Young Leaders
Symposium in Co. Clare (15 June 2000):

Ireland is uniquely placed to understand and empathise with the Asian
historical experience in the face of European expansion into the region.
For centuries the relationship between Europe and Asia was one of
colonisation, exploitation and inequality.

According to Irish official discourse, therefore, the fruition of Irish
nationhood in the European context entails not only a reaffirmation of
the traditional tenets of Irish identity and culture but also redemption of
the historical experience of the Irish nation.

Narrative: Ireland belongs in Europe

Of course, we were always a part of Europe – it is a plain geographical fact
– but perhaps the historical linkages with the Continent were temporarily
weakened in the early decades of independence . . . Accordingly, joining
the EEC was in many ways only a reaffirmation and reassertion of a reality
that to some extent had been lost sight of for some time. (Ahern, 21 March
2000)

Another means by which European integration has been contrasted with
images of colonialism has been the portrayal of Europe in Irish official
discourse as the natural, 'ancient', 'spiritual' and 'cultural' home of the
Irish nation. This particular narrative has two functions: asserting the
long-standing nationhood of Ireland and counteracting arguments

placing Europe as 'other'. It contains three main tenets, each of which will be examined in turn: (1) Ireland is an ancient European nation, (2) Britain's dominance has historically impeded the development of this relationship, and (3) preservation of Ireland's national identity and cultural traditions can only occur in Europe.

Ireland as a European nation

First, speeches and statements made by Irish government ministers on the subject of European enlargement show the narrative of Ireland as an ancient European nation to be as strong as ever, asserting that membership of the European Union is a means of 'renewing friendships' among 'some of the oldest and greatest European nations'.[5] The assertion that Ireland is an ancient nation with historical links to Europe has been a core principle in Ireland's membership of the European Union. Even following disappointment regarding the response of the League of Nations to the Irish petition for self-determination and the tension arising from Ireland's neutrality during the Second World War, relations with 'Europe' were generally positively conceived among Irish nationalists. Ireland's links with Europe predating colonial history implied not only that Ireland previously enjoyed a respected international reputation but also that Europe was a family of nations to which Ireland naturally belonged and had every right, and even duty, to be involved in. The conception that Ireland is a 'natural' part of Europe has featured strongly in Irish official discourse since Ireland's first application for EEC membership in 1961. In this narrative, membership is presented as a rediscovery of Ireland's place in Europe – facilitating continuity between the idealised Gaelic Christian Ireland of the past and the restored Irish nation envisaged for the future.

The notion that Ireland naturally 'belongs' in Europe has enabled EU membership to be presented as a means of *reintegration* into the international community as an active player. For example, the enlightening influence of Irish missionaries in mediaeval Europe (an oft-repeated myth in Irish nationalist discourse) is applied in official discourse in relation to European integration. Taoiseach Jack Lynch's (25 July 1967) statement to the Dáil following Ireland's second application for EEC membership contains an excellent example of the blending of national and European myths:

> Our friends in Europe are fully conscious of the part played by Irish scholars in the defence of those values at a dark moment in Europe's history, just as we cannot but be mindful of our debt to the European nations for the hospitality and encouragement found there by Irish exiles during our own long struggle for national identity. The facts of history and the links of a

common civilisation join our small island to that great land-mass with whose destinies our own are bound up, and we cannot but welcome, support and contribute to any movement aimed at developing and strengthening that European way of life which is a part of our own Irish heritage.

Such images have been particularly used in times of economic uncertainty and even insecurity regarding the success of the European project. In Taoiseach Charles Haughey's 1981 St Patrick's Day message, membership of the European Union is presented as bringing Ireland back not only into Europe but to the heart of world affairs, influencing 'mankind' with its cultural traditions and values.

> When St Patrick came amongst us, we were, as he said in his Confessions, at the very extremity of the then known world. We are no longer so. *The country which he loved has long been part of the mainstream of European culture* and has indeed contributed more than its share to the literature and the general cultural enrichment of mankind. (emphasis added)

The narrative of Ireland's cultural and spiritual contribution to European civilisation reflects an attempt to associate membership of the EU with images of the success of Ireland's historical nationhood. Moreover, it points to Ireland's defence of ideals of civilisation and humanity that are intended to have contemporary resonance with Ireland's defence of the 'European ideal'.

Just as the narrative of Ireland's pre-colonial links with Europe has been used to support the notion that Ireland belongs in Europe, so images from Ireland's pre-colonial past have been also used to support the idea that Ireland's independence will not be compromised in any way through EU membership. In this case, the myth of Ireland's civilising influence in Europe is interpreted in a slightly different way to that explored above, namely with an emphasis on the natural strength and independence of the Irish nation:

> Our greatest memory is of a time when we kept learning and the learned arts alive in Europe. The struggle for independence was always associated in the minds of those who played a major part in it with a renaissance of the Irish spirit and with a time to come when our country's creative potential would be fully realised. (Haughey, 16 February 1980)

European integration counters colonial legacy

Haughey's speech is not unique in its association of the campaign for national independence with European integration, as the statement made by Ahern in Dáil Éireann (29 March 2001a) on the European Council summit in Stockholm illustrates: 'All our patriots were conscious that

Ireland is a European nation'. What this narrative seeks to indicate – especially important, as in this case, in the lead-up to a referendum on an EU treaty – is that European integration is not a betrayal of national identity but, rather, a return to its origins. Reference to images of Ireland as a well-established, united and influential nation in a period long before English colonialism helps to emphasise Ireland's 'natural' place inside Europe and outside the United Kingdom. This merging of historical myths and modern concerns is exemplified in the summary of the effects of EU membership by Ray Burke as Minister for Foreign Affairs (28 October 1997): 'It has reunited us with ancient markets and revitalised links with our continental European neighbours.'

This relates to the second theme in official discourse on Ireland's 'Europeanness' referred to above, namely that British domination inhibited a long-standing and friendly relationship between Ireland and Europe. As de Valera implied in a statement to the League of Nations in September 1935 (emphasis added):

> One of the oldest of the European nations, it is with feelings of intense joy that, *after* several centuries of *attempted assimilation by a neighbouring people*, we find ourselves *restored* again as a *separate recognised member of the European family* to which we *belong*.

Indeed, the positioning of Ireland within the European Economic Community was originally seen as a significant part of extracting Ireland away from British influence. This was set out by Haughey (15 September 1967) as Minister for Finance not long after Ireland's second application to the EEC and shortly before its rejection (see FitzGerald [1991] for more on the circumstances surrounding this application) to an audience particularly concerned with the cultural implications of membership:

> As free and equal partners in the EC we will be able to move *closer to the mainstream of European culture from which our fundamental cultural and spiritual values derive*. This is important. The course of history and the facts of geography have inevitably led to allowing ourselves to be *influenced over-much by our powerful neighbour*. (emphasis added)

EU preserves national culture

Narratives of Ireland's Christian tradition, cultural heritage and historical links with the European continent are frequently invoked alongside assertions of Ireland's need to develop and modernise within the EU. This is related to the third tenet discussed in this part of the chapter, namely that membership of the European Union has been presented in Irish official discourse as the means by which the potential of Irish nationhood is fulfilled. To take one particular element of Irish official discourse in which this is illustrated, the European Union has been presented as enabling Ireland's core moral approach to international affairs to be realised. Upholding the Christian tradition that is recounted in this narrative is not only central to the historical identity of the Irish nation – being 'deeply rooted in [the Irish] people' – but it also affects Ireland's approach to international relations (FitzGerald, 19 September 1977). For instance, FitzGerald (20 August 1978) even speaks of 'recaptur[ing] the deep moral sense and religious feeling' among the diversity of world cultures, implying that consensus on broad ideological principles (not compromise of cultural uniqueness) was to be the basis of agreement and shared activity.

It is not surprising, therefore, that from an early stage emphasis was placed on a shared Christian tradition among the European member-states. The importance of Catholicism to contemporary official nationalism is reflected in the fact that speeches from government ministers during the period of Ireland's EEC applications regularly contained references to the 'spiritual' dimension. This is shown in a speech given by Haughey as Minister for Justice to an audience in University College Galway:

> there is a distinctive European tradition founded on a long history of Christianity which is common to the Six. This we also share . . . I do not therefore fear that we are relaxing our spiritual values and accepting a purely materialistic outlook in joining the Common Market. I think rather that we will be helping to build and strengthen *a new Europe which will be a sanctuary for those spiritual values so highly regarded by us.* (Haughey, 14 December 1962, emphasis added)

The links that had been forged in Irish official nationalism between Irish nationhood and Christian values were put to new use in official discourse on the congruence between European integration and national identity. Haughey's (15 September 1967) comments to the wary audience of the Irish Folk School Movement epitomise this narrative in the way they relate the Pope's teaching to both national integrity and European integration:

> when he speaks of nations having certain unmistakeable characteristics of their own and of the necessity to recognise and respect this individuality, Pope John's precepts [in 'Mater et Magistra'] clearly apply to all. I have no doubt that this is the philosophy which is accepted throughout Europe both in the member States and in the institutions.

Discourse such as this helped to counteract the significant force of opposition to EEC membership in Ireland that had arisen from the belief that it was a purely materialistic enterprise. Such ideological opposition, as expressed by some Marxist commentators, religious leaders and rural community groups, was among the most vehement faced by Fianna Fáil and Fine Gael as pro-EEC parties.[6] Thus, proponents of European membership had to perform a balancing act between emphasising the prospects of prosperity for Ireland in the EEC and stressing that Ireland's traditional values, such as anti-materialism, Christianity and social conscience, would be strengthened by membership.

It is interesting to note that Ireland's cultural heritage, its traditional moral values and national identity have been identified as the natural resources of the nation from which its contribution to the international community arises. At the point of Ireland's application to the EEC, the integrity of these cultural resources was frequently viewed as being under threat. The source of this threat was no longer simply identified as 'Britain', but the even more amorphous 'Anglo-American mass culture'. This 'culture', at a time when mass media was becoming increasingly influential, was portrayed as the counter-opposite of Irish 'native culture', with its 'traditional' 'moral' 'Christian' values and 'ancient' founding principles. Hence, national discourse moved from defining 'Ireland' against 'Britain' to emphasising a different set of fundamental organising and motivating principles to 'Anglo-Americanism'. Those at the forefront of the campaign for Ireland's membership of the EEC presented these 'traditional' and 'moral' principles as a basis of commonality with the European continent.[7] As FitzGerald, then an academic and journalist, wrote in the *Irish Times* (5 January 1963):

> there *is* a danger of our being somewhat swamped by the all-pervasive Anglo-American culture – even at present with all our efforts to isolate ourselves from the world outside – and the more we can reorient ourselves towards Continental influences the more chance we have of resisting Anglo-Americanism. But we must not think only of ensuring the survival of our way of life – we should be thinking of contributing to the rest of the world, and this we can do too by joining Europe and bringing to it our sense of moral values.

Proponents of Irish membership believed that the European Economic Community would revive the 'vitality' of Irish national culture by not only being an alternative to Anglo-American influence, but by strengthening Irish distinctiveness itself.

Model: 'The EU is not them: it is us'[8]

A central argument put forward by the Irish government elite in the lead-up to the 1972 referendum on Irish accession to the EEC was that 'the national cultures of both the larger and the smaller members of the Community can quite clearly be seen to have maintained and even enhanced their separate and distinctive qualities' (Haughey, 7 May 1972). According to Irish official discourse, there are a number of ways in which the distinctive identities of nations, specifically the Irish nation, have been presented as being enhanced through EU membership. Three of these are considered in detail: (1) distinction between Ireland and other member-states, (2) increased confidence in national identity, and (3) realisation of unique nationhood through participation.

National distinctiveness enhanced

First, the concept that integration into a diverse 'community of nations' would make the Irish more 'conscious' of their uniqueness:

> membership of the Community will make us all the more conscious of our national identity and of our *distinct* cultural values and will stimulate us to greater efforts to preserve them . . . [it] will provide a setting more conducive to our *separate* identity and our cultural values . . . Closer contact with [other member-states] will . . . result in a greater awareness of our own *individuality* and a stronger belief in the value and durability of our traditions. (Haughey, 15 September 1967, emphasis added)

This assumption is present in much official discourse on the relationship between north and south in Ireland in the European context. The following extract from an article written by FitzGerald (5 January 1963, emphasis added) depicts the notion that the EEC might encourage all on the island of Ireland to identify their interests and, consequently, their identity as 'Irish':

> I also believe that by facing an external challenge in this way we will come to recognise how much we have failed to integrate together our different national traditions . . . By joining Europe and *facing Europe together we might create that sense of unity at home.*

The flip side of the increased awareness of difference between Ireland and the rest of Europe that will arise through the experience of EEC membership, it is implied, will be a heightened appreciation of the points of commonality among those on the island of Ireland.

FitzGerald (1973: 104–5, emphasis added) reiterated this point ten years later, in a book outlining his vision of a 'new Ireland' in a European context:

> at the psychological level, the more involved Irish people, North and South, become in a wider community, the less significant will appear their internal differences . . . contact with foreigners always tends to accentuate a sense of national identity. *An Irishman never feels more Irish than when*

in an alien environment; his sense of sharing a common culture with his compatriots is then enhanced . . . it is a matter of common experience that a Northern Protestant and a Southern Catholic finding themselves together outside Ireland readily make common cause, conscious of their common Irishness.

It is significant that FitzGerald's prediction says as much about his assumptions regarding the 'common culture' of all those on the island of Ireland as about his vision of the EEC, which is implied to be 'other' and 'foreign' to the identity of Irish 'compatriots'.

Increased national confidence

The European ideal has been consistently related in Irish official discourse to the development of Ireland and, parallel to that, the fulfilment of Ireland as a nation-state. This relates to the second point, namely, that confidence in Irish national identity is increased by Ireland's role in European integration. The two quotations below from leaders of opposing parties – one from Labour's Minister for Finance in the 'rainbow coalition' government, Ruairi Quinn, and the other from Taoiseach Bertie Ahern (to an audience in Malta) – exemplify this point:

Active engagement in European affairs for the first time in our modern history has generated a self-confidence and maturity. (Quinn, 7 May 1997) we are now more confident as a people . . . Ireland's distinctive national identity has in fact been strengthened as a result of our EU membership. (Ahern, 8 January 2001)

This concept is centred on a 'new confidence' that Ireland can 'meet the challenges of development' and 'make an original and worthwhile contribution to the new European Community' (quotations from Burke, 28 October 1997; Haughey, 10 December 1970). The association in official Irish discourse of EU membership with confidence in Ireland's ability to contribute and succeed has been one of its most frequently employed weapons against Eurosceptic opposition. In this way, the Irish governmental elite have exploited the strength of nationalist sentiment in Ireland, assuming that voters will always wish to reflect confidence in Irish nationhood and, therefore, take a positive approach to European integration.

This tactic has been present since the first referendum on accession to the EEC,[9] and was still prominent thirty years later in the first referendum on the Nice Treaty.[10] It is interesting to note that Ahern responded to the 'No' result of the Nice Treaty referendum in 2001 with an assertion of the need for *confidence* in Ireland's position in relation to other members of the European Union:

We must have confidence in our ability to play a distinctive and positive part in this crucial exercise for Europe's future rather than try to opt out because it is too complicated or because we are not confident of our ability to hold our own *vis-à-vis* the larger states. (Ahern, 12 June 2001: 1105)

True realisation of nationhood

Ahern's comment above is related to the final point in this section, namely the concept that Europe has enabled the distinctive qualities of Irish nationhood to move from isolation to realisation in the wider context. The facilitation of an increased Irish role and voice in international affairs was an important goal not only for Irish policy-making but also for Irish national identity. Thus, governmental elite assessments of the success of Irish EU membership have described a 'total transformation of Ireland's place and role in the world' (Dukes, 1988: 6). Alan Dukes (1988: 6, 11) then leader of the opposition Fine Gael, goes on to review the first fifteen years of EC membership in the following terms:

> The Community provided Ireland with both the means and the opportunity to exercise our identity as a *distinctive and identifiable nation among nations* – to influence the shape and direction of European politics . . . The first Irish Presidency, in 1975, presented an opportunity to take a political lead in Community affairs and to establish the *distinctive character of Ireland's political contribution* to the Community. (emphasis added)

Fundamental to this point is the perception that the European Union offers opportunities for the 'talents' and 'ideals' of the nation to be expressed and implemented at a level beyond the state, i.e. on the world stage:

> the separate Irish cultural identity has a worthwhile role to play in the European context – one that could not have been fulfilled if Ireland had remained part of the United Kingdom. (FitzGerald, 22 November 1990)
>
> By availing of the European opportunity, the true talents of our people have been released. That is the foundation on which Ireland's remarkable economic and cultural renaissance has been built. (Ahern, 8 January 2001)

By emphasising the importance of the unique contribution to be made by Ireland in international affairs, Haughey, at this time speaking from the backbenches, is able to include prospective accession to the EEC as an expression of national patriotism:

> Our outlook on life is in many ways distinctive . . . We must be positive and put forward our own alternatives. They must be suited to our character and temperament . . . To be patriotic today is to believe in one's own country, in its capacity to handle its affairs in an enlightened way and to create an acceptable and attractive way of life for its people. It is also, in

our case, to have confidence in our ability to make an original and worth-while contribution to the new European Community. (Haughey, 10 December 1970)

It is interesting to note that points that may have previously been considered a disadvantage to Irish nationhood are seen in the context of European integration as positive characteristics. Hence, the small size and 'colonial past' of Ireland are presented in Irish official discourse as giving Ireland a unique international role and responsibility in the European Union:

> Because of our colonial past, because we have suffered oppression and exploitation, because we have endured famine, there is a widespread sympathetic understanding of these problems in Ireland and a tremendous reservoir of idealism and goodwill seeking to find expression . . . we must voice our concern . . . and maintain and strengthen an independent, distinctive outlook on world issues. (Haughey, 2 November 1985)

In addition, this enhanced role in external affairs is seen as having significant consequences for Ireland's internal self-conception and self-definition in official discourse. Descriptions of Irish society 'opening . . . up', becoming more 'dynamic and outward-looking' and gaining 'broadened . . . horizons' have become increasingly significant elements in official discourse relating to national identity and EU membership, insinuating that Irish national identity is advancing in concurrence with Ireland's globalised economy.[11]

National interests and identity

The fact that Irish governmental elite members can present Irish nationhood as compatible, even fulfilled, through EU membership and, indeed, assert that the impact of membership would be 'uniformly directed towards easing that path to a united Ireland' is related to the integral connection between identity and interests (FitzGerald, 1973: 104). The model of the European 'community' in Irish official discourse is based upon a particular conception of the relationship between national interests and European interests and, thereby, national identity and European identity. Similar to the function of nationalism itself, official discourse has presented this 'community' as uniting both pragmatic and ideological considerations. See, for example, the statement below by Brian P. Lenihan as Minister for Foreign Affairs (1988):

> Ireland saw in Community membership the best means to pursue our economic and social development, and an opportunity to participate in the movement *towards* a *wider* European identity. Our motives were very clearly . . . *a mixture of the practical and the idealistic.* (emphasis added)

The assumption in Irish official discourse that a European identity incorporates rather than replaces national identities arises from the perception that there is congruity between community and national interests. The prediction made by Haughey (26 July 1967) prior to accession encapsulates this belief:

> Our membership of the Community will be separate and independent and our actions as a member will be determined entirely by what we consider to be in the best interests of the Community and by our own needs.

This point is frequently reiterated in Irish official discourse even in circumstances that place pressure on this assumption, as in Ahern's speech in the wake of the failed referendum campaign for 'Nice I' below:

> Since 1973, Ireland has made a positive and distinctive contribution to the Union. And I know that we will continue to do so . . . It is entirely in our national interest to work for the common good in the European Union . . . The Irish people instinctively empathise with the basic principles of partnership and co-operation. (Ahern, 21 June 2001)

Such an assumption relies on substantial ambiguity as to the relationship between the 'national' and the 'European'. Indeed, detailed examination of Irish official discourse since the 1970s reveals not only ambiguity but even inconsistency on this subject.

This inconsistency is evident *within* the official discourse of particular members of the governmental elite, as seen in the following extract from a speech by FitzGerald (30 September 1982):

> In Europe a conscious attempt has been made to create a wider focus of loyalty than the traditional nation-states of Western Europe, in the form of the European Community, but for most of the 260 million inhabitants of this new semi-super State the national loyalties remain strong, and are transcended only to a limited degree and for specific purposes, where a common interest is clearly seen in such an extension.

On the one hand, the *common European* interest is seen as the fundamental deciding factor in the allocation of loyalty that transcends the nation-state. On the other hand, FitzGerald (22 October 1983) asserts a year later, support and loyalty to European policies is conditional on it being in the 'national interest' of Ireland:

> I pledge my Government's positive support for measures necessary to resolve these problems . . . *so long as that cost does not threaten our vital national interest.*

It may be possible to explain this apparent discrepancy in terms of the changed position of the political actor – FitzGerald emphasised the

European interest whilst leader of the opposition and the national interest whilst Taoiseach – but the real significance of this change in emphasis is that it shows the integral flexibility of official discourse on this matter. This is reflected in Ahern's assertion, two decades later, that a common European identity could develop if it was in line with citizens' primary identification with the nation:

> For the foreseeable future, I believe that most people's primary loyalty will remain with their own countries. There is as yet no predominant sense of a common European identity. But provided that what happens at the European level does not go beyond what the citizens of the Member States can identify with, I believe that we can be flexible and innovative. (Ahern, 1 March 2001b)

European identity via national identity

The basis for common European identity and loyalty, according to official Irish discourse, is the satisfaction of *national* interests (particularly those that are shared with other member-states) and fulfilment of Irish national identity. In this way, the development of European identity is founded on recognition of reciprocal and mutually beneficial interests between the nation-state and other member-states. Over the course of Ireland's membership of the EU, there has been movement towards a belief that identity with Europe arises essentially from common enterprise and interests in the Union. The extract below from a speech by Ahern on the subject of 'Europe: the Irish viewpoint' to an audience in Wales exemplifies this point:

> at times it is possible to fall into the trap of talking about Ireland and the EU as if they were two totally separate entities. This is not unusual. Many people throughout Europe talk about Brussels as if it were the remote centre of some alien civilisation. The truth, of course, is that all of the members of the European Union are partners in a common enterprise. The EU is not *them*: it is *us*. (Ahern, 1 March 2001b)

European identity is, therefore, not something separate to or beyond national identity – it is actually created *through* national identity, through the activity of the nation-state at the European level and not vice versa:

> While Ireland belongs to the Union, through our shaping of the Union over the last quarter of a century, the people of Ireland can genuinely claim that the Union belongs to them. (Ahern, 13 December 2000)

> while there is a growing sense of a shared European identity . . . It is with their own country and their own national institutions that people across

Europe, including in Ireland, most directly and most powerfully identify. The evolution of the Union must be consistent with that reality . . . Ireland is determined to play an active and constructive role in charting the future course of the European Union. (Ahern, 21 June 2001)

Such a concept reiterates the view that the community of the European Union is a community of *nations* and that a European identity arises from a national identity. According to Irish official discourse, the European Union is 'us' because the citizens of its member-states have subscribed to its ideal and have drawn together in recognition of their shared interests.[12]

EU partners, American friends

The notion that European identity arises from shared interests and common enterprise raises important issues for the conceptualisation of the European Union as a supranational organisation. Comparisons have frequently been made between the EU and the United States of America in terms of the creation of multidimensional identities (for example, see Adams [1993]). In this respect, it is worth noting that official discourse on Ireland's identification with Europe differs substantially from that regarding its identification with the USA. As noted above, there has been a growing emphasis on the Irish 'diaspora' as Ireland has experienced economic growth and has been seeking to consolidate economic links beyond the European Union. This is, to be sure, not a coincidence. Yet, the Irish diasporic 'community' in the United States has always been frequently acknowledged in official discourse. This is reflected in the image of Ireland's relationship with the United States as being one of 'cousins':

> For over three hundred years, Ireland and America have been bound by special ties of history and friendship . . . no nation looks to another as Ireland does to the United States with such a strong sense of kinship and affection. (FitzGerald, 14 March 1984)

> we are cousins; our countries are linked by a special relationship, not built on mutual calculations of interests, but on human links of kinship and friendship: a unique relationship founded primarily on *people*. (FitzGerald, 15 March 1984)

A distinction is implied here between the 'friendship' of the USA and Ireland and the 'partnership' of the EU member-states based on 'mutual calculations of interest'. These quotations are taken from a speech made by then-Minister for Foreign Affairs (Fine Gael), Peter Barry (11 March 1983), in which he directly addressed the need for governmental motivation regarding Northern Ireland:

Our *friends* in the US do not want us to be inactive. Our *partners* in Europe do not want inactivity.

Irish official discourse has sought to build upon this purportedly unique position by 'endeavour[ing] to reconcile economic differences between Europe and America' (FitzGerald, 3 June 1984). However, Irish official discourse to American audiences on transatlantic relations often contains implicitly unfavourable comparisons with European co-operation:

> our own relations with your great country are based first on human considerations – on people – rather than on the cold concerns of policy. It is on that human dimension, on such old, enduring and unquenchable friendships, that the hope of our world can best rely today. (FitzGerald, 3 June 1984)

An unfavourable comparison with the US has also come to the fore at times of unease in EU-Irish relations. This is evident in a speech given by the then-Tánaiste to an American audience (a highly significant factor)[13] prior to the defeat of the first Nice referendum, in which she described Ireland as being 'spiritually a lot closer to Boston than Berlin' (Harney, 21 July 2000). At around the same time, the American example was applauded by a fellow government minister (although this time from Fianna Fáil rather than the PDs), in contrast to complaints that 'directives and regulations agreed in Brussels can often seriously impinge on our identity, culture and traditions' (de Valera, 18 September 2000).[14] Despite this, visions in Irish official discourse of the European ideal are frequently depicted in similar terms to that of the 'American dream', i.e. people from different nations working together for the common good.[15] This notion is reflected in the changing conceptualisation of Northern Ireland in Irish official discourse during the past thirty years.

Northern Ireland and the European community

> This is a time of great questioning for all of us in Ireland, North and South. We ask ourselves more searchingly than ever before 'what is Ireland?', 'what is it to be Irish?', and 'what is to be the future of our island?'. (Lynch, 17 March 1971)

The focus of this final section of the chapter is on the new conceptualisation of Irish identity that has occurred in Irish official discourse in relation to Northern Ireland. As has already been outlined, a key proposition of this book is that the framework, narrative and model of the European Union has been applied in this redefinition of Irish identity regarding Northern Ireland. Central to this has been the drawing of a clearer distinction between Irish identity (culture, traditions, experience) and Irish nationhood (as a territorial, political entity). To begin, the framework of 'community' (inspired in part by the framework of EU identity) has been applied in Irish official discourse in a way that facilitates improved relations between north and south in Ireland. This has two main dimensions. First is the increased recognition of the plurality of identities and traditions on the island of Ireland, including the elements of British identity among unionists. Secondly, such a development has included the conceptualisation of some form of *community* within what Ahern (29 October 1998) has termed the 'western isles of Europe' (i.e. between Ireland and the United Kingdom). Thus, Irish identity is not directly defined against 'Britishness' in official discourse but is conceived in relation to it in the context of co-operation and equality between different nations.

Such a concept involves a reconfiguration not only of the framework of the Irish nation but also of the narrative of the Irish nation. The narrative of 'diversity in unity' has been crucial in relation to new concepts in Irish official nationalism regarding relations within Northern Ireland and between north and south. This narrative is derived from an amalgamation of the ideals of historical Irish patriots and the founding fathers of a European community based on unity in diversity. The concept of diversity in unity helps to shape the new ideal model of Irish identity or, to be more precise, Irish *identities* which relates to the European model of multidimensional identities. This model has two dimensions in the Irish context, as epitomised in the 1998 Good Friday Agreement. First, there are a variety of identities within the island, British and Irish, all of which are equally valid. Secondly, there is a new recognition of the Irish identity of the Irish diaspora, as individuals with only indirect connection to the territory of Ireland. Each of these aspects of Irish official discourse on identity and Northern Ireland will now be considered in more detail.

Framework: community

The perception that the European Union is a unique international organisation arises to some degree from the perception that it is more than the sum of its parts, that it constitutes a 'community' in its own right. At the core of this community is, according to Ahern (20 May 1998) the acceptance of difference 'through accommodation'. As the EU membership and roles of Ireland and Britain have matured alongside the EU itself, so ideas have developed about the relevance of the EU framework and model for Northern Ireland. One of the key developments in the first thirty years of EU membership regarding the path to peace in Northern Ireland has been co-operation between Ireland and Britain as equal partners in the European Union (see Gallagher, 1985; Gillespie, 2001; Harris, 2001; Meehan, 1998). The success of this co-operation has been in part due to the lessons learnt from the European Union, specifically in the recognition and accommodation of identities as well as interests. Indeed, the Good Friday Agreement marked a significant change in the approach of both governments to Northern Ireland in that it addressed the situation in Northern Ireland through three levels/strands of political co-operation: within Northern Ireland, within the island of Ireland and within the so-called western isles. The construction of a 'community of nations' framework between Britain and Ireland is institutionalised in the British-Irish Council established by the 1998 Agreement:

> The Good Friday Agreement also reflects the positive development of British-Irish relations in recent years . . . The Agreement, for example, provides us all with a unique form for developing new relationships for this new era, the British-Irish Council. (Ahern, 20 June 2001)

This represents a significant development in two areas of Irish official nationalism: (1) the relations between nations represented in the Council and (2) the British identity of unionists in Ireland.

First, the new relations within the western isles reflect a 'deconstruction' of 'Britishness' in both political and ideological terms. Devolution in the United Kingdom has meant that more national identities within the western isles now have political expression and a degree of autonomy in external affairs, including at the European level. As noted above, the Irish governmental elite have responded to devolution in the United Kingdom by seeking to strengthen relations with its constituent nations.

> there is now, for the first time in our respective histories, a framework within which political leaders representing specifically Irish and Scottish institutions of governance, will be able to work together, in pursuit of common ends. The remit of the [British-Irish] Council is to promote the harmonious and mutually beneficial development of the totality of the relationships among the peoples of these islands. (Ahern, 20 June 2001)

It is interesting to note the prominence of 'nationhood' and 'identity' in official discourse on these new relationships within the western isles; the 'Ireland-Wales relationship', for example, is no longer 'eclipsed by the broader British-Irish relationship' (Ahern, 1 March 2001b). The ideological aspects of the 'deconstruction' of British identity is summarised by Ahern (15 April 1999) in his speech to a centre for Irish Studies in London on the 'change in nomenclature' from Anglo-Irish to British-Irish. Ahern sees this change as 'consolidat[ing] an evolution that has been under way since 1985 [Anglo-Irish Agreement]'. It has three specific areas of significance: (1) Irish nationalists 'no longer see England and its rule as the sole issue in relation to Northern Ireland', (2) the 'Britishness of Unionists' is better understood, and (3) 'evolution within the United Kingdom' (Ahern, 15 April 1999). The 'agreed adjustments' in this area therefore reflect the impact of 'the rapid pace of change' not only within and between Britain and Ireland, but in the 'international context in which [they] both operate' (Ahern, 15 April 1999).

As Ahern notes, change in the imagination of 'Britishness' in official discourse has helped facilitate the recognition of the British identity of unionists within the island of Ireland. For reasons noted above, accepting unionism as a version of British identity, rather than a poor imitation of Englishness, is as much a political as an ideological development in Irish official nationalism. Northern unionists' links to Britain were often seen in Irish official discourse as superficial, being based on economic, political or religious interests rather than on unchanging and profound national (essential) identity. This position, as shown above, altered slowly and somewhat equivocally in the late twentieth century towards recognition of a British identity in Northern Ireland. The importance of the British-Irish context in relation to this was recognised by FitzGerald in speeches to audiences in Northern Ireland:

> all the peoples of these two islands have to face the fact that history has linked them together in a very complex relationship which finds no parallels elsewhere. Much British blood runs in Irish veins . . . Moreover we in Ireland, while having our own native culture, share also in Britain's cultural heritage, to which we have in turn contributed . . . None of us – unionists or nationalists in Ireland and Britain – are in any real sense foreign to each other. (26 February 1979)

> The British as well as Irish identity of a million people in Northern Ireland is an added reason for looking seriously at this question of the ultimate shape of Anglo-Irish relations. (22 February 1980)

Difficulties in British-Irish relations were reflected in Irish official discourse on the validity and integrity of the British identity of unionists. Improvements in this area (particularly since the Downing Street Declaration) contributed to the official recognition by the Irish and British governments in the 1998 Agreement of the *legitimacy* of a British identity on the island of Ireland. This development represented a 'paradigm shift' for Irish official nationalism.

Britain's involvement in the Agreement, the endorsement of the constitutional position of Northern Ireland in referendums within Northern Ireland and the Republic and the new British-Irish context all facilitated Irish official acceptance of British identity within Northern Ireland. Moreover, the move from recognising the cultural identity of the residents in Northern Ireland to recognising their political (national) identities also was integrally related to recognition of the legitimacy of

Northern Ireland itself by the Irish governmental elite. Yet, in some ways, Northern Ireland is now more of an 'other' than ever before, falling between Britain and Ireland in terms of politics and identity. For, in post-Good Friday Agreement Irish official discourse, it is not only the political entity but also the identity of Northern Ireland that is differentiated from that of the Republic. This was articulated clearly by Brian Cowen (27 May 2000) as Minister for Foreign Affairs:

> It is that fact of deep and enduring difference which makes Northern Ireland unique. It is neither wholly British in identity, nor wholly Irish, but both British and Irish. To seek to eliminate all traces of Britishness would be as absurd as to seek to eliminate all traces of Irishness.

The 1998 Agreement's recognition of 'a plurality of traditions' in Northern Ireland has consequences for the Republic's approach to north-south relations, most simply stated by Bertie Ahern (21 April 1998) thus: 'Henceforth, we do not insist on press-ganging those who are determined that they are not a part of the nation'. The Agreement did clearly represent a process of adjustment of the framework and ideal model of the Irish nation in Irish official nationalism. This is epitomised, according to the Taoiseach, in the revisions made to Articles 2 and 3 of the Constitution of Ireland:

> In our reformulation of articles 2 and 3, and in the new British-Irish Agreement, it is the people north and South [*sic*] who are sovereign, and who share the territory of Ireland and its title deeds in all the diversity of their identities and traditions. (Ahern, 26 April 1998)

For Ahern to choose the republican commemoration at Arbour Hill as the occasion on which to imply that 'title deeds' of the island are shared between nationalist and unionist makes this ideological adjustment all the more significant, even, perhaps, convincing. Such changes in both the framework and model were supported by new narratives of Irish national identity.

Narrative: unity in diversity

A key aspect of the function of narratives of official nationalism is to enable conceptual and practical change to take place whilst maintaining the impression of stability and consistency in governmental policy. Hence, in a speech to the 1971 Fianna Fáil Ardfheis, made in the context of extreme pressure on official Irish nationalism (not least in wake of the Arms Crisis),[16] Lynch (20 February 1971, emphasis added) called not for a new form of Irish nationalism but for the discovery of its '*true* meaning'. Such a process implied both an affirmation of fundamental elements of Irish nationalism and a new plan for their expression and fulfilment in the changing context. For this to succeed, it was envisaged that Irish nationalists would have to 'clear our minds of many presuppositions, and of much of the debris and clutter of history' (FitzGerald, 26 February 1979). Because a continuum between the 'history' of the Irish nation and its present situation could be identified, it was anticipated that removing historical 'debris' would reveal common ground for a new relationship between north and south:

> The task that faces us is no less than reversing powerful and destructive forces created by hundreds of years of miserable history . . . Together, North and South, let us make the brave choice. However great our differences, however difficult the challenge, let us all together find the courage to break the dominion of history over this island of Ireland. (FitzGerald, 11 February 1982)

> to all those North and South who genuinely seek peace and stability above anything else, to put aside their heritage of suspicions and doubts on the one hand, and unrealistic expectations on the other, and to recognise that North and South are interdependent partners in the vital search for peace and stability. (FitzGerald, 29 June 1984)

What was most significant about this approach was its placing of 'history' as a factor inhibiting the development of the Irish nation, given the traditional significance of collective myth-memories and experience in nationalist discourse. Such a revision of history was not limited to national history, it has also been a theme in Ireland's approach to European integration. See, for example, Andrews' (27 November 1997) urging of European Ambassadors to 'make our own history, conscious of, but not paralysed by either memories of the past or visions of the future.' The Irish governmental elite have presented the motivations and ideals of European unity as of significant relevance to the situation of division and diversity in the island of Ireland.[17] The narrative of 'bloody conflicts' and 'historical divisions' in Europe being overcome through co-operation has been relayed to the Irish population as a model and example for addressing the conflict in Northern Ireland. This is illustrated in official Irish discourse regarding the Good Friday Agreement of 1998. For example, in an address to the European Parliament on the Agreement, Andrews (29 April 1998), as Minister for Foreign Affairs, spoke of the inspiration drawn by the government in its approach to the peace process from 'the European ideal and the concrete achievements of the Union' and commented that Europe has demonstrated 'how age-old rivalries and bloody conflicts can be transcended through new partnership structures'. Andrews (15 May 1998) elaborated on this theme in a speech two weeks later on the subject of the Treaty of Amsterdam:

The complex web of relationships with lies at the heart of the Good Friday Agreement is set in the creative context of our shared membership of the European Union. The Union, which brings together 'peoples long divided by bloody conflicts', illustrates the possibilities for reconciling ancient differences. *The Union's institutional arrangements help to provide the model for blending different histories into a shared future.* (emphasis added)

The holding of the referendum on the Good Friday Agreement and the Treaty of Amsterdam on the same day (22 May 1998) in Ireland facilitated the particularly overt merging of narratives on the EU and the Northern Ireland peace process.

The achievement of 'unity in diversity' in Europe through co-operation was adopted as a model for Irish nationalism in official discourse for two reasons. First, it represented the incorporation of peoples from different political entities in a new undivided entity and, secondly, it demonstrated the success of peaceful, as opposed to violent, means in this achievement. The following extract from an address by FitzGerald (20 August 1978:1, 10) in commemoration of Michael Collins illustrates the presence of these two assumptions in an association of the European ideal and peace in Ireland:

The unity that Collins sought required, as he said, *'diversity in unity'* . . . [Fine Gael's] will be a contribution inspired by Michael Collins's [*sic*] vision – one that will be designed to *encourage the north-east to seek willingly its place in the Irish nation* . . . (10) In adopting *the vision of diversity in unity within Ireland* . . . we shall be echoing here on a large scale what has been attempted in the Europe of the Community [*sic*]. *In Europe, as in Ireland, we need and are actively seeking the many benefits of unity* while doggedly *preserving our heritage* of cultural and social diversity. (emphasis added)

Thus, the mantra of 'diversity in unity' in Irish society signifies a change not specifically in the purported ideal of official nationalism – the incorporation of Northern Ireland into the Irish nation-state – but in the means used to realise it, namely, persuasion rather than intimidation.

Moreover, the European mantra of 'unity in diversity' was interpreted in Irish official discourse as, more than a narrative of the peaceful resolution of political difference, a formula for the creation of an agreed 'whole' from culturally diverse elements:

The EU story is a complex one that requires, and repays, careful telling. It is a tale of a great political adventure in which *countries with diverse cultures* and *a history of mutual conflict* have banded together to create an entity unique in the annals of international relations. (Quinn, 7 May 1997, emphasis added) the [European] Community is a powerful, indeed unique, model of how national and economic conflicts can be resolved in practical partnership directed towards a common goal . . . The division of the continent is ending. (Collins, 8 March 1990)

In this sense, the 'Union' of Europe is viewed as highly pertinent regarding the ideal of a union within Ireland. Thus, the revised Article 3 of the Constitution (emphasis added) makes clear the 'will' of the Irish nation for unification, yet recognises that this will occur through 'peaceful means' and affirms the 'diversity' of the population of the island of Ireland:

It is the firm will of the Irish nation, in harmony and friendship, to unite all the people who share the territory of the island of Ireland, *in all the diversity of their identities and traditions*, recognising that a united Ireland shall be brought about only by peaceful means with the consent of a majority of the people, democratically expressed, in both jurisdictions in the island.

Model: multidimensional Irish identities

The Good Friday Agreement and the constitutional amendments arising from it epitomise a model of Irish identity that reflects the influence of the European model of multidimensional identities. First, there is the concept of diverse identities within Northern Ireland and, by extension, the island of Ireland. These identities are cultural, or 'ethnic', the markers of which include language (hence the provisions for Irish Gaelic and Ulster-Scots) and religion. Secondly, there are diverse national identities within the island of Ireland, as seen in the right of residents in Northern Ireland to be 'British, Irish or both' and to hold dual British and Irish citizenship as natural-born citizens.[18] These identities can be expressed at a regional level (i.e. devolved assembly), national level (i.e. state), inter-regional level (i.e. British-Irish Council) and supra-national level (i.e. European). Each of these levels has significance in political terms and is justified on the basis of interests and identities. Aside from assertions of the dissolving of 'internal differences' between north and south, the European context has been significant in facilitating a conception of identity that goes beyond the territorial boundaries of the state (FitzGerald, 1973: 104). This is reflected in the clarification of Irish identity and nationhood seen in the revised Articles 2 and 3 of the Constitution of Ireland.

Article 2 of the Constitution following the Nineteenth Amendment reads as follows:

It is the entitlement and birthright of every person born in the island of Ireland, which includes its islands and seas, to be part of the Irish nation.

> That is also the entitlement of all persons otherwise qualified in accordance with law to be citizens of Ireland. Furthermore, the Irish nation cherishes its special affinity with people of Irish ancestry living abroad who share its cultural identity and heritage.

The first sentence of this Article continues the unamended Article's non-recognition of the border between Northern Ireland and the Republic in terms of delimiting the bounds of the Irish nation. The crucial difference between them is that the amended Article implies that the residents of Northern Ireland have a *choice* as to whether to define themselves as Irish. Nevertheless, as will be examined in detail in the next chapter, territory remains at the core of Irish nationhood. The second sentence broadens the definition of Irish nationhood through the inclusion of Irish citizens who were not born on the island. The final sentence is of particular interest in terms of the model of Irish identity, for it implies that the 'cultural identity and heritage' of the Irish nation is not territorially bounded. Ahern (20 June 2001) explains this point in Article 2 as arising from the recognition that 'the connection with the Irish abroad is a two-way process'. In 'cherishing' the cultural links with the Irish diaspora, the Irish governmental elite is responding to both 'the new confident identity' and 'resurgent proud consciousness of being Irish' among the diaspora and the international context in which national and cultural identity is as significant as ever (Ahern, 15 April 1999). The model of the Irish nation and identity encapsulated in the revised Article 2 epitomises the uniting of internal and external elements and of continuity and change in Irish official discourse.

Conclusion

> Identities and aspirations are enduring but they are not immutable . . . And, in coming to terms with others, we must question our own assumptions and beliefs. As we start a new century, both unionism and nationalism need to continue to redefine themselves to meet the real needs and hopes of the people of this island. (Cowen, 27 May 2000)

Whilst the inhabitants of Northern Ireland are recognised as different to those of the Republic, they are also seen as distinct from those of Great Britain – a perception that is essentially based on a territorial sense of interest and identity. Hence, the fundamental ideological building blocks of nationalism endure: a unique historical cultural nation, a representative sovereign state, a specific bounded territory. The way in which official Irish discourse has presented European integration has continued to use and arguably strengthen these tenets. Nevertheless, the European context has also contributed to change in official interpretations of core

Table 6.1 'Identity' in Irish official nationalism, 1973–2002

	Framework	*Narrative*	*Model*

Traditional	Nation
	Thirty-two/
	  twenty-six county;
	  political nature
	  of the nation
		Historical culture
		Ancient/mythical;
		  Christian/spiritual;
		  Celtic connections
			Distinct people
			Gaelic/Celtic;
			  Irish diaspora;
			  Unionist other

Approach to European integration	'Community of nations'
	Ireland as
	  European
	  nation; contrast
	  with colonialism;
	  fulfil national
	  identity
		Ireland belongs in Europe
		Historical cultural
		  home in Europe;
		  European
		  integration
		  counters colonial
		  legacy; EU
		  preserves
		  national culture
			'The EU is not them but us'
			National
			  distinctiveness
			  enhanced;
			  increased
			  national
			  confidence; true
			  realisation of
			  nationhood;
			  European
			  partners;
			  European
			  identity via
			  national
			  identity

Approach to Northern Ireland	Community
	Difference accepted
	  through
	  accommodation;
	  'western isles';
	  pluralist society
		Unity in diversity
		Rethinking Irish
		  history; varieties
		  of Irishness
			Multidimensional identities
			British, Irish or
			  both; European;
			  diaspora

nationalist concepts and, moreover, to the notion of how these tenets relate to each other. Official discourse is used to depict these changes as necessary alterations towards finding the true fulfilment of the Irish nation-state. Changes to the conception of not only national identity but also its relationship to territory and state in the context of European integration have affected the definition of what this fulfilment exactly entails, whether in an external or internal context. This is exemplified in the conceptualisation of the ideal of a 'united Ireland' – a notion examined in the ensuing chapter. Table 6.1 summarises the key findings in this chapter on the reimagination of identity in Irish official discourse in the first thirty years of Ireland's EU membership.

Notes

1 The importance of Christianity in Ireland's national identity is also linked to the other 'Celtic nations' in official discourse, with St David's Irish mother and St Patrick's Welsh roots being frequently commented upon (e.g. Ahern, 1 March 2001a).

2 Phrase used by Haughey describing contemporary Europe (11 April 1981). It is significant that this phrase is a well-established, legal and historical (self-) definition of the British Commonwealth, as can be seen in the Anglo-Irish Treaty of 1921 and the 1922 Constitution of the Irish Free State.

3 Quotations taken from FitzGerald (11 February 1982; 22 October 1983; 14 March 1984), Haughey (19 April 1986), Barry (11 March 1983) and Harney (4 June 2001).

4 These phrases were in particularly frequent use in official discourse during the campaign for the 2001 referendum on the Nice Treaty but they have also been prevalent in official statements on EU enlargement. See, for example, Ahern (5 February 2001) and (8 February 2001).

5 Ahern quoted in 'The Battle for Nice', Editorial, *Irish Times*, 10 May 2001.

6 For example, the *Farming Independent* of 1972 carried a story on 'The Conversion of Father Brady', national chairman of Muintir na Tíre, to a pro-EEC position, as he explained: 'My visit to Brussels showed me that the EEC is not the materialistic businessman's arrangement I had imagined. Many people there have a very definite social conscience' (Source: Desmond, 2001.)

7 'Anglo-American mass culture' continued to be considered the 'other' to Irish native culture in official discourse long after Ireland became a member of the EEC, for it provided a counter-balance to accusations that the EEC was founded on materialist principles. For example, see extract below from a speech given by FitzGerald (19 September 1977): 'At the same time the danger of impoverishment of our society through a weakening of traditional values, and the danger of loss of vitality in our native culture as it – like so many others throughout the world – faces the threat of Anglo-American mass culture, are widely felt throughout all groups in our society'.

8 Phrase coined by Ahern (1 March 2001b; 21 June 2001).

9 For example: 'With our tradition of artistic and literary achievement it is foolish to think that we have anything to fear from bringing our culture and our way of life into closer contact with those of Europe' (Haughey, 7 May 1972).

10 For example, Minister of State at the Department of Enterprise Trade and Employment, Tom Kitt's (10 May 2001) remarks that: 'we are strong, confident and forward looking – a nation confident enough in its own culture to maintain its essential position on the European state'.

Also, Ahern (29 March 2001b): 'The basic thrust of the "no" argument is always the same – that we will be swept aside and overwhelmed within Europe. It betrays a fundamental lack of confidence in Ireland and the Irish people.'

11 Phrases taken from Ahern (9 January 2001; 1 March 2001a; 29 March 2001b).

12 This sentiment was present from the early days of Ireland's EEC member-ship, as efforts were made to make national citizens feel that Europe 'belongs' to them. An enchanting example of this is the announcement made in January 1973 in *Eolas* 1 (10), the Government Information Bulletin, that 'Irish school children may help to write the words of [the new] European anthem . . . just one of several EEC activities in which Irish school children may take part'.

13 The importance of the audience in determining the nature of official discourse is also seen in the fact that in an address in honour of Romano Prodi, the President of the European Commission, Ahern (21 June 2001) refers to the 'European family'. Nevertheless, it is generally speaking much more common for Irish official discourse to refer to the EU in terms of a 'partnership'.

14 Síle de Valera (b. 1954): grand-daughter of Éamon de Valera, she was Fianna Fáil TD for Dublin 1977–81, and MEP for Dublin 1979–84, and TD for Clare 1987–2007. She was Minister for Arts, Heritage, Gaeltacht and the Islands (1997–2002) and Minister of State at the Department of Education and Science (2002–06).

15 See, for example, FitzGerald's applauding of the lack of tension between immigrants from the 'two strands' of the 'Irish ethnic tradition' in the United States (16 March 1984). These two strands are defined by FitzGerald as 'the ancient Gaelic, Catholic tradition' and the 'Protestant tradition' (15 March 1984).

16 The 'Arms Crisis': Charles Haughey, then Minister for Finance and Neil Blaney (then Minister for Agriculture) were sacked from office in May 1970 and accused (along with an Irish Army intelligence officer, a Belfast republi-can and a Belgian businessman) of plotting to use government money intended for emergency civilian relief for displaced nationalists in Northern Ireland to purchase arms for the IRA. All defendants were cleared in the sub-sequent trial. For more on the impact of the Arms crisis and trial on Fianna Fáil policy towards Northern Ireland see O'Donnell (2007).

17 For example, a pamphlet published by the Department of Foreign Affairs (1971b) prior to the referendum on accession to the EEC contained the fol-lowing paragraph: 'For centuries men have aspired to a peaceful union of the European peoples. And yet, the history of Europe has been largely a history of wars. The two great wars of this century started in Europe. From the devastation of the Second World War was born a new resolve that such wars should never occur again. The problems of reconstruction were too great for any one country to solve. So countries had to work together, victors and vanquished. The co-operation proved so successful that many Europeans felt that it should be continued.'

18 Both these developments represent the fulfilment of FitzGerald's prescription for resolving conflict in Northern Ireland: 'Such an accommodation must on the one hand recognise the aspiration of the Protestant unionist majority to

retain their British identity, and to be safeguarded against the fear of absorption in an Irish State with a Gaelic, Catholic ethos. But on the other hand it must recognise the aspiration of the nationalist minority to recognition of the equal validity of their Irish identity' (FitzGerald, 30 September 1982).

7

Borders, territory and space

we should be involved in building bridges between North and South, not in the creation of more puerile and more ineffective barriers between the people of this island. (Lynch, 20 October 1971)

This chapter examines the meaning and significance given to 'borders' by official Irish discourse when defining Irish 'territory' and European 'space'.[1] The model of national territory is of a physical, bordered polity made live by the narrative of a common homeland. The framework of European space is also constructed with the aid of an ideal model and narrative in which cross-border co-operation meets shared needs. This chapter explores the way in which the traditional and new frameworks, narratives and models of the territory and European space have been brought together in Irish official discourse since the 1970s. It is structured in the same way as the previous chapter, following a summary of the traditional conception of the Irish territory with an analysis of the way in which this conception has been upheld in Ireland's approach to the EU. The final part of the chapter considers the way in which a 'European' notion of shared space (as a more amenable concept than national territory) has been present in Irish official discourse on Northern Ireland. The idea of changing barriers into bridges (illustrated in the above quotation from Taoiseach Jack Lynch as the border became a Troubles fault line) was one such concept that gradually became less contentious in the Irish context through reference to its 'European' inspiration.

Borders in Ireland

Framework: territory

This country of ours is no sand bank, thrown up by some recent caprice of earth. It is an ancient land, honoured in the archives of civilisation, traceable into antiquity by its piety, its valour, and its sufferings. (Pearse, 1916: 305)

Given the importance of territory in the definition of the Irish nation and in the jurisdiction of the state, the territorial definition of 'Ireland' has been a consistently vital and contentious issue for Irish official nationalism. The ideal correspondence between the 'fiat' (political) and the 'bona fide' (natural, i.e. island) boundaries of the Irish nation, as asserted by republican and constitutional nationalists, became a problem for official Irish nationalism in both ideological and practical terms. Partition meant that the territorial frameworks of the ideal Irish nation and political Irish state did not correspond. The ideal of a 'united Ireland' was thus balanced in Irish official discourse alongside the need to make the twenty-six-county *state* itself 'united [and] sovereign' (de Valera, 21 June 1925). The function of official nationalism to smooth over principle/practice incongruity has been active in this regard, with Irish official discourse presenting reunification as being made attainable via the policies of a twenty-six-county government. Indeed, the persistent identification of the Irish nation as 'the island' has helped to facilitate policy (and constitutional) change regarding Northern Ireland and even to lend credence to the international role of the state. These two areas constitute the focus of the final two parts of this chapter. First, however, it is necessary to examine in more detail the way in which Irish official discourse has traditionally presented the territory of Ireland whilst apparently preserving the integrity of the nation-state.

Grammatical devices

Partition is more than just a *Border*, more than just an *artificially-made* and *artificially-maintained* barrier, more than just an *economically-disruptive* division, more than just a *culturally-divisive* influence, more than just an *historical affront*. (Lynch, 17 January 1970, emphasis added)

The conceptualisation of partition in Irish official discourse, as the extract above implies, affects a wide range of aspects of Irish nation-statehood, including politics, economics, culture and history. The consequent significance of the border between Northern Ireland and the Republic of Ireland is reflected in the capitalisation of 'border' in the transcription of Lynch's speech – a device particularly common in the early 1970s (see, for example, DFA [1972a: 12]). The use of capitalisation in government publications indicates the reification of certain concepts in Irish official discourse. The Irish border and the island of Ireland[2] were in this way often given a significance and status usually reserved for individual places or countries, thus implying that the 'Border' and the 'Island' have their own identity and (international) importance. Although common for the first fifty years of Irish official discourse, this device of capitalisation for emphasis has been used less frequently since the late 1970s, perhaps in line with the growing importance of non-written media.

Yet, nomenclature itself remains a significant element of official discourse and a good indicator of change in Irish official nationalism. Members of both the British and Irish governmental elites have been historically aware of the significance of nomenclature in the realm of national identity. Following Ireland's withdrawal from the Commonwealth, the Irish government issued guidelines prescribing the use of the term 'The Six Counties' in reference to Northern Ireland. In addition, the use of the full title of the United Kingdom of Great Britain and Northern Ireland was forbidden. Although revised in the 1960s, it was not until the late 1990s that the Irish and British governments have agreed 'to conform in official terminology to the general international pattern of using the names for States that they give themselves' (Ahern, 15 April 1999). These guidelines reflect the sensitivity of the Irish government to the significance of terminology and the importance of official discourse as a reflection of the ideological viewpoint of the governmental elite. Even aside from such prescriptions, the difficulty of referring to the Irish state as a nation-state in light of the very existence of Northern Ireland is encapsulated in the different ways in which the two parts of the island are referred to in Irish official discourse.

Frequent reference is made in texts of official discourse to 'the people of this State'. This is more than a statement of fact in that it draws a strong line of connection between the populace of the Irish state with the responsibility of the state. In its application below, FitzGerald is attempting to rally popular support for his new approach to Northern Ireland (note he speaks primarily as an individual rather than on behalf of the government or Fine Gael), in what is styled as a move away from isolationism towards a 'true republicanism':

> If I can bring the people of this State with me along that path, and get them to create down here, the kind of state Tone and Davis looked for, then I believe we would have the basis on which many Protestants in Northern Ireland would be willing to consider a relationship with us, who at present have no reason to do so. (FitzGerald, 27 September 1981)

A similar motivation is also behind references to 'we' or 'us' 'in this part of Ireland', which tend to be used to highlight the collective responsibility of the Republic's population regarding Northern Ireland and, moreover, prospects for reunification.[3]

Other forms of reference to the jurisdiction of the Irish state focus particularly on the notion that it forms only a part of the whole unit of

Ireland. Although 'the North' is often used as a self-consciously 'depoliticised' term for Northern Ireland in Irish official discourse, references to 'the South' are only made in statements that refer also to 'the North'. This affirms the image that Northern Ireland and the Republic are both parts of a 'whole', i.e. the island of Ireland. Yet, the north/south description is not purely territorial and it often appears in texts which acknowledge the different cultural constitutions of the jurisdictions. The fact that FitzGerald can make reference to '*traditional* North/South tensions' (27 September 1977, emphasis added), highlights the association of the geographical areas with different histories, ideologies and cultures. This can be seen in the following extract from a speech by FitzGerald to a Fine Gael Ardfheis (20 May 1978), although at this point he claims to be addressing 'the majority in Northern Ireland':

> when the people in the South speak of Irish unity, they do *not* visualise a unitary State in which the norms of the mainstream Irish tradition of Gaelic nationalism, still less the insights and attitudes particular to the Roman Catholic Church . . . would be imposed upon you.

The phrase 'twenty-six counties' is also used in official discourse with the assumption that the audience will associate this geographical term with a political and cultural entity. It is interesting to note that the phrase is often capitalised, which (for reasons noted above) confirms that it is more than a reference to a geographical area. Indeed, de Valera's (21 June 1925: 5; 16 May 1926: 12) references to a 'sovereign Twenty-Six Counties' and 'mak[ing] good the internal sovereignty of the people over the Twenty-Six Counties' exemplifies the use of the term as a substitute for that of the Irish state. Just as the terms 'North' and 'South' are used together in official discourse, so the term 'twenty-six counties' is used alongside the description of Northern Ireland as the 'six counties'. Thus, the border is conceived as one 'between the Twenty-Six and the Six Counties' – an image which implies that the border is an artificial division within a thirty-two-county Ireland (Irish Transport and General Workers' Union [ITGWU], 1972: 19). The notion of the natural 'fiat' territorial framework of the island of Ireland is rooted in the political and ideological conceptualisation of 'Ireland' in Irish nationalism even prior to independence. For traditional Irish official nationalism, the sea defines the territorial boundaries of Ireland and, therefore, Irish national identity, national political representation and sovereignty should be defined within these shores.

Different nationalist emphases

As noted in chapter 4, territory was an issue of contention between the versions of nationalism existing in modern Ireland prior to 1922, with unionism disputing the republican and constitutional nationalist notions that shared territory is a basis for shared interests and identity. Unionist conceptions of the relationship between territory and statehood can only be understood by looking at its modern roots in the context of the British empire. British imperialism was itself predicated on the belief that statehood was not necessarily territorially defined or confined. In contrast, Irish nationalism (in both its republican and constitutional forms) argued for political autonomy/independence on the basis of the separate territory of Ireland. However, there were some significant distinctions between the two versions of Irish nationalism on the issue of territory. For the republican, an Irish identity was defined by cultural affinities and political will, both of which were seen as incompatible with cultural and political expressions of Britishness on the island of Ireland. Independence (and reunification) for the Irish republican, therefore, meant freedom from British influence in cultural and political terms and freedom to construct a sovereign state that would represent and protect the unique identity of the Irish people. For the constitutional nationalist, an Irish identity was essentially defined on a territorial basis, i.e. by birth of the island, and could therefore be diverse in terms of cultural traditions and political affiliation, although birthplace did provide a certain commonality between all on the island. Independence (and reunification) for the constitutional nationalist therefore meant the opportunity to construct an Irish state that would represent the interests of all Irish people as residents on the island, not as members of one particular cultural group or another.

The significance of these differing ideological assumptions has been evident in the development of Irish official nationalism and the approach of successive governments to internal and external affairs. It is possible to identify distinct elements of republican or constitutional nationalism in the ideological positions of Fianna Fáil and Fine Gael respectively, as political parties who locate their roots in a particular strand of modern Irish nationalism. For example, the following statement by Haughey (19 November 1985) complies with Fianna Fáil's 'republican' demands for British withdrawal from Northern Ireland:

> Fianna Fáil will continue to . . . uphold the democratic nationalist tradition throughout this island . . . We will not be deflected from that role and will continue to work for the reunification of Ireland and the withdrawal of the British presence.

In contrast, FitzGerald's (18 November 1982) call is in line with the self-consciously constitutional approach of Fine Gael to the legitimacy of unionist identity in Ireland:

all of us who share the nationalist aspiration to unity of the people of Ireland, freely achieved by the consent of a majority in the North and in this State, must come together . . . and, in consultation and co-operation with people representative of unionist opinion, devise proposals to put before the people of Northern Ireland which will reflect our vision of the kind of Ireland in which they would have a secure place, and in which their British/Irish identity and their interests would be guaranteed.

However, the principles *shared* by both ideologies have been undoubtedly more significant for Irish governmental discourse and policy. First, they concur that partition of the island of Ireland imposed an *artificial* border and that Northern Ireland is an artificial political and cultural entity. Both presume that Northern Ireland's interests would be better served through *integration* with the Republic rather than union with Britain. And in their manifestation in the official discourse of the Irish state since the late 1960s, both agree that reunification must be achieved 'by peaceful means' and through political *negotiation*, not military action (Lynch, 28 August 1969).[4] Although participation in the government of the Irish state was itself to some degree a statement that reunification would be achieved politically rather than militarily, events in Northern Ireland towards the end of the 1960s forced the governmental elite of the Irish Republic to clarify its official position on reunification. This posed a particular challenge for the Irish governmental elite, not least because it had relied so heavily on narratives to bolster the impression of adherence to the ideological goal of reunification whilst conducting an essentially twenty-six-county based policy. Clarification of the official position of the Irish state on reunification implied a drawing together of ideology and practice in a way not seen since independence.

Narrative: homeland

The island nation

The narrative of an indigenous Gaelic population defending its independence over centuries from invaders from Europe and Britain has, we have seen, been popular in Irish official discourse. The related notion of the island having a distinct cultural and political identity has persisted through continued identification of a 'unique history' and 'uniquely complex heritage' (FitzGerald, 20 August 1978). The very fact that nationalists talk of the island of Ireland as having *a* 'history' and 'heritage' exemplify the reification of the *island* as a cultural and political entity.

the deep conviction of Irish nationalists that the island of Ireland is a natural geographical area forming historically a single cultural and political unity. (FitzGerald, 30 September 1982)

The enduring, incontestable and immutable reality of the island has formed a basis of continuity in Irish nationalist discourse between past, present and future, regardless of how the events on and around this territory are interpreted. Thus, 'the island of Ireland' has been a foundation stone of Irish official discourse, even as members of the Irish governmental elite have sought to construct a more inclusive and moderate approach to Northern Ireland. Cosgrave's (2 July 1973, emphasis added) statement below exemplifies the balance of the traditional (i.e. unity) and the new (i.e. diversity) in the conception of Ireland:

> we hope that our aspiration towards an eventual political unity of the island of Ireland is founded on a reality – on the reality that *Ireland is and has always been a single society* though within this society *there have been, and are, and must remain*, a number of *different traditions*, to which equal respect much be paid.

Indeed, despite the revision of traditional nationalist versions of history, the essential unity of the island remains undoubted. This is seen in the extract below from a speech given by FitzGerald, in which he attempts to distinguish between the indigenous culture of Ireland and Gaelic culture (viewing the ideological reduction of the former to the latter as disinclining unionists from unification). His suggestion that the 'cultural unity' of Ireland was cemented by the 'administrative unity' put in place by colonial rule marks a change in the traditional interpretation of that historical era in Irish official discourse whilst affirming the notion of the essential unity of Ireland:

> The aspiration to a unitary State derived from two sources – first from *the traditional cultural unity of the island* which had always transcended the political divisions of the Gaelic era, and secondly from *the administrative unity of the island achieved by English rule*, a unity which by the time the ideas of nationalism became prevalent was long established in people's minds as the norm. (FitzGerald, 5 June 1982)

North/South disunity

FitzGerald's assertion that colonial rule served to strengthen Irish unity is particularly significant given that one of the most significant points of his revision of Irish official nationalism was the recognition that unity had been weakened by Irish independence. He was not alone in claiming that the process of nation-state building in the twenty-six counties had produced deep alienation between the Republic and Northern Ireland. The development of not only divergent economies and polities but also different 'traditions', 'identities' and 'views' in the two parts of Ireland had, it was argued, resulted in 'psychological barriers between North and South' (FitzGerald, 20 November 1984; Lynch, 6 August 1971; FitzGerald 11 February 1982). The perception that 'the two parts of Ireland [had] drifted apart insensibly' had significant consequences for the ideal of reunification (FitzGerald and Harte, 1979). FitzGerald (20 August 1978) identifies the causes of apathy towards reunification as lying with developments in both Northern Ireland *and* the Republic:

> I know that many in this part of Ireland are today sceptical and some are even bored and others fearful about the possibility of creating a new relationship between North and South . . . The purveyors of the new conventional wisdom tell us repeatedly that no one here [in the Irish state] is really interested in the North anymore.

In the name of Irish unity, therefore, Irish official discourse sought not only to counter the fears of people of Northern Ireland but also counter the indifference of the people of the Republic regarding reunification. Unlike previous assumptions in Irish official nationalism, this new approach was based on recognition of the profound *differences* between 'North' and 'South'. Such differences were highly exacerbated by the emergence of conflict in Northern Ireland, which Taoiseach Liam Cosgrave saw as '*accentuating the mental partition*' and, moreover, 'killing here [in the Irish state] the desire for unity which has been part of our heritage' (13 June 1974, emphasis added). In this context, FitzGerald (20 May 1978), called for 'bridge-building' to 'bring closer together the two parts of this island', arguing against 'the attempt to suggest that North and South are "foreign" to each other'. This apparent digression from his assertion that Northern Ireland and the Republic are different reflects the continuing centrality of the common territory of the island in Irish official discourse's conception of north-south relations.

The unifying power of territory
Indeed, increasing official recognition of the diversity of identities, ideologies, traditions, etc. on the island of Ireland was accompanied by an *emphasis* on the importance of the territory of Ireland as a basis of common history, experience and interests. Recognition of the existence of 'different kinds of Irish people' not only emphasised diversity, it also stressed a conception of 'Irishness' based on territorial residence and not cultural, religious and political affinity (FitzGerald, 16 June 1978). These notions are encapsulated in an address given by Lynch in 1970, which emphasises the territory of Ireland as the basis for Irishness and the natural unity of Ireland:

> We are all Irish in our different kinds of ways . . . I speak now to the Irish people, North and South, Protestant, Presbyterian, Catholic – and simply

Irish . . . We have had invasions piled upon invasions. Danes, Normans, English, Scots, followed into Ireland our earlier migration and *became part of our soil, of our blood and bone, of the green fields we cultivate* . . . we think that a branch has been broken from the Irish tree. (Lynch, 11 July 1970, emphasis added)

The implication in the above narrative is that 'territory' forms a unity between the people in Ireland not only through their physical residence on the island but also their (and their ancestors') cultivation of the land itself. Images of rural life were traditionally common in Irish national-ism's conception of Irish nationhood, with their associated images of simplicity, purity and tradition. These images are also present in a speech given by Lynch, addressed to the population of Northern Ireland:

We share this country not merely because we live on the same island; we share it also because of common history, because of qualities which com-plement each other where they are not the same; because our blood has been intermingled as much as it has been uselessly shed; because we have, all of us, formed and cultivated the land of Ireland and none of us can be removed from what we made. (Lynch, 20 February 1971)

The notions of 'common history', different but complementary 'quali-ties', 'blood' and 'land' are intertwined to present a picture of a people who are fundamentally linked to each other. Hence, the assertion that people north and south 'share this country' is far from apolitical; as this quotation from Haughey shows, the idea of that the residents actively 'share' the territory leads to the notion that they 'belong' to it and thus have responsibility towards its development:

Unionist and Nationalists, Protestant and Catholic all share the one island, and are deeply attached to its soil. All belong and have a contribution to make to our common country. (Haughey, 30 May 1983)

The emotional power of territory

Territory is important in the traditional conception of Irish nation-statehood not only in its political, symbolic or cultural designation but also in ideological, even emotive, terms. This point again highlights the blurring of the distinction between the 'real' and the 'ideal' that occurs in nationalism. For example, in the above extract Haughey (30 May 1983) refers to a deep attachment to the 'soil' of the island shared by all resident on it, thus making a direct equation between the physical reality of territory that forms the literal and metaphorical ground of people's identity and experience. Such a notion is prominent in Irish official dis-course, as it was in pre-independence Irish nationalism, and sustains the belief that territory helps define what it means to be Irish and to hold an

Irish worldview. For this reason, partition is also conceived as an emotive and personal issue as much as political one, as the following extract from a speech given by Lynch to the Fianna Fáil Ardfheis of 1970 highlights:

> No other political topic can generate more emotion in an Irishman's heart that [*sic*] the subject of Partition . . . *Partition is a deep, throbbing weal across the land, heart and soul of Ireland, an imposed deformity* whose indefinite perpetuation eats into the Irish consciousness like a cancer. As I have said, it is impossible for true Irishmen, of whatever creed, to dwell on the existence of Partition without becoming emotional. (Lynch, 17 January 1970, emphasis added)

The final sentence of the above extract returns to the political interpretation of national territory and identity, in that it equates 'true' Irishness with an anti-partitionist sentiment. This notion was present in early Irish official nationalism, as governmental elites struggled to explain the refusal of unionists to join with the Irish state. Hence, de Valera's (17 April 1926, emphasis added) assertion that 'every Irishman' has a 'native' desire for unification:

> in the heart of every Irishman there is a *native undying desire* to see his country politically free, and *not only free but truly Irish* as well, and that the people recently divided are but awaiting an opportunity to come together again and give effective expression to that desire.

Model: demarcated boundaries

It is a legacy of this association of Irishness with a desire for Irish unity that all leading members of the Irish governmental elite find it necessary to stress that reunification remains their ideal objective. Indeed, the task of addressing the discord between the definitions of the Irish 'state' and the Irish 'nation' has been generally dealt with in official Irish discourse by portraying the state as functioning to close the disparity between itself and the territory/people of 'Ireland' beyond its jurisdiction. Thus, whether it is a question of relations with Britain, economic development or participation in the EU, official Irish discourse will not portray any national state policy as making re-unification less feasible. Even when there are significant changes in government policy, this principle remains – or must be *seen* to remain – absolute. This was true with Lynch, who asserted that 'only re-unification can lift from our land the curse of history and restore to our people their natural birthright' (17 January 1970), and remains true even after the Good Friday Agreement. The following statement by Cowen as Minister for Foreign Affairs (27 May 2000) reflects this point, yet it also encapsulates a belief central to progress on the issue of Northern Ireland since the early 1970s, namely that reunification will occur through consensus:

> As an Irish nationalist, it remains my hope that one day there will be a united Ireland. But what we have learned over the past thirty years, is that this united Ireland must be agreed and consensual, both in its achievement and in its administration. And, in coming to terms with others', we must question our own assumptions and beliefs.

Cowen's sentiments reflect the mixture of traditional (the island demarcates the territorial boundaries of 'Ireland') and new (no reunification without consensus) conceptions of Irish unity that have been central to the process encapsulated in the 1998 Agreement. The roots of this process, as suggested above, lay in the early 1970s.

Modifying the goal of unification

> Perhaps we should now begin to change our metaphors when we speak of Northern Ireland. (Cosgrave, 2 July 1973)

In the context of the rising 'Troubles', the Irish governmental elite agreed that the principle of reunification needed to be re-examined in order to offer a clear alternative to the discourse of militaristic nationalism and to present the Republic as a credible negotiator in discussions on Northern Ireland. Clarification was proposed on two subjects: (1) what was meant by the term 'a united Ireland', and (2) what the policies of the parties and government of the Republic were on political unity (see FitzGerald, 20 May 1978; 16 June 1978). First, it was made clear that reunification was expected – reference was frequently made to 'eventual political unity', in a similar vein to the constitutional articles on 'the Nation' (e.g. FitzGerald, 16 June 1978). Second, it was suggested that this unity would not necessarily take the form traditionally assumed by Irish nationalism, i.e. integration of Northern Ireland into the structures of the Republic. For example, Lynch announced that:

> it should be clear that a united Ireland will not be an Ireland in which the present State in the 'South' takes over the 'North' and assimilates it into its existing structures. There should be negotiation, but it should be about a *new* Ireland. (Lynch, July 1972)

This discursive shift in Irish official nationalism over a thirty-year period was, it may be argued, accorded much more profound significance by its proponents than by the assumed beneficiaries (i.e. unionists). FitzGerald (22 February 1980) went so far as to describe the embedding of a more nuanced conception of unification as 'the effective rejection . . . of the traditional nationalist thesis'. Most notably, he identified a new conceptualisation of Irish territory at the core of this 'radical' reconsideration of the nationalist position:

> the reunion sought by the people of the Republic [is] a reunion of peoples and not a re-conquest of territory. (FitzGerald, 22 February 1980)

This notion, we shall note, was articulated in very similar terms by FitzGerald's successors in government when lauding the 1998 Good Friday Agreement.

The significance of this conceptual change is most notable when compared with the official position on territorial unity as outlined at the start of the Troubles. Jack Lynch sought to redress the fraught situation by taking some of the focus off the British government's role and channelling public opinion towards a positive consideration of the way that the Republic could respond. Yet the focus of this reconsideration of the laws and practices of the Irish state remained 'to win the consent of the majority of the people in the Six Counties as to the means by which North and South can come together in a re-united and sovereign Ireland' (Lynch, 20 September 1969). Lynch's successor as Taoiseach, Liam Cosgrave (26 June 1974), continued this theme in his speeches on Northern Ireland, namely to create 'the kind of society in the Republic with which the Northern majority would wish to be closely linked with a view to our common benefit'. Cosgrave saw this ideal society as being achievable only through increased prosperity; as he claimed, '[p]rosperity can bring us a unity of hearts and of purpose' (26 June 1974). Many of his speeches on the subject of drawing north and south closer together were, therefore, premised on the need to first 'increase the material wealth' of the island (2 July 1973). Cosgrave's belief that a (more) united Ireland would arise from more material wealth was integrally connected to his conception of the European Economic Community and the impact of Ireland's membership.

European integration and Irish territory

Framework: within, through and beyond Europe

Irish official discourse has presented the territory of Ireland as being redeemed through being placed within the framework of the European Union. This is due to the link between the reality of the territorial bounds and capacity of the state and the needs and interests of the population of that state. Assessment of the nature of this capacity/interest dichotomy in the late 1960s produced a pro-EEC thesis put forward by the Irish governmental elite on the grounds that membership would: (1) 'promot[e] the economic development of the whole country to its fullest extent' (DFA, 1972d: 3), (2) reduce regional inequality within Ireland, and (3) integrate Ireland into the heart of international affairs. These arguments represent a direct connection being made between Ireland's interests and the development of the European Union.

This association between European and national interests can also be seen nearly fifteen years later, in the Irish Government Information Service's (1987a; 1987b) summary of the necessity of the Single European Act. It supports the Act on the following bases: (1) economic ('Speed up progress towards a truly free internal market'), (2) regional ('Increase the EEC's commitment to spread the Community's prosperity more evenly'), and (3) international ('Make the EEC a world leader' and 'Give Europe a more influential voice on the world stage'). All of these elements have also been presented as highly pertinent to the situation between Northern Ireland and the Republic, as is examined in the final section of this chapter. Right now, we consider the relevance of these three areas in relation to Ireland's position in the framework of the European Union, the narrative used to support this interpretation and the model of Ireland's subsequent territorial position. The focal point of this section is the integral connection made between Ireland's territorially-inspired interests and those of the EU in Irish official discourse.

Territory and economic interests

First, the potential of the territory of Ireland is seen as being achieved through integration into the EEC framework as a 'growing economic area' (DFA, 1972a: 3). This has been so important for the Irish economy for several reasons, many of which arise from the nature of its territory. For example, its small size heightens the sense of the necessity of partic-ipation in the Common Market: '[w]e are a small country with little capacity, at present, to influence events abroad that affect our interests' (DFA, 1972a: 13). Secondly, the close economic ties between Ireland and its British neighbour exacerbated the sense of urgency in this regard, although the likely effects of EEC membership on Ireland's economic relationship with Britain are not elaborated in official government pub-lications in 1971 and 1972. This was possibly due to an unwillingness to add to the impression that Ireland's application came on the coat-tails of Britain – a criticism posed during debates about EEC membership since 1961. The significance of Britain in Ireland's application to the EEC relates to another territorially-based feature of the Irish economy, namely, that Ireland is primarily an exporting country.

> As a nation depending crucially on exports, Ireland stands to gain from the removal of trade barriers. We are more dependent on exports than most of the other members of the EEC. (GIS, 1987d: 1)

These three features – Ireland's small size, close economic ties with Britain and export economy – are brought together in an *Irish Times* article written by FitzGerald in 1963:

> Economically participation in the EEC seems desirable because . . . *the smaller the country the more it needs international trade* because of its greater dependence on goods and services *not obtainable within its own frontiers*. But small countries are at a disadvantage in international trade between sovereign States, as their weakness is easily exploited by larger countries. This is especially true of small countries with large agricultural sectors . . . bigger countries protect their own farming communities by quota or tariff restrictions on imports, or, as in *Britain*, by direct subsidies that force down to uneconomic levels the prices of imported foodstuffs. (FitzGerald, 5 January 1963, emphasis added)

These points are reiterated nine years later in a Department of Foreign Affairs information leaflet prior to the referendum on EEC membership:

> We are *a small country* with little capacity, at present, to influence events abroad that affect our interests. As *a trading country* we are deeply affected by economic and trading developments in Britain and other European countries and in the world generally. (DFA, 1972a: 13)

Integration of the Irish economy into 'one of the great economic groupings of the world' would, the Irish governmental elite contend, effectively overcome the limitations on the Irish economy arising from the position of its territory (i.e. mainly agricultural, small size, geographically 'hidden' behind its neighbour) (DFA, 1972a: 13). The economic development of Ireland has thus been linked in Irish official discourse to the development of the European Common Market.

> Each country – *but especially Ireland* – will gain from having a truly free market stretching right across the EEC. (GIS, 1987a: 2, emphasis added)

Internal regional development was also pivotal to the Irish government's support for European integration. The Department of Foreign Affairs dedicated a large information leaflet to this precise topic in 1972. The leaflet asserts that the EEC accepts Irish requests:

> to give a commitment that it will use all the means at its disposal to help us in removing these [internal economic and social] imbalances and that account will be taken of the special regional problems of Ireland in the further development of a comprehensive Community regional policy. (DFA, 1972d: 7)

Another DFA leaflet of this time points to a different aspect of regional development, those involving north-south relations in the island of Ireland. The EEC policy and impact on regional development are seen as highly significant in this area in that both Northern Ireland and the Republic require a similarly intensive concentration of regional funding and programmes. In this sense, 'the country as a whole' will benefit from EEC membership:

> Both parts of Ireland share many similar problems in relation to underdeveloped regions. Our job is to bring these regions up to the level of prosperity in the more developed areas. In the EEC we shall be pressing for a comprehensive Community policy and action on regional development. This will help the North as much as the South because the country as a whole stands to benefit from a policy and action by the Community for the underdeveloped regions. (DFA, 1972c: 2–3).

This theme is continued in Irish official discourse regarding a number of other areas of Community policy, many of which are considered in the final section of this chapter.

Ireland's international status

The last point regarding the framework of the European Union in relation to territory is the impact that membership is seen as having on redeeming Ireland's international position. It was noted in the previous chapter that the EU is frequently credited in Irish official discourse with 'broadening' the 'horizons' of Ireland (e.g. Ahern, 8 January 2001). This is integrally related to the conscientious disassociation by post-Lemass governmental elites of Irish official nationalism from the isolationism that originally arose from claims for economic and political autonomy. Indeed, Irish official discourse supports EEC membership on the grounds that it would end all traces of isolation in Ireland's international position. Isolation on the world stage is not, however, entirely due to 'fundamentalist' nationalist governmental policies unpopular with other states. The geographical location of Ireland as the 'island behind an island' and 'a small island off Europe' has been reimagined in Irish official discourse regarding EU membership (Ahern, 15 May 1999). In addition, the small size of Ireland is no longer viewed as an impediment to an active and influential role in international affairs. The intrinsic connection between Ireland's integration into Europe and its integration into international affairs means that, according to Irish official discourse, as the EU has developed as 'a political as well as an economic force on the world stage', so too has Ireland (GIS, 1987e: 2).

> Acting together the Community is more effective than any one member could be . . . This co-operation gives Ireland a more effective voice in world affairs, without compromising our independence. (GIS, 1987a: 3)

The contrast drawn here between the negative impact of isolationism and the positive effects of integration acts to confirm the view that the path taken by Irish governmental elite members now is as true to the principles of Irish nationalism as the path chosen by some of their predecessors. In fact, the importance of Irish independence is emphasised not only through the framework of the EU but also within it. See, for example, the summary of EEC membership by the Government Information Service in 1987:

> It has given us an *effective* say in the decision-making of a Community many times bigger than our own country. (Several European countries outside the EEC, such as Norway and Austria, envy this *insider position* that Ireland enjoys). (GIS, 1987c: 2, emphasis added)

From this 'insider position', Ireland is able to influence decisions both within the EU and, as a consequence of this, beyond it. This represents a significant change in the conceptualisation of Ireland's position in international affairs since the 1970s. This has been supported by narratives that have moved away from a vision of the 'small and peripheral' territory of Ireland to one in which this territory is at the centre of global economic and political development (Ahern, 9 January 2001).

Narrative: the European homeland

The narrative of European integration in this area reflects a desire among Irish governmental elite members to move beyond concepts of territory that bound Irish official nationalism to an Anglo-centric focus in terms of politics, economics and international affairs. Still, this narrative is as clearly influenced by the geographical status of the island of Ireland – its location, size, capacity – as any narrative of territory in Irish official discourse that preceded it. Ireland's geographical location on the periphery of the European continent has been traditionally interpreted in Irish nationalist discourse as a clear indicator of its distinctiveness. Its proximity to Britain also gave rise to another traditional tenet of Irish nationalism, namely, its vulnerability to larger countries. This tenet was strengthened by the small size of Ireland. Yet, the fact of Ireland's small territorial size had not only produced a sense of vulnerability in the international sphere, it had also been central in the traditional nationalist identification with other 'small nations'. This was reflected, for example, in the positive response of so many in Ireland to the Allied call in the First World War to defend the rights of 'poor little' Belgium. The small size of Ireland also affected its capacity as an economic player and producer of goods. Although membership of the European Union could not change the facts of Ireland's territorial circumstances, it was possible for Irish official discourse to reimagine these facts in the context of the European Union. The key points of this process are considered here.

Stepping stone to Europe

The territorial location of Ireland beside Britain and beyond the European continent has been reinterpreted in Irish official discourse in recent times as a positive attribute. Even aside from substantial economic growth, the plain fact of EEC membership meant that FitzGerald (20 May 1978) was able to claim in 1978 that the Irish Republic was 'no longer an isolated political unit in a small island off the coast of another island'. This narrative – from isolation to integration – is one that has been consistently supported in Irish official discourse. See, for example, the comments made by Taoiseach Ahern (29 March 1999) to a conference on NATO's 'Partnership for Peace' at a conference of the European Movement in Dublin:

> 'The isolated Republic' was never a beneficial peacetime foreign policy. We have the self-confidence today to co-operate and interact with other countries. Robert Emmet's famous phrase spoke about 'taking our place amongst the nations'.

Perhaps one of the key 'triumphs' of Irish official nationalism in terms of reimagining the significance of the territorial location of Ireland has been in the revival of de Valera's vision of Ireland being 'situated at the very focus of the trade routes between Europe and America – the gateway to the West' (1918: 2) and 'the gateway of the Atlantic . . . the last outpost of Europe towards the West' (1922: 11).[5] This idea is particularly present in speeches aimed at attracting foreign investment in Ireland. For example, in a speech in Washington, FitzGerald (14 March 1984) asserts:

> We fully intend to continue with and are in fact at present supplementing our system of incentives and our welcome for American companies in Ireland, *with that access the location offers to European markets.* (emphasis added)

Haughey (8 October 1982) made a similar claim to an international business audience:

> On an earth made smaller every year by advancing communications we have become a stepping-stone between the Old World and the New, *a bridgehead in Europe for America.* We are, in fact and in reality, a crossroads, and for this reason as well as others we are a good vantage-point from which to view the world. (emphasis added)

This narrative has been utilised in the Celtic Tiger years too, as members of the Irish governmental elite have presented Ireland as 'a natural and profitable gateway to Europe' and 'well-placed to meet the needs of US companies seeking a European basis' (Ahern, 24 November 1997; Cowen, 6 June 2000).

Small nation

Ireland's approach to European integration was also affected by its territorial size, not least in terms of the continuation of the narrative of identification with other small nations in the international realm:

> As a small nation we must voice our concern and join with the other small nations of the world in asserting humanitarian principles. (Haughey, 2 November 1985)

Moreover, the logic of official discourse advocating full co-operation with other states has been that Ireland's geographical size and position necessitates it. As the following extract from a speech by Ahern shows, the arguments against further European integration are classified in official discourse as anachronistic and dangerously quixotic:

> In the real world, all countries, *especially small ones*, operate within very considerable constraints. Nobody can pull the curtains and tell the world to go away. (Ahern, 29 March 2001b, emphasis added)

In contrast, membership of the European Union is portrayed as enabling Ireland:

> a small, insular country, insular literally and, up to then, metaphorically as well to interact on a basis of equality and on a wide range of issues with our fellow-members on the continent, as well as our nearest neighbour (Ahern, 15 April 1999)

Ireland's geographical status (including its size and history) has also been frequently referred to regarding the enlargement of the European Union:

> Ireland is seen [by applicant states] as a small state, with an historical experience not totally different from their own, which, having started from a long way back, has made the best possible use of the support and opportunities given to it to catch up with the European mainstream. (Ahern, 5 February 2001)

Indeed, Ireland's island-status is conceived in official discourse as being transformed in the European context, with its isolation overcome and its distinctiveness enhanced.

The small size of Ireland has also produced a sense of Ireland's physical vulnerability to larger powers. This notion was present in arguments opposed to the derogation of Irish sovereignty through EEC membership, predicting an exploitation of Irish territory similar to that experienced under British colonialism:

> A surrender of sovereignty . . . would mean we would be powerless to prevent the rich folk of Europe from buying as much Irish *land and property* as they wished; it would mean the *surrender of our territorial waters* to highly capitalised fishing concerns in Britain and Europe. (ITGWU, 1972: 20–1, emphasis added)

However, such a protectionist attitude was unpopular with the contemporary Irish governmental elite, who asserted that Ireland's approach to European integration should reflect and build upon its territorial properties. Irish official discourse from this time onwards reflects the conception that Ireland's territorial position gives the state a duty not only to defend what little it has – 'Our responsibilities are those of a small nation with limited resources' (FitzGerald, 14 March 1984) – but also to express its resulting identity on the world stage.

Model: *the liberating boundaries of Europe*

The model of the European Union regarding borders according to Irish official discourse is perhaps more 'progressive' than the models of the EU on the basis of identity or governance. The 'traditional' tenets of Irish territory upheld in the approach of the Irish governmental elite to the EU have been those of fulfilling the potential of Ireland, rather than on strengthening its boundaries (a notion associated with the priority of absolute independence from Britain). In terms of fulfilling Ireland's potential, the model of the European Union has been interpreted in Irish official discourse as enabling Ireland to overcome constraints arising from its territorial qualities. This has been reflected in the Irish elite's presentation of the EU as a broad partnership based on common interests and not limited by territorial position. Indeed, the model of a borderless Europe, in which territorial location, size and capacity do not delimit the level of participation, according to official Irish discourse, is an immensely favourable one for Ireland. This model does not only imply that Ireland's geographical position no longer confines it to the economic and political periphery of Europe, it also enables Ireland to be presented in official discourse at the 'centre' of Europe. Thus, as a 'partner[ ] in a common enterprise', Ireland has been able to play its part 'in assisting and encouraging change across *our shared continent*' (Ahern, 1 March 2001b; 5 February 2001, emphasis added). In addition, the European Union's external as well as internal borders no longer confine the limits of political and economic co-operation. This notion was present in Irish official discourse even prior to accession:

As a member country we will . . . to an extent even be able to influence decisions taken in countries outside the Community. The Community, of which we will form a part, will be one of the great economic groupings of the world, and its views will be listened to by large countries outside it in a way that the views of its individual member countries would not have been. (DFA, 1972a: 13–14).

In the ideal model of European integration, therefore, Ireland's (inter)national potential is realised beyond its borders without its territorial integrity being compromised.

This model reflects to some degree the reconfiguration of an imperial model, in which territory does not restrict the bounds of cultural, economic and political influence. This relates to the point noted in chapter 6, namely, that Irish official discourse has borrowed a phrase used to describe the British Commonwealth in depicting the EU, i.e. 'community of nations'. Given that analogies with imperialism and, thereby, colonialism are made by critics of the EU, Irish official discourse has to make the distinction quite clear. Hence, in the model of the EU, Ireland's territorial limitations (economic, regional, international) are overcome without compromising the features of its territorial identity that are considered central tenets of Irish nationalism (distinctive island status, gateway between Europe and America, role model for small nations). Moreover, the significance for Irish official nationalism of a model in which territorial frontiers are not barriers to partnership and co-operation and in which common interests are of primary significance has not been overlooked.

Northern Ireland and European space

Framework: common space

Turning to the possible effects of EEC membership, although it would be quite wrong to look to this as a panacea for the Irish problem, which will always remain one to be settled by Irishmen in Ireland, such influence as *membership of the Community* will have is likely to be *uniformly* directed towards *easing that path to a united Ireland*. (FitzGerald, 1973: 104, emphasis added)

The way in which EU membership affects the conceptualisation of national territory is fundamental to Irish official discourse on Northern Ireland. For it is on precisely this issue – the conception of Irish territory – that Irish official nationalism faces the greatest challenge in unifying ideals with reality, ideology with practice. The border took on new significance with the emergence of the Troubles in Northern Ireland, as the

Irish government was in the paradoxical position of wanting to confine the conflict to the province of Northern Ireland whilst taking every opportunity to emphasise the need for its involvement in any resolution. The Irish government claimed a right to be involved in resolving the conflict in Northern Ireland for three main reasons. First, Northern Ireland is part of the territory of Ireland, and its residents are thereby entitled to be Irish nationals. Secondly, the conflict in Northern Ireland had 'a negative and divisive' impact on the 'border counties', 'on the rest of the State' and 'on the reputation and morale of the island as a whole' (Cowen, 28 April 2000). Finally, Northern Ireland and the Republic have common interests: 'two parts of a small island linked together so [*sic*] closely as we are economically and socially cannot succeed in developing their full potential without close co-operation' (Cosgrave, 26 June 1974). The context of membership of the European Union has provided Irish official discourse with new opportunities to move these claims from ideological principles to progressive activity.

Island of Ireland as a common market

The primary significance of European integration in this area has been the framework of common 'space', in which co-operation is not delimited by territorial borders. This framework has been applied to the context of the island of Ireland, supported by narratives of overcoming division and models of cross-border co-operation. As it is possible to do in discourse regarding borders (less so in the themes of identity or governance), the pragmatic and expedient consequences of 'common space' are emphasised in Irish official discourse. The creation of the common space of the island of Ireland is stimulated and sustained, for example, by economic 'realities'. This point is clearly expressed in a statement made by Lynch (28 May 1971) to an audience in Dundalk, near the border with Northern Ireland, which is worth quoting at length:

> Ireland and Britain are now very close to entry into the European Economic Community. North and South will find many of its problems and opportunities common to both. *Ireland itself will be one common market* of 4.5 million people and will, in turn, be part of the much larger common market of ten States. *Continental entrepreneurs will not be concerned with political borders* or outmoded political attitudes in this country. And the *Governments of the Common Market countries will not be interested either*. It is Irish people who must diminish the differences between us in step with the dismantlement of tariff walls. It is we who must concert our actions and promote our common interests.

This extract is of direct relevance to the three points outlined above regarding the Republic's approach to Northern Ireland. First, it is assumed that all on the territory are 'Irish'. Second, it is asserted that both have common problems and interests. Thirdly, the border is presented as being irrelevant in terms of trade and commerce that is facilitated by EEC membership. The image of the island of Ireland as a 'common market' in the Common Market draws direct parallels between the practice and ideals of European integration and Irish official nationalism. This not only includes the decreasing economic significance of territorial borders but also an increasing equality between the regions.

> Membership of the Community must by the very force of circumstances lower many of the social and economic differences that exist between the North and South at present. (Haughey, 7 May 1972)

Economic differences between Northern Ireland and the Republic included 'different patterns of industrial development, the competitive rather than complementary character of the two industrial economies, and the somewhat different attitudes towards state enterprise' – all of which, Irish official discourse has asserted, could be overcome by EEC membership (FitzGerald, 1973: 81). The significance of these differences in Irish politics is indicated by a Department of Foreign Affairs (1972c) leaflet, *Ireland North and South in the EEC,* dedicated entirely to identifying the areas in which EEC membership could help overcome these divisions. The ending of tariffs and 'other restrictions on trade between the two parts of the country' resulting from participation in the Common Market is central to the predicted dissolution of economic differences between Northern Ireland and the Republic (DFA, 1972c: 1). An EEC policy singled out for attention is that of regional development, which, under the heading 'Common problems – common actions', the leaflet asserts would 'help the North as much as the South because the country as a whole stands to benefit from a policy and action by the Community for the underdeveloped regions' (DFA, 1972c: 2).

Another positive consequence of EEC membership for bringing north and south closer is the lifting of restrictions on 'people from the South' gaining employment in the north (residents in Northern Ireland were already able to work in the Republic without restrictions) (DFA, 1972c: 2). A number of more indirect implications of EEC policy were also drawn. For example, on the subject of the Common Agricultural Policy, the leaflet simply states that: 'By 1978 when the transitional period following entry will end Irish farmers, North and South, will be working under the same conditions as regards prices and marketing of products' (DFA, 1972c: 1). Other Community policies, including economic, social, transport and trade, are seen as significant because they would 'be in operation uniformly throughout the thirty-two counties'. Yet the point that is perhaps the least directly related to EEC policy is the statement that 'the increased prosperity that membership of the EEC will bring' would enable the Irish government 'to devote more money to social services', as a consequence of which 'the social services gap between North and South will thus be closed' (DFA, 1972c: 3). In summary, the arguments set out regarding the impact of EEC membership on the creation of a common space in the island of Ireland may be classified into three categories: (1) increased cross-border trade of goods and movement of persons, (2) both would be subject to the same policies on 'matters of great importance' in which they have common interests (DFA, 1972c: 2), and (3) imbalance between north and south in areas such as social services and prosperity would be rectified through the economic development of the Republic.

Decreasing barriers

The purpose of the leaflet discussed above was to persuade the Irish electorate that membership of the EEC would not 'involve [the Irish government's] acceptance . . . of the partition of Ireland' nor would it 'adversely affect the national policy for the reunification of this country' (DFA, 1972c: 1). The points it makes about the likely impact of EEC membership on decreasing 'barriers' between north and south were, explicitly or implicitly, referring to its impact on *the* barrier between Northern Ireland and the Republic, i.e. the border. This leaflet was published primarily for public 'information', as one of a series of 'fact sheets' issued by the DFA prior to the 1972 referendum. Again, the 'physical' nature of territory is used to point to the observable, factual ways in which EEC membership affects the territory of Ireland. Irish official discourse has used this to suggest that the 'common space' created in the island of Ireland by EU membership is non-political, moving away from the association of the border, or even territory itself, with divisive political ideologies. This notion is present in a speech by Taoiseach Ahern (14 May 1998) on the Good Friday Agreement to an audience in Dublin Castle (in this instance, not one convened by a tribunal):

> A new beginning to relationships on this island must involve the creation of *a common space* in which our *different cultures* can be experienced, shared and enjoyed by all people of the island, *free from the political overtones* which in the past have alienated different groups and communities from elements of *our common heritage*. (emphasis added).

Ahern implies that political ideologies lie at the heart of the conflict in (Northern) Ireland, rather than cultural difference or religious affiliation.

Thus, the point being made is that, if politics (i.e. the British state and the twenty-six-county state) were to be taken out of the equation, residence in the 'common space' would mean common interests, common action and common identity in a rediscovery of a 'common heritage'. This idea of conceiving of culture as apolitical is actually a highly political statement to make, particularly when made in reference to unionism. For it leads the audience to the implied question of what unionism would be without political identification with Britain, as compared to what nationalism would be in an all-island context. Territory, albeit 'reimagined' in the European context, remains the linchpin of Irish official nationalism.

The revision of articles 2 and 3

The reimagination of Irish territory in relation to Northern Ireland is most clearly evident in the amendments made to Articles 2 and 3 of the Constitution of Ireland following the 1998 Good Friday Agreement. FitzGerald's 'constitutional crusade' of the late 1970s and 1980s had already pointed to these Articles as 'an obstacle to North-South progress' (FitzGerald, 27 October 1978). This call for changes to Articles 2 and 3 was controversial. Many considered Articles 2 and 3 to be of great symbolic significance for Irish nationalism. Haughey (11 October 1981), for example, rejected FitzGerald's proposals on the grounds that irredentism was a fixed feature of Irish nationalism:[6]

> Our Constitution . . . enshrines in Articles 2 and 3 the clear assertion of the belief that this island should be one political unit – a belief stretching far back into history and re-asserted time and time again by the vast majority of our people North and South.

Ultimately, the amendments to Articles 2 and 3 were made in the context of a growing awareness among the Irish governmental elite that they were not *only* a defining point for Irish nationalists but also a sticking point for unionists and, therefore, a barrier to north-south co-operation.

Article 2 of the 1937 Constitution originally read as follows:

> The national territory consists of the whole island of Ireland, its islands and the territorial seas.

Article 2 of the Constitution following the Nineteenth Amendment of the Constitution begins with the following statement regarding the territory of the Irish nation:

> It is the entitlement and birthright of every person born in the island of Ireland, which includes its islands and seas, to be part of the Irish nation.

The territory of the island of Ireland, we reiterate, remains central to the definition of the Irish nation. Yet, to refer again to Andrews' (30 April

1998) phrase, the emphasis has moved from being based exclusively on 'territory' to one on 'people' or, more specifically, the choice of individuals.

This goes some way towards addressing the problem that Article 3 of the 1937 Constitution originally faced, namely accommodating the difference between the 'national territory' and the actual territorial jurisdiction of the Irish state:

> Pending the re-integration of the national territory, and without prejudice to the right of the Parliament and Government established by this Constitution to exercise jurisdiction over the whole of that territory, the laws enacted by that Parliament shall have the like area and extent of the application as the laws of Saorstát Eireann and the like extra-territorial effect.

The element of this Article that was considered most controversial from the standpoint of unionists was the explicit expectation of reunification and the assertion of the 'right' of the Irish government to jurisdiction over the 'whole' of the territory. The anticipation of reunification ('until then') remains in the amended Article, yet the 'threat' is removed through the inclusion of two conditions: (1) it would occur through 'peaceful means' and, (2) with majority consent in Northern Ireland (emphasis added):

> i. It is the firm will of the Irish nation, in harmony and friendship, to unite all the people who share the territory of the island of Ireland, in all the diversity of their identities and traditions, recognising that a united Ireland shall be brought about only by peaceful means with the consent of a major-ity of the people, democratically expressed, in both jurisdictions in the island. *Until then*, the laws enacted by the Parliament established by this Constitution shall have the like area and extent of application as the laws enacted by the Parliament that existed immediately before the coming into operation of this Constitution.

The second part of Article 3 marks a new departure for the 1937 Constitution (although it was present in the 1922 Constitution) in its facilitation of institutions that function on an all-island basis, as envis-aged by the Good Friday Agreement:

> ii. Institutions with executive powers and functions that are shared between those jurisdictions may be established by their respective respon-sible authorities for stated purposes and may exercise powers and func-tions in respect of all or any part of the island.

As the focus of this research is on the Irish governmental elite's interpre-tation and presentation of 'facts', the next part of this chapter analyses the way in which Irish official discourse elucidated and justified these constitutional amendments. The narrative of overcoming divisions in the homeland is at the heart of this discourse.

Narrative: overcome divisions

Justifying the article amendments

Official Irish discourse on the amendment of Articles 2 and 3 exemplifies the attempts of the Irish governmental elite to give the impression of enhancing – *not* compromising – what are deemed to be fundamental nationalist principles. The key principle of reunification remains. In the immediate wake of the 1998 Agreement, the proposed new Articles 2 and 3 were portrayed by Ahern (26 April 1998) as affirming that the Irish nation 'is and always will be a thirty-two-county nation'. This is not particularly surprising given the context of the speech, i.e. at the republican commemoration at Arbour Hill. Nonetheless, in a statement to Dáil Éireann on the proposed Nineteenth Amendment to the Constitution, Ahern (21 April 1998) similarly emphasises an element of the amendments that may be viewed as in line with traditional republican ideals: 'Any British territorial claim to sovereignty . . . becomes irrelevant for the future.' The specified irrelevance of the British *territorial* claim is to be noted, as it allows by omission the rightfulness of the British claim to sovereignty in Northern Ireland through the will of the majority therein. Yet the position of northern nationalists in Ireland is not said to be undermined in any way by the constitutional change. Ahern reiterated this in the same Dáil statement:

> There is no question of anyone being made an alien in their own country. The nation is not territorially disembodied. It is defined in clear terms as a thirty-two county entity. (Ahern, 21 April 1998)

Indeed, the link between the members of the nation and the territory of the nation is affirmed, according to Ahern (21 April 1998) in that:

> The nation is defined in terms of people, but people related to a specific territory, the island of Ireland . . . As a consequence of that, we no longer say, or appear to say, that the territory is ours, not theirs, but rather that it is shared by all of us.

Though the principle of the 'shared ownership of the territory of Ireland' was central to the amendments, Ahern (26 April 1998) stresses to the republican audience at Arbour Hill that:

> the new articles 2 and 3 express noble ideals. They strengthen, not weaken, the bonds that unite the Irish nation, North and South. They declare openly the desire for unity and the democratic, conciliatory and non-threatening spirit in which we wish to achieve it.

Thus, the Taoiseach is presenting the amended Articles 2 and 3 as representing a principle of official nationalism that Cosgrave or FitzGerald, Lynch or Haughey could have recognised and approved of thirty years previously: unity through peaceful means.

Ahern's arguments in support of the amendments arising from the Good Friday Agreement are in line with Fianna Fáil's self-proclaimed role as 'the guardian of the Republican tradition and the Constitution of this State' (Haughey, 12 October 1986). In his speech to the Dáil, Ahern (21 April 1998) portrays the proposed amendments as creating a Constitution that represents Irish republicanism more accurately:

> The reformulation of Articles 2 and 3 reflects modern, progressive Republican thought that is truly pluralist, and keeps faith with the inclusive tradition of Irish nationalists, stemming from Wolfe Tone and the United Irishmen.

The echoes with FitzGerald's 'constitutional crusade' for 'true republicanism' some two decades before are uncanny. It indicates the need in the discourse of the Irish political elite to find moral legitimation of policy change towards Northern Ireland in the re-telling of political legends. This tactic includes fresh interpretations of some of the fundamental tenets of Irish unity. Nowhere is this more explicit than in Ahern's (21 April 1998) post-Agreement claim that the key constitutional article regarding Irish unity was not Article 2 or 3, but Article 1 (which was unaltered by the Nineteenth Amendment). Attached to this argument is a belittling of the importance of Articles 2 and 3 to official nationalism. Ahern (21 April 1998) describes them as primarily a protest against the Boundary Agreement rather than a powerful emblem of Irish nationalism's contention that Northern Ireland should be integrated into the Republic. What is more, Ahern (21 April 1998) goes a step further than usual in claiming deceased national heroes for a contemporary political cause; he suggests that de Valera himself implicitly accepted (through his rejection of 'the use of force' by the Irish state and of 'a forced unity' between north and south) that unification could not occur without consent of a majority in Northern Ireland. Thus, Ahern contends, the revised Article 3 cannot be a betrayal of a key tenet of Irish republicanism but is instead clearly in accordance with – or even the fulfilment of – its long-held principles. His Minister for Foreign Affairs, David Andrews (26 April 1998), agrees: 'In the proposed new Article 3, the aspiration to Irish unity remains undimmed.'

Unite with(in) Europe

The verb 'to unite' has historical resonance in Irish nationalist discourse and this was not missed by the pro-European Irish political elite in its attempts to persuade the Irish electorate to support accession to the EEC. For example, Fianna Fáil campaign advertisements in 1972 carried the slogan 'Unite with Europe'. One of its campaign posters carried the image of Ireland outside of an EEC of which the United Kingdom and, thereby, Northern Ireland was a part, creating a graphic split within the island of Ireland (Desmond, 2001). The implication of this image was that Irish exclusion from the EEC would result in the border being 'permanently entrenched' as an 'international frontier' between not just the Republic and Britain but the Republic and the EEC (Haughey, 7 May 1972; DFA, 1972a: 12; DFA, 1972c: 4). The following extract from a statement to the Dáil by Taoiseach Liam Cosgrave (26 June 1974) affirms the positive implications of EEC membership for realising in practical terms the unity between Northern Ireland and the Republic:

> there are strong common interests which *we* share and which, understandably, at times diverge from the interests of Great Britain, a great industrial power with a minimal agricultural sector. Both parts of Ireland find *themselves* in a very different situation because agriculture is relatively more important in Ireland, North and South, and because neither part of Ireland has the resources *within its own boundaries* to provide adequately for the needs of peripheral areas. (emphasis added)

The language used in this statement is worth examining in more detail in terms of highlighting its complex importance in Irish official discourse on 'unity'. In the space of two sentences, Cosgrave uses two different pronouns to refer to Northern Ireland and the Republic. One the one hand, he uses a pronoun of the first person ('we') to refer to the shared interests of Irish people 'North and South'. This gives the impression that the Taoiseach himself, as a member of the Irish nation, holds a sense of identification with the residents of Northern Ireland. On the other hand, he uses pronouns of the third person (both reflexive, 'themselves', and genitive, 'its') when describing the situation that the two parts of Ireland are in regarding their distinction from Britain and their individual inability to tackle underdevelopment. The effect of this changing use of pronouns is to suggest that the distinction between Ireland and Britain would be clear to an external observer.

The significance of the precise language used in official discourse on Northern Ireland is also recognised by Irish governmental elite members themselves. This is not only in terms of maintaining their nationalist credentials (as may be seen in Ahern's comments at the Arbour Hill Commemoration on 26 April 1998) but also in shaping perception of and *in* Northern Ireland. For example, FitzGerald argues that those in the Irish state are responsible for 'saying or doing things which keep alive the traditional north/south tension' and that 'unwise utterances about Northern Ireland from the lips of politicians in this State have done harm, serious harm' (27 September 1977; 20 August 1978). Since the 1970s, Irish politicians have been conscious of the significance of their rhetoric in effecting some form of reconciliation or bridge-building in overcoming the division between the two parts of Ireland. Membership of the European Union has provided a context and model conducive to such a process, at both a practical and conceptual level.

Model: cross-border co-operation

Common interests

The model of the relationship between Northern Ireland and the Republic of Ireland in the European Union has rested on three tenets. First, because the EU is predicated on the notion that common interests are more important than territorial boundaries, EU membership highlights the *common interests* of north and south. Secondly, membership of the EU thus *lessens differences* and divisions between Northern Ireland and the Republic whilst heightening those between the island of Ireland and Britain. Thirdly, as a result of the *cross-border co-operation* and structures arising from the two previous factors plus the impact of EU membership, reunification of Ireland is made more feasible. Each of these three arguments will be considered in turn, beginning with the notion that the common interests of the two parts of Ireland have 're-emerged under the conditions of EEC membership' (FitzGerald, 16 June 1978). First, it is important to note that recognition of common interests did result in certain levels of co-operation between Northern Ireland and the Republic prior to EEC membership. For example, the Anglo-Irish Free Trade Agreement gave preferential tariff treatment for 'a range of North of Ireland industrial goods than for British goods' (Lynch, 20 February 1971). And in the 1960s, tourist boards of north and south were co-operating for the purpose of ' "selling" Ireland as a unit' (FitzGerald, 1973: 76). Governmental elite members in both Northern Ireland and the Republic had long been aware of the benefits of cross-border co-operation. The context of joint EEC membership facilitated such co-operation in such a way that had previously been inconceivable.

> Participation together in the EEC will certainly encourage the people of this island to concentrate on what they have in common rather than on what divides them. (DFA, 1972b: 3)

Underpinning the identification of common interests between north and south is the assumption that economic interests are themselves integrally related to conditions within a particular territorial unit. This theme in Irish official discourse seeks to highlight the rationale or the logic, rather than the ideology, of a united Ireland. Nevertheless, it leads to the proposal for the political institutionalisation of these common interests. For example, FitzGerald (20 May 1978) calls for an Irish Federation or Confederation 'including a pooling of our joint resources, North and South, in these sectors where we can both be the gainers by common action'. The Irish governmental elite were equally aware of the political implications of common interests in the context of EU membership. It was envisaged that common interests between the Republic and Northern Ireland in the European context in the particular areas of the Common Agricultural Policy and regional aid would form the basis for common action:

> *Within a vast European Community the two parts of Ireland, sharing common interests* in relation to such matters as agriculture and regional policy, *must tend to draw together* – and the fact that on some of these major issues the North and the Republic will have a common interest, divergent from that of highly developed Britain, cannot be without significance in these conditions. (FitzGerald, 1973: 103, emphasis added)

This statement exemplifies the notion that common interests relate to territory and, therefore, that not only are the interests of Northern Ireland and the Republic similar, they differ from those of Britain.

The push/pull of Northern Ireland for British-Irish relations
Irish official discourse on the relationship between Britain and Ireland in the context of EU membership has had to balance the fact that Irish membership was made necessary by British membership with assertions of the strong differences between Britain and Ireland as a whole. One way in which this was achieved prior to accession was through claiming the need for EEC membership on the grounds that to not do so would increase division between the Republic and Northern Ireland:

> Britain has decided to join the EEC. If we were to stay out of the enlarged Community, then the Border would, in effect, become the land frontier between us and the EEC. This would result in the erection of many more economic and trade barriers than exist now. Also, the economic and social development of North and South would inevitably grow even further apart. (DFA, 1972a: 12)

Irish official discourse thus sought to emphasise the drawing together of north and south, and not the Republic's close links with Britain, as a reason for accession:

> The North is joining the EEC; that decision is made. If our people vote in the Referendum in favour of joining, then the whole of Ireland – North and

> South – will be inside the EEC. If not then part of Ireland will be inside the
> EEC and part outside. (DFA, 1972c: 2–4)

Indeed, the close ties between Britain and the Republic were presented
as arising not from the economic dependence of the latter on the former,
but, rather, partition itself.

Due to the Republic's determination to maintain links with Northern
Ireland, partition, according to FitzGerald (1973: 60), had 'played some
part in the close alignment of Ireland with a Britain whose interests have
diverged so notably from those of its smaller neighbour'. This concept is
also behind Lynch's (July 1972) proposal that improvement in the relationship between Britain and Ireland as a result of joint EEC membership would be central to the reunification of Ireland:

> I consider that the only solution is an Ireland united by agreement, in inde-
> pendence; an Ireland in a friendly relationship with Britain; an Ireland a
> member with Britain of the enlarged European Communities.

The fact that Britain and Ireland would move 'into closer political and
economic association' in the EEC represented a move away from previous assumptions that the path to reunification lay in clearer distinction
between Britain and Ireland (ITGWU, 1972: 19). Instead, Irish governmental elite members began to claim that closer association between
Britain and the Republic could help overcome differences between north
and south. This assertion was at the heart of negotiations that led to the
Anglo-Irish Agreement of 1985, the 1995 Framework Documents and
the 1998 Good Friday Agreement (Arthur, 1999: 73–8). Closer links
with Britain in the EU were ultimately envisaged in Irish official discourse as highlighting Northern Ireland's shared interests with the
Republic rather than with Britain.

Representing Northern Ireland in Europe

The common interests of the Republic and Northern Ireland distinct
from those of Britain led to the proposition that the Irish government
was better able to represent the interests of Northern Ireland in the EU.
Even prior to membership, Lynch offered 'to make available to the
Stormont authorities [the Irish government's] knowledge and experience
in relation to EEC matters as the North's problems are much closer to
our own than to Britain's' (28 May 1971). Indeed, the common problems faced by the Republic and Northern Ireland in relation to EEC
membership led to what were described as 'informal exchanges . . .
between officials' in preparation for accession (Lynch, 20 February
1971). Following accession, this developed into assertions that Northern
Ireland's interests were not being adequately represented in the EEC,

indeed that they were being impaired, by being channelled through Britain. By the late 1970s, Britain had gained a reputation for impeding the progress of European co-operation and prospects for its future role in the EEC were being questioned both at a national and European level. This produced uncertainty about the position of Northern Ireland in the EEC. Members of the Irish political elite responded to this situation by asserting that it would do better to be associated with the Republic which, as an enthusiastic and committed member-state, enjoyed 'a role in Europe and the world disproportionate to its size and population' (FitzGerald and Harte, 1979: 20). Irish political leaders argued that Northern Ireland's interests were being obscured through representation by a large member-state with divergent interests (FitzGerald, 26 February 1979). Hence, the view that 'Northern Ireland is effectively not represented in the EEC institutions', especially at the highest levels. For, according to members of the Irish political elite, the representatives of the United Kingdom were not from Northern Ireland and therefore did not bear its interests in mind in EEC negotiations. As a consequence of this, it was claimed, Northern Ireland did not enjoy the full benefits of membership, such as an adequate share of EEC Regional Funds (FitzGerald and Harte, 1979: 12–14).[7]

Cross-border co-operation

The alternative political solution (to Northern Ireland's independence or its full integration in the United Kingdom) established in the 1998 Agreement enables Irish official discourse to claim to uphold the core principles of Irish nationalism (as noted above) whilst implementing new concepts and practices. This again reflects the ability of discourse to balance apparently paradoxical positions. Adherence to the principle of reunification, however, is the primary impression that the governmental elite have consistently sought. This can even be seen in the fact that whilst the border between north and south in Ireland is presented as decreasingly significant in the EU context, the border between Ireland and Britain is not similarly weakened. In this vein, FitzGerald (16 June 1978) asserted that the similarity of the interests of north and south in Ireland, based on shared territory, and their distinction would 'prove a significant factor in the evolution of the political situation between North and South'. However, the path of this evolution, leading to the Good Friday Agreement, reflects the significance of the *new* meaning of borders in the European context that goes a substantial way beyond the traditional concepts of Irish official nationalism.

> Politically and economically, the intrinsic value of North/South co-operation is obvious. (Cowen, 28 April 2000)

Although, as aforementioned, instances of cross-border co-operation in the early 1960s 'ended the taboo that surrounded North-South relations', the impact of the 'Troubles' meant that co-operation became more difficult both at a practical and ideological level (Kennedy, 2000: 367). It is arguably for this reason that even the anticipation of EEC membership was seized upon by the Irish governmental elite as an opportunity to clearly set forth the case for the benefits and timeliness of north-south co-operation at an official political as well as economic level. Arguments for the need for cross-border co-operation particularly emphasised the 'underdeveloped areas of the West and North-West' which, Lynch argued, constituted 'economically and in other ways a homogenous community along Border areas' (ITGWU, 1972: 19; Lynch, 28 May 1971). Indeed, Lynch sought to emphasise the relative insignificance of the territorial border in his assertion that 'the real dividing line in Ireland so far as economic prosperity is concerned has always been an East-West and not a North-South one', arguing that '[r]egional development policies of the EEC will also be helpful to each part of what is largely a single region' (July 1972:1). In this way, the context of EU membership and the notion that EEC/EU common interests override territorial boundaries have been used in official Irish discourse to add weight to the definition of Ireland as a single EU region where the administrations of north and south could 'work together for the benefit of the whole country' (DFA, 1972c:3).

The political and institutional implications of cross-border co-operation have been frequently emphasised in Irish official discourse. For example, in a booklet on the future of the island published in the name of Garret FitzGerald as leader of Fine Gael and Paddy Harte, Donegal TD and party spokesman on Northern Ireland, the cross-border consequences of EEC membership are shown to have potentially political implications (FitzGerald and Harte, 1979: 8):

> This kind of cross-border co-operation, which has been given a further boost by E.E.C. membership, would be considerably facilitated, however, by a political association between North and South.

On some occasions this was used to create the impression that EEC membership would lead to the Republic having a direct input in the administration of Northern Ireland:

> The problems of [*sic*] the North will face in relation to membership of the European Community are much closer to ours over a wide field than they are to British problems. *We would be very happy to make our knowledge available to the Stormont Administration and to enable the North to draw on our experience at any time and on any subject.* There have been occasions, *because of the closer identity of some of the North's problems with*

ours that [*sic*] with Britain's, when informal exchanges have taken place between officials. We regard this as a welcome development and one which we will be glad to pursue. (Lynch, 20 February 1971, emphasis added)

Later in that same year, in a context of strained British-Irish and north-south relations, Lynch strengthened his assertion of the likely significance of EEC membership regarding the Republic's involvement in Northern Ireland with the vision of co-operation on a *formal* basis. In a statement to Dáil Éireann in August 1971, Lynch suggests the establishment of an economic council 'to formalise more the kind of economic co-operation between representatives of the two administrations, especially in the context of our likely membership of the EEC'. This theme has continued and developed since the 1970s; however, it is possible to identify a move away from the traditional concepts of formal co-operation envisaged by Lynch towards a less state-centred vision of cross-border relations. The three strands of the Good Friday Agreement, in which cross-border co-operation is 'multilevel' and covers a wide range of areas, embody this development.

[The Agreement] represents an opportunity for a new beginning – in relationships within Northern Ireland, between North and South on the island and between Britain and Ireland. All of this, of course, is taking place in the context of our shared membership of the EU. (Andrews, 27 April 1998)

The Good Friday Agreement envisaged an ideal situation in which territorial borders would not inhibit co-operation or negotiation, either between Northern Ireland and Ireland or between Ireland the United Kingdom. In a speech to the European Parliament on the Agreement, the Minister for Foreign Affairs acknowledges the role of EU structures as a guide 'in the negotiations of arrangements for co-operation and joint action within Ireland, North and South' (Andrews, 29 April 1998). The significance of the EU in the development of cross-border co-operation on the island of Ireland is sometimes implied rather than directly acknowledged in Irish official discourse. This is shown in the following extract from a speech by Andrews' successor, Brian Cowen (28 April 2000), to members of a Local Authority in Ireland:

[Co-operation] has the potential to make a positive contribution to all aspects of our economic and social life, in all parts of the island . . . Politically and economically, the intrinsic value of North/South co-operation is obvious . . . One of the enormous achievements of the negotiations . . . was the realisation on all sides that North/South co-operation can benefit everybody and need not threaten anybody. This was also a result of that underlying trend . . . towards *working together without reference to the border* or to political affiliation. (emphasis added)

This serves to give the impression that internal territorial borders are *de facto* no longer significant. The logic of this is directed towards the principle of reunification. This has been reflected in statements predicting that a united Ireland would not only be facilitated through the European Community but would be supported by it:

> There would almost certainly be a willingness in the European Community to contribute to investment in economic infrastructure, and firm indications have already been given of U.S. willingness to participate in the economic development of a united Ireland. (Haughey, 30 May 1983)

Nonetheless, in the wake of the Good Friday Agreement, the Irish governmental elite were content to point to the new structures of cross-border co-operation and to imply that that they represent a *process* of territorial integration on the island of Ireland:

> Bodies North and South have come together, in an increasingly structured way, to identify their shared interests and to press for necessary cross-border or all-island action. (Cowen, 28 April 2000)

Conclusion

This chapter has considered some of the ways in which the territory of Ireland has been defined by official Irish nationalism in the twentieth century, particularly since accession to the EEC. It has highlighted the centrality of the principle of reunification in official discourse and its continuity to the present day. The reason for this continuity, and the fact that reunification is the ideal which no Irish government can be *seen* to discard, is essentially because of the significance of 'territory' in Irish nationalism. The framework, model and narrative of the EU have been presented as generally affirming rather than bringing into question nationalist principles of reunification. Thus, instead of becoming less relevant in the context of European integration, the significance of territory and its links to identity and governance has actually been accentuated. Nevertheless, whilst reunification remains an implicit core tenet of Irish official nationalism, changes in the conception of the relationship of territory and borders to identity and governance in the context of European integration have altered the conceptualisation of the meaning of a 'united Ireland' itself. Indeed, the differences between Northern Ireland and the Republic have been explicitly recognised and, therefore, approaches to reunification have been based on the more complex idea of drawing together two distinct entities rather than simply removing an artificial border across a single entity. The core findings of this chapter regarding the reimagination of borders in Irish official nationalism between 1973 and 2002 are summarised in table 7.1.

Table 7.1 'Borders' in Irish official nationalism, 1973–2002

	Framework	*Narrative*	*Model*
Traditional	*Territory* Discrepancy between nation and state frameworks; partition; twenty-six/ thirty-two county	*Homeland* Natural unity; Island; the unifying and emotional power of territory	*Demarcated boundaries* Artificial border; united Ireland
Approach to European integration	*Within, through and beyond Europe* Economic potential fulfilled; regional development for territorial equality; international role	*European homeland* End isolation; gateway between Europe and USA; small size no limitation	*The liberating boundaries of Europe* 'Shared continent'; fulfilment within and beyond EU
Approach to Northern Ireland	*Common space* Common market and space of island; amendments to Articles 2 and 3	*Overcome divisions* Articles 2 and 3 strengthen north-south links; importance of rhetoric in north-south relations	*Cross-border co-operation* Common interests; island distinct from Britain; single region in EU

Notes

1 Earlier and shorter articles on the same subject as this chapter were published in the *European Journal of Political Research* (Hayward, 2006b) and *Irish Political Studies*, 19:1 (2004: 18–38).

2 See, for example, the ITGWU leaflet 1972: 19: 'our [EEC] membership could be a very real force for lasting peace between the communities in this Island'.

3 'Of course it is not sufficient for those of us *in this part of Ireland* to content ourselves with telling the UK government that it must "do something" while ourselves making no effort to assist a solution or even impeding one' (FitzGerald, 27 September 1977, emphasis added).

4 This explicit rejection of the use of military force to achieve reunification by a leader of the republican party of Fianna Fáil contrasts strongly with de Valera's claim (16 May 1926: 12, emphasis added) at the time of his founding of the party: 'We shall at all times be morally *free to use any means* that God gives us *to reunite the country* and win back the part of our Ulster province that has been taken away from us.'

5 This latter quotation is taken from 'Address to the Free Nations of the World' presented by the Irish delegates to the Peace Conference in 1919, an extract of which is quoted in de Valera (1922: 11–13).

6 Seán MacBride (1985: 105) also claimed that any such proposal to amend the Constitution 'would involve a surrender of Ireland's inalienable right to sovereignty, independence and unity'.

7 It is interesting to note that the European context has also been used to discredit arguments for the independence of Northern Ireland, as an alternative to direct rule from London or unification with the Republic. FitzGerald and Harte (1979: 20) surmise that: 'An independent sovereign Northern Ireland would have to come into existence recognising the improbability that it would be admitted to the European Community [given its small size, 'disturbed recent history' and 'doubtful future'], and accepting the economic disadvantages and, to say the least, uncertainties that this would entail.'

8

Governance, state and polity

This chapter examines the conceptualisation of 'governance' in Irish official discourse in relation to both the Irish 'state' and the European
'polity'. 'State' and 'polity' constitute the broad conceptual and institutional supporting frameworks for the meaning and significance of governance in nation-statehood and European Union respectively. The
traditional narrative of the state is national self-determination, i.e. quest
of the nation to decide and direct its own forms of governance. The new
narrative of the European polity is of co-operation between states for
mutual prosperity. The traditional model of the state is sovereignty,
which brings with it the right and ability to act independently in both
internal and external matters. One aspect of the new model of the
European polity is the conception of multilevel citizenship, with the
coexistence of national and European citizenship. This chapter explores
the way in which the traditional and new frameworks, narratives and
models of the state and the European polity have been brought together
in Irish official discourse since the 1970s. After a summary of the traditional conception of the Irish state, the way in which this conception has
been upheld in Ireland's approach to the EU is considered. This then
leads into an analysis of how the conception of the Irish state has been
influenced by the EU-inspired conception of polity in Irish official
discourse on Northern Ireland.

Governance in Ireland

Framework: state

From emotive to interest-led politics

Progression undertaken in the definition of governance within the Irish
state is depicted well in a lecture delivered by FitzGerald (22 November
1990: 13) at Queen's University Belfast. In the lecture, FitzGerald
attempts to explain the course of political development in the Irish state

by highlighting the differences between two types of politics. He draws a distinction between politics that arise from an 'objective assessment of . . . interests' and politics based on 'emotional factors relating often to issues of identity'. FitzGerald identifies the latter as an approach that characterised politics in Ireland in the twentieth century. The establishment of the Irish state and its early policy-orientation were, he suggests, motivated by an emotional commitment to nationalism. This was not necessarily a bad thing; indeed, FitzGerald claims this 'emotive' form of politics was 'the best option at least for the greater part of Ireland' (22 November 1990: 19).[1] Nonetheless, FitzGerald was himself a key player in the state's move away from emotive to interest-based politics from the early 1970s onwards. In the lecture, FitzGerald lauds the Irish state's later rejection of 'the course of action indicated by nationalist emotion', asserting that the 'rapid reassessment of the traditional irredentist attitude' of the state facilitated constructive relations with Northern Ireland and Britain (22 November 1990: 17). Now, FitzGerald claims, the Irish state's policies towards Northern Ireland, European integration and international affairs are based on an objective assessment of interests. This he compares favourably with Britain's 'preoccupation with its identity problem' and out-dated adherence to 'emotional' factors, specifically in relation to the European Union (22 November 1990: 16). Indeed, he asserts, the Irish state's clear-headed, rational approach to European integration places it in an ideal position for making decisions in the EU in the interests of Ireland, north and south. Thus, the politics – based on interests rather than emotion – have perhaps changed, but the justification remains the same: independence, north-south co-operation, international respect.

FitzGerald's lecture encapsulates the conflicting pressures that stimulated reconsideration of the ideals of statehood among the Irish governmental elite. The framework of the Irish state needed to be adjusted in the light of accession to the EEC and political upheaval in Northern Ireland. Lynch (28 May 1971) described this task as 'the most difficult and at the same time most rewarding challenge the Irish people have experienced since the Reformation'. His choice of words was not accidental. Consensus was gaining ground among the Irish governmental elite that a close association between church and state in Ireland made unification with Northern Ireland less likely. As the Taoiseach had explicitly stated to the Fianna Fáil Ardfheis a few months before:

> The Constitution of a united Ireland requires to be [*sic*] a document in which no element of sectarianism, even unconscious or unintended, should occur. (Lynch, 20 February 1971)

The 'special position of the Catholic church was removed from the Constitution in the fifth constitutional amendment (Article 44.ii–iii) following a referendum at the end of 1972. Although this move was made in broad acknowledgement that 'times have changed' (Lynch, 20 February 1971), the Taoiseach also clearly state his belief that, 'this would contribute towards Irish unity' or at least 'be an indication of the outward-looking approach of the Government and the people of Ireland in relation to unity' (2 November 1972).

FitzGerald's (5 June 1982) 'constitutional crusade' some years after was predicated on similar motivations which had been disappointed by this constitutional amendment, believing that it did not go far enough in rectifying the 'clearly deficient' 'political structures in Ireland'. Moving beyond the ground laid out by Lynch, FitzGerald identifies these deficiencies as residing in two core areas. First, the system of government in Ireland was 'inadequately geared to meet modern needs' (FitzGerald, 20 May 1978). A crucial element of *modernising* the Irish state lay in the relationship between political and economic development. FitzGerald (19 September 1977) welcomes EEC membership as facilitating this change, not least through a revival of the private sector, the previous weakness of which had forced the Irish state to undertake unsuitable 'entrepreneurial roles'. The second area of concern was that the position of the Irish government was inconsistent and uncertain in its approach to Northern Ireland (FitzGerald, 5 June 1981). Members of the governing elite were aware that any clarification of the state's approach to Northern Ireland would make it more vulnerable to criticisms that it was abandoning traditional nationalist principles. Official discourse on this subject, therefore, emphasised continuity between traditional and contemporary concepts of the Irish state, not least through the use of narrative.

Narrative: national self-determination

Revising republicanism

FitzGerald (11 February 1982) sought, in his words, to 'frame a Constitution embodying the highest traditions of true republicanism'. The following extract from an interview given by FitzGerald on RTÉ radio (27 September 1981) encapsulate the rhetoric and logic of this argument:

> I want to lead a crusade, a Republican crusade, *to make this a genuine Republic*, on the principles of Tone and Davis. If I can bring the people of this State with me along that path, and get them to create *down here*, the kind of state Tone and Davis looked for, then I believe we would have the

basis on which many Protestants in Northern Ireland would be willing to consider a relationship with us. (emphasis added)

Before dissecting the implications of this rhetoric, it is worth noting that historical figures of Irish republicanism are often invoked in official discourse as a stamp of legitimacy on the discourse, particularly if it appears to diverge in some way from traditional conceptions of Irish nationalism. Although Tone, perhaps because of his denominational and geographical background, is open to be claimed, so to speak, by all the political parties in Ireland,[2] the historical roots of the main parties are evident in their choice of patriot to refer to. Fianna Fáil politicians tend to refer to Pearse, Connolly and de Valera,[3] Fine Gael politicians allude more often to Griffith, Collins, O'Higgins[4] and (a favourite of Garret FitzGerald) Davis.[5] However, following 'the principles of Tone and Davis' leads FitzGerald to a rather different interpretation of statehood than that held by many of his predecessors and contemporaries. This is no coincidence – the narrative of 'true republicanism' as articulated by FitzGerald in the early 1980s is deliberately quite distinct from the type of republican ideals previously advocated by Fianna Fáil. Indeed, it is intended to form the conceptual basis for a type of state quite unlike that associated with de Valera's republican nationalism.

The way in which FitzGerald's conception of 'true republicanism' differed from that of his political opponents is exemplified in the difference between the tenets of the discourse put forward by FitzGerald and that of Haughey. FitzGerald (5 June 1982) states his fundamental point clearly in a speech to a Belfast conference of the SDLP:

The simplistic nationalist concept of a unitary State, republican in form and with total sovereignty over its own affairs no longer reflects, therefore, the reality of what exists or of what is aspired to. In varying degrees these concepts have been modified as the years have passed.

The fact that such principles were shared by the SDLP was a fundamental factor in reviving north-south co-operation between political parties, leading to the New Ireland Forum (1983) which had a positive impact on the future of the peace process itself. However, although supportive of the New Ireland Forum, Haughey did not concur with many of FitzGerald's assertions of the need for fundamental changes to the Irish state structures and constitution. Rejecting both FitzGerald's claim to represent 'true republicanism' and his 'constitutional crusade', Haughey (12 October 1986) reiterated the 'republican' credentials of Fianna Fáil in defence of the constitution, particularly Articles 2 and 3:

Fianna Fáil today is more than ever left alone as the guardian of the Republican tradition and the Constitution of this State, in which that

tradition is enshrined. We are a constitutional party in the fullest sense, in
that we support totally and unequivocally the Constitution of our country.

This is not to say that Haughey was a more 'fundamentalist' republican
than Lemass and Lynch – many of his speeches, for example, build upon
their recognition of the need to 'accommodate the interests, identity and
aspirations of all the traditions on this island' (Haughey, 9 March 1982).
However, he did differ with FitzGerald on the question of how this was
to be done and on the extent of change needed in the Irish state to achieve
it, not least because of his emphasis on Britain's responsibility. The different ideological positions of FitzGerald and Haughey is exemplified in
their contrasting interpretations of the principles of republican figureheads such as Tone. See for example, Haughey's (12 October 1986)
summary of Tone's ideology:

> Wolfe Tone's basic thesis is still valid. It is only when the power and influ-
> ence of the London Government have been withdrawn from Irish affairs
> that the interests of all the people on this island can be secured.

Within ten years of this speech, official nationalism in Ireland was to bear
little resemblance to the version that Haughey was defending. The fact
that the substance of the discourse of Ahern is closer to that of FitzGerald
or Bruton than de Valera or even Haughey points to predominance of
internal and external pressures for change over the traditions of particular political parties.

Revising self-determination

This is evident in the changing interpretations of the narrative of national
self-determination. The new meaning of this term as set forth in Irish official discourse is discussed in the final part of this chapter; in order to
prepare the ground for a comparison, the traditional tenets of national
self-determination are now elaborated. In a speech on the Good Friday
Agreement, Ahern (29 October 1998) states:

> The view is propagated that the right [to self-determination] can only be
> fulfilled by full political independence, but that is not the position.

This marks a clear deviation from the traditional interpretation of
national self-determination. Indeed, the view Ahern is rejecting, i.e. that
self-determination is fulfilled by full political independence alone, is one
propagated by his predecessors.[6] For example, Haughey (9 March 1982)
often equated national self-determination with the complete independence of the island:

> We look forward to, and will actively seek to bring closer, the day when
> *the rights of self-determination* of *all the people of Ireland* will again be

exercised in common, and when the *final withdrawal of the British* military and political presence takes place. (emphasis added)

Haughey's depiction of Britain's position in Northern Ireland as preventing the fulfilment of national self-determination reiterates a core principle of Irish republican nationalism.[7] The ambiguity of the term, however, became increasingly clear following the independence of the Irish state. This is evident even within a speech made by Haughey around this time in which, although arguing that (thirty-two county) national self-determination was still to be achieved, he boasts of the development of a (twenty-six county) 'independent and sovereign nation' in Ireland. In a typically ironic twist of nationalism, Haughey (26 February 1983) states that the development of the sovereign twenty-six county state is underpinned by the 'national philosophy' of Fianna Fáil, central to which is the right of national self-determination, 'a right that is possessed and should be exercised in common by all the people of Ireland'. The building of a 'national life' in the twenty-six counties is predicated on the demand for a thirty-two-county state. And so, although the twenty-six county state came to be increasingly upheld as 'national' (a process traced in chapter 5), Northern Ireland is said to have 'failed as a political entity' (Haughey, 16 July 1982). Such a traditional understanding of national self-determination would not divide the island into two legitimate and separate political jurisdictions. By the turn of the century, Bertie Ahern's conception of national self-determination is also all-island based but, as will be shown, he defines this in terms of upholding the political will of a majority in the Republic *and* a majority in Northern Ireland. This represents a remarkable adjustment in the ideal model of the Irish state's relationship to nation and territory.

Model: sovereignty

Sovereignty and citizenship

One of the most significant indicators of the conception of the connection between state and nation is the definition of citizenship. A comparison of the traditional conception of citizenship with that of more recent interpretations brings to light a process of change in Irish official nationalism. In traditional republican discourse, statehood essentially facilitated vital international recognition of the nation; it was vital because, as de Valera (1918: 2) conceded, 'unfortunately it is not the peoples, but their governments, that count'. Citizenship, according to this discourse, was based on membership of the nation, 'a Free and Gaelic Ireland', rather than the jurisdiction of the state (de Valera, 1922: 14). Yet the political nature of 'the Nation' is central to this concept, as evident in de

Valera's (1918: 4) statement: 'the one test of citizenship [is] that they place Ireland and her interests before those of any other nation'. In this way, unionists are seen as opting themselves out of citizenship of the Irish nation, for 'they are proud to have upheld here an enemy's flag for 300 years. Are these Irishmen or Englishmen – which?' (de Valera, 1918: 4). According to republican discourse, the move from being 'subject of an Imperial Province' to 'citizen of an independent sovereign State' should remove all ambiguity about national allegiance because the rights and duties of citizenship were coterminous with the duties and rights of the state towards the citizen (de Valera, 1926: 2).

According to the republican ideal, the 'allegiance and service' of the citizen was rewarded by the 'Nation'/state's duty 'to assure that every citizen shall have the opportunity to spend his or her strength and faculties in the service of the people'. Similarly, whilst every citizen had a right to 'an adequate share of the produce of this Nation's labour', 'the Nation' had a right to the 'willing service' of its citizens. Moreover, it was 'to the public right and welfare' that 'all right to private property' should be subordinated (de Valera, 1922: 13). It is possible to see this interpretation of citizenship in some later instances of elite discourse, for example, Seán MacBride's (1985: 22) comment:

> Until comparatively recently, the purchasing of Irish goods was regarded as part of the essential requirement of good citizenship and was considered a civic duty in order to promote employment. Now, no one seems to care.

MacBride bemoans the move towards a notion of citizenship that underplays the duties of the citizens towards the nation-state and instead asserts the duties of the state towards its citizens.

Such a change was embodied in Lynch's (28 May 1971) description of the state's role as 'the guardian of the civil and religious liberties of all the citizens of the nation' and Cosgrave's (26 June 1974) statement on behalf of the government:

> Our primary obligation is to safeguard the institutions which have been entrusted to us as elected representatives of the people and to safeguard the lives and property of our citizens.

A speech made by Haughey (11 October 1981) in reply to Fine Gael's 'constitutional crusade' also epitomises a change in the notion of citizenship, despite being given on the occasion of the unveiling of a memorial to de Valera: 'Our Constitution has been availed of time and time again by individual citizens to assert some particular right or liberty'. This move away from a communitarian to a more individualistic notion of citizenship in the 1970s was a highly significant element in the reconsideration of the position of the Irish state in relation to Northern Ireland. It also complemented the ideals of European integration, with Irish official discourse able to present the EU as another means of enhancing the 'rights and liberties' of Irish citizens.

Sovereignty and neutrality

Membership of the European Union also related to another central area of the model of Irish statehood, i.e. sovereignty. At the foundation of the state, Irish republicans asserted that sovereignty is a nation's inalienable right according to 'immutable natural law' (de Valera, 1922: 6). This was reiterated nearly thirty years later in the Bipartisan Declaration adopted by the Dáil which 're-affirm[ed]':

> *the sovereign right* of the people of Ireland to choose its own form of Government and, through its democratic institutions, to decide all questions of national policy, *free from outside interference*. (Costello and de Valera, 10 May 1949, emphasis added)

This declaration reflects the importance of the principle of sovereignty in Irish official discourse and, more specifically, the determination to maintain its expression in the international arena through a policy of military neutrality. The link between neutrality and sovereignty has been a fundamental tenet of Irish nationalism in the twentieth century. As Ahern (29 March 1999) notes: 'Neutrality in Ireland's case has been an important expression of sovereignty'. Neutrality has been considered an important expression of Ireland's 'natural' independence from Britain; wartime gave the Irish elite an opportunity to assert a distinct position in international affairs even prior to the establishment of the Irish state. Thus, de Valera declared in 1918: 'As a nation, Ireland in its present position should stand neutral as regards all powers but England.' The desire to stand independently from its dominant neighbour on the world stage was reiterated by de Valera to the League of Nations in 1936: 'All the small states can do, if the statesmen of greater states fail in their duty, is resolutely to determine that they will not become the tools of any great power.'

The fact that de Valera is speaking in defence of 'small states' points to a core element of Irish neutrality – that it is not only an expression of independence, it is a *tactic* in international affairs. As small states (in economic and territorial terms) cannot hope to compete for influence or a strong voice on the world stage on equal terms with large states, neutrality is a means of making their foreign policy noticeable. For example, Haughey (2 November 1985) lauds the qualities of small nations and their unique role in international affairs and asserts: 'We must pursue a policy of positive neutrality and maintain and strengthen an independent, distinctive outlook on world issues.' Haughey's urging of Ireland to not only 'maintain' but to 'strengthen' an independent outlook in international relations is notable in the context of European integration. As will be discussed below, membership of the European Union has generally been presented in Irish official discourse as compatible with Irish neutrality. This is essentially because a core tenet of the Irish governmental elite's approach to EU membership has been that it complements, even fulfils, the sovereignty of the Irish state.[8] Hence, Ahern (8 January 2001) is able to encourage another small state, Malta, that Ireland's 'European experience' has not lessened the 'neutral and independent-minded' character of the Irish state.

European integration and the Irish state

Framework: independence through interdependence

Realising independence

A new approach to independence developed in official Irish nationalism in the first thirty years of EU membership. This may be summarised as the perception that the independence of the Irish state is not 'an end in itself' and that the state has actually had to move 'beyond independence' in order to fulfil its needs (Ahern, 22 April 2001). The European Union has been presented in Irish official discourse as facilitating both the affirmation of Irish independence and the move 'beyond' it. Accession to the EEC was itself, Commissioner Peter Sutherland (1988: 4) claims, 'the ultimate expression of our hard-won independence'. Moreover, the Irish state has moved beyond this point as membership of the EU enabled it to overcome the underdevelopment 'that had not been cured by political independence' (Ahern, 29 October 1998). In addition, EU membership enhanced Irish independence by integrating Ireland into a 'wider economic and political environment' and enabling it 'to interact on a basis of equality' with fellow members (Sutherland, 1988: 4; Ahern, 15 April 1999). The subsequent broadening of 'Irish political and cultural horizons' and 'internationalisation of the Irish economy' are related to the role of the EU in Ireland's adjustment to a context of interdependence (Ahern, 15 April 1999; 9 January 2001). Ahern (9 January 2001) tells an audience in the prospective member-state of Cyprus that, 'in an era of globalisation, there is no feasible alternative to the route of modernisation and openness', and he notes the necessity of this adjustment. Nevertheless, he is quick to assert that, 'while being aware that in today's world interdependence is more than ever a reality', the Irish government and people 'cherish our independence' (Ahern, 9 January 2001; 8 January 2001).

The European Union, therefore, is envisaged as simultaneously enhancing Ireland's independence in the international sphere and its interdependence with other states. In this way, Ireland's independence – securing its own future and gaining control over its external situation – has been achieved *through* membership of the European Community. This portrayal of Ireland's position in the EU again reflects the complex nature of official nationalism (able to present two apparently divergent factors as complementary). It also points to the unique nature of the community and polity of the EU, whose development is presented in Irish official discourse as conjoined with that of the nation-state. As a government information leaflet on the Single European Act claimed:

> Being part of *that* kind of community is very much in Ireland's interest. This co-operation gives Ireland a more effective voice in world affairs, without compromising our independence. (GIS, 1987a: 2, 3)

Meeting national interests

The projects of the nation-state and the European Union are also seen as complementary in the area of 'interests'. The perception that membership of the European Community is about the fulfilment of national interests has remained a core tenet of Irish official discourse. Haughey's (7 May 1972) exclamation – 'I cannot understand how any patriotic Irishman or woman can oppose our going into Europe' – is integrally related to his assurances that EEC members would work together 'for our mutual benefit'.[9] In the context of moving from a net recipient to a net contributor within a twenty-seven member EU, the Irish governmental elite has continued to acknowledge that 'the EU has been good for Ireland in direct, material ways'. Yet it has also sought to counter suggestions that Ireland's membership is one-dimensional, assuring both a national and international audience that Ireland's experience of the EU 'by no means ends there' (Ahern, 29 March 2001b).

For, in a way similar to going 'beyond independence', EU membership has been presented as extending Ireland's horizons 'beyond [its] own national interests' by giving Ireland 'the means and opportunity to influence the evolution of the European Union' itself (Ahern, 9 January 2001). The notion of the interconnection of the interests of Ireland and those of the EU is reflected in Andrews' (20 April 1998) support for the Treaty of Amsterdam: 'It is in our best interests as a people to retain our place at the forefront of the Union's development.' See also Minister for Foreign Affairs Ray Burke's (28 October 1997) synopsis of Ireland's EU membership:

We have benefitted from membership by virtue of better access to wider markets and enhanced appeal to foreign investors on account of our location within the EU. We have also contributed actively to the advancement of European integration and will continue to do so.

Thus, official discourse has attempted to argue (as in these quotations from two Ministers for Foreign Affairs, from Fianna Fáil and Labour) both that the EU has provided 'a constructive external framework within which to pursue [Ireland's] national interests', and that, in response, Ireland has 'helped to determine the paths which the Union will take' (Burke, 2 October 1997; Spring, 7 February 1997).

Presenting European and national interests as mutually complementary has been a theme of Irish official discourse since accession, when EEC membership was perceived as an 'historic opportunity to break out of the disadvantageous, circumscribed position we have been in for centuries' (Haughey, 7 May 1972). The pursuit of further European integration was therefore seen as related to the fulfilment of Irish national interests. One important measurement of this was the growth of EEC initiatives for regional development – a priority area for the Irish economy, as noted in chapter 7. As a consequence, the EEC's 'continuing inability to reduce the serious regional imbalances within its borders' had, according to Haughey (26 March 1981), 'created doubts in some minds as to the political will of Europe to progress towards its fundamental aim of closer union'. Disappointment in Ireland at the progress of European integration continued until the late 1980s. The resulting frustration was expressed during a Dáil Debate on the Dooge Report, in which Haughey (26 June 1985) outlined a 're-appraisal' of Ireland's membership of the EEC. Haughey's comments centred on a call for the formation of an 'alliance' with other less developed member-states to campaign for 'effective redistributional Community policies'. Yet the way he phrased this argument, with a combination of what may be termed pro-interdependence and pro-independence rhetoric, perfectly encapsulates the 'productive paradox' at the core of Ireland's relationship with the European Community:

> *In discussing the future direction of the European Community today, we are also discussing the future of the Irish nation.* Ireland's place is in Europe. But history has taught us that we must never rely on others to ensure our interests and our welfare . . . *There is no case to be made for sacrificing our vital interests solely for the sake of being regarded as 'good Europeans'* . . . We remain one of the less favoured regions of the EEC and we should have no illusions about it. (Haughey, 26 June 1985, emphasis added)

In the very different economic context of the late 1990s, the European Union was portrayed less as a foundation for inter-state co-operation and more as 'a constructive external framework within which to pursue [Irish] national interests' (Burke, 2 October 1997). The explicit prioritising of national interests in Ireland's approach to the EU is partly a response to changes that are occurring within the Union itself. For example, one of the 'two major objectives' of Irish foreign policy for the early twenty-first century was defined by Cowen (31 May 2000, emphasis added) as 'to *promote and protect Ireland's interests in the EU as it deepens* its level of integration and prepares for Enlargement'. Perceptions of the relationship between national and European interests continue to adjust alongside perception of the 'European polity' and, specifically, Ireland's place within it. Nevertheless, Irish official discourse consistently projects the image of Ireland as an enthusiastic and committed member-state. This image persists, despite evidence – in the form of referendum results, opinion polls and voter turnout at elections to the European Parliament – to the contrary. Indeed, it is even more strongly reiterated at such times, as seen in the following quotations from speeches given by Taoiseach Bertie Ahern in the lead-up to and the aftermath of the first referendum on the Treaty of Nice:

> the Irish people are among the most positive in Europe about the EU
> . . .We are strongly committed and enthusiastic members . . . Excited
> reports of growing Irish Euroscepticism are well wide of the mark. (Ahern,
> 1 March 2001b)

> I wish to state that the Government, the vast majority of the members of
> this House and in my view the vast majority of the Irish people are com-
> mitted to Ireland's full and active membership of the European Union, and
> to the Union's enlargement. (Ahern, 12 June 2001)

The two-way 'relationship' between Ireland and the EU has been consistently emphasised, not least as confirmation that Irish sovereignty is not diminished but enhanced by EU membership. The idea that the relationship between Ireland and the EU is mutually beneficial, rather than one of Irish dependence, works to affirm the image of a confident, independent state within the EU. Ahern's quotation of Chancellor Schröder's statement that, 'Ireland has experienced solidarity from the EU and now shows this very solidarity back to the Union as well', is a good example of this relationship being seen as both recognised and practised.[10]

The nation-based EU polity

Despite frequent reiteration of the broad success of European integration, successive members of the Irish governmental elite have not attempted to clarify the form and nature of the 'political entity' they envisage. With the exception of FitzGerald's (20 May 1978) statement of anticipation of a

'Federal Europe' (which is in any case focused primarily on the future status of Northern Ireland rather than the EU), Irish official discourse has not generally engaged specific terms regarding the political blueprint of the EU. Although occasionally willing to set out what they do *not* envisage for the European polity – such as Ahern's (14 May 2001a) statement that 'rapid movement towards a more federal Europe would be neither desirable nor feasible in the foreseeable future' – members of the governmental elite have not engaged in detailed discussion of the ideal framework of EU governance. Instead, the 'unique' nature of the EU and its institutions has been affirmed, with a particular emphasis on its relationship to the nation-states within it. For example, Ahern states that the EU 'is a totally new form of political institution', 'based on the identification of common interests and the cherishing of cultural and national identities' and 'reflecting the unique circumstances, histories and needs of the people of Europe' (30 April 1998; 8 January 2001). As elaborated in chapter 6, the European Union has consistently been lauded in Irish official discourse for being based on 'the recognition rather than the suppression of individual national identity and culture' (Haughey, 2 December 1981). Indeed, a central pillar of Ireland's support for European integration has been the assurance that political union in Europe was to be '*the creation of the peoples* and *governments* that are members of the Community' (Haughey, 26 July 1967, emphasis added). Nearly twenty years later, Haughey's (26 June 1985) vision of the European polity was even more explicitly state centred: 'At this stage European Union can only be based on the sovereign nation-states of Europe'.

The notion of nation-states providing the 'building blocks' for European Union has been a consistent theme in Irish official discourse on European integration. For example, although FitzGerald (7 September 1976, emphasis added) sees the experience of the first years of EEC membership as '*not* suggest[ing] that governments left to themselves are likely . . . to become a major source of European dynamism', he argues for a European polity of which the nation-state is the 'building block':

> In the United States of Europe of the future the building blocks of the nation-states will retain much more of their present roles, especially in the social and cultural areas, devolving upwards only those economic and political functions which could no longer, in the world of the 21st century, be exercised effectively at the nation-state level. (FitzGerald, 7 September 1976)

It is worth unravelling this conception of governance in a future EU polity based on a principle of subsidiarity. Whilst the European level of governance would perform economic and political functions that can no

longer be performed effectively at a national level, the nation-states
oversee social and cultural policies: 'the *national governments*, whose
essential role, above all as the *guardians of the cultural identities* of their
peoples, will survive indefinitely' (FitzGerald, 7 September 1976, emphasis added).

The political and economic functions of governance are thus distinguished from the cultural and ideological ones. The significance of the
state's 'essential' role in relation to the nation is, however, preserved
'indefinitely'. Twenty-five years later, Ahern (21 June 2001, emphasis
added) echoes FitzGerald's emphasis on the role of the nation-state in
relation to the identity of the European polity:

> the basic building block of Europe, *the core political reality, is the nation
> state*. It is with their own country and their own national institutions that
> people across Europe, including in Ireland, most directly and most power-
> fully *identify*. The evolution of the Union must be consistent with that
> reality.

Moreover, Ahern (9 January 2001, emphasis added) asserts 'it is essential that *the Government*, and all other *domestic* social and economic
players, recognise the continuing critical importance of the policy
choices they make and the actions they take'. Whilst Ahern (1 March
2001b; 5 February 2001) recognises that 'EU membership has been a
vital part of our success', he is also quick to point to the central role of
the state, noting that the EU does not offer 'a magic wand' or a 'magic
formula for effortless success'. Ultimately, the EU polity is conceived as a
framework within which Ireland manages its 'own affairs as a sovereign
independent State' (Ahern, 15 April 1999).

Narrative: self-determination through co-operation

The European project

> The European story also calls to mind the changes that have come about
> within Irish society, and the revolution in attitudes that has occurred
> during our first quarter century of European involvement. (Quinn, 7 May
> 1997)

If the nation-state forms the 'building block' of the European polity, narratives of the historical roots and ideological motivation of the European
political project serve not only to enhance the EU's legitimacy but also
to reflect Ireland's experience of EU membership. Even if not explicitly
outlined, such narratives are referred to in most examples of official Irish
discourse on the European Union. To take a specific case, the Irish government's support for enlargement of the European Union has centred

on drawing links between, as the Minister of State in the DFA (O'Donnell, 20 November 1997) put it, the EU's historical 'vocation to promote peace, security and progress' and Ireland's own experience of membership:

> the entire process of European integration bears witness to the fact that *peace* and *co-operation* can supplant age-old rivalries. *History has shown*, both *in our own case* and that of other entrants into the Union, that *nations have joined the European project* in order *to draw strength* from its collective *ideals*, its *economic* coherence, and its *democratic* dynamic. (Ahern, 9 January 2001, emphasis added)

Examination of a range of excerpts of official discourse, in which the 'European project' is defined, highlights the repetition of particular themes, namely 'democracy' and 'prosperity'. For example, Andrews' (20 May 1998) description of the European Union as 'a project for peace, security and prosperity founded on principles of democracy and human rights'. These principles went, according to Ahern, 'hand in hand' as the fundamental purposes of the 'founding fathers of the Union' were 'to rid Western Europe of the scourge of war, and to make its people better off' (8 January 2001; 1 March 2001b). The following quotation is an extract from a Seanad statement by Ahern (8 February 2001) on the meeting of the European Council at Nice. Its focus on the 'moral' nature of the European project reflects a core theme in the government's subsequent campaign for the ratification of the Nice Treaty:

> The European Union has an historic duty to underpin freedom and democracy, and to promote prosperity and partnership, throughout Europe. It was itself founded for those very purposes.

The fact that 'the precise form' of the end result of the 'project' of European integration has remained unclear, or not agreed, at both a European and national level, has made the use of 'positive' discourse in support of the project even more vital (Haughey, 26 July 1967). Minister for Finance Ruairi Quinn (7 May 1997) justifies this ambiguity by reasoning that:

> The EU story is a still unfolding one . . . there are new twists all the time, for the EU does not, and cannot, stand still. It needs to evolve to meet its peoples' changing needs.

The result of the first Irish referendum on the Treaty of Nice in June 2001 may be seen as reflecting the insufficiency of the narrative of the EU as a project for 'democracy' when the democratic credentials of the evolving EU polity were in question. Yet, although the first referendum on an EU treaty to be defeated since Irish accession, the debates surrounding Nice

I were not the first to include apparent disillusion with the European project among the Irish population. Indeed, international events within the first few years of Irish accession combined with internal disagreement within the EEC to produce a situation of stagnation and blighted hopes for the new member-state. In response to uncertainty surrounding the precise nature of the EU polity, the Irish governmental elite have presented the member-states as 'ensuring' the maintenance of democracy in the EU (Ahern, 21 March 2000).[11] Irish official discourse thus represents the EU as a project in which individual states co-operate in seeking democracy and prosperity in Europe.

Batting the European ball

The 'nation-state' is, therefore, central to both the EU polity under construction and to the defence of its common ideals. This was epitomised in the mid-1970s to late 1980s, when Irish criticism of the EEC often centred on its perceived betrayal of the European ideal through a drift into a 'dreary sea of trivialities' and 'partisan self-interests' (Haughey, 24 June 1976).[12] In response to the frustrating lack of progress, Irish official discourse placed Ireland in the role of defending the European ideal. As a consequence, the projection in official discourse of the European ideal and narrative holding great meaning and value for Ireland remained consistent and unambiguous throughout this period – and the apparent rapport between Ireland and Europe was maintained.

For more than a decade from the mid-1970s, Irish official discourse upheld an image of the European ideal as a focus of expectation whilst directing blame for the disappointing progress of European co-operation towards the larger member-states. In 1979, Commissioner Dick Burke (1979: v) explains the 'faltered' pace of European integration in terms of the economic recession, the strain of enlargement in 1973, a weakening of the EEC institutions and:

> a renewed tendency (in some member-states) to see things in national terms and to look for national solutions to problems, at the expense of the Community perspective.

This last point was supported by Haughey who made scathing criticisms of the European Community for its failure to deliver the economic rewards of membership that Ireland had anticipated – a deficiency that Haughey interpreted as directly related to the influence of individual member-states in the EEC. To be more precise, Haughey, along with the Irish political elite in general, resented the negative impact that Britain's 'Eurosceptic' stance had on the progress of EEC policy development. Indeed, there is continuity between Ireland's postcolonial self-conception and the image of Ireland defending grand ideals from being subsumed by the interests of dominant states. Haughey's criticisms are framed as arising from a concern to defend the 'European' ideal although his central objections and motivations were undoubtedly centred on uniquely Irish concerns. Hence, frustration at the stalling tactics of Britain is expressed in his lamentation 'there are no political leaders to take this floundering concept [of European union] by the shoulders' (24 June 1976).[13] On occasions, in his criticism of other member-states, Haughey (1 May 1980) even goes as far as to downplay the significance of national interests in the EEC:

> The Community cannot be complacent or negative in its approach, and, above all, members should not seek solutions separately or nationally . . . While national objectives obviously can never be far from our minds, they, in the reality of today's conditions, can never be the final motivation. To my mind, Europe and its peoples depend on each other now in a way which is without precedent in history.

However, a close connection exists between Haughey's self-appointed role as campaigner for the 'Community ideal' (a role replicated by many other leading members of the political elite) and Ireland's national interests. Haughey's (13 December 1974) comments as a backbench TD during a Dáil Debate on the 1974 Paris Summit, reflect the notion that the highest ideals and interests of the European Community essentially complemented those of Ireland:

> We have a fundamental interest in ensuring that the Community progresses, that integration proceeds and that the overall objectives of the Community are pursued. We have just as vital an interest in that as we have in any particular matter where our immediate interest is concerned. . . In pursuing a particular line which in the short term would appear to be very much in our own interests, it could also happen that it was in the overall interest of the Community.

On the occasions that Irish national interests were seen as conflicting with EEC decisions, Haughey presents Ireland as defending the ideals of the EEC whilst criticising its practice. Take, for example, the way in which Haughey (26 March 1981), now Taoiseach, conveys dissatisfaction with the outcome of the Maastricht European Council of March 1981 (which dealt with agricultural policy, an area of fundamental importance to Ireland) in terms of suspicion of other member-states' commitment to the European project:

> What is happening in agriculture is aggravating the Community's greatest failure to date – its continuing inability to reduce the serious regional imbalances within its borders. *This failure has created doubt* in some

minds *as to the political will of Europe* to progress *towards its fundamental aim of closer union.* (emphasis added)

In the wake of another European Council meeting, the Athens Summit,
the outcome of which included decisions on agricultural surpluses and
levies that went against Ireland's negotiating stance, Haughey (7
December 1983), as leader of the opposition, makes a similar com-
plaint:

> It is a depressing truth that Europe today is far more a group of national
> member states . . . [the Summit] was simply a question of each individual
> member State stating its position and demand. The Community ideal and
> spirit have been diminishing . . . It seems to me that Heads of Government
> go to European Councils more as ambassadors and spokesmen for their
> own national interests than as European leaders committed to an ideal of
> European integration.

Haughey is deflecting criticism of his government for its failure to secure
Ireland's interests by claiming a 'moral victory' in terms of valuing the
'Community spirit' above divisive national demands. This tactic epito-
mises the integrally state-centred approach to European integration in
Irish official nationalism.

Model: European democracy through national sovereignty

National mediator between EU and its citizens

If, according to official Irish discourse, the nation-state is the building
block of the EU polity, it is also the mediator between the EU and its citizens. This has significant implications for the meaning and practice of
democracy within the EU polity, and is exacerbated by ambiguity about
the type of polity that the EU is to be and the location of governing power
within it. On the one hand, official discourse presents the national government as pushing the EU towards becoming a more democratic entity;
on the other hand, it presents the national state as defending the national
interests of Irish citizens in the context of the EU. This theme is most
clearly expressed during referendum campaigns on EU treaties, as seen
in the assertion, repeated by Ahern (1 January 1998) and Andrews (20
May 1998), that the Treaty of Amsterdam would 'enable the Union to
address more effectively the direct concerns of its citizens'.

However, new rights for EU citizens have not been laid out in official
Irish discourse (with the exception of consumer rights). The duties of
EU citizenship have only been indirectly referred to, as the Minister for
Foreign Affairs Brian Cowen (3 May 2001) urged the electorate to vote
in referendums on EU treaties 'not just for themselves, but also on behalf

of our fellow Europeans'. To the extent that voting in such a referendum fulfils a 'duty of community solidarity', the Irish electorate may be said to be experiencing a sense of participation in the polity of the European Union (Ahern, 29 October 1998). Yet a sense of 'belonging' to the Union as its citizens is not specifically encouraged or directed by Irish official discourse. The Irish governmental elite rarely credits the EU alone for such developments; instead, it frequently points to the central role that it has played in the construction of a more democratic Union. For example, Labour's Minister for Finance, Quinn (7 May 1997), claims that the Irish Presidency revised the draft Maastricht Treaty to include 'a promise of greater transparency and openness in the operation of the Union and its institutions'. This is essential, Quinn argues, 'if the Union's workings are to be understood and accepted by its citizens' and thus redress the fact that 'the citizen tends to feel at a distance' from the EU.

The distance between the EU and its citizens exists at many levels, including in comprehension of the EU's functioning, involvement in its development and identification with its foundational principles. Attempts to maintain support for European integration have focused on showing that 'the EU is continuing to deliver results' (Ahern, 1 March 2001b). Official discourse also uses analogies of nation-statehood to support the image of the EU as democratic and relevant to its citizens; for example, 'the European Union has all the ingredients of domestic politics' (Quinn, 7 May 1997). Yet the Irish governing elite is wary of giving the impression that the EU is in competition with the nation-state, or threatening to expand into its particular realm of combining governance with a collective identity. This tension is seen in Cowen's (19 May 2001) response to questions on the shape of the future EU: 'European institutions, despite the fact that they have an everyday importance on lives of citizens in Europe, are not seen in the same way as national institutions or local institutions.'

Thus, whilst Irish politicians have been unable to ignore the 'genuine anxieties and concerns about the future' felt by the electorate towards the European Union, they are still focused on the role of the nation-state in the process of change that this demands (Ahern, 8 June 2001). Hence, Ahern's (8 June 2001, emphasis added) focus on 'democratic accountability *in each member-state*' and Harney's (4 June 2001) reassurance that the securing of 'Ireland's interests in Europe and the world' will be carried out by '[t]he political leaders you trust', namely the *Irish* political leaders. This notion arises from the Irish governmental elite's conception of the sovereignty of the Irish state and the way it relates to the processes of European integration.

Pooling sovereignty

De Valera's political heirs began to accept from the late 1950s onwards that his aim of 'a glorious world mission' for the Irish nation, if it was to be anything more than a 'spiritual' mission, was incompatible with the principle of absolute sovereignty (de Valera, 1918: 2). Eight years into EEC membership, in a statement made to a meeting of the European Council, Haughey (1 May 1980) asserted that the objective of 'world peace and stability' could only be achieved through the *co-ordination of policies* by small and medium-sized states. Membership of the EEC was presented in official discourse as an – or, rather, *the* – opportunity to modernise Ireland through interaction and equality with other states. Shifting norms in international relations, combined with ideals of post-war Europe, provided the contextual framework for membership of the European Community that was based on 'a willingness to share sovereignty with a number of our neighbours' (FitzGerald, 5 June 1982).

The declining virulence of the *ideal* of sovereignty (to be defended by the state as an inalienable right of the nation) has been accompanied in official Irish discourse by a growing emphasis on the *utility* of sovereignty. This was evident in the lead up to the first referendum on the Treaty of Nice in 2001, when the government coined a new definition of 'true sovereignty':

> not a theoretical concept but measure of how successfully we can protect and promote our basic national interests and our social and economic well-being as a people. (Ahern, 29 March 2001b; also Cowen, 14 May 2001)

This definition of sovereignty was used by the government to justify its support for further European integration, as the above quotation continued:

> our consistent policy towards the EU over the past thirty years has done far more to achieve both purposes than any narrow policy of isolationism would have.

It also supports a move away from adherence to the concept of absolute sovereignty towards sharing sovereignty for practical ends:

> Pooling sovereignty to the EU has made it possible for us to project our values and goals more effectively in the wider world and to have some degree of influence over those global trends which are shaping the future. (Ahern, 1 March 2001b)

At the core of Ireland's relationship with the EU, therefore, has been the sovereignty of Ireland. In this way, the EU has been presented as enhancing Ireland's ability to play an independent and 'distinctive role' in

Europe, for the benefit of Ireland, its citizens and the EU itself (O'Donnell, 15 August 1997).

Neutrality and the EU

Tensions within Irish official discourse regarding the political project of European Union and the sovereignty of the Irish nation-state are evident on the subject of Irish neutrality and the impact of EU integration on Ireland's 'distinctive' foreign policy. Although there were concerns raised regarding the implications of accession to the EEC for Irish neutrality, the Irish governmental elite consistently argued that the two were compatible. This is primarily because of a fairly ambiguous definition of neutrality rather than a highly restricted conception of the EEC. For instance, Haughey (15 September 1967) explicitly states that the European Union involves 'economic harmonisation, political solidarity and common defence arrangements'. Indeed, he goes beyond this to claim that a common defence policy is a necessary element of political union:

> We mean that we are fully aware that the Community as defined in the Treaty of Rome is intended to serve as a foundation for political unity and that we support this objective and are anxious to play our part in making it a reality . . . But, there is *one aspect about which we have no doubt*: political union without the capacity and means to defend that union would be utterly meaningless in the world in which we live today. The achievement of *political union, to my mind, necessarily implies the formulation of a common defence policy and the working-out of common defence arrangements*. (26 July 1967, emphasis added)

As late as 1981, Haughey was reiterating that, as a result of Ireland's pro-European stance, Ireland was willing to be involved in common defence arrangements in Europe:

> In the event, therefore of the European States being organised into a full political union, we would accept the obligations, even if these included defence. We could not, and would not, wish to opt out of the obligations and aims inherent in the achievement of European unity. (11 March 1981)

However, the above statements should be analysed in the same light as the ones Haughey made regarding defending the European ideal. For when the EEC did begin to take steps in this direction, within nine months of the above comments being made, Haughey's (2 December 1981) approach changed dramatically.

> Both the Community and Ireland will be losers if the pace is forced in this manner. The Community has nothing to gain by striving to become a military bloc or a superpower . . . It already has considerable economic and

political influence, much of which will be lost if it seeks to enter power politics. Ireland's entry to the Community was of great significance, as it showed that a neutral country could be a member of the EEC. Will this no longer be the case?

The issue of a common EEC stance on international affairs and Irish neutrality came to the fore the following year during the Falklands crisis. Haughey (23 May 1982) describes Ireland's response to the situation in terms of 'behaving as responsible, mature citizens of the world' – an expression of neutrality which he distinguishes from 'our Anglo-Irish relations, and even our position as a member of the European Community'. With specific regard to Ireland's position in a developing EEC, Haughey appears to backtrack on his previous assertions. For example, he bemoans what he describes as 'an attempt to push political union out in front' towards a 'defence oriented' Europe. Quite how seriously Haughey (6 December 1984) views this development is reflected in his conclusions:

> If Europe is not to be an independent entity in world affairs, then we Irish would be better off to retain our own independent voice as the most constructive contribution we can make to world peace and stability. It is not enough to say that we would have reservations about the military aspects of European union.

Haughey's absolute rejection of the link between political union and common defence arrangements is also evident in his assertion that the formalisation of political co-operation 'will have the definite effect of making the operation of an independent foreign policy like Ireland's more difficult' (4 December 1985). In the same statement to the Dáil on the draft European Act, the Taoiseach opposes 'any attempt to effect a wholesale transfer of sovereignty to the EEC institutions' on the grounds that it would leave 'a small country like Ireland in a dangerously exposed and vulnerable situation, apart altogether from its implications for our neutrality'.

This statement epitomises the fundamental point about Irish neutrality it is, as noted above, an emblem of Irish sovereignty and an expression of Ireland's 'freedom of decision' (Haughey, 19 April 1986). The assertion in a government information booklet that 'Ireland's defence policy will continue to be a matter for Ireland alone' encapsulates the correlation of sovereignty and neutrality (GIS, 1987f: 3). The continued importance of this principle of Irish official nationalism is reflected in the Declaration on Neutrality attached to the Single European Act before Ireland ratified it.[14] Indeed, neutrality arises as a point of debate in Ireland around every referendum on a European treaty precisely because it is seen as a sign of Irish sovereignty. The raising of this issue represents the clash less of two principles of Irish official nationalism than of two types of ambiguity: the meaning of Irish sovereignty in an interdependent context and the meaning of the European polity in relation to national independence.

Northern Ireland and the European polity

Framework: polity

Constitutional change

It was noted in the first section of this chapter that members of the Irish governmental elite from the early 1970s onwards pointed to the need to reconsider the structures of the Irish state as a means of responding to the situation in Northern Ireland. FitzGerald's 'constitutional crusade' focused on the role of the Irish state in exacerbating and (ideally) over-coming tensions between north and south. The purported motivation behind this campaign was the desire for re-unification and the changes called for by FitzGerald (27 October 1978) were predicated on the removal of 'obstacles' to this end:

> And as we in this State are seeking this association, the onus is on us to ensure appropriate modifications of any features of our Constitution, laws or practices which represent a genuine psychological obstacle to more open-minded unionists, who might in the absence of this psychological obstacle be willing in time to consider a different relationship between North and South.

As the above quotation shows, central to this movement was the belief that the foundational policies and laws of the Republic contributed to and maintained the exclusion of 'a part of the Irish people'. In contrast to the traditional discourse that placed the blame for partition and responsibility for changing the status of Northern Ireland with the British government, FitzGerald (27 September 1981) claims 'it was *we* who have divided this island' and therefore:

> The responsibility for action to change the situation and to remove the fun-damental obstacle to progress thus lies primarily with the people of the Irish State themselves. (FitzGerald, 5 June 1982)

The constitutional review subsequently initiated by FitzGerald in 1982 highlighted two key elements in the Constitution that impeded prospects for 'progress':

> The creation of a climate . . . to accommodate the different aspirations and fears of the two sections of the community in Northern Ireland, requires

action by the Irish State to make such changes as would be *necessary to create a pluralist society* within the territory of the State, *and to remove the claim to sovereignty over Northern Ireland* contained in the Constitution. (FitzGerald, 30 September 1982: 24, emphasis added)

However, any change that would be made to the Constitution of Ireland in terms of its view on the constitutional status of Northern Ireland could, it was recognised, only be made in the broader context of development in the Republic's relationship with both Northern Ireland and Britain. In the uneasy context of the early 1970s, there was not the political will amongst the British or the Irish governments to make a dramatic gesture in this way. Hence, Cosgrave's (13 March 1974) statement following a meeting with his British counterparts:

The Government were well aware that differences exist in the constitutional law of the Republic of Ireland and of the United Kingdom as to the status of Northern Ireland but they considered that it would not be helpful to debate those constitutional differences.

Nevertheless, incremental change in this position occurred on both sides over the ensuing decades, particularly in relation to a growing conception (in both the Republic and Britain) of Northern Ireland as a political entity in and of itself, not simply an uncomfortable British appendage or Irish lost property. As a result, the principle of majority consent within Northern Ireland for any change to its constitutional position to occur became a fundamental tenet of the policies of both governments. This principle was originally encapsulated in the Fine Gael statement on Northern Ireland (12 September 1969); later it was explicitly stated in the communiqué issued by Haughey's government following the Downing Street talks (Haughey, 21 May 1980)[15] and the communiqué issued by FitzGerald's (6 November 1981) government following the London summit.[16]

Despite his endorsement of the principle when Taoiseach, the highly sensitive nature of this issue and its implications for Irish official nationalism is apparent in Haughey's (15 May 1985) later criticism of a speech made by FitzGerald (22 March 1985). FitzGerald accepts that there could be 'no change in the constitutional status of Northern Ireland, involving a transfer of sovereignty, without the consent of a majority of the people in Northern Ireland'. Haughey decries this acceptance as 'essentially an endorsement of the British guarantee [in the 1949 Ireland Act of Northern Ireland's position in the UK]'. Haughey (19 November 1985) also criticises the Anglo-Irish Agreement for 'accepting British sovereignty over part of Ireland'. This is because of the affirmation in the Anglo-Irish Agreement (15 November 1985) that 'any change in the status of Northern Ireland would only come about with the consent of a majority of the people of Northern Ireland' (Article 1a). The principle of majority consent is also reaffirmed in the Joint Declaration for Peace (15 December 1993). Yet it was not until the Good Friday Agreement that the electorate of both jurisdictions endorsed this principle in referendums, marking the culmination of a thirty-year process of redefining Northern Ireland's constitutional status among the Irish governmental elite.

The EU and the Northern Ireland debate

At the heart of this reconsideration of Northern Ireland's constitutional status was the belief that the context and logic of the European Union necessarily changed the conceptualisation of political and governmental structures between EU member-states. At first, however, the EEC was seen primarily as a means of 'internationalising' the problems in Northern Ireland, taking it beyond a 'domestic' issue for the British government. Hence, even prior to accession, Lynch (20 October 1971) welcomes the establishment of a committee in the Council of Europe at Strasbourg to recommend 'appropriate legal and administrative provisions which would guarantee the involvement of the Northern minority in all decision-making and administrative processes'. Prior to the Sunningdale talks, Taoiseach Liam Cosgrave also diagnoses that 'the central issue in Northern Ireland has always been the absence of a basic consensus' and subsequently calls for 'the development of a system of institutions within the North that will be acceptable to its people, of both communities' (2 July 1973; 21 June 1973). However, following the collapse of the power-sharing institutions in Northern Ireland in 1974, the Irish government became increasingly aware that a 'solution' within Northern Ireland would have to be supported by a framework beyond it. The Irish governmental elite began to view the framework of the EEC as being instrumental to restructuring relations within the island of Ireland.

The model, example and context of EEC membership is evident in the proposal for an all-island council, and Taoiseach Lynch (6 August 1971) even comments that the EEC was 'particularly relevant' for such a development. Successive Irish government members suggested the establishment of an all-island council to complement the activities of the separate institutions north and south through formal co-operation, particularly in the economic arena. This supra-state council was envisaged as far more than a talking-shop by Lynch, who dismissed the proposition by Prime Minister Callaghan's goverment for 'a council for all Ireland' by comparing it unfavourably to the Council of Ireland laid out in the 1920 Government of Ireland Act. Lynch (6 August 1971) argues that the original Council of Ireland 'would have had real powers and was intended to have its powers extended eventually to the point where it would replace both the Parliament of the South and of the North and itself become the Parliament of all Ireland'. Lynch thus refuses to consider any all-island institution that does not have 'real powers or known or overt functions'. Fine Gael Taoiseach Cosgrave (2 July 1973) similarly supports the proposal for 'an effective Council of Ireland' which could respond to the aspiration of the minority of Northern Ireland 'which seeks reconciliation between North and South'. He envisages this council engaging 'the common interests of north and south in joint projects of common benefit'. In a sentence that encapsulates his prioritising of practical issues and, again, the antici-pation of increasingly formal co-operation between north and south, Cosgrave (2 July 1973) asserts that the council 'would accustom both parts of Ireland and all communities in the island to working together on pragmatic issues'.

New modes of governance

Another form of institutional arrangement based on common interests that was suggested by some members of the Irish governmental elite was (con)federalism. Although Lynch expresses an interest as early as 1969 in discussing possible federal arrangements with Britain as a 'solution' to Northern Ireland (see 28 August 1969; 20 September 1969), FitzGerald was the first party leader to clearly outline the implications of such an arrangement. In a booklet on the future of north-south relations, FitzGerald and Harte (1979: 23), the Fine Gael spokesman on Northern Ireland, explicitly reject the idea of a unitary state of Ireland for the reason that 'it would run counter to the reality of the existence today of two different political communities'. FitzGerald and Harte also dismiss the idea of a federation of the four provinces of Ireland (as suggested by Fennell 1972) for being 'contrived [and] administratively cumber-some'.[17] Yet they favour the establishment of a confederal government to which specific functions relating to the common interest of north and south would be delegated 'for the good of all the people of the island' (1979: 25–7, 23). Significantly, the areas under confederal control would be 'where the material interests of both parts of Ireland, *especially within the EEC*, are similar, and are often sharply differentiated from those of Britain' (FitzGerald, 30 September 1982: 22, emphasis added). Thus, many of these areas of common interest, such as economic policy, secu-rity and external relations, were seen as 'intrinsically linked with the EEC'. One by-product of this arrangement would be that both the states of Northern Ireland and the Republic would have 'a large measure of autonomy' but 'subject to EEC constraints' (FitzGerald, and Harte 1979: 27, 13). It is clear, then, that the this 'Irish Confederation', in which '[s]overeignty in respect of different matters would reside in different places, according to the needs of the occasion' was conceived very much in the context of the EEC (FitzGerald, 5 June 1982: 24).

These proposals – for an all-island council or an Irish confederation – are notable for their exclusion of Britain in the conceptualisation of a new constitutional position for Northern Ireland. This is essentially a legacy of the non-British principle of Irish official nationalism's definition of the ideal polity for the island of Ireland. This was made clear in a speech given by Lynch (20 February 1971) rejecting the 'formalisation' of the British-Irish relationship whilst admitting its significance:

> *The relationship between Ireland and Britain requires no formalisation.* Indeed, the attempts, for centuries, to bind the relationship into formulas which took no account of Irish nationhood, failed. Since the failure was admitted 50 years ago the relationship between Britain and the South has become all the stronger for being a mutually valuable one without over-tones of conquest. The remnant of that conquest, which is an aspect of the division of Ireland remains the only but dangerous disaffection in what has become otherwise a unique condition between independent countries. (emphasis added)

This extract epitomises the approach taken by the Irish government to its relationship with Britain in the early 1970s. The Irish governmental elite wanted more influence in the affairs of Northern Ireland without damaging the relationship between the two sovereign states. This objective benefited directly from joint membership of the EEC, for the Community provided a *new context* for relations between Britain and Ireland as well as a *new model* for inter-state co-operation. As Taoiseach Charles Haughey (29 May 1980) noted:

> what is now required is a willingness on the part of the two sovereign Governments . . . to address the problem jointly by setting a wholly new context and encouraging progress towards a settlement . . . steps can now be taken to establish a new framework for a solution. This would take full account of all that has changed in the relations between the two islands and in Western Europe since Northern Ireland was first established.

Indeed, the most significant element of the new framework of governance for Northern Ireland has been due in part to the connection between change in western Europe and in Europe's 'western isles', i.e. Ireland and the United Kingdom.

New British-Irish relationship

This connection has been central to the recent peace process in Northern Ireland, as confirmed by Ahern (29 March 2001b):

> The strong relationship between the two Governments has been the bedrock on which the peace process, and the Good Friday Agreement, have been built – and, of course, the EU has very generously supported us in building reconciliation and in stimulating North/South links.

Ahern asserts that the new British-Irish relationship had been 'greatly enhanced' by the EU context in which the two states were enabled 'to see each other in a more rounded way, drawing on our joint experience as EU partners', which highlighted their 'many shared interests and objectives' (8 January 2001; 29 March 2001b). The institutional expression of this partnership between Britain and Ireland regarding their shared interest in establishing peace in Northern Ireland was the British-Irish Council, which Ahern (9 January 2001) describes as reflecting 'complexity' of relationships within the western isles of Ireland and the United Kingdom. Thus, what FitzGerald and Harte (1979: 34) define as the 'innovatory spirit' of the European Union towards institutional arrangements is embodied in the 'unique form' of the British-Irish Council and the 'new era' of relations between the western isles that it heralds (29 March 1999, Ahern, 1 March 2001a,).

In a comment made in a lecture in Edinburgh, Ahern (29 October 1998) even considered that the British-Irish Council could develop into 'a loose confederation'; however, he was quick to affirm that such an arrangement would 'fully respect[] sovereignty'. The fact that this comment was made to a Scottish audience is no coincidence, for the implementation of devolution to Scotland and Wales in the United Kingdom represents (according to Nairn [2000]) the *rising* prominence of nationhood and, indeed, sovereignty in the contemporary European context. The British-Irish Council embodies what may be termed this 'productive paradox': the enhancing of national sovereignty through supranational institutions. In finding a 'solution' for Northern Ireland, official discourse in Ireland has been able to marry the concepts of interdependence and inter-state co-operation with those of independence and sovereignty through the use of ideals and images associated with the European project itself.

Narrative: partnership

Images of co-operation

Schuman and Monnet rightly saw that by working together we, the peoples of Europe, could ensure that never again would our continent be ravaged by war. I share this vision, and it enjoys the strong support of the Irish people. (Ahern, 9 May 2001)

There are two ways in which parallels can be drawn between the narratives of European integration and narratives of conflict resolution in official Irish discourse: (1) the identification of common images/analogies, and (2) the use of common words/phrases. Central to the project of European integration is the narrative of co-operative partnership as opposed to conflict. The image of European integration as an alternative to war is given credibility by references to the historical roots of the European Union. FitzGerald (11 July 1985) uses such imagery during a Dáil debate in which he likens the Anglo-Irish Agreement to the origins of the European Union. 'We have begun to transcend a part of our history that has been dangerously limiting and even positively dangerous', he argued, 'not many countries can transcend their history in this way'. Yet, the significant exception was that of France and Germany, who 'now have a relationship that no one could have foreseen forty years ago'. Reminders of previous conflicts in Europe are frequently used to maintain support for the vision of European integration. They have also been used to stimulate support for the peace process in Northern Ireland, as seen in Ahern's statement on the inauguration of the Memorial Peace Park at Messines (11 November 1998):

> As the 20th century draws to a close, we hope that we will never again see the bloody conflict between nations that scarred the battlefields of Europe over so many centuries. Ireland's contribution to that must above all be a determination to work the Good Friday Agreement in all its aspects . . . and to ensure that the fundamental political differences on this island are in future peacefully restored.

Ahern's description of the conflict in Ireland as one of 'political differences' is significant in itself, not least because it implies that these tensions can, indeed must, be resolved through political means. Indeed, during the campaign for the ratification of the Good Friday Agreement, Ahern (20 May 1998) claims that Ireland reflected 'the essence of the European model' in its acceptance of difference 'in the fullest sense – through accommodation'. The European Union is, therefore, presented as embodying the political and peaceful resolution of 'age old European rivalries' (Burke, 2 October 1997). This supports Lynch's (20 September 1969) declaration that: 'Differences in political outlook or religious belief need not set people apart . . . and are no barrier to effective and constructive co-operation.' Thus, although few members of the Irish political elite, either then or now, would confidently ascribe to FitzGerald's (20 May 1978: 12) vision of the 'evolution of the European

Community into a Federation of States', the technique of drawing parallels between the EU and Northern Ireland is common to official
discourse:

> In speaking of a united Europe, and of the Federal Europe we look forward
> to in the future, we remind ourselves by these words 'United' and Federal'
> of our own domestic problem of unity within Ireland, perhaps to be
> achieved through a Federal structure.

Shared language of peace

FitzGerald's highlighting of the significance of two particular words for
both the EU and Ireland leads into the second point, namely the use of
similar words and phrases in Irish official discourse regarding both
European integration and Northern Ireland. For example, in a speech to
the UN General Assembly, Cowen (14 September 2000) describes the
task of the Irish government as 'to work with others in peace, partnership and in a spirit of mutual tolerance and respect, building together a
better future for all the people of Ireland'. The tools used to build this
future are, according to Ahern (20 May 1998), those of 'negotiation,
compromise and agreement'. Significantly, this language is also present
in Ahern's speeches to republican audiences, such as at the Arbour Hill
Commemoration (26 April 1998) in which Ahern reaffirms his desire for
a united Ireland, but states that:

> We can only bring about a united Ireland through a process of co-
> operation and engagement. But that closer *co-operation, engagement and
> friendship* is good in its own right, whatever results. While I hope to live
> to see a united Ireland brought about in *friendship and harmony*, we can
> only at this stage lay the foundations for a closer coming together of North
> and South, whatever form it takes. (emphasis added)

It is important to note, however, that terms such as these are not new to
Irish official discourse on the subject of Northern Ireland. It would be
most accurate to conclude that the European project has given *moral
weight and context* to this type of narrative, supporting the Irish governmental elite's attempts to draw a distinction between its approach to
Northern Ireland and that taken by republican paramilitaries, for
example. Hence, the phrases of Ahern may be seen to echo those of his
predecessor Jack Lynch (17 January 1970), speaking in a context of
heightening pressure for military action by the Irish state in response to
events beyond the border:

> Until the ugly blooms of mistrust and suspicion which poison the atmos-
> phere have died and the ground is planted with the fresh, clean seeds of
> friendship and mutual confidence, re-unification can never be more than

an artificial plant rather than a burgeoning, blossoming flower. And so, as I have said, our course is clear: amity, not enmity, is our ideal; persuasion, not persecution, must be our method; and integration, not imposition, must be our ultimate achievement.

Particular language forms and phrases, such as 'peace', 'confidence' and 'friendship', are therefore applied in official discourse as a means of expressing recommendation of a particular course of action.

Concurrent self-determination

Disagreement within Irish nationalism, as discussed above, regarding the Irish state's approach to Northern Ireland arises from different conceptions of the meaning of Irish national self-determination. The meaning of 'total independence' of the Irish 'nation' has been frequently associated with 'the right of the Irish Government . . . to influence developments in Northern Ireland' and, thereby, a 'fading out of the British involvement in Irish affairs' (Haughey, 26 September 1982; Barry, 11 March 1983: 11). However, in more recent times, the interpretation of 'self-determination' itself has been 'internationalised' as part of the process of internationalising the search for peace in Northern Ireland. The Hume-Adams statement of 1993 recognised that 'while the Irish people have the right to self-determination, they are divided on its exercise' (quoted in Ahern, 21 April 1998). The Irish government established a 'new position' on self-determination with the Good Friday Agreement, part of the backdrop to which was 'the state of international law on self-determination', including the various forms of self-determination recognised in the UN Declaration on the Principles of International Law (1960). Ahern (29 October 1998) notes this background before concluding that 'whatever country or region one is talking about, independence, union or devolution, provided they are freely chosen, are all equally valid expressions of the national right to self-determination'. Moreover, Ahern claims:

> We regard the Belfast Good Friday Agreement, as endorsed by the people of Ireland, North and South in concurrent referendums, as a valid expression of national self-determination. That broader understanding might be helpful in resolving many international disputes.[18]

By defining the approval of the Good Friday Agreement 'on both sides of the border' as 'a concurrent act of self-determination by the people of Ireland as a whole', Ahern seeks to 'remove any false vestige of democratic self-justification for further acts of violence' (21 April 1998; 29 March 1999). His claim represents an attempt to signify resolution (in both senses of the word) in the approaches of republican and constitutional nationalism (as they are present in Irish official nationalism) to Northern Ireland. In effect, Ahern was echoing de Valera's (1926: 9) assertion that 'the supreme constitution is the natural right of the Irish people to rule themselves'. By affirming that the people of Ireland, north and south, have been given this opportunity by the Good Friday Agreement, Ahern hopes to gain support for the actual constitutional changes that the Agreement necessitated. In a statement to Dáil Éireann (21 April 1998), Ahern approves the 19th Amendment to the Constitution on the basis that the principle of national self-determination is not compromised in any way:

> The foundation stone of this State, as well as of the peace process, the right to national self-determination in its full political, social and cultural meaning, remains untouched in Article 1, to which de Valera attached most importance, and would not let go even in the context of a united Ireland.

By reimagining the meaning of national self-determination in the international context, the Irish governmental elite has been able to present change in Northern Ireland's constitutional status as a move towards the realisation of traditional tenets of Irish official nationalism.

Model: multilevel citizenship

In a statement encapsulating a tenet of official Irish discourse on Northern Ireland since the establishment of the Irish state, Lynch (17 January 1970) surmised:

> it is up to us to prove beyond doubt that as citizens of a free, united Ireland [the citizens of the Six Counties] would have nothing to fear.

However, the assumption behind this statement – that common citizenship meant the integration of Northern Ireland into the Republic – was soon to be overtaken by recognition in the late 1970s of the significance of Britain, and British identity, in establishing an 'agreed' Northern Ireland. Thus, the proposal for common or dual citizenship in Britain and Ireland developed alongside co-operation between the two states in this period. Whilst it represented explicit recognition by the Irish government of the sovereignty of both states 'in their own jurisdictions', the proposal for common citizenship 'for the people of these islands' was also intended to lead to a legal basis for claims of common interests and identity between north and south in Ireland (FitzGerald and Harte, 1979: 38; FitzGerald 25 February 1979, 26 February 1979).

In 1982, legislation was introduced that extended voting rights to British citizens living in the Republic and calls were made for the British government to formally recognise 'the right of people in Northern

Ireland to carry Irish or British passports' (FitzGerald, 5 June 1982: 23).[19] FitzGerald (5 June 1982: 23) also asserts that new structures arising from such legislation 'could seek to make provision to enable the two parts of Ireland to undertake together the things they can do better on a joint basis', including within the EEC. The north-south co-operation envisaged by the Irish governmental elite within the framework of British-Irish and European relations was complemented by the contemporary removal of obstacles to the employment of Irish citizens from the Republic in the Northern Ireland civil service. Such changes led Reynolds (30 June 1994: 28) to affirm the connections between co-operation and common citizenship in the wide European realm and that within the island of Ireland:

> We have a shared identity as *fellow citizens of the European Union*. It is the view of the Irish Government that we should, to the greatest extent possible, treat the island of Ireland as a single unit when formulating and implementing policy on European Union matters. (emphasis added)

Yet it is the formal recognition of dual citizenship 'regardless of [Northern Ireland's] future status' included in the 1998 Agreement that marks a most significant development in the model of British-Irish relations with regard to Northern Ireland (Ahern, 26 April 1998). At the heart of this change is the new conceptualisation of sovereignty in the context of European integration.

New sovereignty

> The old simple verities about sovereignty have perforce in the modern world had to give away [*sic*] to acceptance of the fact that no modern state can exercise total sovereignty in the sense of being free to act in an untrammelled way in its relations with its neighbours. (FitzGerald, 5 June 1982)

Ahern (29 October 1998) marks the new direction of official Irish nationalism in a lecture delivered in Edinburgh in which he draws parallels between the experiences of Scotland and Ireland. Ahern's lecture expresses support for Scotland's newly-established political institutions and praised its 'distinctive political culture'; however, he also notes 'the futility of empty flag-waving and chauvinism that hankers after a world of unfettered national sovereignty that has long disappeared'. In its place, Ahern (29 October 1998) welcomes 'the new interdependence', integral to which was the transformation of Europe into 'partners rather than . . . rivals'. Closer to home, the loosening of the bonds between the practice and discourse of the Irish government and 'traditional concepts or forms of sovereignty or government' has facilitated a new approach to Northern Ireland (FitzGerald, 20 August 1978).

In a statement that combines European rhetoric with the prioritising of practical interests, Ahern (3 February 1998) claims: 'On the North-South axis . . . what we are talking about is pooling sovereignty to mutual advantage.' It was noted in the second part of this chapter that Irish official discourse has moved from a focus on the ideals of sovereignty to one on the *utility* of sovereignty in the European context. This shift in emphasis has been central to the reimagination of north-south and British-Irish relations and the establishment of new institutions to represent these relations. The new model of governance arising from practical interests represented by the EU has been applied to the case of Northern Ireland by the Irish governmental elite without appearing to compromise the ideals of the traditional model of Irish sovereignty and statehood.

Conclusion

This chapter has examined the conceptualisation of the Irish state in official discourse and the ways this has interacted with the conceptualisation of the European Union as a political project and polity. The fact that Ireland's accession to the EEC occurred at a time of significant upheaval in Northern Ireland intensified the search for a satisfactory meaning and role for the Irish state by members of its governing elite. Over time, it appears that membership of the European Union has enabled a blurring of boundaries between 'traditional' and 'new' concepts of statehood in official Irish discourse. According to official Irish discourse, the EU has enabled Ireland to adapt to the global politics of '*interdependence*' by making it a 'mature *sovereign* state' (Ahern, 9 May 2001, emphasis added). The maintenance of this apparent paradox has been central to the Irish governmental elite's approach both to European integration and Northern Ireland. Just as an emphasis on the traditional tenets of Irish statehood has supported Ireland's role in the EU, so an emphasis on the impact of EU membership has been used to bolster a new approach to Northern Ireland. The key tenets of the reconceptualisation of governance in Irish official nationalism that is behind this are set out in table 8.1. This technique, however, relies on a strong sense of connection between the Irish population and the Irish governmental elite. Popular suspicion, even disinterest, in the very processes of governance was reflected in the result of the 2001 referendum on the Nice Treaty, when the government failed to convince the electorate that giving away sovereignty to the EU with one hand in effect meant gaining it on the other. The contradictions and paradoxes that exist within Irish official discourse regarding the meaning of Irish statehood are now proving difficult to balance.

Table 8.1 'Governance' in Irish official nationalism, 1973–2002

	Framework	*Narrative*	*Model*

Traditional	State
	Emotive politics to
	  to interest politics;
	  'constitutional
	  crusade'
		National self-
		  determination
		'True
		  republicanism'
			Sovereignty
			Citizenship –
			  duty and rights;
			  Neutrality

Approach to
  European
  Integration
	Independence
	  through
	  interdependence
	Nation-state
	  building block;
	EU promote
	  national interests;
	  contribute to EU
		Self-determination
		  through co-
		  operation
		Broadening
		  horizons;
		  confidence;
		  defending EU
			European
			  democracy
			  through national
			  sovereignty
			Full sovereignty;
			  neutrality;
			  mediating EU to
			  citizens

Approach to
  Northern
  Ireland
	Polity
	Constitutional
	  change; new
	  models of
	  governance;
	  British-Irish
	  Council
		Partnership
		From conflict to
		  co-operation;
		  new meaning of
		  national self-
		  determination
			Multilevel
			  citizenship
			Citizenship –
			  British, Irish or
			  both; utility of
			  sovereignty

Notes

1 Even the trade protectionism arising from this political outlook had the positive effect, FitzGerald (1990: 21) contends, of preparing Ireland for free trade within the European Community by providing a base for an export-oriented industrial sector.

2 For example. 'We can do the same and create within Ireland and for ourselves a fundamental law, a legislation and an administration which will restore the Irish nation that Tone dreamed of in Belfast almost 200 years ago' (Lynch, 28 May 1971).

3 For example 'As the heirs of Pearse and Connolly and de Valera, we have, needless to say, very little in common with those who still hanker after imperial glories in splendid isolation' (Ahern, 22 April 2001).

4 'Fine Gael is the inheritor of the original Sinn Fein tradition of Arthur Griffith' (FitzGerald, 19 September 1977: 7); 'as Leader of Fine Gael. I inherit an inspiring tradition – a tradition which was fired into a long life of service to the Irish people by the painful but constructive decisions of the founding fathers of this State, Griffith, Collins and O'Higgins' (FitzGerald, 20 May 1978).

5 A quotation from Davis most frequently repeated by FitzGerald in the early 1980s was: 'Conciliation of all sects, classes, and parties who oppose us, or

who still hesitate, is *essential* to moral force' (references include FitzGerald 27 September 1981: 7, 18 November 1982: 9, 30 May 1983: 9).

6 For example: 're-asserting the *inalienable right of the Irish Nation to sovereign Independence*, re-affirming the determination of the Irish people to achieve it, and guaranteeing within the independent Nation equal rights and equal opportunities to *all its citizens*. Believing that the time has arrived when Ireland's voice for the principle of *untramelled* National self-determination should be heard above every interest of party or class' (de Valera, 1922: 6, emphasis added).

7 'Ireland's enemy is the power that denies Ireland self-determination' (de Valera, 1918: 1).

8 The link between Ireland's small size, international affairs and Irish sovereignty is made in a Department of Foreign Affairs leaflet (1972a: 13) on the necessity of EEC membership: 'We are a small country with little capacity, at present, to influence events abroad that affect our interests . . . This seriously restricts our freedom of action and is a very real limitation on our national sovereignty.'

9 The Irish government's emphasis on the non-threatening and mutually beneficial nature of Ireland's membership is reflected in the analogies for the EEC used in a governmental publication on the Single European Act (GIS, 1987e: 1): 'The EEC is like a golf club (without a bias against women!) or a residents' association. Its members have come together for their mutual benefit.'

10 Ahern (29 March 1999) was quoting from German Chancellor Schröder's address on his visit to Dublin in March 1999.

11 'The challenge for me as a Leader and for other political leaders and opinion formers in society in Ireland is to maintain momentum behind the European project and to ensure that the Union's development is relevant to the interests and aspirations of our citizens' (Ahern, 21 March 2000).

12 In his summary of the first fifteen years of Ireland's EEC membership, Lenihan (1988) is forced to admit: 'The period since 1973 has not been an easy one for the Community . . . As a result the demands of national interests predominated over those of the Community as a whole well into the 80s [*sic*].'

13 Haughey (22 June 1983) was making a similar argument seven years later whilst (not coincidentally) in Opposition: 'The EEC is still a great political concept. It still has the incalculable capacity to achieve economic and social progress. Its leaders today, however, are not measuring up to their responsibilities. They are failing the people of Europe.'

14 The Declaration on Neutrality read as follows: 'The Government of Ireland note that the provisions of Title 111 do not affect Ireland's long established policy of military neutrality and that co-ordination of positions on the political and economic aspects of security does not include the military aspects of security or procurement for military purposes and does not affect Ireland's right to act or refrain from acting in any way which might affect Ireland's international status of military neutrality' (GIS, 1987g: 16).

15 The Communiqué included the following statement: 'While agreeing with the Prime Minister [Thatcher] that any change in the constitutional status of Northern Ireland would only come about with the consent of a majority of the people in Northern Ireland, the Taoiseach [Haughey] reaffirmed that it is the wish of the Irish Government to secure the unity of Ireland by agreement and peace.'

16 At this summit, the Taoiseach, FitzGerald (6 November 1981), agreed 'that any change in the constitutional status of Northern Ireland would require the consent of the majority of the people in Northern Ireland, and the British Prime Minister agreed to support the passing of legislation if that consent were given'.

17 For a more recent example of the argument for an Irish federation, see Caul (1995).

18 Ahern's suggestion that the new conceptualisation of self-determination in Ireland could be applied in the resolution of other conflicts itself reflects awareness of the significance of language in politics and the importance of external models and influences in inter-state co-operation.

19 It is significant that Haughey's (15 January 1982) announcement of this legislation was followed by an affirmation of links between north and south: 'All the people of Ireland share the same basic Christian values. There is far more in common between them than separates them. They move freely from one part of the island to another. They share business and sport. They recognise each other as fellow countrymen anywhere in the world when they meet. *They have common interests in the European Community*' (emphasis added).

9

Conclusion

The case of Ireland epitomises the enduring power and potential of official nationalism even (perhaps especially) in a context of immense upheaval. Official nationalism both responds to and shapes popular perception; it draws together past, present and future; it affects and it is an effect; it builds support for what *is* by asserting what *ought* to be; it is a pillar of continuity and a force for change. Official discourse plays a crucial role in giving voice to this process. The contradictory nature of nationalism is made manifest in the complexity of official discourse. Politicians' redefinition of key words, their elaboration of the same myths in different contexts, their changing of core principles on the pretext of bringing goals closer – indeed, their repositioning of those very goals . . . all these discursive tactics enable the 'nation-state' to remain the critical constant in a changing global environment.

Symbiotic discourses

Through examination of official discourse we have seen the 'productive paradoxes' within Irish nationalism which have enabled significant adjustments (some would say concessions) to be made in touchstone areas of state sovereignty, i.e. Northern Ireland and European integration. These changes have been made in and around the three ideological pillars of identity, borders and governance. Some traditional conceptions of nation, territory and state have been reinforced in official discourse on the EU, whilst some new 'EU-inspired' conceptions of community, space and polity have been utilised in justifying the concessions necessary for political agreement on the island of Ireland. Table 9.1 gives an indication of these processes as set out in Irish official discourse around the time of the 1998 Agreement.

The concept of identity traditionally associated with nationhood (with an historical culture of a distinct people group) has been blended with new concepts of community in the EU context, in which diverse multidimen-

Table 9.1 Connections between discourses on the EU and Northern Ireland

Discursive themes	*Identity*	*Borders*	*Governance*
Traditional framework of nation-state	Nation	Territory	State
Traditional narrative of nation-state	Historical culture	Demarcated boundaries	Self-determination
Traditional model of nation-state	Distinct people	Island	Sovereignty
Summary of approach to European Union using 'traditional' themes	National identity forms building block of EU	National territory redeemed through integration	National democracy central to EU democracy
Summary of approach to Northern Ireland using' new' themes	Diversity in unity	Decreasing significance of partition	Collaborative institutions
New model of European Union	Multidimensional identities	Cross-border co-operation	Multilevel citizenship
New narrative of European Union	Unity in diversity	Overcome divisions	Partnership
New framework of European Union	*Community*	*Space*	*Polity*

sional identities are united. The concept of national territory with its demarcated boundaries has become adjusted to the European concept of space created by cross-border co-operation. The idea of the self-determined, sovereign state has been modified through participation in the European polity, with new forms of citizenship and partnership at multiple levels. These conceptual amalgamations have been revealed most clearly in Ireland's relationship with Northern Ireland and the European Union. With regard to Ireland's approach to the EU, the traditional elements of identity, borders and governance are still emphasised: nations are the EU's building blocks, the island of Ireland is a European region, and the EU's democratic legitimacy is attained through national means. In relation to Northern Ireland, EU-inspired concepts of identity, borders and governance have been applied so that the territorial border is increasingly insignificant, with collaboration and diversity across the island. The findings from these themes are summarised in the chapter sections below.

All in all, Irish official nationalism has redefined the island of Ireland – its identity, borders and governance – in the European context.

Identity

The traditional framework for identity in Irish official nationalism is the nation. The processes of nationalisation (begun before independence) and nation-state building (after 1922) sought to draw together the cultural and the political dimensions of nationhood. This was done by constructing a model of the nation as a distinct people group and supporting it with narratives of its historical culture. In asserting the political right of the nation to independence from Britain, the 'natural' cultural difference between Irishness and Britishness was also emphasised. As the border between Northern Ireland and the Free State became confirmed by the consolidation of the political structures either side of it, so also did the cultural distinction between the two jurisdictions become more established, if only by default. Just as nationalism appears to be relevant to every area of collective life, so the differences between the Irish nation and the 'other' of Northern Ireland, Britain and other states were evident, according to Irish official discourse, on a vast range of levels: from religious observance to economic policies.

The traditional tenets of Irish identity underlying the meaning of Irish nationhood were those that bolstered the legitimacy of the Irish state, albeit a twenty-six-county one. Bunreacht na hÉireann epitomised these tenets. Hence, the spiritual elements of Irish nationhood were reflected in the constitutional recognition of the 'special position' of the Catholic Church. The Gaelic/Celtic ancient heritage was reflected in the positioning of Irish Gaelic as the official language of the state. More specifically, the nation was presented as epitomised in the twenty-six-county state but also extending beyond its borders to include the six counties of Northern Ireland. The tensions that this produced within Irish official nationalism came to the fore in the late 1960s, when this constitutional claim was seen by some as an obligation and by others as a threat regarding the Irish government's responsibility to act.

The way that the Irish governmental elite chose to act regarding Northern Ireland prioritised the integrity of the twenty-six-county state. Nevertheless, as Ireland's position in the wider sphere began to alter, so did its position in relation to Northern Ireland. Membership of the EEC not only broadened Irish horizons in economic terms, it also, according to Irish official nationalism, gave Irish identity a boost in terms of confidence, distinctiveness and fulfilment of national interests. Whilst Irish identity was enhanced on the European stage, it was also gaining more credibility in the context of the 'western isles' of Ireland and the United Kingdom, as negotiations for a future settlement of Northern Ireland began to acknowledge the need for recognition of British as well as Irish identity within Northern Ireland. In uncoupling the political and cultural elements of nationhood, Irish official discourse has been able to present not only unionist identity but EU membership as compatible with Irish nationhood. Traditional myths of Ireland's civilising role in the Dark Ages and its spiritual obligations in the international realm,[1] for example, have been used to legitimise European integration. In relation to Northern Ireland, through a reinterpretation of traditional narratives (e.g. 'true republicanism') and an application of new concepts from the European experience, Irish official discourse has been able to support a new approach towards accommodation within Northern Ireland, as well as in the other two strands. Examination of Irish official discourse in relation to Irish identity and nationhood highlights the fact that traditional and new elements of Irish official nationalism are accommodated side by side.

Borders

The traditional framework for borders in Irish official nationalism is the definition of the territory of the Irish nation-state. The border between Northern Ireland and the Irish state has been a central defining point for Irish official nationalism, even when its existence is deliberately disregarded. An all-island definition of 'Ireland' was made simultaneously more significant and more complex with the entrenchment of partition. Indeed, a core point of change in Irish official nationalism in the late twentieth century arose from the recognition that its anti-partitionism actually helped to fortify the border. Even after thirty years of EU membership, the principle of reunification remained upheld by members of the Irish governmental elite, but the means by which to achieve it have changed. Moreover, the actual conception of what reunification means has substantially altered.

This change (encapsulated in the 1998 Good Friday Agreement) was described at the time by the Irish Minister for Foreign Affairs as a shift in 'the centre of gravity' from 'land' to 'people' (Andrews, 30 April 1998: 1); reunification now explicitly depends on the choice of a majority within Northern Ireland. In placing reunification as a matter of choice for unionists rather than a right of nationalists, Irish official nationalism has made a significant move away from the conflation of Irish identity with a political desire for reunification. Indeed, it is possible to disagree with Minister Andrews and note that Irishness is now more than ever defined on a territorial basis. For the core elements of constitutional change in relation to Irish identity – including the possibility that all in the island of Ireland may be defined as Irish plus the recognition of the Irish diaspora – are still ultimately connected to the territory of Ireland. The cultural, historical and political significance of the territory of the island of Ireland remains a core tenet of Irish official nationalism.

Other areas of Irish territory, such as its economic productivity, its geographical positioning and trade routes, have all been affected by Ireland's membership of the European Union. Official discourse in Ireland has presented European integration as a means of lifting the confines that have been placed on Irish economic, political, cultural, spiritual, etc. influence by decreasing the significance of internal European borders and, moreover, giving Ireland a clearer voice on the world stage. This has been applied to the situation in Northern Ireland, with north-south co-operation developing at a number of levels, even to the degree of the conceptualisation of the island of Ireland as a single European region. This is an example of the new conception of borders in the EU being applied to reaffirm the traditional notion of Irish territory. At the same time, membership of the European Union has been presented as enhancing the integrity of Irish territory through, for example, making its small size an important quality rather than an impediment, giving it a special position between Europe and the United States, and facilitating regional equality within Ireland. The traditional tenets of Irish official discourse on borders – reunification, the island borders of Ireland, the importance of the land in society and economy, small nation principles – have been merged with new concepts of territory in the contemporary context, in which borders are not barriers but bridges.

Governance

The traditional framework for governance in Irish nationalism has been the state. The state is, according to official nationalism, the institutional expression of the nation and the administrative centre of the territory. Connections between the nation, territory and state are clearly represented in the particular citizenship policies of a state. Recent changes have led towards a multilevel conception of citizenship in the context of the 'western isles of Europe', with dual British and Irish citizenship by birthright for residents of Northern Ireland. The state also represents the nation and territory of Ireland in the international realm. Neutrality is a signifier of the sovereignty and distinctive foreign policy of the Irish state. Changing conceptions of the impact of EU membership on Irish neutrality epitomise the fact that the priority is the sovereignty of the nation-state. The definition of neutrality in the EU context changes according to

the interpretation of the Irish governmental elite as to the impact of the
EU's development on Irish sovereignty. Indeed, the definition of sovereignty itself changes in a similar way. Chapter 8 traced a development
from an emphasis on what FitzGerald (1990) terms an 'emotive' conception of the ideal of sovereignty to an 'interest-based', pragmatic definition
of the utility of sovereignty. This has enabled Irish official nationalism to
present a pooling of sovereignty in the EU context as enhancing Irish sovereignty in real terms. It has also supported the establishment of institutions for cross-border and intergovernmental co-operation within the
'western isles'.

The traditional narrative supporting governance in the nation-state is
that of national self-determination. Since prior to independence, this narrative was interpreted as legitimating the search for political institutions
of governance that would reflect the particular distinctive qualities of the
Irish people. It was consequently interpreted as having application on a
thirty-two-county basis, i.e. the demand for an all-island state. However,
the meaning of self-determination has been reinterpreted in the contemporary context in a way that supports the Good Friday Agreement's
principle of majority consent within Northern Ireland and within the
Republic of Ireland. The will of all on the island is being recognised, the
proponents of the new interpretation of self-determination assert.
However, this definition of self-determination accepts the division of
the island into two distinct jurisdictions. Yet, the new institutions of
co-operation within the western isles are presented as making this fact
less significant than ever. This institutional change is related to the
context of multilevel co-operation in the European Union.

The EU is presented as enabling the traditional principles of sovereignty, independence and self-determination of the Irish state to be
realised to a greater degree than ever. Whilst partnership at the European
level has been interpreted as a means of expanding the role of the nation-
state, it has been applied in Irish official discourse on Northern Ireland
to facilitate progress beyond the confines of traditional interpretations of
state sovereignty etc. This is exemplified in the relationship between
Britain and Ireland. On the European stage, Ireland is presented in official discourse as a committed, ideal member-state, enjoying equality with
and the confidence of other member-states – in frequent contrast to the
obstructionism of Britain. Ireland's co-operative foreign policy contrasts
favourably with Britain – a long-held feature of Irish official nationalism.
In the internal context, the new equality between the states means that
exclusive sovereignty over Northern Ireland is not so important in
the global context of interdependence. As 'fellow citizens' of the EU,
distinctions between British and Irish are not so significant. Closer

examination of the meaning of European citizenship does, however, point back to state sovereignty. Irish official discourse has consistently pointed to the centrality of the nation-state in determining the relevance and consequence of European citizenship. Moreover, the democracy of the EU is seen as being not only constructed but also defended by the Irish governmental elite. This has significant implications for the definition of the future European Union and Ireland's position within it.

'No to Nice'

The core finding of this research is that there is a symbiotic relationship between the nation-state and the European Union in Irish official nationalism. However, after nearly thirty years of relatively uneventful EU membership, questions were raised regarding the success of this process given the rejection of the Treaty of Nice in the first referendum in June 2001. To what extent does this represent dissolution of the close ties between nation-state and European Union in Irish official nationalism? Until the June 2001 referendum on the Treaty of Nice, all referendums on EU treaties since accession had passed with a significant majority. Yet this majority had been in decline since the 1992 referendum on the Treaty of European Union (see table 9.2a). Table 9.2b demonstrates fact that the ratification of the Nice Treaty was prevented in 2001 by a substantial decrease in the proportion of the population voting 'Yes' rather than by an increase in the proportion of the population voting 'No'. Indeed, the proportion of the population voting 'No', as FitzGerald (23 June 2001) notes, was actually less than in 1998. The percentage of the population voting against EU treaties has been relatively stable at around 18–19 per cent since the early 1990s. The biggest increase in this was in May 1998 on the Treaty of Amsterdam, which could be related to a protest vote at the decision to hold the referendum on the same day as that on implementing the Belfast Agreement which was seen as a sneaky attempt by the Irish government to bring a 'Yes' vote in on the coat-tails of enthusiasm for agreement in Northern Ireland (Gilland, 1999). The decreasing voter turnout appears to be directly related to the declining 'Yes' vote. Thus, the Nice Treaty referendum result reflects not so much increasing disaffection with European integration as decreasing *interest* in the European Union. Explanations for the result, therefore, should begin with an examination of the fundamental weaknesses of the government's campaign for a 'Yes' vote, of which there are three.[2]

In the first instance, the government's standpoint on the subject of the future EU, and specifically Ireland's position within it, was unclear and inconsistent. This lack of clarity was exacerbated by the government's

Table 9.2a Results of referendums on certain constitutional amendments

Date	Amendment	Referendum	For (%)	Turnout (%)
May 1972	3rd	Accession to EEC	83	71
May 1987	10th	Single European Act	70	44
June 1992	11th	Maastricht Treaty	69	57
May 1998	18th	Amsterdam Treaty	62	56
May 1998	19th	Belfast Agreement	95	56
June 2001	24th	Nice Treaty (I)	46	35
Nov 2002	26th	Nice Treaty (II)	63	50

Source: Data source: Coakley (1999: 372) and the Referendum Commission (www.referendum.ie).

Table 9.2b Irish referendum results on EU treaties showing decline in voter turnout(%) [3]

Date	Referendum	For	Against	Turnout
May 1972	Permit EU membership	83.1 (58.9)	16.9 (11.9)	70.9
May 1987	Single European Act	69.9 (30.7)	30.1 (13.2)	43.9
June 1992	Maastricht Treaty	69.1 (39.6)	30.9 (17.7)	57.3
May 1998	Amsterdam Treaty	61.7 (34.7)	38.3 (21.5)	56.2
June 2001	Nice Treaty (I)	46.1 (16.0)	53.9 (18.8)	34.8
Nov 2002	Nice Treaty (II)	62.9 (31.1)	37.1 (18.4)	49.5

Note: Bracketed figures beside percentage of recorded votes show actual percentage of electorate.

Source: Referendum Commission (www.referendum.ie).

reliance on rhetoric rather than information to gain support for EU membership. This was reflected in low levels of knowledge on the Treaty. The Irish government sought to inspire citizens to vote 'Yes' to a treaty that 85 per cent of the electorate did not fully comprehend.[4] The government's failure to challenge the 'No' campaign with a clear alternative vision of Ireland's place in Europe centred on the fact that there *is* no clear vision in the government on the future shape of the EU and Ireland's position within it. It did not bode well for the government's campaign when in a Dáil debate on the eve of its launch, Ahern (8 May 2001: 1147) refused to state his views on Chancellor Schröder's recently-announced proposals for a European federation:

> *I am not willing to provide any views as yet* on what course the debate on the *future of Europe* should take. We must deal with the Nice treaty in the first instance and *then* give consideration to the debate on the future of

Europe, which will take place during next year and the year after . . . *The debate in this country will not take place in any form* – this was agreed by all the groups – *until* the Nice Treaty *has been ratified*. That is the position. (emphasis added)

The government's campaign on the Nice Treaty was subsequently founded on tenuous position of asserting generalities whilst avoiding discussion of the most significant general issue: the future shape of the EU. As a consequence, the government's campaign was characterised by a lack of information as to its view of the purpose, implications and likely impact of the Treaty of Nice on Ireland and the EU. No press release, speech or statement by government ministers in the course of the referendum debate specifically outlined the actual terms of the Treaty of Nice. Hence, people were ultimately left to be moved to vote by the thought of what they might lose – which, according the anti-Treaty placard slogan, was 'power, money and freedom' – rather than by what might be gained from ratification or, indeed, from European integration.

The negative impact of these flaws was exacerbated by the second factor contributing to the failure of the 'Yes' campaign, namely the dissent within the government regarding future European integration that became most apparent at the time of the 2001 referendum. This dissent may be primarily understood as arising from perception in the government that the public was concerned about the preservation of Irish sovereignty and the quality of democracy within the EU. The government made a deliberate attempt to address voter disillusion with the EU by presenting itself as an independent voice in the EU, rather than a pawn in the EU political project. This was epitomised in an article written by Tánaiste Mary Harney (4 June 2001) arguing for a 'Yes' vote whilst attempting to express the government's empathy with those who felt alienated from and suspicious of the EU:

> You say you don't like what's coming out of Europe . . . You say you think Ireland's interests cannot be secured, despite our best efforts. I understand all these concerns . . . Asserting our voice is the way to keep the EU democratic.

The explicitly negative complaints of fellow government ministers Charlie McCreevy, Frank Fahey and Síle de Valera, and ministers of state, Éamon Ó Cuiv and Willie O'Dea, counteracted the positive intentions of Harney's arguments.[5] The fact that this dissent became most apparent after the referendum result suggests that it represents an attempt by politicians to disassociate themselves from an unpopular government policy rather than long-held, direct objections to European integration, as is the case in Britain and Denmark.

The disclaimers posted by some politicians over their referendum campaigns once the result was announced epitomised one reason for the final point of weakness in the 'Yes' campaign, i.e. a breakdown of trust between citizens and the political system. Official discourse failed to redress, even exacerbated, the popular sense of alienation from and distrust of not only the European Union but, moreover, the practice of democracy itself. Thus, the result of the Nice Treaty referendum highlighted the risks involved in the Irish government's emphasis on its pivotal role in linking the EU to its citizens (as discussed in chapter 8). For the fact that both referendum campaigns, involving all national politicians, intense media coverage and public debate ultimately failed to inspire two-thirds of the electorate to vote implies that the core democratic channel between the citizen and the political system is weak even at a national level. The government may have been correct to identify a sense of popular alienation from the EU but this was to a significant degree an extension of the widespread disillusion present in Ireland regarding domestic politics in general, following a succession of high-profile cases of political corruption at the highest levels.

Official discourse may place the government at the heart of European integration, but the success of this policy relies upon the electorate's engagement and identification with national politics. In this way the first Nice referendum shows that the task of addressing popular disconnection from the European Union cannot be adequately fulfilled before voter engagement in national politics is restored – a task that requires an entirely different approach to that taken to date by the government. MacCarthaigh (2006) shows that many of the measures introduced since the post-Nice I Laeken summit (December 2001) to address the EU's democratic deficit strengthen the role of national parliaments in the EU system of governance. There is now, he points out, an even greater requirement for governments to tend to the (perceived and actual) accountability of parliaments in building trust of the European Union. More 'local' measures introduced to this end included the establishment of the National Forum on Europe. Although successful in terms of providing a forum for public discussion on the EU, it has not led to complete clarity regarding the government's own position on the future shape of the European Union. The relatively small amount of publicity that it has received also indicates a continuing lack of public interest in European integration and certain unwillingness to place the EU high on the public agenda. The conduct of the government's campaign for the second referendum on Nice was, therefore, not substantially different to its forerunner except perhaps in terms of the underlying current of urgency. It showed an inadequate response to the direct issues raised by

'No to Nice': still no direct answers about the future shape of the EU, intimations of lagging faith in EU partners, wariness of pinning colours to the EU mast. If the 2001 referendum saw some chickens coming home to roost, the 2008 referendum on the Lisbon Treaty witnessed the hatching of their eggs.

Conclusion

The result of the first Nice Treaty referendum does not represent the end of a symbiotic fit between the Irish nation-state and the European Union; on the contrary, it highlights the importance of the relationship between official nationalism and European integration for two reasons. First, it reflects the projection of national issues – disillusionment with the democratic process, suspicion of the government's position on neutrality after joining Partnership for Peace, desire to protect economic achievements, distrust of politicians – onto the European level. Secondly, the key weaknesses leading to the 'No' vote or, rather, the decline of the 'Yes' vote – ambiguity regarding the future of the EU, dissent within the government on this issue, disconnection between citizens and the governmental elite – reflect at a national level problems that exist at the European level. Few EU member-state governments would have been confident to put the Nice Treaty to the vote, for reasons exemplified in the rejection of the Constitutional Treaty by the French and Dutch electorates in 2005 and in the subsequent decision by all member-states but Ireland (constrained by the *Crotty v. An Taoiseach* judgment) to revise that consolidating Treaty in such a way so as to avoid a referendum on it in the future. The fact that the European Union has reached a crucial time of change and decision is reflected in the indecision and uncertainty among and within its member-states. If the EU is to become a stronger community, common space and polity, it will require democratic connections between citizens and the EU that may include but also go beyond the national political institutions. Such connections will ultimately need greater levels of public information on the EU, new dynamics and channels of political representation and enhanced significance for European citizenship. The fact that the main revisions to the Treaty as agreed in Lisbon in 2007 have included the removal of proposed symbols and signifiers for an EU community indicates the 'Catch 22' situation that member-state governments believe themselves to be in.

Dancing at the crossroads

As the Irish governmental elite adds its voice to demands for developing the qualities of traditional statehood (such as democratic accountability, citizens' rights and executive decision-making by directly-elected representatives) in the European Union, it must also alter its notion of the central role of the nation-state within it. So, as the EU matures, new conceptions of identity, borders and governance will be accommodated in official discourse. Yet it may become increasingly difficult for the Irish political elite to claim the fulfilment of the Irish nation, territory and state through advancing European integration. It is becoming harder for citizens to trace the link between the development of the EU and the development of the Irish state. This is due in some part to the 'disconnect' between the narratives of the 'whys and wherefores' of European integration and the public perception of the actual decisions and activities of the EU. It is also due to the changing relevance and reception of traditional ideas of nation-statehood itself. It is striking that Irish official discourse on the subjects of Northern Ireland and the European Union after the period examined in this book, i.e. since 2002, tends to refer less often to the very idea of nation-statehood. This is exemplified in the fact that the phrase 'the economy' is now frequently substituted for the term 'nation-state'.[6] This is not due solely to the Celtic Tiger phenomenon. It is also connected to growing perception (encouraged by official discourse from Britain as well as Ireland) that the 'Northern Ireland question' has been as good as answered.[7] Despite Mr Paisley's growing familiarity with southern territory and politicians, the restoration of devolution in 2007 led, if anything, to a decreasing profile for Northern Ireland as a topic of media and political concern. Debates about Irish citizenship, identity and territory are now much more likely to be about immigration than partition. This was exemplified in the passing of the 2004 referendum changing the conditions of Irish citizenship.[8] In the new deliberation of Irish nationhood, Northern Ireland was not a stolen land but a precariously open back gate.

The ardour of Ireland's marriage with Europe has been due to the potency of Irish official nationalism – itself a consequence of the historical constraints faced by Irish sovereignty, not least of which were economic underdevelopment and partition. As these internal and external pressures have become less virulent, Ireland has become more 'comfortable' with its position in the world, in relation to Britain and with the status of Northern Ireland. This poses a new challenge for the Irish governmental elite and will necessitate a further adjustment of Irish official discourse on European integration. Progress made during Ireland's first thirty years of EU membership has demonstrated the potential of both traditional and new discourses of Irish nation-statehood. The events hailed by the *Irish Times* in December 1999 as heralding the 'birth of a new Ireland' did constitute a remarkable and unique development in the institutional and constitutional status of cross-border and British-Irish relations. These were but the visible products of profound and substantial change in the official definition of the island of Ireland within the EU. For as the geopolitical, economic and historical context has changed, so too has the projected meaning of Irish identity, borders and governance. Perhaps the singular principle that remains steadfast in official nationalism is that the nation-state must be continually redefined in order to remain a constant. This is the ultimate 'productive paradox', sustaining not only national democratic politics but European integration at large.

Notes

1 This type of thinking was reflected even in relation to EU enlargement to 25 and 27 member-states, as the Irish government claimed the supporting enlargement was a 'moral' imperative and duty for the Irish people (Ahern, 8 February 2001: 2, 21 June 2001: 3).

2 For detailed analysis of the debate around the Nice Treaty in Ireland and the meaning and implications of the referendum results see Holmes (2005), Hayward (2002 and 2003) and O'Brennan (2003). Further analysis of Irish governmental discourse around the first referendum is available in Hayward (2001).

3 Table based on figures adapted in part from Coakley (1999: 372).

4 The results of an MRBI/*Irish Times* poll taken at the end of 2001 showed that only 15 per cent of respondents said they had a good understanding of the issues involved in the Treaty of Nice (*Irish Times*, 2 June 2001). This is notably better than the results of a similar poll on the text of the Lisbon Treaty taken six weeks before the referendum in June 2008, which showed that just 5 per cent of people questioned believed they understood the Treaty (Referendum Commission research, reported in *Irish Times*, 29 April 2008). All results in percentages. Data from MRBI/*Irish Times* poll results of 29–30 May 2001, reported in *Irish Times*, 2 June 2001.

5 McCreevy, the Minister for Finance hailed the result as 'a healthy sign' and affirmed his criticisms of the European 'federal project'. In an interesting use of rhetoric on national identity, he said that Irish people had shown for 'several hundred years' that they 'did not lie down easily' (*Irish Times*, 6 and 16 June 2001). Minister for the Marine, Fahey, complained that the EU's Common Fisheries Policy was 'top-down, bureaucratic, complex, remote and centralised' (*Irish Times*, 19 June 2001). In correspondence with her previous criticisms of EU integration, the Minister for Arts, Heritage, the

Gaeltacht and the Islands, Síle de Valera, said that the result was, 'a warning sign' to all political parties that Irish people were 'not in favour of further European integration'. In a remarkable confession of hypocrisy that reveals the fervour of the post-referendum backlash, the Minister of State for Agriculture and Rural Development (also a grandchild of Éamon de Valera's), Éamon Ó Cuív, after calling for a 'Yes' vote in the referendum, publicised the fact that he voted against the ratification of the Nice Treaty (*Irish Times*, 11 and 22 June 2001).

6 For example, in his address to the Arbour Hill commemoration in 2007, Bertie Ahern (22 April 2007) described north-south co-operation in terms of developing an 'all-island economy' and the peace process as a badge of honour for Ireland's modernity rather than its nationhood: 'North/South co-operation will benefit all as will the further development of the island economy. A growing and prospering Northern Ireland will be good for this entire island . . .We have already shown that with our commitment to significant cross-border investment. I have also told Dr Paisley we fully support the idea of a corporation tax reduction for Northern Ireland. We understand the issues that this raises for the British Government. But radical and innovative moves are needed to transform the Northern Ireland economy. Corporation tax reform could make a real difference and we hope that it can be achieved . . . An island economy that is built on co-operation between North and South will help us all gain that extra competitive edge that we need in the global economy. The Celtic Tiger and the dynamism of Ireland's economy are widely recognised around the world. The success of the peace process adds a new and very valuable dimension to the story of modern Ireland.' A certain paradigm shift has taken place that a Taoiseach's speech to his most traditionally republican audience presents reform of corporation tax as a British-irritating, 'radical and innovative move' for Irish policy towards Northern Ireland.

7 For an example of the use of past tense in relation to Northern Ireland, see Bertie Ahern's (15 May 2007) speech to the Joint Houses of Parliament: 'Today, I can say to this Parliament at Westminster as John Kennedy said in Dublin: "Ireland's hour has come". It came, not as victory or defeat, but as a shared future for all. Solidarity has made us stronger. Reconciliation has brought us closer. Ireland's hour has come: a time of peace, of prosperity, of old values and new beginnings. This is the great lesson and the great gift of Irish history.'

8 The Twenty-seventh amendment of the Constitution was passed in a referendum in June 2004 by a majority of 79 per cent (turnout 60 per cent). It amended Article 9 (which made Irish citizenship a birthright to all born on the island of Ireland) to add the condition of having at least one parent holding (or being entitled to hold) Irish citizenship.

Afterword

The 'Irish problem' has long been a euphemism in EU circles for the con-tested status of Northern Ireland. The term took on a new meaning overnight on 12 June 2008, after which the 'Irish problem' debated across Europe was Ireland's second rejection of an EU treaty (Lisbon) and the consequent stalling of European integration.[1]

The breakdown of results for the referendum on the Treaty of Lisbon (46.6 per cent 'Yes' to 53.4 per cent 'No') was almost identical to that of the first referendum on the Treaty of Nice in 2001. The difference this time, and a crucial one, was that the turnout was 53.1 per cent – higher than for either referendum on the Treaty of Nice. This disproved the theory (maintained by the pro-European political parties) that most Irish voters are 'Yes' voters by default and that they simply had to be encour-aged out to vote; these parties actually had to compete (against a more effectual if typically disparate 'No' campaign) in persuading people *how* to vote. Yet criticisms made in the concluding chapter of this book regard-ing the conduct of the 'Yes' campaign for Nice I (such as lack of clarity, information and preparation) apply equally well to this case, some seven years on. Our foremost consideration, however, should be that the Lisbon result (and turnout) indicates that the passing of Nice II was not a 'cor-rection' of the blip of Nice I but a temporary reprieve; indeed, it may be said that it was not Nice I but Nice II that was the 'blip'.[2] This is of grave importance given that a 'Lisbon II' type referendum has the most credence among a variety of suggestions (from a two-speed EU of 26 + 1 to an EU of 27 − 1) as to how European integration might proceed.[3] In any case, proposals to get around the 'Irish situation' via clever legal tricks or polit-ical sleights of hand are short-sighted, given the certainty that other member-states would face similar difficulties in a referendum on any Lisbon or any other EU treaty. Such knowledge adds piquancy to this debate and makes its conclusion all the more consequential.

Apart from the legacy of the *Crotty* judgment, what makes Ireland such a notable case study is that it *is* such a pro-European member-state.

Judging by the research presented in this book, it is evident that the 'No' to Lisbon does not represent a dramatic about-turn in Ireland's approach to European membership. In fact, the path from 'model member-state' to 'bad boy of Europe'[4] is unbroken and direct, bedded in Ireland's official approach to European integration. Three key features of this path are briefly outlined here: the lack of a 'vision' of European integration, the mediating role of the national political elite, and the public response to Irish official discourse on the EU. Thus, the purpose of this afterword, written in the immediate wake of the Lisbon referendum, is to consider how Irish nationalism's symbiotic relationship with European integration can be not merely reprieved but readjusted.

Lack of European vision

With nationalism as the driving force behind Ireland's EU membership, there appeared little need for the Irish political elite to outline a 'grand vision' of the future of Europe. There was no Irish blueprint for the 'ideal Europe'; indeed, Ireland's vision of the EU got more blurred as the EU grew in stature. The fundamental criterion for mainstream Irish political support for further integration has been that national interests are better served within it than apart from it. But that argument was won in 1972 – it has not essentially been a matter for debate since that time – and it does not address the crucial issue, some thirty-five years and eighteen additional member-states later, as to at what point Irish national interests may conflict with the sum of those of other member-states (however they be calculated). It is not just the lack of message but the presentation of the message that has generated doubt. If Irish political leaders struggle to articulate to a local audience what kind of Europe they want to see, what limits it should have and what position Ireland should take within it, voters may wonder how the Irish position could be discerned, let alone respected, in a forum of twenty-seven member-states.

Irish elite as mediators of the EU

A reliance on a nation-based discourse to lead Ireland's approach to EU integration has meant that national politicians have stood in the 'gap' between the EU and the Irish people. But have they actually played a role of a bridge or of a barrier between the two? Certainly, Irish politicians have been adept at taking the credit for the EU's successes and blaming the EU for the failures of national policies.[5] The conduct of 'Yes' campaigns in referendums tend to be national affairs, with 'European' voices generally sidelined.[6] Most damaging, however, has been the contribution of the mediating role of national politicians to the lack of public knowledge of the EU. The text of the Treaty of Lisbon was opaque and not understood by most Irish citizens (according to Commissioner Charlie McCreevy, 'there would only be a few experts in Ireland capable of reading it', himself not included).[7] Such incomprehension of the particular – in a context of economic uncertainty, global insecurity, and cabinet change – exacerbated popular suspicion of politicians and painted the EU itself as a symbol of the feared 'unknown'. [8]

The reverberations of official discourse

The Eurobarometer survey taken in the weeks before the referendum confirms that the Irish public maintains EU membership to have benefited the country (82 per cent) and to be a 'good thing' (73 per cent).[9] On the latter question, Ireland is second only to the Netherlands, whose rejection of the Constitutional Treaty confirms that pro-European views are compatible with doubts about EU treaties. This is reflected in the self-description of Ireland's 'No' campaigners as 'pro-European'.[10] To see EU membership as a good and beneficial thing and to vote 'No' to an EU treaty does not imply some kind of schizophrenic – or indeed selfish, ungrateful or petulant – voting behaviour. The Irish see EU membership as important and envision Ireland at the heart of the EU project. Moreover, popular thinking conceives Ireland as favourably respected by fellow member-states, with an ability to 'punch above its weight'. In this sense, it may be said that the Irish population took Irish official discourse more seriously than those who espoused it, i.e. believing that Ireland's reputation as a 'good European' was neither fragile nor conditional. The counterintuitive argument that this status could only be maintained by Ireland *reducing* its say in EU decision-making was difficult for the 'Yes' campaign to elaborate alongside typical referendum slogans such as 'Vote Yes for a better Ireland and a better Europe'.[11]

On a related point, the official discourse of successive Irish governments about a 'new Ireland in a new Europe' became so embedded in public consciousness that it lost its impact. Such discursive motifs are not primarily intended to inform but to inspire, to give confidence and motivation to move popular thought in a particular direction. But when consensus has shifted in line with this new thinking, the lack of substance and meaning in these terms becomes evident. This is not dissimilar to the way in which John Hume's discourse about the future of an 'agreed Ireland' with 'three strands' and 'two traditions' became so successful (taken up by both governments and other political parties) that it helped create a situation in which the SDLP party came to be seen as lacking innovation or lustre. It is not inconceivable that Sinn Féin, which has done well from adapting principal elements of Hume's discourse for post-Agreement Northern Ireland, will reap political benefits from tuning core elements of Irish official discourse on the EU for a fresh constituency.

On the subject of Northern Ireland: the conflict provided an implicit motivation for deeper European integration, not least to internationalise the problem, dilute Britain's control over Northern Ireland and to facilitate stronger cross-border links. The EU appears to many to have done what it can in relation to these areas; and reunification has been, in effect, decommissioned as a powerful and urgent theme of Irish nationalism. The weight and momentum that 'Northern Ireland' gave to both European integration and Irish nationalism has thus dissipated.

Conclusion

In responding to a Dáil question by Sinn Féin's Parliamentary Group Leader on Ireland's position in the European Council in the week after the Lisbon referendum, Taoiseach Brian Cowen, in rather frustrated tones, highlighted the inevitable disappointments and sacrifices involved in high-level negotiations. His implicit reference to the Good Friday Agreement illustrated the links made in the blend of idealism and pragmatism that has characterised Irish official discourse on Northern Ireland and the EU.

> All of us, including Deputy Ó Caoláin [Sinn Féin] and his party, have been involved in negotiations. One does not get what one sets out to achieve at the beginning. One has to listen to the points of view of others and try to see if one can move from where one is to another position in a way that is agreeable to all. That is the point. Everybody can have a view about what the European Union is or is not but at the end of the day the agreement of everybody is required. This means entering into these discussions in good faith, with a view to trying to confirm what I understood everybody in this jurisdiction was claiming, namely, that we are pro-Europe and pro-European Union and do not want to be marginalised, isolated or disadvantaged in the European Union. My job, as Taoiseach, is to try to uphold our national interests and maintain our position in the Union, while recognising that the people made a decision last Thursday.[12]

The Irish government's task of balancing pragmatism with idealism in relation to such momentous issues as reunification and European integration has centred on Irish official nationalism. This has been for the most part a successful strategy, but it depends on ceaseless adaptation to contextual change. The official redefinition of the 'island of Ireland' epitomises how this can be done, with the European Union playing a vital supporting role. Irish official discourse on the EU itself, however, has not adjusted to the transformed domestic and international scene or, indeed, to what the EU has actually become. After many years of membership, Ireland's relationship with the EU has come of age: Irish citizens, as European citizens, are ready to engage with it as a political entity in its own right. It is on this basis that the Irish political elite should bring the European Union centre stage in national debate and on these grounds that the European political elite should welcome the challenge.

Notes

1 Jean-Guy Giraud, 'Le règlement du problème irlandais', *Brève sur le traité de Lisbonne* No 186, August 2008. www.europarl.europa.eu/paris/4/uploads/pdf%20breves/breves186.pdf.

2 I owe thanks to Colin D. Shaw for this insight.

3 '[German Foreign] Minister suggests Ireland take a "break" from EU', *Irish Times*, 16 June 2008.

4 'France and Germany put the squeeze on Cowen', *Irish Times*, 21 June 2008.

5 'Roche criticises "communication deficit" in EU', *Irish Times*, 29 April 2008.

6 The active role played by Pat Cox, the Irish MEP who became Head of the European Parliament, in Irish EU referendums is the exception that proves this rule.

7 Comments by Commissioner McCreevy made at a public meeting on 'Ireland and the European Union: our joint economic future', European Commission Representation in Ireland, Dublin, 23 May 2008 (*Irish Times*, 24 May and 19 June 2008)

8 'It wasn't all about Lisbon. The people are fearful and in foul mood. And they have spoken' (front page headline, *Sunday Independent*, 15 June 2008).

9 Eurobarometer 69, First Results, June 2008, http://ec.europa.eu/public_opinion/archives/eb/eb69/eb_69_first_en.pdf.

10 'Ganley insists "this is a pro-European message"', *Irish Times*, 14 June 2008.

11 'The EU Treaty paves the way for a more effective EU which can serve the needs of Europe', Brian Lenihan, Minister for Finance, Bray, 21 April 2008, www.fiannafail.ie/article.phpx?topic=123&id=8883&nav=Local%20News.

12 'EU summits: Supplementary questions', *Dáil Debates*, 656(4), http://debates.oireachtas.ie/DDebate.aspx?F=DAL20080617.xml&Node=H4-1&Page=3.

References

Official documents (in chronological order)

Articles of Agreement for a Treaty between Great Britain and Ireland (Anglo-Irish Treaty) (1921) London, 6 December 1921, www.nationalarchives.ie/topics/anglo_irish/dfaexhib2.html.[1]

Constitution of the Irish Free State (Saorstát Eireann) Act (1922), www.irishstatutebook.ie/1922/en/act/pub/0001/index.html.

League of Nations (Guarantee) Act (1923) 18 August 1923, www.irishstatutebook.ie/1923/en/act/pub/0041/index.html.

Irish Nationality and Citizenship Act (1935), www.irishstatutebook.ie/1935/en/act/pub/0013/index.html.

Executive Authority (External Relations) Act (1936), www.irishstatutebook.ie/1936/en/act/pub/0058/index.html.

Bunreacht na hÉireann, Constitution of Ireland (1937), www.constitution.ie/reports/ConstitutionofIreland.pdf.

Emergency Powers Act, First Amendment to the Constitution (1939), www.irishstatutebook.ie/1939/en/act/pub/0028/index.html.

Republic of Ireland Act (1948), www.irishstatutebook.ie/1948/en/act/pub/0022/index.html.

Accession of Denmark, Ireland and the United Kingdom (1973) Brussels, 1 January 1973, Official Journal L 1973/2, 1, EN, 1–27.

The Northern Ireland Constitution (1974) White paper of the Northern Ireland Office (Cmnd. 5675), 4 July 1974, http://cain.ulst.ac.uk/hmso/cmd5675.htm.

New Ireland Forum report (1984) Dublin: Stationery Office, http://cain.ulst.ac.uk/issues/politics/nifr.htm.

Anglo-Irish Agreement (1985) Hillsborough, 15 November 1985, http://cain.ulst.ac.uk/events/aia/aiadoc.htm.

Single European Act (1986) Luxembourg and The Hague, 29 June 1987, Official Journal L 1987/169, 1, EN, 1–29.

Treaty on European Union including the Protocols and Final Act with Declarations (1992) Maastricht, 7 February 1992, http://eur-lex.europa.eu/en/treaties/dat/11992M/htm/11992M.html.

Joint Declaration on Peace (Downing Street Declaration) (1993) London, 15 December 1993, http://cain.ulst.ac.uk/events/peace/docs/dsd151293.htm.

A New Framework for Agreement (1995) London, 22 February 1995, http://cain.ulst.ac.uk/events/peace/docs/fd22295.htm.

Government White Paper on Foreign Policy (1996) Department of Foreign Affairs.

Treaty of Amsterdam amending the Treaty on European Union, the Treaties establishing the European Communities and certain related Acts (1997) Amsterdam, 10 November 1997, http://eur-lex.europa.eu/en/treaties/dat/11997D/htm/11997D.html.

The Agreement: Agreement Reached in the Multi-Party Negotiations (1998) Belfast, 10 April 1998, http://cain.ulst.ac.uk/events/peace/docs/agreement.htm.

Treaty of Nice amending the Treaty on European Union, the Treaties establishing the European Communities and certain related Acts (2001) Nice, 12 March 2001, http://eur-lex.europa.eu/en/treaties/dat/12001C/htm/12001C. html.

Agreement reached at St. Andrews (2006) St. Andrews, 13 October 2006, www.standrewsagreement.org/agreement.htm.

Treaty of Lisbon amending the Treaty on European Union and the Treaty establishing the European Community (2007) Lisbon, 13 December 2007, http://eur-lex.europa.eu/JOHtml.do?uri=OJ:C:2007:306:SOM:EN: HTML.

Official information publications

Department of Foreign Affairs, EEC Information Service (1971a) *Ireland and the Common Market: Industry and Employment*. Dublin: Department of Foreign Affairs.

Department of Foreign Affairs (1971b) *The Common Market and How It Works*. Dublin: Department of Foreign Affairs.

Department of Foreign Affairs (1972a) *'Into Europe': Ireland and the EEC*. Dublin: Department of Foreign Affairs.

Department of Foreign Affairs, EEC Information Service (1972b) *Ireland and the EEC: The Cost of Living*. Dublin: Department of Foreign Affairs.

Department of Foreign Affairs, EEC Information Service (1972c) *Ireland North and South in the EEC*. Dublin: Department of Foreign Affairs.

Department of Foreign Affairs (1972d) *Ireland and the Common Market: Regional Development*. Dublin: Department of Foreign Affairs.

Department of Foreign Affairs (2001) *Ireland in the World* (information website on Ireland and international relations), www.irlgov.ie/aboutireland/eng/irelandworld.asp.

European Commission (1999) *Eurobarometer 50*. Brussels: European Commission, http://ec.europa.eu/public_opinion/archives/eb/eb50/eb50_en.pdf.

European Commission (2006) *Eurobarometer 66: Public Opinion in the European Union*. Brussels: European Commission (Directorate General Communication), http://ec.europa.eu/public_opinion/archives/eb/eb66/eb66_en.pdf.

European Commission (2007) *Eurobarometer 67: Public Opinion in the European Union*. Brussels: European Commission (Directorate General Communication), http://ec.europa.eu/public_opinion/archives/eb/eb67/eb67_en.pdf.

European Communities (1997) *A New Treaty for Europe: Citizen's Guide*. (Amsterdam, 17 June 1997) Luxembourg: Official Publications of the European Communities.

Government Information Bureau (1972–73) *Eolas: An Information Bulletin*. Dublin: Stationery Office.

Government Information Service (n/d, *c*.1987a) *Why the Single European Act?* Dublin: Department of the Taoiseach.

Government Information Service (n/d, *c*.1987b) *The Single European Act: Why Ireland's Economy Depends on It*. Dublin: Stationery Office.

Government Information Service (n/d), *c*.1987c) *The Benefits of Being in the EEC: The Benefits the Single European Act will Guarantee*. Dublin: Stationery Office.

Government Information Service (n/d, *c*.1987d) *Freer Trade in the EEC: The Benefits for Ireland*. Dublin: Stationery Office.

Government Information Service (n/d, *c*.1987e) *The Single European Act: The Facts*. Dublin: Stationery Office.

Government Information Service (n/d, *c*.1987f) *Ireland's Neutrality: Six Key Questions about the Single European Act*. Dublin: Stationery Office.

Government Information Service (1987g) *The Single European Act: A Brief Guide*.

Texts of official discourse

Ahern, B. (24 November 1997) Speech by the Taoiseach at the American Chamber of Commerce Ireland business luncheon, www.dfa.ie/home/index.aspx?id=27015.

Ahern, B. (1 January 1998) Statement by the Taoiseach on the twenty-fifth anniversary of Ireland's accession to the EU, www.taoiseach.gov.ie/index.asp?locID=375&docID=1265.

Ahern, B. (3 February 1998) Speech by the Taoiseach on a motion in the Dublin University Law Society 'That this House believes the joint paper represents the best chance for as agreement in N. Ireland'. Trinity College Dublin.

Ahern, B. (3 March 1998) Address by the Taoiseach to the Council of the Institute of European Affairs, Dublin www.taoiseach.gov.ie/index.asp?locID=375&docID=1015.

Ahern, B. (30 March 1998) Address by the Taoiseach to the fifteenth plenary of the British-Irish Inter-Parliamentary Body in the Slieve Russel Hotel, Ballyconnell, Co. Cavan, www.taoiseach.gov.ie/index.asp?locID+375&docID+997.

Ahern, B. (21 April 1998) Speech by the Taoiseach on the second reading of the Nineteenth Amendment of the Constitution bill, Dáil Éireann, *Dáil Debates*,

489, 1027–43, http://historical-debates.oireachtas.ie/D/0489/D.0489. 199804210007.

Ahern, B. (26 April 1998) Speech by the Taoiseach at the Fianna Fáil Arbour Hill commemoration, www.dfa.ie/home/index.aspx?id=26976.

Ahern, B. (30 April 1998) Address by the Taoiseach to the EU Heads of Mission, Dublin, www.taoiseach.gov.ie/index.asp?locID=375&docID=998.

Ahern, B. (14 May 1998) 'The Good Friday Agreement and cultural diversity', speech by the Taoiseach, Dublin Castle, www.taoiseach.gov.ie/index. asp?locID=375&docID=1228.

Ahern, B. (20 May 1998) Address by the Taoiseach to the IMPACT biennial conference, Co. Clare, www.taoiseach.gov.ie/index.asp?locID=375&docID=-1145.

Ahern, B. (29 October 1998) 'The Western Isles of Europe at the millennium', *The Lothian European Lecture* delivered by the Taoiseach, Edinburgh, www.taoiseach.gov.ie/index.asp?locID=375&docID=1030.

Ahern, B. (11 November 1998) Statement by the Taoiseach on the Memorial Park at Messines, www.taoiseach.gov.ie/index.asp?locID=375& docID=1273.

Ahern, B. (29 March 1999) Opening address by the Taoiseach at a European Movement national conference on 'Partnership for Peace', Dublin, www.irlgov.ie/taoiseach/press/current/29-03-99.htm (accessed January 2001).

Ahern, B. (15 April 1999) 'Ireland and Britain: a new relationship for a new millennium', address by the Taoiseach at the Irish Studies Centre, University of North London, www.irlgov.ie/taoiseach/press/current/15-10-99.htm [*sic*] (accessed January 2001).

Ahern, B. (15 May 1999) Speech by the Taoiseach to the Federation of Irish Societies annual congress, Leicester, www.irlgov.ie/taoiseach/press/current/ 15-05-99.htm (accessed January 2001).

Ahern, B. (21 March 2000) 'Ireland and the EU: future prospects', address by the Taoiseach to the Institute of European Affairs, Dublin, www.irlgov.ie/ taoiseach/press/current/21-03-2000.htm (accessed January 2001).

Ahern, B. (13 December 2000) Statement by the Taoiseach on the European Council in Nice, 7–11 December 2000, Dáil Éireann, *Dáil Debates*, 528, 444–52, http://historical-debates.oireachtas.ie/D/0528/D.0528.2000121300 17.html.

Ahern, B. (8 January 2001) 'Ireland's experience of EU membership', speech by the Taoiseach to the Malta Chamber of Commerce, Valletta, www.taoiseach.gov.ie/index.asp?locID=369&docID=479.

Ahern, B. (9 January 2001) 'Ireland's experience of EU membership', speech by the Taoiseach to the Chamber of Commerce, Cyprus, www.taoiseach. gov.ie/index.asp?locID=369&docID=482.

Ahern, B. (5 February 2001) Speech by the Taoiseach at the European Movement Ireland 'European of the Year' Award, Dublin, www.taoiseach. gov.ie/index.asp?locID=369&docID=470.

Ahern, B. (8 February 2001) Seanad statement by the Taoiseach on the European Council in Nice, Seanad Éireann. *Seanad Debates,* 65:2, 160–66, http://historical-debates.oireachtas.ie/S/0165/S.0165.200102080008.html.

Ahern, B. (1 March 2001a) 'A new relationship for a new era', address by the Taoiseach to the National Assembly for Wales, Cardiff, www.irlgov.ie/taoiseach/press/current/01-03-01.htm (accessed May 2001).

Ahern, B. (1 March 2001b) 'Europe: the Irish viewpoint', keynote address by the Taoiseach to the *Wales, Europe and the World* Forum, Newport, Wales, www.irlgov.ie/taoiseach/press/current/01-03-01b.htm (accessed May 2001).

Ahern, B. (17 March 2001) Address by the Taoiseach at the American Ireland Fund dinner, Washington, www.taoiseach.gov.ie/index.asp?locID=369&docID=506.

Ahern, B. (29 March 2001a) Statement by the Taoiseach to the Dáil on the outcome of the Stockholm European Council, *Dáil Debates,* 533, 1084–89, http://historical-debates.oireachtas.ie/D/0533/D.0533. 200103290007.html.

Ahern, B. (29 March 2001b) Speech by the Taoiseach at the Founders' Dinner, Institute of European Affairs, Dublin, www.irlgov.ie/taoiseach/press/current/29-03-01b.htm (accessed May 2001), also: http://www.eurosceptic.com/sources_of_information/speeches/bertie_ahern. htm.

Ahern, B. (22 April 2001) Speech by the Taoiseach at the annual Arbour Hill commemoration, www.taoiseach.gov.ie/index.asp?locID=369&docID=541.

Ahern, B. (8 May 2001) The Taoiseach answers questions on the European Council meeting in Gothenburg, Dáil Éireann, *Dáil Debates,* 535:4, 1147–49, http://historical-debates.oireachtas.ie/D/0535/D.0535.200105080002.html.

Ahern, B. (9 May 2001) Speech by the Taoiseach at the launch of the Nice Treaty referendum campaign, www.taoiseach.gov.ie/index.asp?locID=369&docID=484.

Ahern, B. (14 May 2001a) The Taoiseach answers questions about the Treaty of Nice, Department of Foreign Affairs press release, ww.dfa.ie/home/index. aspx?id=26458.

Ahern, B. (14 May 2001b) Speech by the Taoiseach at a state reception in honour of His Eminence Desmond Cardinal Connell, Dublin Castle, www.taoiseach.gov.ie/index.asp?locID=369&docID=500.

Ahern, B. (8 June 2001) Statement by the Taoiseach on the outcome of the Nice Treaty referendum, www.taoiseach.gov.ie/index.asp?locID=369&docID=495.

Ahern, B. (12 June 2001) Statement by the Taoiseach on the outcome of the referendum on the Nice Treaty, Dáil Éireann. *Dáil Debates,* 537:5, 1103–06, http://historical-debates.oireachtas.ie/D/0537/D.0537.200106120015.html.

Ahern, B. (20 June 2001) Address by the Taoiseach to the Scottish Parliament, Edinburgh, www.scottish.parliament.uk/nmCentre/news/news-01/pa01-043. htm.

Ahern, B. (21 June 2001) Speech by the Taoiseach at a state dinner in honour of President and Mrs Prodi, Dublin Castle, www.gov.ie/taoiseach/press/current/21-06-01.htm (accessed June 2001).

Ahern, B. (11 February 2002) Speech by the Taoiseach at a reception in honour of an economic delegation from Wales led by First Minister, Rhodri Morgan, Dublin Castle, www.taoiseach.gov.ie/index.asp?locID=367&docID=694.

Ahern, B. (22 April 2007) Speech by the Taoiseach at the annual Arbour Hill commemoration, http://cain.ulst.ac.uk/issues/politics/docs/dott/ba220407.htm.

Ahern, B. (15 May 2007) 'Ireland and Britain: a shared history – a new partnership', speech by the Taoiseach to the joint Houses of Parliament at Westminster, www.taoiseach.gov.ie/index.asp?locID=558&docID=3427.

Andrews, D. (27 November 1997) 'A moment of definition draws near', speech by the Minister for Foreign Affairs to ambassadors of the European Union, Dublin, www.dfa.ie/home/index.aspx?id=27012.

Andrews, D. (20 April 1998) 'Minister for Foreign Affairs highlights advantages of Amsterdam Treaty', Department of Foreign Affairs press release, www.dfa.ie/home/index.aspx?id=26979.

Andrews, D. (26 April 1998) 'An unbeatable chance to work together for a better future', article by the Minister for Foreign Affairs, *News of the World*, www.dfa.ie/home/index.aspx?id=26977.

Andrews, D. (27 April 1998) 'Minister of Foreign Affairs calls for EU support to help consolidate Northern settlement', Department of Foreign Affairs press release, www.dfa.ie/home/index.aspx?id=26975.

Andrews, D. (29 April 1998) 'Minister for Foreign Affairs praises role of the EU in peace process', speech to the European Parliament in Brussels, www.dfa.ie/home/index.aspx?id=26974.

Andrews, D. (30 April 1998) 'A passage over the threshold', address by the Minister of Foreign Affairs to the Council of Europe on the Good Friday Agreement, www.dfa.ie/home/index.aspx?id=26972.

Andrews, D. (15 May 1998) 'The Amsterdam Treaty', speech by the Minister for Foreign Affairs to an ICTU Conference, www.dfa.ie/home/index.aspx?id=26965.

Andrews, D. (20 May 1998) 'Minister Andrews gives five good reasons for a resounding Yes to Amsterdam', Department of Foreign Affairs press release, www.foreignaffairs.irlgov.ie/home/index.aspx?id=2691.

Barry, P. (11 March 1983) Speech by the Minister for Foreign Affairs at a function marking twenty-one years of membership of Dáil Éireann by T. O'Donnell, Limerick. (Source: Fine Gael collected papers, Institute for British-Irish Studies [IBIS], University College Dublin.)

Burke, R. (1979) 'Foreword by Commissioner Richard Burke', in J. Cooney, *The Race for Europe*, Dublin: Dublin University Press, v–viii.

Burke, R. P. (2 October 1997) 'Article by the Minister for Foreign Affairs on the occasion of the signing of the Treaty of Amsterdam', Department of Foreign Affairs press release, www.dfa.ie/home/index.aspx?id=27049.

Burke, R. P. (28 October 1997) Remarks by the Minister for Foreign Affairs to representatives of the Foreign Press Association, London, www.dfa.ie/home/index.aspx?id=27032.

Collins, G. (8 March 1990) 'The future of our changing Europe', address by the Minister for Foreign Affairs to the Irish Council of the European Movement Conference. Dublin.

Cosgrave, L. (2 July 1973) 'Northern Ireland', text of a speech given by the Taoiseach. (Source: Government Documentation N.I.2.)

Cosgrave, L. (13 March 1974) 'The status of Northern Ireland', statement by the Taoiseach, Dáil Éireann, *Dáil Debates*, 271, 7–12, http://historical-debates.oireachtas.ie/D/0271/D.0271.197403130002.html.

Cosgrave, L. (13 June 1974) Speech by the Taoiseach, Dún Laoghaire. (Source: Government Documentation N.I.8.)

Cosgrave, L. (26 June 1974) Text of a statement by the Taoiseach to Dáil Éireann, *Dáil Debates*, 273, 1571–81, http://historical-debates.oireachtas.ie/D/0273/D.0273.197406260010.html.

Costello, J. A. and de Valera, E. (10 May 1949) *Bipartisan Declaration* (on partition) unanimously adopted on the proposition of the Taoiseach and the leader of Fianna Fáil. (Source: MacBride, 1985: 78–9, 110–11.)

Cowen, B. (28 April 2000) Address by the Minister for Foreign Affairs at the annual conference of the Local Authority Members Association, Kilkenny, www.dfa.ie/home/index.aspx?id=26635.

Cowen, B. (27 May 2000) 'Nationalism and the Act of Union', address by the Minister for Foreign Affairs to Conference of the British Irish Association and Institute of British-Irish Studies, Dublin. (Source: Publication of conference proceedings by British Irish Association, 2000: 13–19.)

Cowen, B. (31 May 2000) Statement by the Minister for Foreign Affairs to the select committee on foreign affairs, www.dfa.ie/home/index.aspx?id=26619.

Cowen, B. (6 June 2000) Speech by Minister for Foreign Affairs at luncheon in honour of H.E. Mr Goh Chok Tong, Prime Minister of the Republic of Singapore, Iveagh House, www.dfa.ie/home/index.aspx?id=26613.

Cowen, B. (15 June 2000) Address by Minister for Foreign Affairs to the fourth Asia Europe Young Leaders Symposium (AEYLS) at Ennis, Co. Clare, www.dfa.ie/home/index.aspx?id=26612.

Cower, B. (14 September 2000) Statement by the Minister for Foreign Affairs during the General Debate at the fifty-fifth session of the General Assembly of the United Nations, www.foreignaffairs.irlgov.ie/home/index.aspx?id=26581.

Cowen, B. (3 May 2001) 'Treaty of Nice', opening statement by the Minister for Foreign Affairs, Seanad Éireann, *Seanad Debates*, 166, 721–27, http://historical-debates.oireachtas.ie/S/0166/S.0166.200105030005.html.

Cowen, B. (14 May 2001) 'Let's share in EU's great future', article by the Minister for Foreign Affairs, *Irish Examiner*, www.dfa.ie/home/index.aspx?id=26459.

Cowen, B. (19 May 2001) 'Brings combativeness to bear on his brief', interview with the Minister for Foreign Affairs by Vincent Browne, *Irish Times*.

Cowen, B. (27 May 2001) 'Treaty of Nice: it will give the EU peace and stability', article by Minister for Foreign Affairs, *Sunday Business Post*, www.dfa.ie/home/index.aspx?id=26448.

De Valera, E. (n/d, *c*.1918) *Eamonn [sic] De Valera States His Case*. Reprint as a pamphlet text of an interview published in *Christian Science Monitor*, May 1918. Dublin: Sinn Féin.

De Valera, E. (1922) *The Testament of the Republic*. Dublin: Irish Nation Committee.

De Valera, E. (21 June 1925) Speech delivered by the leader of anti-treaty Sinn Féin at the grave of Wolfe Tone. (Source: de Valera, 1926: 1–2.)

De Valera, E. (17 April 1926) Extract from an interview given by the leader of anti-treaty Sinn Féin to the representative of the United Press. (Source: de Valera, 1926: 18–24.)

De Valera, E. (16 May 1926) Speech delivered at the inaugural meeting of Fianna Fáil at La Scala Theatre, Dublin. (Source: de Valera, 1926: 3–14.)

De Valera, E. (1926) *A National Policy*. Dublin: Fianna Fáil.

De Valera, E. (16 September 1935) Speech by the President of the Executive Council at the League of Nations on the Abyssinian Crisis. (Source: Mitchell and Ó Snodaigh 1985: 212, doc. 124.)

De Valera, E. (1936) Statement by the President of the Executive Council to the League of Nations. (Source: MacBride, 1985: 41.)

De Valera, E. (28 January 1942) Speech by the Taoiseach on the arrival of U.S. troops in Northern Ireland, *Irish Press*. (Source: Mitchell and Ó Snodaigh, 1985, Doc.137, 231.)

De Valera, E. (17 July 1945) Statement by the Taoiseach on the constitutional status of the state (Vote 65 – External Affairs), Dáil Éireann. *Dáil Debates*, 97 2569–74, http://historical-debates.oireachtas.ie/D/0097/D.0097.194507170021.html.

De Valera, S. (18 September 2000) Address by the Minister for Arts, Heritage, the Gaeltacht and the Islands, Boston College, Massachusetts, 18 September 2000. (Source: *Irish Times*, 20 September 2000.)

Dillon, J. (17 October 1963) 'Dillon urges EEC integration', article by the leader of Fine Gael, *Irish Times*.

Dukes, A. (1988) 'How Ireland has coped with its new role', article by the leader of Fine Gael, *Community Report: 'Ireland in the EC, First Fifteen Years 1973–1988'*, 8: 3, 6, 11.

Fine Gael (12 September 1969) *Political Party Statement on Northern Ireland*.

FitzGerald, G. (5 January 1963) 'The Common Market', article in *Irish Times*. (Source: Desmond, 2001.)

FitzGerald, G. (1973 [1972]) *Towards a New Ireland*. Dublin: Torc Books.

FitzGerald, G. (7 September 1976) 'European Integration', address by the Minister for Foreign Affairs of Ireland to the Europa Institute at the University of Amsterdam, University of Amsterdam: Occasional Papers of the European Instituut, 3, 1976.

FitzGerald, G. (19 September 1977) 'The role of Fine Gael', address by the leader of Fine Gael, Cork. (Source: *The Role of Fine Gael: Speeches by Garret FitzGerald*. Dublin: Fine Gael, (n/d) *c*.1977: 7–14.)

FitzGerald, G. (27 September 1977) 'Northern Ireland', extract from a speech by the leader of Fine Gael, Moylough, Co. Galway. (Source: *The Role of Fine Gael*, 1977: 15–17.)

FitzGerald, G. (20 May 1978) Presidential address by the leader of Fine Gael to the Fine Gael Ardfheis. (Source: Fine Gael collected papers, IBIS, UCD.)

FitzGerald, G. (16 June 1978) 'Brussels and Washington: new perspectives on the Northern Ireland issue', speech by the leader of Fine Gael to the Foreign Policy Association, New York. (Source: Fine Gael collected papers, IBIS, UCD.)

FitzGerald, G. (20 August 1978) Address by the leader of Fine Gael at Michael Collins commemoration, Beal na Blath. (Source: Fine Gael collected papers, IBIS, UCD.)

FitzGerald, G. (27 October 1978) 'A new direction for Ireland', speech by the leader of Fine Gael, College Historical Society, Trinity College Dublin. (Source: Fine Gael collected papers, IBIS, UCD.)

FitzGerald, G. (25 February 1979) Address by the leader of Fine Gael to the East Belfast branch of the Social Democratic and Labour Party, Europa Hotel, Belfast. (Source: Fine Gael collected papers, IBIS, UCD.)

FitzGerald, G. (26 February 1979) 'Unity and the union', speech by the leader of Fine Gael, Law Society, Queen's University Belfast. (Source: Fine Gael collected papers, IBIS, UCD.)

FitzGerald, G. (22 February 1980) 'Northern Ireland as we enter the '80s', speech by the leader of Fine Gael, Portora School, Enniskillen. (Source: Fine Gael collected papers, IBIS, UCD.)

FitzGerald, G. (5 June 1981) Speech by the leader of Fine Gael, Roscommon. (Source: Fine Gael collected papers, IBIS, UCD.)

FitzGerald, G. (27 September 1981) 'Towards a new Ireland', transcripts of an interview with the Taoiseach on the RTÉ Radio 1 programme *This Week* (interviewer Gerald Barry). Issued by Government Information Service. (Source: Fine Gael collected papers, IBIS, UCD.)

FitzGerald, G. (6 November 1981) Communiqué issued by the Irish Government following the Taoiseach's summit with the British Prime Minister, London. (Source: Mansergh, 1986: 358.)

FitzGerald, G. (11 February 1982) 'Northern Ireland', speech by the Taoiseach to Fine Gael workers, Mansion House, Dublin. (Source: Fine Gael collected papers, IBIS, UCD.)

FitzGerald, G. (5 June 1982) Speech by the leader of Fine Gael to the Social Democratic and Labour Party Conference, Europa Hotel, Belfast. (Source: Fine Gael collected papers, IBIS, UCD.)

FitzGerald, G. (30 September 1982) 'Reconciliation in a divided community', *Heinz Fellowship Lecture* delivered by the leader of Fine Gael, University of Pittsburgh. (Source: Fine Gael collected papers, IBIS, UCD.)

FitzGerald, G. (18 November 1982) Speech by the leader of Fine Gael, Dublin South East constituency meeting, Shelbourne Hotel, Dublin. (Source: Fine Gael collected papers, IBIS, UCD.)

FitzGerald, G. (30 May 1983) Speech by the Taoiseach at the first meeting of the Forum for a New Ireland, Dublin Castle. (Source: Fine Gael collected papers, IBIS, UCD.)

FitzGerald, G. (22 October 1983) Address by the Taoiseach to the Fine Gael Ardfheis, Ballsbridge. (Source: Fine Gael collected papers, IBIS, UCD.)

FitzGerald, G. (15 December 1983) Speech by the Taoiseach on the Haagerup Report, Dáil adjournment debate, Dáil Éireann, *Dáil Debates*, 348, 2460–80, http://historical-debates.oireachtas.ie/D/0346/D.0346.198312150020.html.

FitzGerald, G. (14 March 1984) Speech by the Taoiseach at a dinner on the occasion of his visit to Washington. (Source: Fine Gael collected papers, IBIS, UCD.)

FitzGerald, G. (15 March 1984) Speech by the Taoiseach to the joint Houses of Congress, Washington. (Source: Fine Gael collected papers, IBIS, UCD.)

FitzGerald, G. (16 March 1984) Reply by the Taoiseach to the toast by President Reagan at White House luncheon. (Source: Fine Gael collected papers, IBIS, UCD.)

FitzGerald, G. (3 June 1984) Address of the Taoiseach at a dinner in honour of President Reagan, Dublin Castle. (Source: Fine Gael collected papers, IBIS, UCD.)

FitzGerald, G. (29 June 1984) 'My message to the northern unionists', article by the Taoiseach, *Belfast Telegraph*. (Source: Fine Gael collected papers, IBIS, UCD.)

FitzGerald, G. (20 November 1984) 'Summit between the Taoiseach and the British Prime Minister, 18–19 November 1984', statement by the Taoiseach to Dáil Éireann, *Dáil Debates*, 354, 164–70, http://historical-debates. oireach-tas.ie/D/0354/D.0354.198411200082.html.

FitzGerald, G. (22 March 1985) Speech by the Taoiseach to the Diplomatic and Commonwealth Writers' Association. (Source: Mansergh 1986: 948.)

FitzGerald, G. (11 July 1985) Statement by the Taoiseach during an adjournment debate on talks between the British and Irish Governments, Dáil Éireann, *Dáil Debates*, 360:7, 1455–56, http://historical-debates.oireachtas. ie/D/0360/D.0360.198507110003.html.

FitzGerald, G. (22 November 1990) 'What makes politics tick? Interests, ideals or emotions?', *John Whyte Memorial Lecture*, delivered by the former Taoiseach, Queen's University Belfast. Belfast: Queen's Politics Occasional Paper 3, 1990.

FitzGerald, G. (23 June 2001) 'Treaty campaign has a mountain to climb', *Irish Times*.

FitzGerald, G. and Harte, P. (1979) *Ireland: – Our Future Together*, co-authored by the leader of Fine Gael and the Fine Gael spokesman on Northern Ireland. Dublin: Fine Gael.

Harney, M. (21 July 2000) Remarks by the Tánaiste at a meeting of the American Bar Association in the Law Society of Ireland, Dublin, www.entemp.ie/press/2000/210700.htm.

Harney, M. (4 June 2001) 'Let enlarged EU work effectively', article by the Tánaiste and Leader of the Progressive Democrats, *Irish Times*.

Haughey, C. J. (14 December 1962) 'The Common Market', speech by Minister for Justice, University College Galway. (Source: Mansergh, 1986: 12–13, doc. 7.)

Haughey, C. J. (26 July 1967) 'The second application for EEC membership', statement by the Minister for Finance in Dáil Éireann, *Dáil Debates*, 230, 1098–1117, http://historical-debates.oireachtas.ie/D/0230/D.0230. 196707260006.html.

Haughey, C. J. (15 September 1967) 'Cultural identity and the European Community', address by the Minister for Finance at the opening of the annual assembly of the Irish Folk School Movement, Bray. (Source: Mansergh, 1986: 80–2, doc. 29.)

Haughey, C. J. (10 December 1970) 'New tensions of change', speech by the Fianna Fáil TD, *Cairde Fáil* function, Wynn's Hotel, Dublin. (Source: Mansergh, 1986: 142–5, doc. 45.)

Haughey, C. J. (7 May 1972) 'Ireland's place among the nations of Europe: an historic opportunity', speech by the Fianna Fáil TD to election workers, Dublin North-East constituency, Edenmore. (Source: Mansergh, 1986: 161–3, doc. 52.)

Haughey, C. J. (24 June 1976) 'The European Community and the economic crisis: an inadequate response', speech by the Fianna Fáil TD to the Publicity Club of Ireland, Broc House, Dublin. (Source: Mansergh, 1986: 224, doc. 71.)

Haughey, C. J. (16 February 1980) 'Northern Ireland: a failed political entity', presidential address by the Taoiseach to the Fianna Fáil Ardfheis. (Source: Mansergh, 1986: 327–38, doc. 92.)

Haughey, C. J. (1 May 1980) 'The Community in disarray', statement by the Taoiseach on a meeting of the European Council in Luxembourg, Dáil Éireann, *Dáil Debates*, 320, 423–31, http://historical-debates.oireachtas.ie/D/ 0320/D.0320.198005010006.html.

Haughey, C. J. (29 May 1980) 'Downing Street talks', statement by the Taoiseach, Dáil Éireann, *Dáil Debates*, 321, 1052–64, http://historical-debates.oireachtas.ie/D/0321/D.0321.198005290004.html.

Haughey, C. J. (11 March 1981) 'Defence policy', statement by the Taoiseach, Dáil Éireann, *Dáil Debates*, 327, 1393–1400, http://historical-debates.oireachtas.ie/D/0327/D.0327.198103110048.html.

Haughey, C. J. (17 March 1981) 'The cultural unity of Ireland', St. Patrick's Day message by the Taoiseach. (Source: Mansergh, 1986: 450–1, doc. 115.)

Haughey, C. J. (26 March 1981) 'Employment, agriculture and the EEC', statement by the Taoiseach on the Maastricht European Council, Dáil Éireann, *Dáil Debates*, 328, 380–89, http://historical-debates.oireachtas.ie/D/0328/ D.0328.198103260071.html.

Haughey, C. J. (11 April 1981) 'The spirit of the nation', presidential address by the Taoiseach to the fiftieth Fianna Fáil Ardfheis. (Source: Mansergh, 1986: 462–81, doc. 119.)

Haughey, C. J. (11 October 1981) 'Eamon de Valera and the colonial mentality: a reply to the constitutional crusade', speech by the leader of Fianna Fáil at the unveiling of the de Valera memorial, Ennis. (Source: Mansergh, 1986: 522–5, doc. 126.)

Haughey, C. J. (2 December 1981) 'The Genscher-Colombo proposals for a European Act', statement by the leader of Fianna Fáil on the outcome of the European Council Meeting in London, Dáil Éireann, *Dáil Debates*, 331, 909–24, http://historical-debates.oireachtas.ie/D/0331/D.0331.198112020 054. html.

Haughey, C. J. (10 November 1981) 'The faltering initiative', speech by the leader of Fianna Fáil on the outcome of the London Summit. (Source: Mansergh, 1986. 538–48, doc. 131.)

Haughey, C. J. (7 January 1982) 'The Church of Ireland and the libertarian tradition', speech by the leader of Fianna Fáil at a fund-raising function, Jury's Hotel, Dublin. (Source: Mansergh, 1986: 572–3, doc. 125.)

Haughey, C. J. (15 January 1982) ' "The Unionist case": Fianna Fáil's reply', letter by the leader of Fianna Fáil to Robert McCartney. (Source: Mansergh, 1986, 573–81, doc. 136.)

Haughey, C. J. (9 March 1982) 'Ireland's right to self-determination', speech by the Taoiseach on the nomination of members of government, Dáil Éireann, *Dáil Debates*, 333, 33–45, http://historical-debates.oireachtas.ie/D/0333/D. 0333.198203090005.html.

Haughey, C. J. (17 March 1982) 'St. Patrick's Day in the White House', speech by the Taoiseach, Washington. (Source: Mansergh, 1986: 606–8, doc. 141.)

Haughey, C. J. (23 May 1982) 'Rolling devolution: the Prior initiative', Interview by the Taoiseach, RTÉ. (Source: Mansergh, 1986: 612–3, doc. 142.)

Haughey, C. J. (16 July 1982) 'Northern Ireland: a lack of consultaton', speech by the Taoiseach, adjournment debate, Dáil Éireann, *Dáil Debates*, 337, 3090–3113, http://historical-debates.oireachtas.ie/D/0337/D.0337. 198207160005.html.

Haughey, C. J. (26 September 1982) 'The renewed political struggle in Ireland', speech by the Taoiseach at the Wolfe Tone commemoration ceremony, Bodenstown. (Source: Mansergh, 1986: 672–3, doc. 153.)

Haughey, C. J. (8 October 1982) 'A crossroads of the world', speech by the Taoiseach at the opening of the world business council conference, Killarney. (Source: Mansergh,1986: 683–8, doc. 156.)

Haughey, C. J. (26 February 1983) 'Back on the high road', presidential address by the leader of Fianna Fáil to the Fianna Fáil Ardfheis. (Source: Mansergh, 1986: 733–42, doc. 166.)

Haughey, C. J. (30 May 1983) Speech by the leader of Fianna Fáil at the opening of the New Ireland Forum, Dublin Castle. (Source: Mansergh, 1986: 752–8, doc. 171.)

Haughey, C. J. (22 June 1983) Statement by the leader of Fianna Fáil on the European Council at Stuttgart, 17–19 June 1983, to Dáil Éireann. (Source: Mansergh, 1986: 758–62, doc. 172.)

Haughey, C. J. (7 December 1983) ' The superlevy negotiations', statement by the leader of Fianna Fáil on the outcome of European Council meeting in Athens, Dáil Éireann. (Source: Mansergh, 1986: 785–7, doc. 178.)

Haughey, C. J. (6 December 1984) 'The third Irish Presidency: the outcome of the Dublin European Council', statement by the leader of Fianna Fáil, Dáil Éireann, *Dáil Debates,* 354, 1841–53, http://historical-debates.oireachtas.ie/D/0354/D.0354.198412060003.html.

Haughey, C. J. (1 March 1985) 'Strengthening the Irish-American connection', speech by the leader of Fianna Fáil at the first annual dinner of the friends of Fianna Fáil in America, New York. (Source: Mansergh, 1986: 914–19, doc. 202.)

Haughey, C. J. (15 May 1985) 'The Bilderberg Conference', reply to the Taoiseach's statement on his visit to North America, Dáil Éireann, *Dáil Debates,*358, 1118–30, http://historical-debates.oireachtas.ie/D/0358/D.0358.198505150043.html.

Haughey, C. J. (26 June 1985) Speech by the leader of Fianna Fáil, debate on the Dooge Report, Dáil Éireann, *Dáil Debates,* 359, 1962–81, http://historical-debates.oireachtas.ie/D/0359/D.0359.198506260003.html.

Haughey, C. J. (2 November 1985) 'Young people and the future', address by the leader of Fianna Fáil to the tenth national youth conference of *Ógra Fianna Fáil,* Metropole Hotel, Cork. (Source: Mansergh, 1986: 1002–07, doc. 220.)

Haughey, C. J. (19 November 1985) 'The Hillsborough Agreement', statement by the leader of Fianna Fáil, Dáil Éireann, *Dáil Debates,* 361, 2580–2600, http://historical-debates.oireachtas.ie/D/0361/D.0361.198511190109.html.

Haughey, C. J. (4 December 1985) 'The draft European Act', statement by the leader of Fianna Fáil on the European Council at Luxembourg, 2–3 December 1985, Dáil Éireann, *Dáil Debates,* 362, 1166–82; http://historical-debates.oireachtas.ie/D/0362/D.0362.198512040033.html.

Haughey, C. J. (19 April 1986) 'Reviving the spirit of the nation', presidential address by the leader of Fianna Fáil to the Fianna Fáil Ardfheis. (Source: Mansergh, 1986: 1102–14, doc. 233.)

Haughey, C. J. (12 October 1986) 'The deterioration in the Northern situation', speech by the leader of Fianna Fáil at the annual Wolfe Tone commemoration ceremony, Bodenstown, Co. Kildare. (Source: Mansergh, 1986: 1158–60, doc. 243.)

Kitt, T. (10 May 2001) 'Ireland is a model for other nations', article by the Minister of State with Responsibility for Labour, Trade and Consumer Affairs, *Irish Sun.*

Lenihan, B. P. (1988) 'First fifteen has put Ireland ahead', article by the Tánaiste and Minister for Foreign Affairs, *Community Report,* 8:3, 2–3.

Lenihan, B. J. (21 April 2008) 'The EU Treaty paves the way for a more effective EU which can serve the needs of Europe', Speech by Minister for Finance, Bray, Co. Wicklow, www.fiannafail.ie/article.phpx?topic=123&id=8883&nav=Local%20News.

Lynch, J. (25 July 1967) 'European Economic Community', statement by the Taoiseach to Dáil Éireann on Ireland's second application for EEC membership, *Dáil Debates,* 230, 742–82, http://historical-debates.oireachtas.ie/D/0230/D.0230.196707250030.html.

Lynch, J. (28 January 1969) Speech by the Taoiseach to the Fianna Fáil Ardfheis. (Source: M. Kennedy, *Division and Consensus*, 2000: 319).

Lynch, J. (28 August 1969) Statement on Northern Ireland by the Taoiseach. (Source: J. Lynch, *Irish Unity, Northern Ireland, Anglo-Irish Relations: August 1969–October 1971*. Dublin: Government Information Bureau, 1971: 6–8.)

Lynch, J. (20 September 1969) Speech by the Taoiseach, Tralee. (Source: Lynch, 1971: 9–12.)

Lynch, J. (17 January 1970) Presidential address by the Taoiseach to the Fianna Fáil Ardfheis. (Source: Lynch, 1971: 15–16.)

Lynch, J. (11 July 1970) Address by the Taoiseach over Radio Teilefís Éireann. (Source: Lynch, 1971: 22–3.)

Lynch, J. (1971) *Irish Unity, Northern Ireland* and *Anglo-Irish Relations: Speeches, August 1969–October 1971*. Dublin: Government Information Bureau.

Lynch, J. (20 February 1971) Presidential address by the Taoiseach to the Fianna Fáil Ardfheis. (Source: Lynch, 1971: 41–8.)

Lynch, J. (17 March 1971) Speech to the Society of the Friendly Sons of St Patrick, Philadelphia. (Source: Lynch, 1971: 49–50.)

Lynch, J. (28 May 1971) Speech by the Taoiseach, Dundalk. (Source: Lynch, 1971: 55–9.)

Lynch, J. (6 August 1971) Speech by the Taoiseach in Dáil Éireann (Vote 3 – Department of the Taoiseach), *Dáil Debates*, 255, 3860–72, http://historical-debates.oireachtas.ie/D/0255/D.0255.197108060005.html.

Lynch, J. (20 October 1971) Statement by the Taoiseach opening the special debate on the Northern Ireland, Dáil Éireann. (Source: Lynch, 1971: 87–106.)

Lynch, J. (July 1972) 'Northern Ireland in the context of Anglo-Irish relations', article by the Taoiseach, *Eolas: an information bulletin* (issued by the Government Information Bureau), 1:4, 1.

Lynch, J. (2 November 1972) Statement by the Taoiseach on the second stage of the Fifth Amendment to the Constitution, Dáil Éireann, *Dáil Debates*, 263, 422–5, http://historical-debates.oireachtas.ie/D/0263/D.0263.19721 1020005.html.

O'Donnell, L. (15 August 1997) 'The important role of small nations in world affairs', speech by the Minister of State at the Department of Foreign Affairs, Humbert summer school, Ballina, www.foreignaffairs.irlgov.ie/home/index.aspx?id=27072.

O'Donnell, L. (20 November 1997) 'Small states and European security', Opening address by the Minister of State at the Department of Foreign Affairs at the Royal Irish Academy's nineteenth Annual Conference, Dublin, www.dfa.ie/home/index.aspx?id=27016.

Prodi, R. (22 June 2001) 'Our common future', speech by the President of the European Commission, University College Cork, www.ireland.com/ newspaper/special/2001/prodicork/index.htm.

Quinn, R. (7 May 1997) Address by Minister for Finance at the presentation of the European Journalism Awards, Iveagh House, www.foreignaffairs.irlgov.ie/home/index.aspx?id=27106.

Reynolds, A. (30 June 1994) 'The European Structural Funds in Ireland', address by the Taoiseach at conference on 'Equity in development: the European structural funds in Ireland'. (Source: joint publication of conference proceedings by the Community Workers Co-operative and the Northern Ireland Council for Voluntary Action, Belfast and Dublin, 1994.)

Robinson, M. (2 February 1995) 'Cherishing the Irish diaspora', address by Uachtarán na hÉireann to joint sitting of the Houses of the Oireachtas. *Dáil Debates*, 448, 1145–56, http://historical-debates.oireachtas.ie/D/0448/D.0448.199502020002.html.

Spring, D. (7 February 1997) 'Reflections on Ireland's EU Presidency 1 July 1996–31 December 1996', address by the Tánaiste and Minister for Foreign Affairs to law students, University College Cork, www.dfa.ie/home/index.aspx?id=27137.

Sutherland, P. (1988) 'Why the good news may only be starting', article by the European Commissioner, *Community Report*, 8:3, 4–5.

Books and articles

Adams, W. (1993) 'Nation over ethnic groups: a European look at the America experience', in P. Krüger (ed.) *Ethnicity and Nationalism: Case Studies in Their Intrinsic Tension and Political Dynamics*. Marburg: Hitzeroth, 91–6.

Alter, P. (1987) 'Symbols of Irish nationalism', in A. O'Day (ed.) *Reactions to Irish Nationalism*, 1–20.

Althusser, L. (1971) *Lenin and Philosophy and Other Essays*, trans. B. Brewster. London: Monthly Review Press.

Amery, L. S. (1912) 'Home Rule and the colonial analogy', in S. Rosenbaum (ed.) *Against Home Rule*, 128–52.

Anderson, B. (1991 [1983]) *Imagined Communities*. London: Verso.

Andrews, C. J. (1979) *Dublin Made Me: An Autobiography*. Dublin: Mercier Press.

Armstrong, J. (1982) *Nations before Nationalism*. Chapel Hill: University of North Caroline Press.

Arthur, P. (1999) ' "Quiet diplomacy and personal conversation": Track two diplomacy and the search for a settlement in Northern Ireland', in J. Ruane and J. Todd (eds), *After the Good Friday Agreement: Analysing Political Change in Northern Ireland*. Dublin: University College Dublin Press, 71–95.

Austin, J. L. (1962) *How to Do Things with Words*. Oxford: Clarendon Press.

Ball, T., Farr, J. and Hanson, R. L. (eds) (1989) *Political Innovation and Conceptual Change*. Cambridge: Cambridge University Press.

Barker, R. (2001) *Legitimating Identities: The Self-presentations of Rulers and Subjects*. Cambridge: Cambridge University Press.

Bassin, M. (2001) 'Imagined communities/constructed geographies: the flexibilities of homeland', paper delivered at *Territory and Nation*, Tenth Annual Conference of the Association for the Study of Ethnicity and Nationalism, London School of Economics and Political Science, 23 March 2001.

Beetham, D. and C. Lord (1998) *Legitimacy and the European Union.* London: Longman.

Beramendi, J. G., R. Máiz, and X. M. Núñez (eds) (1994) *Nationalism in Europe: Past and Present, Vol. II.* Santiago de Compostela: Universidade de Santiago de Compostela.

Beresford, C. (1912) 'Home Rule and naval defence', in S. Rosenbaum (ed.) *Against Home Rule,* 189–94.

Berger, P. and T. Luckmann (1967) *The Social Construction of Reality: A Treatise in the Sociology of Knowledge.* London: Penguin.

Bew, P. and H. Patterson (1982) *Seán Lemass and the Making of Modern Ireland 1945–66.* Dublin: Gill and Macmillan.

Bhabha, H. K. (1990) *Nation and Narration.* London: Routledge.

Billig, M. (1987) *Arguing and Thinking: A Rhetorical Approach to Social Psychology.* Cambridge: Cambridge University Press.

Billig, M. (1995a) *Banal Nationalism.* London: Sage.

Billig, M. (1995b) 'Socio-psychological aspects of nationalist: imagining ingroups, others and the world of nations', in K. Benda-Beckman and M. Verkuyten (eds) *Nationalism, Ethnicity and Cultural Identity in Europe.* The Netherlands: ERCOMER, 89–105.

Bottomore, T. B. (1966 [1964]) *Elites and Society.* London: Penguin.

Boyce, D. G. (1991 [1982]) *Nationalism in Ireland.* London: Routledge.

Brass, P. R. (1991) *Ethnicity and Nationalism: Theory and Comparison.* Newbury Park: Sage.

Breuilly, J. (1993 [1982]) *Nationalism and the State.* Manchester: Manchester University Press.

Breuilly, J. (1996 [1994]) 'Approaches to nationalism', in G. Balakrishnan (ed.) *Mapping the Nation.* London: Verso, 146–74.

Breuning, M. and J. T. Ishiyama (1998) 'The rhetoric of nationalism: rhetorical strategies of the Volksuni and Vlaams Blok in Belgium, 1991–1995', *Political Communication,* 15:1, 5–26.

Brown, G. and G. Yule (1983) *Discourse Analysis.* Cambridge: Cambridge University Press.

Brown, T. (1981) *Ireland: A Social and Cultural History, 1922–1979.* London: Fontana.

Brubaker, R. (1996) *Nationalism Reframed: Nationhood and the National Question in the New Europe.* Cambridge: Cambridge University Press.

Bryant, D. C. (1953) 'Rhetoric: its function and its scope', *Quarterly Journal of Speech,* 39, 401–24.

Burgess, M. (2000 [1989]) *Federalism and European Union: The Building of Europe, 1950–2000.* London: Routledge.

Burton, F. and P. Carlen (1979) *Official Discourse: On Discourse Analysis, Government Publications, Ideology and the State.* London: Routledge and Kegan Paul.

Calhoun, C. (1997) *Nationalism.* Buckingham: Open University Press.

Castletown, Lord (1892) [Contribution] *Unionist Convention for the Provinces of Leinster, Munster and Connaught (June 1892)*. Report of the Proceedings, Lists of Committees, Delegates etc. Dublin: Hodges, Figgis and Co. Ltd.

Caul, B. (1995) *Towards a Federal Ireland*. Belfast: December Publications.

Chilton, P. (2003) *Analysing Political Discourse: Theory and Practice*. London: Routledge.

Christiansen, T., K. E. Jørgensen, and A. Wiener (1999) 'The social construction of Europe', *Journal of European Public Policy*, 6:4, 528–44.

Clery, C. (1979) 'The effects of the European Monetary System on Anglo-Irish relations', *Political Quarterly*, 50:2, 182–91.

Close, P. (1995) *Citizenship, Europe and Change*. Basingstoke: Macmillan.

Coakley, J. (1999) 'The foundations of statehood', in J. Coakley and M. Gallagher (eds) *Politics in the Republic of Ireland*, 1–31.

Coakley, J. and M. Gallagher (eds) (1999) *Politics in the Republic of Ireland*. London: Routledge in association with PSAI Press.

Cobban, A. (1969) *The Nation-state and National Self-determination*. London: Harper Collins.

Collier, A. (1993) *Critical Realism*. London: Verso.

Collins, S. (2000) *The Power Game: Fianna Fáil since Lemass*. Dublin: O'Brien Press.

Colum, P. (1959) *Arthur Griffith*. Dublin: Browne and Nolan.

Connor, W. (1994) 'Elites and ethnonationalism: the case of Western Europe', in J. G. Beramendi, R. Máiz and X. M. Núñez (eds) *Nationalism in Europe*, vol. II, 349–61.

Cronin, M. and Regan, J. M. (eds) (2000) *Ireland: The Politics of Independence, 1922–49*. Basingstoke: Macmillan.

Crotty, R. (1986) *Ireland in Crisis: A Study of Capitalist Colonialist Underdevelopment*. Dingle: Brandon Book Publishers.

Cunningham, M. (2008 [1997]) 'The political language of John Hume', in C. McGrath and E. O'Malley (eds) *Irish Political Studies Reader: Key Contributions*. London: Routledge, 136–49.

Davis, R. P. (1974) *Arthur Griffith and Non-violent Sinn Féin*. Dublin: Anvil.

Dedman, M. J. (1996) *The Origins and Development of the European Union, 1945–1995*. London: Routledge.

Delanty, G. (1995) *Inventing Europe: Idea, Identity, Reality*. Basingstoke: Macmillan.

Delanty, G. (2006) 'Borders in a changing Europe: an analysis of recent trends', *Comparative European Politics*, 4:2, 183–202.

Delanty, G. and P. O'Mahony (2002) *Nationalism and Social Theory: Modernity and the Recalcitrance of the Nation*. London: Sage.

Delors, J. (1992) *Our Europe: The Community and National Development*. London: Verso.

De Paor, L. (1997) *On the Easter Proclamation and Other Declarations*. Dublin: Four Courts Press.

Desmond, B. (2001) 'Reflections on the EEC referendum, 1972', paper presented at a Department of Politics Seminar, University College Dublin, 19 January.

De Valera, E. (1922) *The Testament of the Republic*. Dublin: Irish Nation Committee.

De Valera, E. (1926) *A National Policy*. Dublin: Fianna Fáil.

Diez, T. (1999) 'Speaking "Europe": the politics of integration discourse', *Journal of European Public Policy*, 6:4, 598–613.

Diez, T., M. Albert and S. Stetter (eds) (2008) *The European Union and Border Conflicts: The Power of Integration and Association*. Cambridge: Cambridge University Press.

Dobson, L. (2001) 'Citizenship, political authority and constitutionalism in the European Union: a normative theoretical approach', *Journal of European Integration*, 23:4, 335–71.

Dooge, J. and R. Barrington (eds) (1999) *A Vital National Interest: Ireland in Europe, 1973–1998*. Dublin: Institute of Public Administration.

Durkheim, E. (1982) *The Rules of Sociological Method*. London: Macmillan.

Eagleton, T. (1991) *Ideology: An Introduction*. London: Verso.

Eder, K. and B. Giesen (eds) (2001) *European Citizenship: National Legacies and Transnational Projects*. Oxford: Oxford University Press.

English, R. (1998) *Ernie O'Malley: IRA Intellectual*. Oxford: Clarendon.

English, R. (2006) *Irish Freedom: The History of Nationalism in Ireland*. London: Macmillan.

Fairclough, N. (2001 [1989]) *Language and Power*. Harlow: Pearson Education.

Fairclough, N. and R. Wodak (1997) 'Critical discourse analysis', in T. A. Van Dijk (ed.) *Discourse as Social Interaction*. London: Sage, 258–84.

Farr, J. (1989) 'Understanding conceptual change politically', in T. Ball, J. Farr and R. L. Hanson (eds) *Political Innovation and Conceptual Change*, 24–49.

Farrell, B. (1988) (ed.) *De Valera's Constitution and Ours*: *Thomas Davis Lectures*. Dublin: Gill and Macmillan for RTÉ.

Farrington, C. (2007) 'Reconciliation or irredentism? The Irish government and the Sunningdale communiqué', *Contemporary European History*, 16:1, 89–107.

Fennell, D. (1972) *A New Nationalism for the New Ireland*. Belfast: Comhairle Uladh.

FitzGerald, G. (1973 [1972]) *Towards a New Ireland*. Dublin: Torc Books.

FitzGerald, G. (1991) *All in a Life. An Autobiography*. Dublin: Gill and Macmillan.

FitzGerald, G. (1998) 'The Irish constitution in its historical context', in T. Murphy and P. Twomey (eds) *Ireland's Evolving Constitution, 1937–97: Collected Essays*. Oxford: Hart Publishing, 29–40.

Foley, J. A. and S. Lalor (1995) *Gill and Macmillan Annotated Constitution of Ireland (with Commentary)*. Dublin: Gill and Macmillan.

Forsyth, M. (1981) *Unions of States: The Theory and Practice of Confederation*. Leceister: Leicester University Press.

Foster, R. F. (1989 [1988]) *Modern Ireland, 1600–1972*. London: Penguin.

Foucault, M. (1972) *The Archaeology of Knowledge*. London: Tavistock.

Foucault, M. (1974 [1966]) *The Order of Things*. London: Tavistock.

Foucault, M. (1977) *Language, Counter-memory and Practice*. Ithaca: Cornell University Press.

Friedman, J. (1992) 'Narcissism, roots and postmodernity: the constitution of selfhood in the global crisis', in S. Lash and J. Friedman (eds) *Modernity and Identity*. Oxford: Blackwell, 331–63.

Gadamer, H.G. (1996 [1960]) *Truth and Method*. London: Sheed and Ward.

Gaffney, J. (ed.) (1996) *Political Parties and the European Union*. London: Routledge.

Gallagher, E. (1985) 'Anglo-Irish relations in the European Community', *Irish Studies in International Affairs*, 2:1, 21–35.

Gallagher, M. (1999) 'The changing constitution', in J. Coakley and M. Gallagher (eds) *Politics in the Republic of Ireland*, 71–98.

Garvin, T. (1982) 'Change and the political system', in F. Litton (ed.) *Unequal Achievement*, 21–40.

Garvin, T. (1987) *Nationalist Revolutionaries in Ireland, 1858–1928*. Oxford: Clarendon.

Garvin, T. (1996) *1922: The Birth of Irish Democracy*. Dublin: Gill and Macmillan.

Geddes, A. (1995) 'Immigrant and ethnic minorities and the EU's "democratic deficit" ', *Journal of Common Market Studies*, 33:2, 197–217.

Gellner, E. (1983) *Nations and Nationalism*. Oxford: Blackwell.

Giddens, A. (1985) *A Contemporary Critique of Historical Materialism, ii: The Nation-state and Violence*. Cambridge: Polity Press.

Gilland, K. (1999) 'Referenda in the Republic of Ireland', *Electoral Studies*, 18:3, 430–8.

Gillespie, P. (1996) 'Diversity in the Union', in B. Laffan (ed.) *Constitution-building in the European Union*, 29–70.

Gillespie, P. (2001) 'From Anglo-Irish to British-Irish relations', M. Cox, A. Guelke and Fiona Stephen (eds) *A Farewell to Arms? From War to Peace in Northern Ireland*. Manchester: Manchester University Press.

Gilligan, C. (2007) 'The Irish question and the concept of 'identity' in the 1980s', *Nations and Nationalism*, 13:4, 599–617.

Gilroy, P. (1987) *'There Ain't No Black in the Union Jack': The Cultural Politics of Race and Nation*. London: Hutchinson.

Girvin, B. and G. Murphy (eds) (2005) *The Lemass Era: Politics and Society in the Ireland of Seán Lemass*. Dublin: UCD Press.

Goodman, J. (2000) *Single Europe, Single Ireland? Uneven Development in Process*. Dublin: Irish Academic Press.

Graham, C. (2001) *Deconstructing Ireland: Identity, Theory, Culture*. Edinburgh: Edinburgh University Press.

Green, J. R. (Alice Stopford) (1911) *Irish Nationality*. London: Williams and Norgate.

Greenfeld, L. (1992) *Nationalism: Five Roads to Modernity*. Cambridge, Mass.: Harvard University Press.

Grey, E. (1912) 'Preface', in H. Spender, *Home Rule*, iii–vii.

Haas, E. B. (1968 [1958]) *The Uniting of Europe: Political, Social and Economic Forces 1950–1957*. Stanford: Stanford University Press.

Haas, E.B. (1997) *The Rise and Decline of Nationalism*. Ithaca: Cornell University Press.

Habermas, J. (1976) *Legitimation Crisis*, trans. T. McCarthy. London: Heinemann.

Hajer, M. (1995) *The Politics of Environmental Discourse*. Oxford: Oxford University Press.

Häkli, J. (1999) 'Cultures of demarcation: territory and national identity in Finland', in G. H. Herb and D. H. Kaplan (eds) *Nested Identities*, 123–50.

Hall, J. A. (1995) 'Nationalisms, classified and explained', in S. Periwal (ed.) *Notions of Nationalism*. Budapest: Central European University Press, 8–33.

Hall, S. (1990) 'Cultural identity and diaspora', in J. Rutherford (ed.) *Identity: Community, Culture and Difference*. London: Lawrence and Wishart, 222–37.

Halliday, M. (1978) *Language as Social Semiotic*. London: Edward Arnold.

Hanafin, P. (2001) *Constituting Identity: Political Identity Formation and the Constitution in Post-Independence Ireland*. Aldershot: Ashgate.

Harkness, D. (1996) *Ireland in the Twentieth Century: Divided Island*. Basingstoke: Macmillan.

Harris, C. (2001) 'Anglo-Irish elite cooperation and the peace process: the impact of the EEC/EU', *Irish Studies in International Affairs*, 12, 203–14.

Harvey, D. (1995 [1989]) *The Condition of Postmodernity: An Inquiry into the Origins of Cultural Change*. Cambridge: Blackwell.

Hayward, K. (2002) 'Not a Nice surprise: an analysis of the debate on the Nice Treaty in Ireland', *Irish Studies in International Affairs*, 13, 167–86.

Hayward, K. (2003) ' "If at first you don't succeed . . .": the second referendum on the Treaty of Nice, 2002', *Irish Political Studies*, 18:1, 120–32.

Hayward, K. (2006a) 'Reiterating national identities: the approach of the European Union to conflict resolution in Northern Ireland', *Cooperation and Conflict*, 41:3, 261–84.

Hayward, K. (2006b) 'National territory in European space: reconfiguring the island of Ireland', *European Journal of Political Research*, 45:6, 897–920.

Hayward, K. (2007) 'Mediating the European ideal: cross-border programmes and conflict resolution on the island of Ireland', *Journal of Common Market Studies*, 45:3, 675–93.

Hayward, K. and K. Howard (2002) 'Europeanisation and hyphe-nation: renegotiating the identity boundaries of Europe's western isles', Working Paper No. 18, Institute for British – Irish Studies University College, Dublin.

Hederman, M. (1983) *The Road to Europe: Irish Attitudes, 1948–61*. Dublin: Institute of Public Administration.

Hederman O'Brien, M. (2000) 'The way we were', in R. O'Donnell (ed.) *Europe: The Irish Experience*. Dublin: Irish European Association, 6–17.

Hennessey, T. (1998) *Dividing Ireland: World War One and Partition*. London: Routledge.

Henry, R. M. (1920) *The Evolution of Sinn Féin*. Dublin: Talbot Press.

Herb, G. H. (1999) 'National identity and territory', in G. H. Herb and D. H. Kaplan (eds) *Nested Identities*, 9–30.

Herb, G. H. and D. H. Kaplan (eds) (1999) *Nested Identities: Nationalism, Territory, and Scale*. Oxford: Rowman and Littlefield.

Hillery, P. (1999) 'Negotiating Ireland's entry', in J. Dooge and R. Barrington (eds) *A Vital National Interest*, 18–30.

Hindess, B. and P. Hirst (1975) *Pre-capitalist Modes of Production*. London: Routledge and Kegan Paul.

Hirst, P. (1996) 'Democracy and civil society', in P. Hirst and S. Khilnani (eds) *Reinventing Democracy*. Oxford, Blackwell, 97–116.

Hobsbawm, E. J. (1990) *Nations and Nationalism since 1780: Programme, Myth, Reality*. Cambridge: Cambridge University Press.

Hobsbawm, E. J. (1995 [1994]) *Age of Extremes: The Short Twentieth Century 1914–1991*. London: Abacus.

Hobsbawm, E. J. and T. Ranger (eds) (1983) *The Invention of Tradition*. Cambridge: Cambridge University Press.

Hobson, S. G. (1912) *Irish Home Rule*. London: Stephen Swift and Company.

Hoffmann, S. (1966) 'Obstinate or obsolete? The fate of the nation-state and the case of western Europe', *Daedalus*, 95, 863–909.

Holmes, M. (ed.) (2005) *Ireland and the European Union: Nice, Enlargement and the Future of Europe*. Manchester: Manchester University Press.

Hook, S. (1940) *Reason, Social Myths and Democracy*. New York: Humanities Press.

Howard, K. (2007) 'Accidental diasporas: a perspective on Northern Ireland's nationalists', in A. Ní Éigeartaigh, K. Howard and D. Getty (eds) *Rethinking Diasporas: Hidden Narratives and Imagined Borders*. Newcastle: Cambridge Scholars Publishing, 78–89.

Howarth, D. (1998) 'Discourse theory and political analysis', in E. Scarborough and E. Tanenbaum (eds) *Research Strategies in the Social Sciences: A Guide to New Approaches*. Oxford: Oxford University Press, 268–93.

Howarth, D. and Y. Stavrakakis (2000) 'Discourse theory and political analysis', in D. Howarth, A. Norval and Y. Stavrakakis (eds) *Discourse Theory and Political Analysis: Identities, Hegemonies and Social Change*. Manchester: Manchester University Press, 1–23.

Hroch, M. (1995) 'National self-determination for a historical perspective', in S. Periwal (ed.) *Notions of Nationalism*, 65–82.

Hurst, M. (1987) 'Ireland and the Ballot Act of 1872', in A. O'Day (ed.) *Reactions to Irish Nationalism*, 33–59.

Hutchinson, J. (1987) *The Dynamics of Cultural Nationalism: The Gaelic Revival and the Creation of the Irish Nation State*. London: Allen and Unwin.

Irish Transport and General Workers' Union (1972) *The Question Posed: How Would You Fare in the Common Market?* Dublin: ITGWU.

Jackson, A. (1996) 'Irish Unionism', in D. G. Boyce and A. O'Day (eds) *The Making of Modern Irish History: Revisionism and the Revisionist Controversy*. London: Routledge, 120–40.

Jameson, F. (1989 [1981]) *The Political Unconscious*. London: Routledge.

Kaplan, D. H. (1999) 'Territorial identities and geographical scale', in G. H. Herb and D. H. Kaplan (eds) *Nested Identities*, 31–49.

Keane, J. (1995) 'Nations, nationalism and European citizens', in S. Periwal (ed.) *Notions of Nationalism*, 182–207.

Kearney, R. (1997) *Postnationalist Ireland: Politics, Culture, Philosophy*. London: Routledge.

Keating, M. (1997) 'Stateless nation-building: Quebec, Catalonia and Scotland in the changing state system', *Nations and Nationalism*, 3:4, 689–717.

Keatinge, P. and B. Laffan (1999) 'Ireland: a small open polity', in J. Coakley and M. Gallagher (eds) *Politics in the Republic of Ireland*, 320–49.

Kennedy, L. (1992) 'Modern Ireland: post-colonial society or post-colonial pretensions?', *Irish Review*, 13, 107–21.

Kennedy, M. (2000) *Division and Consensus: The Politics of Cross-Border Relations in Ireland, 1925–1969*. Dublin: Institute of Public Administration.

Kohn, H. (1965 [1944]) *The Idea of Nationalism: A Study in Its Origins and Background*. New York: Macmillan.

Kornprobst, M. (2005) 'Episteme, nation-builders and national identity: the reconstruction of Irishness', *Nations and Nationalism*, 11:3, 403–22.

Kornprobst, M. (2007) 'Dejustification and dispute settlement: irredentism in European politics', *European Journal of International Relations*, 13:4, 459–87.

Laclau, E. (1990) *New Reflections on the Revolution of Our Time*. London: Verso.

Laclau, E. and C. Mouffe (1985) *Hegemony and Socialist Strategy: Towards a Radical Democratic Politics*. London: Verso.

Laclau, E. and C. Mouffe (1987) 'Post-Marxism without apologies', *New Left Review*, 166, 79–106.

Laffan, B. (1996a) 'The politics of identity and political order in Europe', *Journal of Common Market Studies*, 34:1, 81–102.

Laffan, B. (ed.) (1996b) *Constitution-building in the European Union*. Dublin: Institute of European Affairs.

Laffan, B. and R. O'Donnell (1998) 'Ireland and the growth of international governance', in W. Crotty and D. E. Schmitt (eds) *Ireland and the Politics of Change*. Harlow: Addison Wesley Longman, 156–77.

Laffan, B., R. O'Donnell, and M. Smith (2000) *Europe's Experimental Union. Rethinking Integration*. London: Routledge.

Laughland, J. (1998 [1997]) *The Tainted Source: The Undemocratic Origins of the European Idea*. London: Warner Books.

Lee, J. J. (ed.) (1979) *Ireland 1945–70: Thomas Davis Lectures.* Dublin: Gill and Macmillan for RTÉ.

Lipgens, W. (1982) *A History of European Integration: vol. I, 1945–1947.* Oxford: Clarendon.

Litton, F. (ed.) (1982) *Unequal Achievement:. The Irish experience 1957–1982.* special edition of *Administration*, journal of the Institute of Public Administration of Ireland, 30:2–3.

Litton, F. (ed.) (1987) *The Constitution of Ireland 1937–1987*, special edition of *Administration*, journal of the Institute of Public Administration of Ireland, 35:4.

Llobera, J. R. (1994) *The God of Modernity: The Development of Nationalism in Western Europe.* Oxford: Berg Publishers.

Loughlin, J. (2001) 'Ireland: from colonized nation to "Celtic Tiger" ', in J. Loughlin (ed.) *Subnational Democracy in the European Union: Challenges and Opportunities.* Oxford: Oxford University Press, 61–82.

Lynch, J. (1971) *Irish Unity, Northern Ireland* and *Anglo-Irish Relations: Speeches August 1969 – October 1971. Dublin*: Government Information Burea.

Lynd, R. (1919) *Ireland a Nation.* London: Grant Richards.

Lynd, R. (1934 [1916]) 'Introduction' to *The Reconquest of Ireland* by J. Connolly. Dublin: Irish Transport and General Workers' Union.

MacBride, S. (1985) *A Message to the Irish People.* Dublin: Mercier Press.

McCall, C. (1999) *Identity in Northern Ireland: Communities, Politics and Change.* Basingstoke: Palgrave.

McCall, C. (2007) ' "Hello stranger": the revival of the relationship between Ireland, Northern Ireland and Scotland', *Journal of Cross Border Studies in Ireland* (Armagh: Centre for Cross-Border Studies), 2, 7–21.

MacCarthaigh, M. (2006) 'Conceptualising the role of national parliaments in the EU system of governance', *Administration*, 54:3, 69–94.

MacDonagh, O. (1989) *The Emancipist: Daniel O'Connell, 1830–1847.* London: Weidenfeld and Nicolson.

MacLaughlin, J. (2001) *Reimagining the Nation-state: The Contested Terrains of Nation-building.* London: Pluto Press.

McLoughlin, P. (2006) ' ". . . it's a United Ireland or Nothing"? John Hume and the Idea of Irish Unity, 1964–72', *Irish Political Studies*, 21:2, 157–80.

Macmillan, G. M. (1993) *State, Society and Authority in Ireland: The Foundations of the Modern Irish State.* Dublin: Gill and Macmillan.

Maher, D. J. (1986) *The Tortuous Path.* Dublin: Institute of Public Administration.

Mann, M. (1995) 'A political theory of nationalism and its excesses', in S. Periwal (ed.) *Notions of Nationalism*, 44–64.

Mansergh, M. (ed.) (1986) *The Spirit of the Nation: The Speeches and Statements of Charles J. Haughey (1957–1986).* Dublin: Mercier Press.

Marcussen, M., J. Risse, D. Engelmann-Martin, H. J. Knopf and K. Roscher (1999) 'Constructing Europe? The evolution of French, British and German nation-state identities', *Journal of European Public Policy*, 6:4, 614–33.

Marsh, M. and B. Wessels (1997) 'Territorial representation', *European Journal of Political Research*, 32:2, 227–41.

Maye, B. (1997) *Arthur Griffith*. Dublin: Griffith College Publications.

Meehan, E. (1993) *Citizenship and the European Community*. London: Sage.

Meehan, E. (1997) 'Political pluralism and European citizenship', in P. B. Lehning and A. Weale (eds) *Citizenship, Democracy and Justice in the New Europe*. London: Routledge, 69–85.

Meehan, E. (2000) ' "Britain's Irish Question: Britain's European Question?": British-Irish relations in the context of the European Union and the Belfast Agreement', *Review of International Studies*, 26; 1, 83–97.

Mezo, J. (1994) 'Nationalist political elites and language in Ireland (1922–1937)', in J. G. Beramendi, R. Máiz and X. M. Núñez (eds) *Nationalism in Europe*, vol. II, 209–22.

Miller, D. (1973) *Church, State and Nation in Ireland, 1898–1921*. Dublin: Gill and Macmillan.

Miller, D. (1989) *Market, State, and Community: Theoretical Foundations of Market Socialism*. Oxford: Oxford University Press.

Milward, A. S. (1992) *The European Rescue of the Nation-state*. London: Routledge.

Milward, A. S. and V. Sørensen (1993) 'Interdependence or integration? A national choice', in A. S. Milward, F. M. B. Lynch, R. Ranieri, F. Romero and V. Sørensen (eds) *The Frontier of National Sovereignty: History and Theory, 1945–1992*. London: Routledge, 1–32.

Mitchell, A. and P. Ó Snodaigh (eds) (1985) *Irish Political Documents 1916–1949*. Dublin: Irish Academic Press.

Mitrany, D. (1965) 'The prospect of integration: federal or functional', *Journal of Common Market Studies*, 4:2, 119–45.

Monnet, J. (1978) *Memoirs,* trans. R. Mayne. London: Collins.

Moran, D. P. (1905) *The Philosophy of Irish Ireland*. Dublin: James Duffy.

Moravcsik, A. (1999) 'Is something rotten in the state of Denmark? Construction and European integration', *Journal of European Public Policy*, 6:4, 669–81.

Münch, R. (1996) 'Between nation-state, regionalism and world society: the European integration process', *Journal of Common Market Studies*, 34:3, 379–401.

Murphy, A. B. (1999) 'Rethinking the concept of European identity', in G. Herb and D. H. Kaplan (eds) *Nested Identities*, 53–73.

Murphy, G. (2001) ' "A measurement of the extent of our sovereignty at the moment": sovereignty and the question of Irish entry to the EEC – new evidence from the archives', *Irish Studies in International Affairs*, 12, 191–202.

Murphy, J. A. (1979) ' "Put them out!" Parties and elections 1948–69', in J. Lee (ed.) *Ireland 1945–70*. Dublin: Gill and Macmillan, 1–15.

Murray, J. (1952) 'This growing sense of Europe', *Studies: An Irish Quarterly Review*. 41, 268–80.

Murray, S. (ed.) (1997) *Not on Any Map: Essays on Postcoloniality and Cultural Nationalism*. Exeter–University of Exeter Press.

Nairn, T. (2000) *After Britain: New Labour and the Return of Scotland*. London: Granta Books.

O' Brennan, J. (2003) 'Ireland's return to "normal" EU voting patterns: the 2002 Nice Treaty referendum', *European Political Science*, 2:2, 5–14.

O'Day, A. (ed.) (1987) *Reactions to Irish Nationalism, 1865–1914*. Dublin: Gill and Macmillan.

O'Donnell, C. (2007) *Fianna Fáil, Irish Republicanism and the Northern Ireland Troubles, 1968–2005*. Dublin: Irish Academic Press.

O'Dowd, L. (1991) 'Intellectuals and the national question in Ireland', in G. Day and G. Rees (eds) *Regions, Nations and European Integration: Remaking the Celtic Periphery*. Cardiff: University of Wales Press, 125–42.

O'Dowd, L. (2002) 'Transfrontier regions and emerging forms of European governance with special reference to Ireland', in G. Bucken-Knapp and M. Schack (eds) *Borders Matter: Transboundary Regions in Contemporary Europe*. Aabenraa: Danish Institute of Border Region Studies, 75–92.

O'Dowd, L. (2003) 'The changing significance of European borders,' in J. Anderson, L. O'Dowd and T. M. Wilson (eds) *New Borders for a Changing Europe. Cross-Border Cooperation and Governance*. London: Frank Cass, 13–36.

O'Dowd, L. (ed.) (1996) *On Intellectuals and Intellectual Life in Ireland: International, Comparative and Historical Contexts*. Belfast: Institute of Irish Studies, Queen's University Belfast and Royal Irish Academy.

O'Dowd, L. and T. M. Wilson (eds) (1996) *Borders, Nations and States: Frontiers of Sovereignty in the New Europe*. Aldershot: Avebury.

Offe, C. and H. Wiesenthal (1979). 'Two logics of collective action: theoretical notes on social class and organizational form', *Political Power and Social Theory*, 1, 67–113.

O'Halloran, C. (1987) *Partition and the Limits of Irish nationalism: An Ideology Under Stress*. Dublin: Gill and Macmillan.

O'Hegarty, P. S. (1998 [1924]) *The Victory of Sinn Féin: How It Won It and How It Used It*, introduction by T. Garvin. Dublin: University College Dublin Press.

O'Leary, P. (2000) 'Davitt, Parnell and Pearse: the impact of Irish political nationalism in Wales, 1860–1914'; unpublished paper presented to the Department of Celtic Studies, University College Dublin, 20 November.

O'Mahony, P. and G. Delanty (1998) *Rethinking Irish History: Nationalism, Identity and Ideology*. Basingstoke: Macmillan.

O'Malley, E. (1979 [1936]) *On Another Man's Wound*. Dublin: Anvil Books.

O'Neill, M. (ed.) (1996) *The Politics of European Integration: A Reader*. London: Routledge.

Özkirimli, U. (2000) *Theories of Nationalism: A Critical Introduction*. London: Macmillan.

Paasi, A. (1996) *Territories, Boundaries and Consciousness: The Changing Geographies of the Finnish-Russian Border*. Chichester: John Wiley and Sons.

Parker, N. (1998) 'Integration: Amsterdam and after', *Political Quarterly*, 69:1, 85–8.

Paseta, S. (2000) 'Ireland's last Home Rule generation: the decline of constitutional nationalism in Ireland, 1916–1930', in M. Cronin and J. M. Regan (eds) *Ireland: The Politics of Independence*, 13–31.

Patterson, H. (1999) 'Seán Lemass and the Ulster Question, 1959–65', *Journal of Contemporary European History*, 34:1, 145–59.

Pearse, P. H. (1916) *The Spiritual Nation*. University College Cork: Corpus of Electronic Texts Edition. www.ucc.ie/celt/online/E900007.012/text002.html (accessed 24 February 2001).

Penrose, J. (2002) 'Nations, states and homelands: the power of territory and territoriality in nationalist thought', *Nations and Nationalism*, 8:4, 277–97.

Percy, Lord (1912) 'The military disadvantages of Home Rule', in S. Rosenbaum (ed.) *Against Home Rule*, 195–203.

Periwal, S. (ed.) (1995) *Notions of Nationalism*. Budapest: Central European University Press.

Pinder, J. (1995) 'European citizenship: a project in need of completion', in C. Crouch and D. Marquand (eds) *Reinventing Collective Action: From the Global to the Local*. Oxford: Blackwell, 112–22.

Prenter, S. (1892) [Contribution] *Unionist Convention for the Provinces of Leinster, Munster and Connaught (June 1892)*, report of the proceedings, lists of committees, delegates etc. Dublin: Hodges, Figgis and Co. Ltd.

Radaelli, C. and V. A. Schmidt (eds) (2005) *Policy Change and Discourse in Europe*. London: Routledge.

Redmond, J. (1898) *Historical and Political Addresses, 1883–1897*. Dublin: Sealy, Bryers and Walker.

Regan, J. M. (2000) 'The politics of utopia: party organisation, executive autonomy and the new administration', in M. Cronin and J. M. Regan (eds) *Ireland: The Politics of Independence*, 32–66.

Risse, T. and A. Wiener (1999) ' "Something rotten" and the social construction of social constructivism: a comment on comments', *Journal of European Public Policy*, 6:5, 775–82.

Risse, T., D Engelmann-Martin, H. J. Knopf and K. Roscher (1999) 'To euro or not to euro: the EMU and identity politics in the European Union', *European Journal of International Relations*, 5:2, 147–87.

Rosamond, B. (1999) 'Discourses of globalization and the social construction of European identities', *Journal of European Public Policy*, 6:4, 652–68.

Rosenbaum, S. (ed.) (1912) *Against Home Rule: The Case for the Union*. London: Kennikat Press.

Ruggie, J. (1993) 'Territoriality and beyond: problematizing modernity in international relations', *International Organization*, 47:1, 139–74.

Said, E. (1991 [1978]) *Orientalism*. London: Penguin.

Sawyer, R. (1993) *We Are But Women: Women in Ireland's History*. London: Routledge.

Schlesinger, P. (1992) 'Europeanness: a new cultural battlefield?', *Innovation*, 5:1, 12–22.

Schlesinger, P. (1999) 'Changing spaces of political communication: the case of the European Union', *Political Communication*, 16:2, 263–79.

Schmidt, V. A. (2000) 'Democracy and discourse in an integrating Europe and a globalizing world', *European Law Journal*, 6:3, 277–300.

Schmitter, P. C. (1970) 'A revised theory of regional integration', *International Organization*, 24, 232–64.

Schuman, R. (1950) Speech in the consultative assembly of the Council of Europe, 10 August, quoted in M. O'Neill (ed.) *The Politics of European Integration*, 35; also: www.ena.lu/europe/formation-community/robert-schuman-council-europe-strasbourg-1950.htm (accessed 3 August 2007).

Seale, C. (ed.) (1998) *Researching Society and Culture*. London: Sage.

Searle, J. (1995). *The Construction of Social Reality*. London: Allen Lane.

Seton-Watson, H. (1977) *Nations and States*. London: Methuen.

Seymour, W. D. (1888) *Home Rule and State Supremacy* or *Nationality Reconciled with Empire*. London: Kegan Paul, Trench and Co.

Shils, E. (1957) 'Primordial, personal, sacred and civil ties', *British Journal of Sociology*, 8:2, 130–45.

Shirlow, P. and M. McGovern (1998) 'Language, discourse and dialogue: Sinn Féin and the Irish peace process', *Political Geography*, 17:2, 171–86.

Simons, H. W. (ed.) (1989) *Rhetoric in the Human Sciences*. London: Sage.

Sinnott, R. (1995) *Knowledge of the European Union in Irish Public Opinion: Sources and Implications*. Dublin: Institute of European Affairs, Occasional Paper 5.

Sinnott, R. (1999) 'The electoral system', in J. Coakley and M. Gallagher (eds) *Politics in the Republic of Ireland*, 99–126.

Sitter, N. and K. Henderson (2006) 'Political developments in the EU member states', *Journal of Common Market Studies annual review*, 44:1, 171–98.

Skinner, Q. (1989) 'Language and political change', in T. Ball, J. Farr and R. L. Hanson (eds) *Political Innovation and Conceptual Change*, 6–23.

Skotnicka-Illasiewicz, E. and W. Wesolowski (1995) 'The significance of pre-conceptions: Europe of civil societies and Europe of nationalities', in S. Periwal (ed.) *Notions of Nationalism*, 208–27.

Smith, A. D. (1986) *The Ethnic Origins of Nations*. Oxford: Blackwell.

Smith, A. D. (1991) *National Identity*. London: Penguin.

Smith, A. D. (1992) 'National identity and the idea of European unity', *International Affairs*, 68:1, 55–76.

Smith, A. D. (1995) *Nations and Nationalism in a Global Era*. Cambridge: Polity Press.

Smith, B. (1995) 'On drawing lines on a map', in A. U. Frank, W. Kuhn and D. M. Mark (eds) *Spatial Information Theory (Proceedings of COSIT 1995)*. London: Springer Verlag, 475–84.

Smith, C. A. and K. B. Smith (2000) 'A rhetorical perspective on the 1997 British party manifestos', *Political Communication*, 17:4, 457–73.

Smith, D. E. (1990) *Text, Fact and Femininity: Explaining the Relations of Ruling*. London: Routledge.

Sofos, S. A. (1996) 'Culture, politics and identity in Former Yugoslavia', in B. Jenkins and S. A. Sofos (eds) *Nation and Identity in Contemporary Europe*. London: Routledge, 251–82.

Spender, H. (1912) *Home Rule*. London: Hodder and Stoughton.

Spinelli, A. (1972) *The European Adventure*: *Tasks for an Enlarged Community*. London: Charles Knight and Co.

Spinelli, A. and E. Rossi (1941) 'The Ventotene Manifesto', quoted in M. Newman, *Democracy, Sovereignty and the European Union*. London: Hurst and Company, 1996: 16.

Sutherland, C. (2005) 'Nation-building through discourse theory', *Nations and Nationalism*, 11: 2, 185–202.

Taylor, P. (1975) 'The confederal phase', *World Politics*, 27:3, 336–60.

Tilley, V. (1997) 'The terms of the debate: untangling language about ethnicity and ethnic movements', *Ethnic and Racial Studies*, 20:3, 497–522.

Tilly, C. (ed.) 1975) *The Formation of National States in Western Europe*. Princeton: Princeton University Press.

Tishkov, V. A. (2000) 'Forget the "nation": post-nationalist understanding of nationalism', *Ethnic and Racial Studies*, 23:4, 625–50.

Tonkiss, F. (1998) 'Analysing discourse', in C. Seale (ed.) *Researching Society and Culture*. London: Sage, 245–60.

Tonra, B. and D. Dunne (1997) *A European Cultural Identity: Myth, Reality or Aspiration?* Dublin: Institute for European Affairs.

Tully, J. (1995) *Strange Multiplicity: Constitutionalism in an Age of Diversity*. Cambridge: Cambridge University Press.

Van Amersfoort, H. (1995) 'Institutional plurality: problem or solution for the multi-ethnic state?', in S. Periwal (ed.) *Notions of Nationalism*, 162–81.

Walker, B. M. (2007) ' "Ancient enmities" and modern conflict: history and politics in Northern Ireland', *Nationalism and Ethnic Politics*, 13:1, 103–28.

Wallace, W. (1982) 'Europe as a confederation: the Community and the nation-state', *Journal of Common Market Studies*, 21:1, 57–68.

Wallace, W. (1990) *The Dynamics of European Integration*. London: Pinter.

Walsh, B. (1979) 'Economic growth and development, 1945–70', in J. J. Lee (ed.) *Ireland 1945–70*, 27–37.

Ward, A. J. (1994) *The Irish Constitutional Tradition. Responsible Government and Modern Ireland, 1782–1992*. Washington: Catholic University of America Press.

Weber, M. (1968) *On Charisma and Institution-building*, introduced by S. N. Eisenstadt. London: University of Chicago Press.

West, N. C. (1926 [1921]) *The Truth about Ireland*. Dublin: Mahon.

Whyte, J. H. (1971) *Church and State in Modern Ireland*. Dublin: Gill and Macmillan.

Williams, T. D. (1979) 'Irish foreign policy, 1949–69', in J. J. Lee (ed.) *Ireland 1945–70*, 136–51.

Wistrich, E. (1991 [1989]) *After 1992: the United States of Europe*. London: Routledge.

Wittgenstein, L. (1953) *Philosophical Investigations*, trans. and ed. G. E. M. Anscombe and R. Rhees. Oxford: Blackwell.

Wodak, R., R. de Cillia, M. Reisigl and K. Liebhart (1999) *The Discursive Construction of National Identity*, trans. A. Hirsch and R. Mitten. Edinburgh: Edinburgh University Press.

Yiangou, G. (2001) 'Analysing the prospects of an overarching European collective identity', *Studies in Ethnicity and Nationalism*, 1:2, 37–49.

Younger, C. (1981) *Arthur Griffith*. Dublin: Gill and Macmillan.

Note

1 All internet addresses were accessed and correct as of January 2008, except where otherwise indicated.

Index

Note: 'n.' after a page number indicates the number of a note on that page.